THE
CHINESE

A Study of a
Hong Kong Community

Volume One

THE
CHINESE

A Study of a
Hong Kong Community

Cornelius Osgood

Volume One

THE UNIVERSITY OF ARIZONA PRESS
TUCSON · ARIZONA

About the Author...

Cornelius Osgood, Professor of Anthropology and Associate Director of the Peabody Museum of Natural History, Emeritus, at Yale University, served on the Yale faculty from 1930 to 1973. He made his first trip to China in 1935 and his field work there and in Korea resulted in three previous volumes. Although the Far East has been the area of his greatest interest, he is equally known for his many monographs resulting from anthropological studies in Alaska, Canada, and South America. The present work is based on some fifteen months of field research during four trips to Hong Kong, as well as on many years of the teaching of Chinese culture.

We wish to acknowledge the generous support of the National Science Foundation, which funded much of the research behind these volumes as well as assisting with the costs of publication.

THE UNIVERSITY OF ARIZONA PRESS

I.S.B.N.-0-8165-0418-0
L. C. No. 74-77207

For

my darling

Hsiao Ling

给我的親愛的小玲

Contents

Part II. The Growth of a Settlement

ILLUSTRATIONS IN VOLUME ONE

VOL. 1; ILLUSTRATIONS *(cont'd)*

TABLES IN VOLUME ONE

CONTENTS OF OTHER VOLUMES IN THIS SET

VOLUME TWO

Part IV. The Town of Lung Shing

VOLUME THREE
Part V. Summary and Analysis of the Culture of Lung Chau

Reference Material

General Preface

The Chinese may be misleading as a title for an ethnography of an island lying offshore from the famous one that has given its name to the British Crown Colony attached to the southeast coast of China. Still, if one were attempting to sample the Chinese culture of the whole of Hong Kong, or for that matter, the traditional culture of China itself, the little island on which our studies were undertaken would probably prove to be as typical a locale as one could well find. Lung Chau, or Dragon Island, as I have named it, shares the mixture of refugee Chinese peoples from various mainland backgrounds that is so characteristic of Hong Kong. Lung Chau also has areas of farming more typical of the New Territories than of the main island that lies only three minutes away and on which within a half hour one can skirt the well-known Peak and reach the heart of the largest European controlled metropolis in Asia with its impact of Western culture that has reached not only to the most remote parts of the four-hundred-square-mile Colony but far beyond. Hong Kong, we should note, was originally a maritime settlement, and its wealth came by way of the sea. Hong Kong means Fragrant Harbor, a name that actually designated the narrow strait created by the shore of little Lung Chau, most of whose people still take their wealth from the sea.

There are those who will say that to claim that the populace of Lung Chau is typical of Hong Kong or that it represents Chinese culture in general is erroneous. I quickly agree. There is actually no segment of China that is typical of the whole country, or even one locality of Hong Kong that portrays the entire Colony. Lung Chau, for example contains few if any elite, no cultivated class whose members bear the great tradition of Chinese arts and literature. The inhabitants of Lung Chau are common people, as are the overwhelming majority of all those in the Colony and in China itself. Lung Chau, furthermore, is generally more conservative than the Hong Kong cities, its economics are tied particularly to fishing, there is no rice grown on the island, and there are no large aggregates of people representing ancient lineages, such as distinguish the walled towns of the New Territories, in what was originally part of the Kwangtung mainland. Nothing more is asserted than that this work presents a study of the residents, about 9,000 Chinese, who were residing on

Lung Chau between 1960 and 1966. On the other hand, if one wishes to understand the Chinese of East Asia who live outside the boundaries of the People's Republic, one might reasonably begin with this volume.

This report may be considered a community study, but the integration of the people of Lung Chau is different from that in most groups that have been the objects of research by social scientists. In the ordinary village or small town, the majority of the residents present an aspect of a culture that has been basically unified by time. Each adult knows many others, speaks the same language, and can generally anticipate the behavior of his associates in response to established stimuli. On Lung Chau, to the contrary, a considerable number of the older people speak mutually unintelligible languages, and most of them have lived the early part of their lives in a completely different environment with associates now seldom seen. There is little of the security that comes to families occupying the same vicinity for generations.

In large degree, the culture of Lung Chau exemplifies that of the central coast of Kwangtung which has Canton as its main city, but apart from the not unusual pockets of Hakka people, there is on Lung Chau the conflict of intrusive enclaves from the districts of northeast Kwangtung and of Fukien Province, as well as the impact of the distinctive and formerly outcast boat peoples. Lung Chau is a stewpot in which contributions of cultural spice from various strangers is creating a new and distinctively Hong Kong dish, and one that is especially fascinating to those who are interested in knowing just how such dishes are made.

The approach to the study of Lung Chau is that of the traditional ethnographer with perhaps an extra emphasis on people as human beings. In this case, the ethnographer wants to know how an individual behaves, what he produces in the material world, and what are his views about things. To satisfy this purpose, the ethnographer records his observations and the results of his interrogations with respect to a specific aggregate of people within a definable area and within a reasonable limit of time. To do this accurately while introducing only the minimum of personal bias or distortion is an essential part of the method. The ethnographer has to present the facts without a misleading coating of value judgments, reserving a final part of the work for summary statements of a more personal and subjective nature. The separation has not been completely made, but any variations from the overall pattern should become immediately obvious.

Clearly this account is not strictly sociological nor does it contain a statistical treatment of various traits that might be usefully compared with data elsewhere. Neither has there been any highly detailed analysis of special aspects of culture such as have created hope among some ethnologists that broadly applicable scientific laws may be deduced from them. Here, the usual wide range of culture has been dealt with piece by piece despite the interminable difficulties of trying to comprehend the intellectually and technically different worlds that may be exemplified by descriptions of the procedures involved in the operation of a temple in one case or in the manufacture of threadlike vermicelli in another. With the foundations of general ethnography laid, various specialized studies could well follow with richly rewarding results. Admittedly, what may have been accomplished over six years, including four periods of field research totaling about fifteen months, can hardly be more than marked cloth on which the embroidery has yet to be begun.

Although the ethnographic approach has in this case been primarily descriptive, there has been a conscious and clear concern for the historical development of culture, not only in the longer view which extends back beyond the inception of the research, but in that more immediate interaction which may be thought of as the process of acculturation. It is hard to conceive of another cultural situation in which growth and change have been characterized by such speed as has been exhibited during recent years in Hong Kong and, of this, Lung Chau is an excellent example. A revolution of this kind cannot be overlooked even if one wishes to do so.

It would be remiss not to make clear that the final form of the research was not foreseen in advance. Indeed, if the expansion of effort had been anticipated, I probably would not have been venturesome enough to have initiated it. Beginning with the study of a few families isolated on the south shore of the island, my attention was drawn to the suburb from which they came. This involved me in the historical development of the latter settlement, but before either study could be finished, it became essential to view the whole rural area of Lung Chau in its relation to the town. Thus I became enmeshed in the procedures of understanding the primitive industries in a third outlying section of the island.

Inevitably, as one might suspect, it became impossible to exclude the town, for while its linkage with farmers might appear intermittent and casual, the connection of the simple industrial plants was dependent and direct. Thus the study of Lung Shing, or Dragon Town, became the fourth and most elaborate part of the research.

This pattern of development is reflected in the arrangement of the data which accordingly has been divided into five parts subtitled as follows.

Part I.   The Origin of a Farming Community
Part II.   The Growth of a Settlement
Part III.   A Suburb with Small Industries
Part IV.   The Town of Lung Shing
Part V.   A Summary and Analysis of the Culture of Lung Chau

To recapitulate, I can say that Part I is the result of the investigation of a small group of families, chiefly Hakka and principally engaged in vegetable farming in an isolated valley on the south shore of Lung Chau. This hamlet has been called Chung Nam Wan. The research emphasizes the character of the individual lives of the residents and presents the details of their physical and material surroundings. The origin and history of the hamlet has been outlined, and the culture considered historically in terms of its elements. The initial research, undertaken in 1960, was virtually finished in manuscript form within eight months. In the summer of 1961, considerable additional material was obtained and incorporated in a rewritten manuscript completed in 1962 except for some final corrections and adjustments to integrate it with the other segments of the series.

Part II is primarily a culture-historical study of a second isolable and suburban community which has been named Tung Pak Wan. This predominantly Cantonese settlement has been described in terms of its growth which could be entirely encompassed within thirty-five years. Each of its eighteen households has been examined in the order of their establishment. Of principal concern have been the motivations for settlement and the effect of family relationships and friendships on them. Of special interest is the formation of religiously and politically oriented cliques, Christian and Communist. Some aspects of the society that appear significant for understanding cultural change have been summarized and compared. The field work was initiated in 1960, largely completed in 1961, and was in manuscript form by the end of the summer of 1963. With additions, it was rewritten in the spring of 1966.

Part III consists of a study of a third suburban community which has been called Sai Mi Wan, the *Wan*, as in the previous names, meaning *Bay*. The community has as its distinction a number of primitive Chinese industries, most of which are carried on by individuals who came from the regions of Swatow and Amoy and who speak the languages of those areas. As in the case of the other suburbs, the origins and history, as well as certain cultural aspects of the various households have been summarized, while emphasis has been placed on the fast-disappearing technologies which distinguish this sub-area. Field work for Part III was begun in 1961, and a manuscript including all the then available data completed in 1962. Another period of research was devoted to Sai Mi Wan in 1963, after which the manuscript was rewritten in essentially final form in 1964.

Part IV, The Town of Lung Shing, differs from the previous three parts in that its plan evolved over the years. The original research was undertaken simply to integrate the studies of the three peripheral communities which depend on the town in a large degree economically and more distinctly for schools, doctors, and organized entertainment. First, a survey of the urban culture was undertaken. Then emphasis was placed on those aspects of the culture most meaningful for an understanding of the lives of the inhabitants in the dependent settlements. Finally, it was decided to study the town as a whole for its own sake. This latter effort also differed from the previous research in that, whereas in the suburbs almost every individual served as an informant, such inclusiveness was clearly impossible to achieve among a group of more than eight thousand individuals submerged in the few blocks of old buildings along the ancient main street or hidden in the shack slums which cling to the hillside behind it. The method by which I have tried to picture the life of the whole town can most quickly be comprehended by examining the table of contents of Part IV.

In 1960, the data for Part IV consisted of little more than a crude plan of the major arteries of Lung Shing with a list of the shops and the stalls that were crowded together along them. The following summer, this survey was completed with more attention to detail, while notes were also taken on the schools, amusements, and various industries in which the people of the outlying districts were involved. Then, in the winter of 1963-64, I lived in the town of Lung Shing for seven months and my interests were largely absorbed by it. By the fall of 1965, a manuscript of approximately one hundred and seventy-five thousand words on Lung Shing had been completed. Finally, I returned for the first nine weeks of 1966 to collect additional data. This period was so rewarding that Part IV had to be almost entirely rewritten to include the emendations and new material, an effort that was concluded that year.

Part V, the summary and analysis, is an attempt to bring together the essential facts of the six-year study and to provide comments on selected aspects of the culture of Lung Chau not only from the viewpoint of the island as a whole, but also in terms of their historical development over centuries. Notes were accumulated for Part V beginning in 1963, but this final section did not really take form until after the other parts were completed in 1966. Only editorial changes in the five parts of the manuscript have been made since the end of 1967.

In concluding this preface, it should be candidly stated that the method of presentation is not patterned on analogous works in the social science field, even those by the author himself. This can be a disconcerting fact to scholars, especially if the contribution does not immediately strike one as being singularly superior. I can only offer apologies to my academic colleagues for the lack of the ingenuousness that makes an improved copy more effective in the scientific world and, at the same time, hope that some compensation may result from such enlightenment as may be given the ordinary intelligent reader for whom these volumes have been at least equally designed.

PART I

The Origin of a Farming Community

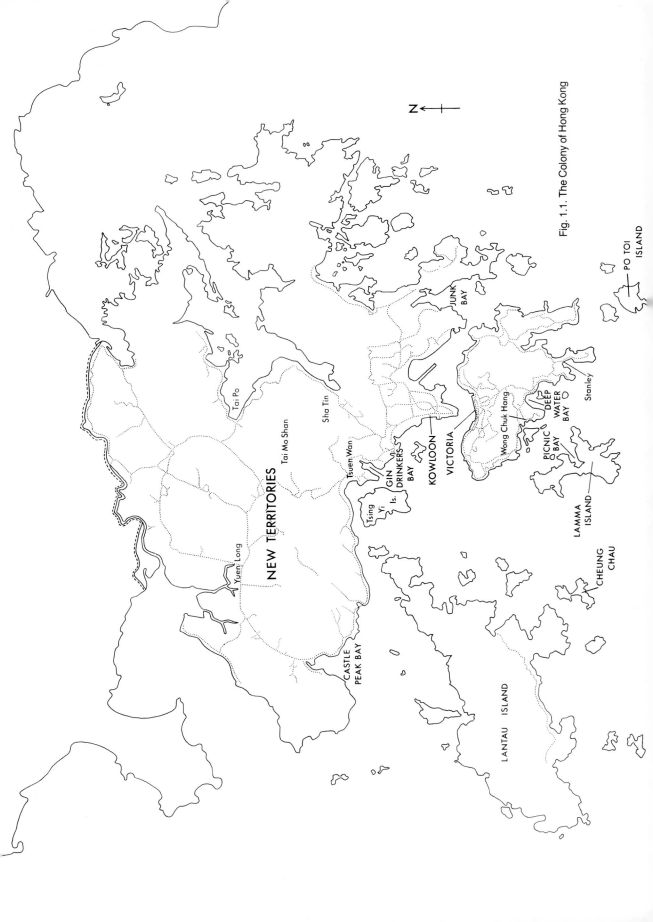

N

Fig. 1.1. The Colony of Hong Kong

PO TOI
ISLAND

NEW TERRITORIES

Tai Po

Sha Tin

Tai Mo Shan

Tsuen Wan

GIN
DRINKERS
BAY

Tsing
Yi Is.

KOWLOON

VICTORIA

Wong Chuk Hang

JUNK
BAY

DEEP
WATER
BAY

Stanley

PICNIC
BAY

LAMMA
ISLAND

CHEUNG
CHAU

Yuen Long

CASTLE
PEAK BAY

LANTAU ISLAND

Preface to Part I

Hong Kong delighted me so much on a casual visit in 1938 that disappointment seemed certain if I ever went back. Its capital city, a luminous gem in a mountain slope setting, flashes out over the sea as an incomparable jewel. It is a vortex of population in which people command admiration for their intelligence in the struggle to better their lives and deserve respect for their courage in facing death or disaster. I am glad I returned.

Almost certainly the attempt to carry out a community study in the Colony of Hong Kong would not have been undertaken had it been possible to have continued such work in China itself. The dictates of chance seem curious enough to relate. Following a visit to China in 1935, plans were developed for extended, cooperative research on a village in Hopei to begin in the summer of 1938—but the Japanese occupation intervened. Fearful even then that the chance to record traditional Chinese culture would disappear, I reacted to frustration by going to Yünnan via Hong Kong and Hanoi, thus skirting the Japanese military operations involved in the attack on Canton. Arriving ahead of the great influx of refugees, I found that it was possible to spend a few undisturbed weeks in a small village near Kunming, one which had retained so many nineteenth century characteristics that my reports of them were at first regarded as incredible by a Chinese colleague who joined me near the end of the season. This visit to Yünnan was a priceless experience.

The war which was torturing China exploded into a holocaust, and there was no further chance of field work in Asia until the late 1940s. Then the American need for knowledge of Korea led to an attempt to undertake research there in 1947 but, recognizing that the work might be stopped before it began, application had also been made for a six-month visa to initiate a project in Hong Kong, permission for which was graciously given, a significant gesture considering the circumstances of the Colony at that time. As things turned out, the primary plan was successful, and several years passed in the process of producing a volume on the Koreans and their culture.

By the time it was feasible to return to the Far East again, China was politically controlled by the Communists, a group who could not be expected to sponsor anthropological research by an American, even if the

United States Department of State had not placed severe sanctions on a citizen's undertaking it. Scholarship inevitably suffers from the presumptuous dictates of politics.

The situation having been surveyed once again, the most logical place for a study of Chinese culture appeared to be the old mainland villages of Kwangtung which had come under the jurisdiction of the stable British government by the lease of the New Territories in 1898. During 1954, a few days' visit to Hong Kong were sufficient to show that the Colony was suffering from the greatest inundation of people in its history. Tens of thousands of refugees were crowded onto roofs, sleeping in the streets, or clutching at shack space on precipitous hills because of this tidal wave. It was not the best time to observe the normal social functioning of an ancient society.

Again the project was put off, but after devoting several years to the completion of research elsewhere, I again felt the magnet of China against the metal of my interest. Hong Kong had made miraculous readjustments and was effectively absorbing its befriended millions. For the ethnographer, time was no longer endless, and he made his decision.

To some people, the many attractions of metropolitan Hong Kong would make it seem an ideal place from which to work out. But it is not. The movement of material things is too fast, whereas the intellectual and spiritual progress which befits a great center of civilization has been slow. Officials are too busy with the urgencies of technical changes, and they wisely resist the too frequently unrewarding distractions presented by visitors. In the summer, Hong Kong can also be challengingly hot, while research assistants with the desired intellectual qualifications and necessary physical stamina are difficult to find. On the other hand, if one can succeed in resolving multifarious problems, Hong Kong is a marvelous locale for the ethnographer. As I have already stated, I am glad I returned.

What was accomplished during a season of ninety-two days was little enough, and this introductory monograph of the series represents only a part of the data recorded. The first week was memorable with an arrival on June 5, a Sunday, and the next day a holiday. On Tuesday there was a tropical downpour, and soon afterward wind stopped the ferries. Then Typhoon Mary, which was said to be the worst storm in twenty-three years, struck the island. Fortunately, it was all an invaluable experience for the future historian and, although rain later ruined some days of field work, the weather was, on the whole, merely unpleasant. The summer of 1960 happened to contribute some of the highest temperatures recorded in Hong Kong for the previous sixty years. It may be evident, however, that the ethnographer tried to work diligently. For him there was always the excitement of intellectual discoveries which are in themselves the great motivation as well as reward. That his Chinese assistant survived, however, seems a diminutive miracle.

Since the hamlet which is the subject of this monograph was visited only on thirty-nine days during that first season, it will be understood why more details were essential. Fortunately, it was possible to return to Hong Kong the next year, and thus fill some of the gaps in the information. Although vegetable gardening is not the most typical activity in the Colony, it is basic, and the ethnographer hopes that becoming acquainted with a few farming families will be, as it proved for him, the best introduction to an understanding of the Chinese of Hong Kong.

It may be noted that the following text of these volumes has been written with the substitution of the editorial pronoun *we* in place of the singular form as a gesture of acknowledgment to the participation not only of my interpreter-assistants but to the hundreds of informants whose statements have been edited, evaluated, and entwined in this developing and detailed account of Lung Chau.

As in all complex stories, to comprehend the descriptive setting may be effortful in the beginning, but one's horizon of knowledge—given a touch of literary faith and a tittle of intellectual courage—should be expected to widen rapidly thereafter. In contrast, any later and seeming simplicity in the writing cannot be claimed as fortuitous.

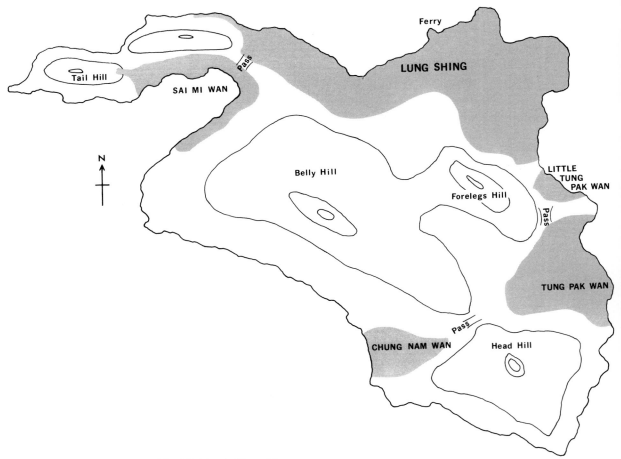

Fig. 1.2. Island of Lung Chau

1. Introduction

The country. Lung Chau is an imaginary name for an island rising off the south shore of the greater island of Hong Kong (Endsheet 1.1 and Fig. 1.2). It is perhaps somewhat less than a mile and a quarter long and, were a measurement taken perpendicular to such a line, the greatest width would approximate half of that distance. Actually, the total area of the island is 263 acres.* From a series of projections into the sea, the land rises into ridges and prominences, one of which is well over six hundred feet in height, and another, five hundred. Like most of the southern half of the main island, Lung Chau, or Dragon Island, is built primarily of Repulse Bay volcanics, and it has minor outcroppings of Tai Mo Shan porphyries and Tai Po grandiorite which are all of the Jurassic geological period. The hills appear treeless from even a short distance away, but they hide a few stunted specimens which project from the rough grass and scrub. Where there are farms, one finds guava trees and a lesser number of papayas, mulberries, and palms. To the people who live on the island, the most commonplace representatives of the fauna are the rats. If there are any larger wild mammals, our informants did not know of them. Snakes are indigenous, and some of them are claimed to be poisonous. There are also lizards and frogs. Because of the efforts made to control malaria, mosquitoes have been effectively reduced, and flies appear in notable quantities only where large numbers of pigs are being kept. Garden insects also prove a pest. Among birds, the people pay most attention to hawks, although dozens of other species may be recognized by those sophisticated enough to identify them.

The climate, one may presume, is not appreciably different from other areas of Hong Kong which lies somewhat less than a hundred miles south of the Tropic of Cancer (Fig. 32.1). We repeat the familiar figure of 84.76 inches which represents the average rainfall in the Colony, three-quarters of which occurs during the five months from May to September.† In midsummer when the humidity hangs a little below 100 per cent, hoeing

---

*The figure of 263 acres (.410 square mile) comes from the Crown Lands and Survey Office, but a different source gives .455 square mile. *Gazetteer*, 1960: 97.

†The data on climate are from the *Hong Kong 1959 Report*, 1960: 313–14.

vegetable fields is no pleasure. Actually, the temperature rarely goes above 95°F, or below 40°F in winter, the monthly means being 82°F in July and 59°F in February, with an annual average of 72°F. As for the summer of 1960, it was often so hot and humid that even the Chinese complained. On August 22, when the temperature reached a record 95.7°F, the day was not noticeably uncomfortable. It is when the humidity holds at 97 per cent while the temperature stays above 90°F that one loses weight.

There had been no census taken in Hong Kong for twenty-nine years when Lung Chau was first studied, and even those professionally preparing to measure the population were naturally unwilling to make guesses. However, an official census for the Colony gave the population of the little island as 8680 for March 7, 1961. Most of the population live in the town, but there are several hundred individuals who reside apart from the others and occupy discernible areas in the suburbs of Lung Chau, so to speak, and it is in the most isolated of these communities that we concentrated our first study.

History. The historical background of Lung Chau can best be given in terms of the Colony as a whole which in recent years has become the home of over three million Chinese, most of whose ancestors were born in the province of Kwangtung of which Hong Kong was originally a part. Therefore such details as we have been able to discover will be summarized in the historical section of Part IV, The Town of Lung Shing, where they seem to be more pertinent. We shall merely note here that in 1841, when the island of Hong Kong was occupied by the British, its total population was believed to be less than ten thousand.[1] Before that date there is more than inferential evidence that Lung Chau was inhabited, although the size of the settlement and anything concerning its composition is unknown. It may safely be presumed that there were only a few hundred people at most, while Chung Nam Wan itself was uninhabited. The harbor which Lung Chau helps to provide, however, is one of the best for small boats in the Colony, and it is true, even to this day, that the occupants of the island have in some measure been linked to the ancient fishing population. These latter people, living on their small vessels, have been traditionally assigned to two groups: the Tanka, originally speaking a non-Chinese language, it is thought, but now their own dialect of Cantonese, and the Hoklo whose language belongs to the Min subdivision of Chinese.* Exactly how much they have contributed to the population structure of Lung Chau is unknown. Today, most of the people on the small island speak one

---

1. Sayer, 1937: 203.

*We use the term Hoklo to refer only to the boat people speaking a Min language.

of the Cantonese dialects, but some of them know as their primary language Ch'ao An, Hakka, Fukienese, or other subdivisions of Chinese. These non-Cantonese speaking residents form a relatively high proportion of those farming in the peripheral sections of Lung Chau and a group consequently significant for this study as we shall see later.

Purpose of the work. Contributors to anthropological literature do not always make their purposes clear. It is possible, however, that to grope blindly may be the natural manner of development in an adolescent discipline. Also an awareness of ultimate goals perhaps tends to divert a simple explanation of immediate efforts to a statement of the author's ideals, for the little he accomplishes often seems hardly enough. Here, to avoid confusion, we shall try to present the case for motivations and then relate our results to them.

First among several objectives is the description of culture as replete in its details as is possible. The ideas and values of human beings must be known if one is to be realistically aware of their behavior, and the entire performance of society must be shown on a stage made comprehensible by a recognition of the cultural products. It is taken as a premise that the greater the understanding of the people of one society by another, the greater the possibility for meaningful communication, beneficial exchanges, increased appreciation, and the reduction of fear. No better example could be chosen than the need for mutual comprehension by the members of the Chinese and English-speaking worlds.

Second among objectives is the analysis of cultural content for the purpose of developing more precise concepts for use in the description and exposition of human society. Refinement and coordination of data lead to a more sophisticated awareness of culture and enable the research worker to gauge the validity of his records with increasing accuracy. It is assumed that such analyses may be most effectively and objectively undertaken when one culture is studied by a member of another. The analysis of Chinese culture by an Englishman, or vice versa, should provide a most illuminating viewpoint.

Third among goals is the ideal of reconstructing the developmental history of a culture. It is believed that, given a sufficient knowledge of the elements by which a culture is designated, a mosaic of interrelationships can be formed that will provide clear inferences of change both in time and in space. If an expression of pattern in the multiple causations can be formalized, so much the better, and in some distant future, no doubt this will be possible. For historical studies, Hong Kong with its sharply delineated boundaries and its clearly documented period of mushroom-like growth, presents a magnificent laboratory.

As for the immediate effort and what has been accomplished in Part I, the text will best speak for itself. The primary and manifest purpose is to present an ethnographic account of an isolated segment of Hong Kong society; the fact that the segment proved tiny is to some degree chance. Later, certain aspects of culture will be surveyed in the small village to which the more closely examined hamlet is juxtaposed. Both of these social units are in more or less degree related to the town and to the metropolis of which they are satellites.

In this simple study, which provocatively suggests some enlargement, there has been no presumption of any significant refinement of concepts. Even vegetables may not have been exactly identified. Offered here is only the concomitant of perspiration, not genius, and one is not expected to esteem it too much. There is, however, an effort to discern in an elemental way the process of social growth, the proliferation of the village tree, and what happens when seeds are blown over the hill. We shall try to explain how in one locality it was done, but first how we managed to learn of Chung Nam Wan.

The prelude to research. To find a distinct portion of Hong Kong society that can be studied within a brief period of time is not easy. Since the men of the village families often work away from home, it becomes essential to engage a woman to act as an entrepreneur and interpreter. The isolated settlements of the New Territories, ideal in some respects, present the task of getting to and from them because of the very fact of their isolation. To reside in one raises difficulties with respect to obtaining short term living accommodations consistent with long hours of work and, even if the anthropologist can accept the drawbacks of discomfort, it cannot be expected that a woman accustomed to more comfortable standards of living will do so. Furthermore, at this period, houses were not often immediately available in the villages of Hong Kong. Seeking for a solution, we found our efforts both physically exhausting and mentally disquieting. In short, when we could neither find an assistant with the necessary intellectual qualifications who would live in such a village, nor a village not so removed that we could commute to it, the gray shadows of frustration closed down upon us. Unless we abandoned our purpose altogether, the discovery of an isolatable social unit close to metropolitan Hong Kong impressed us as the least impractical choice of the two solutions that were offered.

For days we moved about Hong Kong Island itself questioning whoever gave the chance for conversation, asking the stranger if he knew of any small community for some reason set apart. In each case we were informed that there was none in the immediate locality, but on the opposite side of the island there was thought to be such a hamlet. On the opposite side of the island, however, we received the same answer.

One noon after asking our usual questions of a social worker on a ferry bound on the three-minute journey to an offshore island, and after politely assuring her that we had already searched on the other side of Hong Kong, we left her and walked rather disconsolately through the town. The narrow streets and throngs of people overwhelmed us. Plagued by our problem, aimless wandering led us higher and higher through the thin and dirty passages used by the poor of the town to gain access to their artlessly constructed homes wedged against one another on the face of the hill. When we had reached the highest of these cliff-clinging houses several hundred feet above the sea, the barking dogs below us and the charm of angular sails on distant blue water impelled us to climb through the underbrush and rocks to the summit. There, the quiet and beauty of Hong Kong was drink for our thirst and, deciding that discouragement deserved a holiday, we descended on the far side to a place where we could see a narrow path encircling the bare hill below. Then we followed a parallel course around the island until, having passed over a ridge, we looked down at a nearly vertical coomb with a semicircle of sand beach where it slipped into the ocean. To our surprise, we saw smoke rising between the trees and, after choosing a more favorable location for surveillance, we counted three or four houses. Hot and thirsty, we continued our circumambient journey, wishing that three or four houses made a village.

Several days later while debating in our mind whether to continue studying Hong Kong culture as a whole or to depart for Taiwan, it occurred to us that an unconscious insistence on finding a community of at least a hundred people was an arbitrary and unnecessary prerequisite for the research that had been planned. We immediately telephoned to the most reconcilable and qualified of our potential assistants and asked if she would be willing to transit a very small mountain on foot twice a day, providing it could be arranged for her to be home for dinner with her family by seven. She said that she was sure that she could climb.

Our doubts were relieved the next day when she almost left us behind with her sure-footed grace. We also found the path previously seen, so we had only to climb a precipitous three hundred feet as we circled water-torn gashes in the orange-colored earth, noting here and there a grave on the barren slope. Suddenly we discerned that a slight physical barrier set off nearly twenty more houses from the town. Fortune seems to come to those who climb hills. As we went on we tried to explain the requirements of our research. If among the dwellings originally seen there were a few families amenable to answering the questions of visitors, we would devote a few weeks to gathering information from them, after which we would

Fig. 1.3. The Descent to Chung Nam Wan

move back across the gap and try to tie in the larger, if apparently less integrated, community.

Then in the glaring tropical sun we stumbled and slipped down the precipitous trail into the settlement to which we have given the gratuitous name of Chung Nam Wan (Fig. 1.3). Nervously, we contemplated what our reception would be. Would the few inhabitants be suspicious and intolerant of our curiosity?

That day we visited each of the families, and in each someone said in his own polite way how grateful they all were for our coming. Chung Nam Wan, they told us, was so isolated that they rarely had the privilege of entertaining guests and they insisted that it would be a pleasure to tell us whatever it was that we wanted to know.

We returned again and again, widening our knowledge of the life of these people. In the pages that follow, the effort has been made to pass on some meaningful part of what was discovered. Perhaps to the anthropologist, the record will not seem large, nor to the people who now live in Hong Kong will descriptions of the commonplace strike them as worth the recording. If human beings have the chance to survive, however, the day probably will come when such simple accounts may be valued as the rare record of what has been but no longer exists.

2. The Setting of the Hong Kong Hamlet

The Lin family. Standing in the three hundred foot high gap in the center of Lung Chau, we can look westerly down into the small valley of Chung Nam Wan with its half a dozen buildings and its concisely laid out vegetable fields, some of which are high and detached, but most of which are juxtaposed on both sides of a tiny stream near the place where it debouches onto a narrow sandy beach (Fig. 2.1). As we begin the descent following the precipitous path, we cannot see the older houses clearly because of guava or palm trees around them that cut off the view, and the most recent additions rest concealed by a projection of the hills. In some places steps have been cut into the clay for better footing, but usually an irregular series of rocks suffices to keep one from falling. When it rains, it is safer to walk with bare feet. About a quarter of the way down, we pass to the south of the two upper fields of the family we shall call Lin. On the far side of the nearer field with its several vegetable beds we can perceive the beginning of a ravine where the previously-mentioned tiny stream has its source in the rocks. About a hundred feet beyond the ravine is another field of the Lin family cut from the steep hillside and terraced with a smooth wall of stone (Fig. 2.2). Conspicuous at the near end of the upper bed of that field are adjoined concrete reservoirs, one for water and the other for pig fertilizer.

Continuing on down the path, we reach the stream and pass a third field on the left with a basin for water at the bottom. A few yards below, the defile seems to narrow and we come upon the two buildings of the Lin family with the stream running between them (Figs. 2.3 and 2.4). The structure on the southerly side is quickly ascertained to consist of a rectangular, gable-roofed, central room about twelve by thirteen feet in size constructed of stones reinforced with cement. On the upper end is a shed-roofed, twelve-and-half-foot extension, the front part of which houses the family chickens, while the rear part serves as a kitchen. Extending from the lower end of the main room is a smaller, shed-roofed pigsty, a rough nine or ten feet square, for which there are unfortunately no longer tenants. Just below this structure is the fourth and last group of terraced vegetable fields of the Lin family.

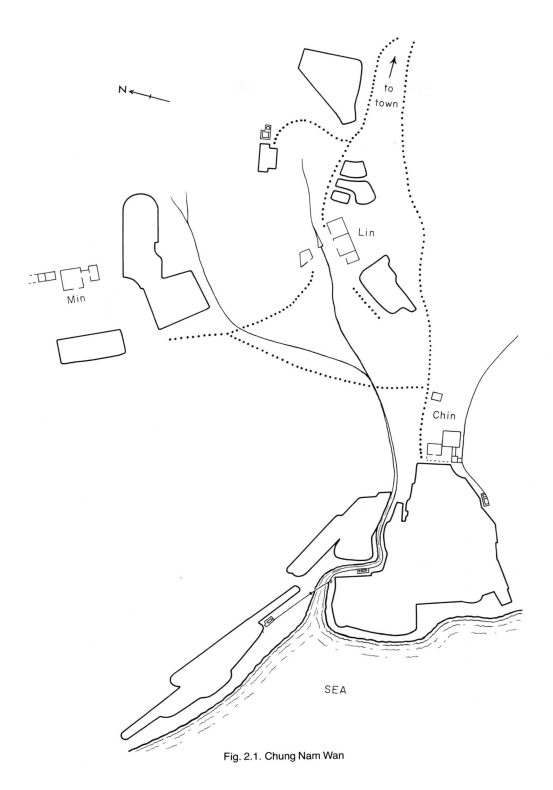

N

to
town

Lin

Min

Chin

SEA

Fig. 2.1. Chung Nam Wan

Fig. 2.2. The Upper Terraces of the Lin Family

Fig. 2.3. The Lins at Home

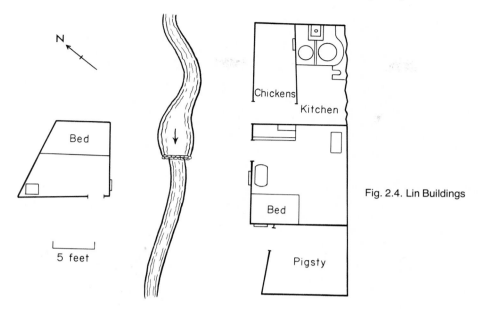

N

Bed

5 feet

Chickens

Kitchen

Bed

Pigsty

Fig. 2.4. Lin Buildings

Directly in front of the kitchen door, the tiny stream in its three-foot-wide gully has been dammed in order to create a pool in which to wash dishes and clothes, as well as to provide an easy crossing place to the opposite bank where the Lins have another rock and cement building. This structure, like the main house, is seven feet from the near bank of the stream. It was originally made to house pigs, and little care was taken in its construction. No two sides are quite parallel, and all four are of different lengths varying from about seven to eleven feet. Mrs. Lin and her four-year-old (Ch)* adopted daughter sleep in this small house, the rear half of which is entirely blocked off by the commonplace bed made of planks extended on a pair of sawhorses with a reed mat spread on top and a mosquito net suspended from the three rafters that hold up the tin and tarpaper roof. In the west corner of the room stands a small table made by nailing four legs to a box. There are also two of the family's four small square stools, but stools may be removed from one building to another or used to sit on outside. A board shelf runs two-thirds of the way along the north wall and characteristically holds four or five bottles, a glass, two cups, a battered thermos for drinking water, a few gourds, and several paper notebooks in which Mr. Lin enters his record of deliveries to the market. From a nail above the middle of the shelf is suspended a kerosene lamp eight inches high with a dirty glass chimney.

---

*Ages have all been given according to Chinese reckoning and are occasionally so marked to refresh the memory. In Chinese style, this girl is said to be four as she was one-year-old when born and became two on New Year's Day a few weeks later. By the English system, she would be called two.

The southeast wall is perforated by a small window which faces the tiny stream and the main house. On the wall southwest of the window hangs an 8″ by 10″ mirror next to an 11″ by 14″ framed piece of glass containing a photograph of Mr. Lin with his daughter.* Above the mirror, an alarm clock tells the time and below it there is a calendar with a sheet imprinted with both Chinese and European reckoning to be pulled off each day, a duty punctiliously performed by Mr. Lin when he returns from the market in the morning. Mr. Lin enjoys a cup of wine when the opportunity offers, and it was the restaurant where he usually drinks that provided the calendar.

A few other items might be noticed which have a tendency to be permanent fixtures of the house. There is the small and seldom used abacus which hangs from the highest rafter, the five-sided loose-woven tray suspended from a nail which, when put over a pail of boiling water, serves as a steamer for cakes at New Year's. Then there is a blanket, an old red winter coat, and the small pillow on the corner of the bed. Also on the wall near the door are a row of hangers, contrived by either driving nails through empty wood spools, or winding the nails with layers of tin foil. Through the door one looks southwest over the fields of the Chin family toward a blue vista of sea, with usually a junk or two sailing past the islands in the distance.

Recrossing the tiny stream to the main room of the first building where Mr. Lin sleeps and the family eats its meals, such distinction in appearance as there is reflects little more than the slightly larger size and a concomitant increase in the furnishings. The floor is concrete as are those in all bedrooms and pigsties in the settlement. Six three-quarter-inch planks, more or less seven feet long and as many inches wide, placed on a pair of sawhorses provide a bed 24″ off the floor. Under the bed one might note a pair of rubber boots 15″ high belonging to Mr. Lin, a length of spout pipe for a fertilizer spray bucket, and an old can, once painted red, containing the remnants of burned incense sticks. To the right of the door as one enters stands a round drop-leaf table that is 30″ in diameter. The leaves are folded down. On it, the family regularly eats its meals. Two of the small square stools adjoin it. There is a window above the table and another above the bed.

---

*The writing of numerals in Arabic has epistemological meaning in these volumes and should be borne in mind as part of the field work method. Arabic numbers, with the exception of *one* by itself, have been specifically used for exact ruler measurements up to 99 inches. They also serve to indicate the days and the months of the Chinese calendar (e.g., 5th of the 5th month), thus distinguishing it from the Western. Also, specific prices and percentages have been written in Arabic. By this method, an effort has been made to distinguish exact calculations from those that are approximations of various kinds (e.g., paced distances). The system is not absolute, especially as any numeral of three or more digits has usually been written in Arabic, but it should readily establish a quantitative guide in the mind of the reader.

To the left of the door as one enters and extending along the northeast wall is a heavy table made of two planks 1½" thick and 60" long. One of the planks is 20" wide and the other 6", and they rest on a pair of sawhorses 27" high. The table had to be heavy as it was formerly used for making dumplings, a business in which the Lin family was once briefly involved. At the moment, however, the surface is largely covered with an assortment of cans and bottles, a child's doll, a tube of toothpaste, and a bag marked CARE which has been re-used to hold noodles. Some of these things are in a wood box turned on its side on the table to provide an additional surface. Under the table are two tin funnels, a spouted tin kerosene can, some empty bottles, a small charcoal stove with a pot on it, a tin plate, and another tin can containing incense sticks, most of which have been burned.

Against the southeast wall, resting on stones a few inches off the floor is a homemade case for dishes constructed by turning on its side a wood box which Mr. Lin purchased in Lung Shing, or Dragon Town, the business center of the island, for $.50.* In it are eleven porcelain rice bowls, two handsome but inexpensive dishes bearing underglaze designs of a blue fish with green scales, a deep bowl for soup, two shallower ones, two small dishes, and five porcelain spoons, one of which has a painted bowl. There is also a small brown stoneware spouted pot of the type the Chinese commonly used for medicine but which the Lin family uses for tea when they have any. Besides these ceramic vessels, there are also three gaily-colored enamelware plates, which are a well-known product of Hong Kong, and a container with a cover of the same material which serves to protect leftover food.

On the floor near the rear wall next to the collection of dishes is a wood tub 21" in diameter and 10" high which is primarily used for bathing the small daughter. Close to it is a gasoline can with the top cut out in which water is carried. Then there are two stoneware jars 20" in diameter and equally high. One has a delightful dragon preserved on the yellow slip. Both are imposing, brown-glazed vessels of a type that were purchased from a food store in Lung Shing for from three to five dollars each after their original contents, such as pickled eggs from China, had been sold. They function as excellent protectors of edibles from the voraciousness of the ubiquitous Hong Kong rats. Piled on top of one of the jars is a burlap bag full of clothes and, on the other, are two basketry suitcases containing various personal objects. Leaning against the jars is a slightly battered folding cot.

---

*All statements of cost are in Hong Kong money, a dollar of which was equivalent to approximately U.S. $.17½ and British ls 3d during the period of our research. See Appendix D.

Against the rear wall hang clothing, including a pair of the small daughter's shoes and a pointed straw hat bearing the two-character name of the place where it was made; also a Chinese balance made of wood (steelyard) for measuring the weights of things, two baskets with loop handles, three dishrags, a night lantern, a moldy gourd, and a raincoat. On the southwest wall above the bed is a rolled up mosquito net. Farther along is a black umbrella, more clothing on hooks, and a green net bag full of Small Daughter's costumes. It is almost curious that on the northwest wall there is nothing hanging at all. On the northeast wall, however, there is a large soft-brimmed straw hat with a spray of flowers painted on it next to a calendar with a picture of a girl whose costume is distinguished by red pants. To these items one can add string and several spare lamp chimneys. More interesting is a faded orange-red paper bearing black Chinese characters that may be translated as "Four seasons always good," an optimistic expression, the assertion of which, it may be hoped, will have some influence on the state of one's affairs.

Also on the northeast wall above the heavy table an elaborate shelf 34″ long and 16″ wide is supported on two vertical sticks from which two additional pieces slant out to the front edge which is held at one corner by a wire that angles back and is fastened to a roof beam. That this is a special piece of furniture is indicated by the one-inch strip of wood running around and above the shelf rim and another over twice that width below that has a border festooned with a continuous series of semicircular segments. These decorative additions are painted red and prepare one to recognize the religious nature of the picture of Kun Yam (Kuan Yin),* the Chinese Goddess of Mercy, in a 10″ by 14″ frame and the matching framed red paper with three columns of five gold characters bearing an auspicious message.† On the shelf itself are six wine cups (half of which have fallen over in conspicuous disarray), two small plates, a broken fan, a cardboard box with toothpicks, three small tin cans painted red, full of the remnant red slivers of burned incense sticks, a glass kerosene lamp which is only 7″

---

*The problem of transliterating Chinese characters into the English alphabet is one that cannot be resolved to everyone's satisfaction, or even to our own. What we have done throughout this study is to use the system adopted by Eitel for the Cantonese dialect (Eitel, 1883), adding the Mandarin equivalents from Giles' *Chinese English Dictionary* (Giles, 1912) in parentheses when available. The purpose has been simply to make the words meaningful to both Cantonese and Mandarin speakers who read English. In cases of doubt, the corresponding Chinese characters are given in Appendix G. Exceptions have been made in certain cases, such as the words for the commonest costumes and for geographic terms as will be noted later. Also as a major exception, we have added Herklots' transliteration after Eitel's in the list of locally grown vegetables as Herklots has published a special paper on that subject (Herklots, 1947). Chinese words, such as amah, feng-shui, and kaoliang, that have been adopted into English and listed in *Webster's New International Dictionary* are treated simply as English. Clearly, our procedure has weaknesses, but to have presented consistently in any better fashion the agglomeration of Chinese dialects used by our informants would have overtaxed our ability as well as our patience.

†Such religious sayings are not always readily translated into meaningful English.

high to the top of its chimney, and a small statue of Kun Yam (Kuan Yin). From the existence of this altar, it is clear that the Lin family has an identification with the traditional religion of southeast China, if not with Buddhism itself.

Kitchens are crude adjuncts to the main rooms of the houses in Chung Nam Wan, and that of the Lin family has a slightly haphazard appearance because of the enclosure for chickens built on in front and extending the length of the kitchen. The joint depth of these secondary rooms is equal to that of the main part of the house. A second look reveals that part of the irregularity results from the fact that the shed roof of the kitchen section slopes southeast into the hill, whereas that of the chicken roost slopes northeast. Inside, the kitchen is not what would be called light and airy, although there is a northeast window with a square opening almost two feet on a side and another somewhat larger one which leads into the chicken room. Certainly the fact that the rear, or southeast, wall remains a vertical cut of the hill without benefit of any laid stone or cement adds to the initial dismal effect which, however, quickly disappears as one participates in the activities of the household and enjoys the easy hospitality of its occupants.

The stove for pig food in the north corner is the largest object one sees in the kitchen and it has the characteristic form of the region (Fig. 2.5). Built of cement, the imposing right-hand section stands 24" high and its circular cooking depression is 27" in diameter. The left-hand section is a similar stove but only 18" high. The essential difference between them is that the latter burns wood and the former burns grass. One large, pyramidal chimney topped by a six-inch metal stovepipe extending through the roof serves both. Since, as has already been stated, there no longer are

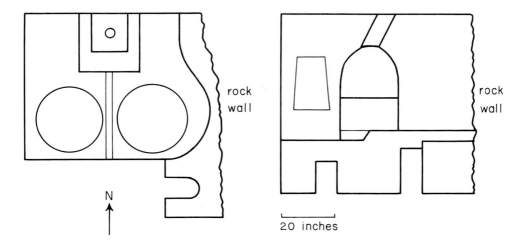

Fig. 2.5. Lin Stoves

pigs to be fed, it is not so strange to find on top of the stove, a pile of grass, a metal basin with rice for the chickens, a cover half over the cooking depression and, on the cover, a sleeping cat.

Cooking for the family is actually done in a small fireplace—a kind of built-in pot stove a little less than two feet square and a foot and half high—along the southeast wall. Both stoves were constructed by a mason who was called in for the purpose. Also in the dark of the kitchen one can find pans, a broom, food jars, and a miscellany of broken and unused oddments which challenge description but do not deserve it.

On one's way out, one may notice the old boxes and baskets in the chicken house, the front wall of which is made of flattened tin cut from old gasoline cans that may be purchased in Lung Shing, the town on the north side of the island, for twenty cents each. The boxes and baskets are empty because the chickens usually spend the day pecking at the earth in front of the small house originally built for pigs on the other side of the tiny stream, an area from which they are prevented from returning at will by a small wood-framed, wire gate.

The shelter for pigs which is the southwesterly wing of the main house is a rough nine by ten feet and not quite square. Its shed roof, matching that of the kitchen, slopes back toward the hill. The southwest wall of poured concrete was originally only two and a half feet high, but the southeasterly third has since been filled up by flat fragments of rock. There is a drain from the cement floor running to a fertilizer basin outside used as a toilet by the family. Small Daughter may sit on a pot in the house, but the others do not. Since the demise of the pigs, the sty has become a ramshackle storeroom. Inside, one can see a chicken basket hanging from the roof, another on the floor containing a hen that is brooding. There are four more old baskets of various kinds on the floor, one of which has a mat resting on it, a second a broken wood tray. Near one corner stands a fifty-gallon* drum in which pig food formerly was cooked. There is also a good pick-mattock leaning against the wall, and two wood fertilizer buckets are hanging above it. Nearby is a dipper for fertilizer. A pile of grass to be used as fuel completes the roster of items in the room.

The people who inhabit or utilize the buildings just described have had a complicated life, as have had many human beings in the colony, but it has not deprived them of their charm. Mr. Lin was born in the province of Kwangtung, as was his wife. Both of them are Hakka, but they speak Cantonese. They emigrated to Hong Kong after World War II.

Mr. Lin is a slightly-built man with the wide cheekbones and narrow forehead frequently found among southeastern Chinese. He has a low bridge to his nose and his nostrils are wide. His ears are large and he has

---

*Or forty imperial gallons, the U.S. measure being used throughout the text.

clear brown skin, a pair of brown eyes, unusually fine teeth, and a smile—a very frequent smile (Fig. 2.6). He does not know either his height or his weight, but he measures five feet five inches. He was born about 1917.

Mr. Lin's favorite costume for a hot summer day consists of a white shirt with elbow length sleeves tucked into a pair of faded blue shorts that end above his knees and are worn over underpants. To this outfit, he may

Fig. 2.6. Mr. Lin and His Daughter

add green plastic sandals with straps and a large straw hat of one type or another. With the heat at its exceptional worst, Mr. Lin has been known to reduce his costume to only his underpants and his smile. On other days, Mr. Lin has made himself conspicuous in a checked shirt, dark glasses, and a pith sun helmet someone has given him. Mr. Lin has a real sense of humor.

Fig. 2.7. Mrs. Lin Washing in the Stream

Fig. 2.8. The Sam Fu

Mrs. Lin is a sweet woman about four years older than her husband and she works almost incessantly (Fig. 2.7). There are a few streaks of gray in her hair. She has a broad nose and a large mouth in an animated, somewhat wrinkled, oval face. When she laughs she tries to keep her mouth closed, for of her incisors, only one upper and one lower have survived. Of further distinguishing marks, one might note the large scar on the front of her lower right leg, and one long nail on the thumb of her left hand.

Mrs. Lin always dresses in the Chinese jacket and trousers called sam fu* (Fig. 2.8). Usually they are of the black, gum-coated silk material so common in Hong Kong, but sometimes of blue cotton so many times washed as to be almost white. The jacket fastens down the right side, and beneath it is an under jacket which buttons down the front and has two patch pockets over the stomach. Then there are underpants. Mrs. Lin customarily works barefooted and has her trousers rolled up to her knees. She wears on her head the distinguishing broad-brimmed straw hat of the Hakka with a hole in its crown and a 4½″ black cloth band hanging down like a fringe from its edge (Fig. 47.3). She has had it for over ten years and it shows wear. She would like a new one, but her husband thinks the seven dollars that Hakka hats cost is too much. They are not sold on Lung Chau, and one has to cross the strait to obtain them. Mrs. Lin says that she likes her Hakka hat because it is cool. When it rains, she replaces it with a small, plain one of bamboo.

Small Daughter, like most young children in Hong Kong, wears European style dress, most often an abbreviated kind of overall with the halter over a shirt. One day it is a green-figured shirt tucked into pink-figured pants, another day a white shirt and undershirt plus red overalls with a blue horse's head on the bib, but there are other combinations as well. Underclothes in summer are an unneeded accessory. Small Daughter is not above asking for dresses and rings. It is said that only a girl would ask for clothes and jewelry.

The Lin family buys clothing only when it wears out, and this means perhaps one set for the adults each year. The best outfit is saved for special occasions, while the older ones serve for work and as a costume in which to sleep. Finally, when nothing is left except rags, pieces of cloth may be coiled up and burned on a stick of wood under the beds on summer nights in order to keep some of the mosquitoes away. The cloth is purchased, and the dressmaking is all done in Lung Shing, for Mrs. Lin would not know how to do it herself.

Compared with other Chinese, those of the southeast coast are exceptionally clean, and there is no commoner sight than the washing of clothes. Mrs. Lin washes hers and her daughter's with great regularity, as well as some of her husband's, but he frequently does his own, squatting at the bridge over the stream and scrubbing his pants on a large flat stone with a

---

*Our simplified spelling of the names for the two common Chinese costumes does not follow the rule: sam fu would be sham fu (shan k'u) and cheong sam would be ch'eung sham (ch'ang shan).

brush well-covered with soap which he keeps in a can. A neighbor, who does not wash clothes, says that Mr. Lin on occasions even washes some of Mrs. Lin's wearing apparel which action is attributed to the fact that she works so hard and has so little time. Nevertheless, the commentator, a man, considers such behavior most unusual.

The family also bathes every day. Mr. Lin says everyone in Chung Nam Wan takes a bath every day, winter and summer, which is the theory if not the fact. Small Daughter, for example, may skip a day in winter. She has her bath in the wood tub before she goes to bed. Mrs. Lin takes hers in the kitchen in Cantonese style by pouring water over her shoulders while she squats in the tub. Some hot water is used. Her husband does likewise, but not at the same time. Mr. Lin uses a three-gallon bucket of water. He wets himself all over, soaps himself, and then spreads water over himself with a rag to wash off the soap. He says that he would itch and could not sleep without a bath. He has one rag which he ordinarily uses for his hands and face, and another for his bath. Small Daughter warns him not to confuse them, her recognition of the difference being perhaps the simple correlate of her concern. The parents, it is claimed, brush their teeth every morning, using a toothpaste named "Darkie."

Mr. Lin also purports to shave almost every day and can produce a small amount of chin whiskers and a mustache if he does not. Something provokes him to ask why the ethnographer does not go to a barber. Twice a month, he himself pays $1.20 for a haircut in Lung Shing, but the service includes shampooing and shaving as well, and a little oil on the hair. He states that the shop does not smell good.

Mrs. Lin wore her long black hair in a bun at the back of her head until the week before our arrival. Then she had it bobbed in Lung Shing for a dollar and brought back the hair that was cut off, although her husband did not know why, whereas any woman can guess. Two or three years ago Mrs. Lin bought a small bottle of perfume which she liked very much, but she has used it all. She also likes a white summer flower (probably a yulan) to put in her hair. Such an ornament, however, can be purchased only across the strait on the main island.

Mrs. Lin wears small gold loop earrings every day and she has a silver wedding band on the third finger of her left hand. Of necklaces or bracelets, her husband says she has none. Mr. Lin has no jewelry at all.

The Min family. Having introduced the Lin family, we can move on to visit the home of the people we shall call the Mins (Fig. 2.9). To do this we need only to cross the tiny stream, pass through the gate, and follow the path which leads from the front of the Lin's former pig house around a rib of the hills for two or three hundred feet toward the north. Remaining at the same height of approximately a hundred feet above the sea, we

Fig. 2.9. The Approach to the Mins' House from the Lins

cross a dry gully and skirt the bottom of seven terraced fields which extend eighty feet up the steep slope. Thus passing their untended vegetable beds, we come suddenly upon a view of the Min house and pig pens which impress us first by the professional efforts that have gone into their construction, and, secondly, by the relative bareness of the surroundings. The few trees, except for one willow, have not grown high, and the home has obviously not been lived in as long as the others in Chung Nam Wan. The Min dogs bark louder than those of the Lin family and one has the feeling that the people they intend to protect are possibly a little less secure. This is understandable since Mrs. Min is alone with her five young children, the oldest of whom is no more than eleven (Ch) (Fig. 2.10). Mr. Min, as we have already learned from the Lins, is a builder in concrete and, because of the demands for his services caused by a recent typhoon, he is often away from early in the morning until late in the evening. We are nonetheless immediately invited to have tea, the children yelling at the dogs which, still whimpering uneasily, hide under the bed in one of the two rooms into which the ten-by-sixteen-foot house is almost equally

Fig. 2.10. The Min Children

divided (Fig. 2.11). The structure, containing a considerable amount of stone (Fig. 2.12), is unquestionably well-built as one can perceive from the smoothness of the cement floor, from the two evenly-spaced windows at the front and the one at each end, and from the flat, steel-reinforced concrete ceiling.

The division of the house is cleverly contrived by installing six-foot high pieces of quarter-inch masonite in a grooved frame so that one of them, about two feet wide, will slide as a door. The only deficiency is that a person must be careful not to trip over the frame in passing from one room to another. The south room which one enters from the front or rear door contains a three-by-six-foot double-decked bed extending along the south wall from the southwest corner.* First and Second Daughter sleep on the lower level, but the upper is not regularly used for fear the children might fall out.

---

*The so-called west or front door of the house actually faces twenty degrees south of west.

[34]

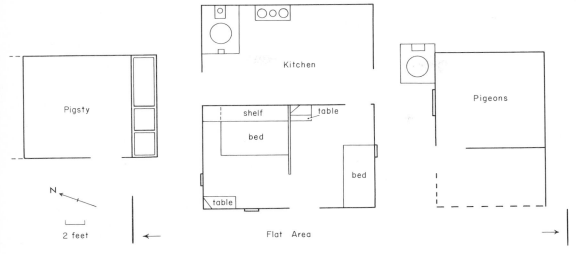

Kitchen

shelf table

bed

bed

table

N

2 feet ← Flat Area →

Fig. 2.11. Min Buildings

Pigsty

Pigeons

Fig. 2.12. Front View of the Min House

In the opposite corner along the east wall is a one-by-two-foot table, not counting the 9″ drop leaf which is held open by a swinging fifth leg. A foot and a half above this table is a triangular shelf 17″ on two sides. There are also three stools in the room with 12″ by 9½″ wood tops and steel rod and strap supports which fold flat. More unusual is a folding canvas chair with a wood frame so relatively comfortable that it can make a person sleepy to look at it.

On the table are a group of dishes that have supplied a recent meal and some of the older children's school books. On the shelf above is a circular enamel tray on which rest three plain water glasses, a small teapot, and two toothbrushes. In the teapot are three more toothbrushes. Next to the tray are a package of Bristol cigarettes, a box of matches, and four various-sized bottles. Over the top of the six-foot partition dividing the house appear the legs of a pair of man's blue pants and next to it are hooked two black umbrellas, one of which is the kind that opens automatically. From neither the south nor the west wall hang anything, but on the east one, with a horizontal strip of wood to furnish support, a frame color print of Christ between Mary and Joseph leans out. Behind it has been stuck a slender tin handpump which functions to draw kerosene from a can. Directly below the picture hangs a calendar with a sheet to be torn off daily beneath a picture of a female cinema star. Next to the calendar, a wire net basket has been suspended with some "chicken-egg flowers" (probably "chicken-crown flowers," an amaranth) in it. These, we may add, when boiled in water will provide a tonic to make people feel better when it rains a great deal.

The other, and slightly smaller, half of the house is largely filled by a typical bed made of planks resting on two sawhorses. It extends from the southeast corner along the east wall and is an inch or two short of five feet wide. On it Mr. and Mrs. Min sleep each night as well as the three younger children, First Son, and Third and Fourth Daughter, the last named having been in the family only eight months. In the northwest corner extending along the west wall is a four-legged rectangular table with a top 38″ by 14″. On it is a thermos bottle, a half-gallon glass bottle used for boiled water (later demolished by First Son who dropped it on the cement floor), three smaller bottles, an enamel cup, and a drinking glass. Under the table are several wood boxes and next to them along the south wall, a 10″ by 13″ rectangular metal container two feet high for the storage of rice, and finally a wood box turned on its side which contains half a dozen pairs of children's shoes. There are more shoes of various kinds under the bed.

Above the table three triangular shelves, like those in the south room but only fourteen to sixteen inches on the shorter sides, have been fixed. They hold a miscellaneous collection of small cans, bottles, and boxes, the latter containing materials for sewing. There are also two alarm clocks, one of them broken. Another shelf made of two boards totaling a foot and a half wide extends above the bed from the partition the full length of the east wall to rest on a wood strip running the full length of the north wall. On the shelf are two woven bamboo suitcases, a white cotton blanket, four cardboard cartons, and a composition suitcase. These contain the family clothes.

Resting on the wood strip just mentioned, and near the triangular corner shelves, are two picture frames, the first with a photograph of Mr. and Mrs. Min and four of their children; the other, twenty-one small photos of members of their families and of friends. On the same north wall hang a man's blue shirt and darker blue trousers, and above the window, a hand mirror and pair of scissors. Against the west wall in proximity to the middle corner shelf is a slender kerosene lamp and, near it, a second mirror suspended from the same nail as a calendar with a sheet for each day. South of the window on the same wall hangs a Chinese wood steelyard, with a man's blue shirt over it. In the corner by the door is a "six-bunch" cocoanut fiber broom. A last look shows the upper part of the blue pants mentioned previously as hanging over the partition dividing the house.

If we go out the rear door of the south room, we find ourselves in the kitchen which is set into the hill behind the house. It is of the same length as the latter and nine and a half feet deep, a measurement which happens to correspond with the height of the shed roof where it joins the house (as well as that of the house itself). The roof slopes down to about seven feet at the natural rear wall which once was cemented but has deteriorated badly. For a moment one is surprised by two large rocks suspended by a rope from the central of the three rafters; then one realizes that the threat of a recent and serious typhoon was the cause of this precaution. The kitchen has the feeling of being subject to winds as there are three-foot-wide openings at each end without any doors. The floor is of earth unevenly tamped down.

Facing west from the northeast corner of the kitchen is a large and excellently made cement stove designed for cooking pig food with sawdust as fuel (Fig. 2.13). It is over five feet long and nearly four feet wide. Mr. Min made it himself, a special art not practiced by all masons. Some 16" south of the large stove is a smaller one with three fire pits used for cooking the family meals. It runs somewhat less than five feet along the wall and is only a foot and an half wide. It contrasts with the pig food stove in being less than two-thirds as high, in having no chimney, and in presenting its structure in rather dilapidated condition. Actually, since the number of pigs being kept is considerably less than formerly, the left hand fire pit is used to cook for them, whereas the family rice is regularly prepared on the right hand burner.

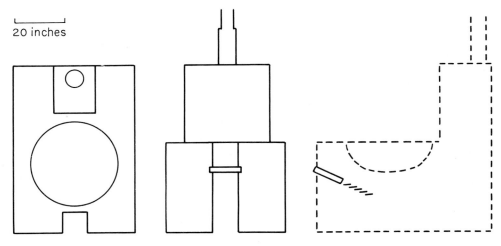

20 inches

Fig. 2.13. Min Pig Food Stove

In the southeast corner of the kitchen is a table so flimsy and crude that it questionably deserves the name. On it, however, rest two soot-blackened kettles, the top for the circular metal drum in which the pigs' food is cooked, a wood paddle for stirring the food, and an empty burlap bag. Under the table are three baskets containing sawdust, two of them large and covered with burlap; also there is a basket for a chicken. Three more baskets hang from the corner post.

Against the west wall, which is that of the house, is a large stoneware jar which formerly served to hold salt for the pigs. Above it on shelves made in a niche which was originally a window in the south room of the house are some porcelain rice bowls, a can containing an assortment of chopsticks, an enamel cup, bowl, and some shallow dishes, a covered aluminum pail for transporting cooked food, three bottles, a box of matches, and a rag. A "five-bunch" cocoanut fiber broom leans near the door.

On the floor in front of the small stove is a platform of planks which enables Mrs. Min to keep her feet out of the water when it rains. Near the south end of the stove is a small pile of kindling and a contemplative chicken. The remainder of the contents of the kitchen rest on top of the unused pig's food stove. To the left of its chimney are some rusty tin cans and a stoneware dish, to its right, eight glass bottles, two tin cans, a stone lantern, a deep blue enamel kettle and cover, and a stoneware ginger jar with a spoon stuck in the salt it contains. On the front of the stove a kitten is sleeping.

If we walk out of the kitchen to the north, we encounter the end of a row of six pigsties continuing on a line parallel with those of the back and front walls of the kitchen, the sties having the same depth of approximately ten feet (Fig. 2.14). Along the full width of the end of the sties and four feet from the kitchen is a cement tank 28″ wide and a little over three feet deep. This tank, which has smooth four-inch walls, is divided into three sections, the largest of which is next to the hill and twice the length of the others. It was built to hold pig food. The middle basin serves to store water brought from the well for use in the kitchen. The third, also for water, remains empty.

The six pigsties are almost identical in construction but the four farthest away are in various states of disintegration, the roofs having been blown off by storms at one period or another. This is not surprising since the roofs consist of only a wood frame covered with tin that rests freely on top of eight-inch cement columns seven feet high. The surviving roofs support rocks which were added to counteract a typhoon. Except for the natural wall of the hill at the rear which has been faced with cement, and the wall nearest the kitchen, the remainder are only 32″ high, thus creating half open pens. At the front of each pen is an entrance blocked by planks which slide down in grooves for the purpose. Inside the front wall of each pen is a cement trough for food. The floors are flat, well-made, and

Fig. 2.14. Interpreter in front of Min Pigsties

have a pebbled surface purposefully created in the cement. At the front next to the entrance is a drain so that when the pens are washed clean, the refuse can flow out into an open concrete duct which continues along in front of the pens and finally descends into a fertilizer basin, a 48″ by 52″ rectangle, which serves also as the family toilet.

If we leave the kitchen in the opposite direction, we enter a small nook created by a pigeon house which lies five and half feet to the south. In the northeast corner of the nook is a second pig food stove designed to burn grass. It is about two-thirds as long and wide as the one in the kitchen and only about half as high. Set into its top is a concave iron pan 32″ in diameter which has unfortunately been broken. Now deposited in it is a nearly globular stoneware jar 10″ in diameter. It has heavy brown glaze, a small spout, and a wood cover. The jar once held an expensive kind of vinegar which is believed to be an excellent addition to certain foods when cooked for pregnant women.

The pigeon house mentioned as creating the nook is a ten-foot long concrete building with a shed roof sloping back nine feet against a vertical cut in the hill which has been faced with cement. The roof consists only of loosely-spaced boards with tarpaper on top, then more boards, some pieces of tin, and finally rocks. There are windows in each of the well-made south and north walls, and adjacent to the north window a door opens west into an area completely enclosed with chicken wire extending six feet west of the front wall. Pigeon raising did not prove profitable to the Mins, and the wire enclosure has been adopted for chickens by the simple addition of a series of boxes turned on their sides and some boards raised off the ground on stones for the chickens to sit on. Actually, below the terrace which extends twenty feet out in front of the Min home, the chickens have a house of their own, but a recent typhoon blew it over, and Mr. Min has been too busy to undertake any domestic repairs. The terrace, it should be mentioned, continues along in front of the pigpens, but the latter area is wired off and devoted to fruit trees.

Mrs. Min, who presides over her brood of five children, is a pleasant-faced woman given to laughter and inclined to be a little bit plump. She does not know her weight or how tall she is, but it was not difficult to determine the latter as 62½″. Most people would recognize that she has the oval face and harmonic features of the Shanghai area from which she came, and no one could fail to appreciate her beautiful teeth. She is about thirty years old (Ch), and about seven years younger than her husband, a slightly built man of medium height, with a nice Cantonese face. As for the physical characteristics of the children, it means little that to one person, Third Daughter is a perfect image of her mother. Another disagrees. Besides, the children are constantly changing in the numerous ways children do. Perhaps it is a careless thing to say, but the Min family, taken as a whole, is the handsomest one in Chung Nam Wan. Technically, two of Mr. Min's father's father's brother's sons are also members of the household, for they are not married and have no other permanent home. Unless they are out of work, however, neither one is apt to appear in Chung Nam Wan. When one does, he sleeps in the upper bunk of the double-decked bed. The situation of having to accommodate both uncles at one time has never been faced.

Like all the other women in the settlement, Mrs. Min wears a sam fu with an underjacket and panties, but not a brassiere. She, as do her children, uses Japanese style plastic (or rubber) slippers with the thong between the toes. At home, their feet are most often bare. Mrs. Min admits she would like to dress well if she could afford to, and her attitude is suggested by the fact that she is the only mother in Chung Nam Wan to

Fig. 2.15. The Cheong Sam

wear anything but dark cloth on ordinary occasions. In her navy blue sam fu with white polka dots, she looks particularly well. The material cost $1.10 a yard and required four,* the tailoring only $2.00 because it was done by a friend, whereas double that amount would not be an unreasonable price. Mrs. Min, incidentally, says that once when she lived in Canton, she had a cheong sam (the Chinese long dress with a high collar and split skirt) (Fig. 2.15), but she would no longer have any use for one.

---

*Cottons are usually twenty-nine inches wide, silks thirty-six inches or more. The latter will leave enough left over for a child's dress.

In passing, it may be noted that winter clothes differ little from those worn in summer except that black gummed silk is not used in the cool part of the year. Sam fu have longer sleeves in winter,* are made of heavier cotton, and the sam may possibly be padded. Sweaters can be added.

The children wear European style clothing. For example, First Son has blue shorts and a light white cotton undershirt one day while Third Daughter wears pink pants and a pink undershirt. The baby is decked out with a red shirt embellished with green flowers. Sometimes it goes naked except for a rolled blue cloth string around its middle which is used to keep pants on when pants have no elastic. The preference for European costume for children is dictated by the fact that dresses take less material. It requires only two yards, for example, to make a dress for First Daughter, whereas a sam fu would take three. The latter states a positive preference for sam fu, however, as soon as she grows up. She thus shows that she wishes to conform to the usual custom, for adolescent village girls are seldom seen in skirts.

Mr. Min was seen only in dark trousers and a white undershirt but, as has been noted, he was away most of the time.

Clean clothes are considered essential and with five children in the house, washing them is a daily chore whether it is raining or not. Mrs. Min usually does the laundry in the early afternoon using a tin pail, and the clothes are soon hanging on lines draped across the wire face of the pigeon house (Fig. 2.12). Then before dinner at night all the children have a bath inside the pigeon house, or sometimes at the well. No tub is used; they are just well soaped and water is poured over their heads. Soap is essential. As Mrs. Min says, "How can one take a bath without soap?" She and her husband also bathe in the privacy of the pigeon house. Mr. Lin confided that the Min family was distinguished for using warm water for a shorter period than the other Chung Nam Wan families. All use some hot water when the weather is cold, but the Mins do not trouble to heat water after the 3rd month.†

The girls all have bobbed hair, as does their mother whose hair was first cut short at the age of twelve. She goes to a hairdressing shop in Lung Shing just before the Chinese New Year's Day and for $3.00 has her hair cut, washed, and given a permanent curl by an electric machine. Other than this annual visit, the necessary care is provided at home. The children are taken to a barber to have their hair cut. This costs $.70 each for the three younger children and $1.20 for the two older. It also may be noted that fingernails in the family are cut, never filed.

---

*Mrs. Min requires four and three-quarters yards.

†The use of Arabic numerals for months indicates the latter are the Chinese lunar months.

Mrs. Min no longer owns any earrings, bracelets, or rings. When she came to Hong Kong she sold everything. At about age eight (Ch) she was taken to a gold earring shop where a man rubbed the front and back of her ear lobes with ginger and then the pins of gold earrings were thrust through. The process hurts, and she cried, but she was happy with her new ornaments. One reason she sold them was that she was fearful during her worst days in Hong Kong that some thief would tear them out of her ears. The holes have not closed again. She also sold a wrist watch, a gold ring set with jade, and a gold bracelet.

Although there is a path leading directly down from the gap to the Chin house (that to the Lin and Min homes turns off westerly from it), it is possible to go to the Chins directly from the Min door and that we shall do. From the flat in front of the Min house, there is an excellent view of the Chin buildings and fields occupying the best and least vertical land in the coomb (Figs. 2.16 and 2.17). From the southeast corner of the flat we dip past the Min dry gully and come directly upon a well which Mr. Min cut into the rock and shored around with cement (Fig. 2.18). The work is nicely done, and the dependable supply of water is cool and inviting. The well is about a yard in diameter and holds approximately fifty gallons. Mrs. Min empties and washes the well once a week. When emptied, it will fill in about three hours. It is the best source of water in Chung Nam Wan and, in the dry season, the other families use it. While mentioning the Min

Fig. 2.16. The Chin Home from the Mins

Fig. 2.17. The Chin Vegetable Fields

Fig. 2.18.
The Min Well

Fig. 2.19. The Min Estate from the Chins

well, it may be noted that it has been the source of distubance to the Chin family, but we shall elaborate on that circumstance later. Looking back from beyond the well, one can see the whole of the Min estate (Fig. 2.19).

The Chin family. Crossing the tiny stream, we rise to the Chin path and turn down it between guava trees that have grown high above one's head, passing a former pig house in which sleeps a hired man, until in another fifty-six steps we reach the main dwelling. It is not unlike the Min house, being well-built of concrete, but there are a few differences. First of all, it seems almost closed in by trees, palms, papayas, and guavas, plus an important mulberry which shades the partly cemented flat area seven feet wide in front of the house (Fig. 2.20). Secondly, the roof is gabled and was made by pouring a five-inch concrete slab (or should we say two of them?) over tightly joined roof boards supported by a ridge pole seven inches in diameter and by three purlins that are two inches smaller on each slope. The height of the ridge pole is about nine and a half feet above the cement floor. Thirdly, there are decorative elements. The roof which overhangs the front wall by ten inches has a gutter with flower motifs impressed at the corners. Also the westerly* front wall has been roughed over with pearl gray cement in a decorative fashion.

The Chin house is slightly more than a foot longer than the Min house and exactly one foot less in width which makes the area covered ten

---

*Actually the wall, termed westerly for easy orientation and comparison with other houses, faces twenty degrees south of west toward the sea as does the Min's.

Fig. 2.20. The Chin House

square feet larger but, perhaps because of the surrounding trees, it appears smaller (Fig. 2.21). Certainly it is darker, for there are only two
windows, one at the right of the door as one looks in from the flat and one
diagonally across from it in the rear wall. These windows each have three
vertical steel bars set into the concrete and a steel cross piece, as well as
paired wood sashes with two panes of glass, one above the other. The
front window swings out, while the rear one swings in. The Min windows,
one might interpolate, were almost identical except that they have four
bars and all of them swing out, whereas the Lin windows have no bars at
all and neither glass nor wood shutters.

Going inside through the double doors which swing inward, we find a
single room. The floor is fairly smooth concrete and the walls even
smoother. In the corners to the right and left, and stretching along the end
walls, are a pair of standard beds made by laying a series of planks on
sawhorses. On them are colored mats, and it is commonplace for those
driven inside by a violent rainstorm to use them to sit on as there are only
a couple of standard square wood stools. Indeed the beds take up so much
space, there is only room for a table which is two feet wide and a little bit
longer and stands against the wall opposite the door. The table is 30″ high
and has an area between its four legs and below the top which is closed off

[46]

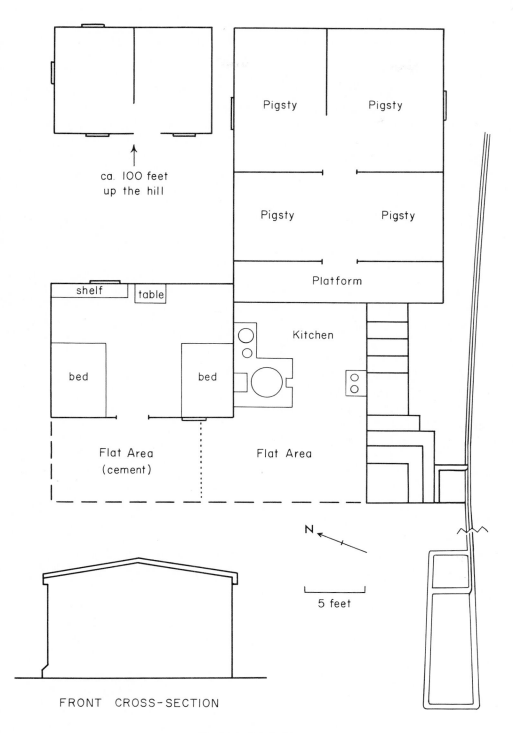

ca. 100 feet
up the hill

Pigsty   Pigsty

Pigsty   Pigsty

Platform

shelf   table

Kitchen

bed   bed

Flat Area
(cement)

Flat Area

N

5 feet

FRONT CROSS-SECTION

Fig. 2.21. Chin Buildings

and has a screen door. This area is used to protect remnants of cooked food from the flies. In the southeast corner is a bamboo carrying pole three inches in diameter and eight feet long. Such an implement is used by two men to carry a young pig over the hill or an old one down to a boat.

Along the north half of the rear wall is a ten-inch plank shelf six feet long and 44″ above the floor. On it stand a half dozen empty bottles, a package of "snail killer," several cans, an enamel tray with a cup upside down, a brown stoneware jar, a thermos bottle, four bottles of orange drink and 7-Up, a lampshade for a kerosene street lamp such as is used to guard excavations, a small kerosene lamp inside it, some cigarettes, a flashlight and batteries, plus three small flat tins. At the end of the shelf hangs a section of bamboo made into a container for chopsticks.

Six inches below the north half of this shelf, another only three feet long and four inches wide is suspended by wires. On it are two pairs of shoes, Mr. and Mrs. Chin's best. From the shelf, an enamel wash basin hangs.

The walls themselves have been pasted over with sheets of Chinese newspaper, now fragmentary and peeling off. As an upper border there are 10″ x 7″ paper flags of the Republic of China (Taiwan), five on the north wall, four on the east, and three on the west. Suspended above the shelf on the rear east wall is a calendar with a sheet for each day, a pair of Chinese style scissors, two toothbrushes (each on its own nail), another flashlight, a mirror, Mr. Chin's stainless steel Swiss Repco wristwatch, and a small triangular case with sewing implements. South of the rear window is a strip of wood with four hooks from which towels hang. On the ledge of the window is a spray gun, a bottle of disinfectant, two cans, and a patented type clothespin with a spring. Over the window is a framed colored picture of Jesus, and a little to the north a frame containing a number of family photographs. The front, or west, wall displays an umbrella and some of Mr. Chin's clothing north of the door. Against the north wall is stretched a wire with three soft-brimmed straw hats behind it. Two have Chinese shop names and "Chin" painted on them in white Chinese characters, the latter an addition by the youngest Chin brother. Hanging over the wire is a piece of blue cotton clothing and a black raincoat. The flagless south wall is empty.

The flat cement area outside the front of the house extends to the south end of the house where it is bordered with stone, as it is also on the west edge which drops off a foot and a half or more in some places to the vegetable fields below. On the northwest corner lies an old gravestone which was placed there for a seat. The cemented area stops three feet short of the south end of the house because the wife of the builder, according to her own statement, could not decide where she wanted the kitchen. There does not seem to have been any great choice, and the kitchen

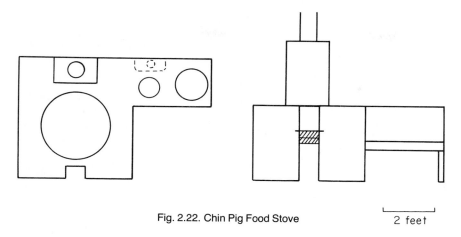

Fig. 2.22. Chin Pig Food Stove

2 feet

developed as a crudely covered ten-and-a-half by eight-and-a-half-foot area juxtaposed lengthwise to the south end of the house. In the kitchen, as by this time might be expected, stands a pig food stove (Fig. 2.22). It is built against the wall of the house and extends 87″ from the west corner. The right hand three feet of the stove, however, is a narrow extension only two feet wide set up on a four-inch concrete slab. Built into it is a 16″ opening for pots, and another that is only 10″ in diameter. The separate chimney for this part of the stove has collapsed. The main section of the stove built to cook pig food is similar to that of the Min family, except that it was not constructed to burn sawdust. It is 58″ deep, 51″ wide, and 36″ high. It has the usual concave iron pan and pyramidal base for the chimney. The pan is 29″ in diameter. Like all the other large pig food stoves in Chung Nam Wan, it is not being used. When a sow litters, however, all pig food must be cooked, and then a large stove is essential.

At the south end of the kitchen is a small rock and cement stove with two burners of which only one is in good shape. On this stove almost all of the cooking is done (Fig. 2.23). Near it one can see a large basket containing sawdust, a pair of long-handled steel pincers used for tending the fire, two five-gallon cans including one with a wood top, a round portable kerosene stove, a broken metal cooking pan cover 27″ in diameter and a foot high which has been adopted to hold sawdust, a worn out broom, four covered aluminum saucepans of various sizes, two sickles, and a small long-handled brush.

On the pig food stove rest five shallow dishes, one deep bowl, and a large cup, all of enamelware. Beside them are three glass bottles, an earthenware jar with an aluminum saucer on top, and an old wood bucket. On the adjacent extension of the stove is a mixed pile of old iron and bottles. If one is a member of the Chin family, one does not see this

Fig. 2.23. Mrs. Chin Cooking

unappealing aggregation essentially as junk; indeed, one does not make any appraisal at all.

Outside the kitchen, the family shed roof which slopes toward the sea is extended seven feet over the flat area by means of a series of parallel bamboo poles which on some occasion may have supported a leaf or mat covering spread out to provide shade (Fig. 2.24). The rough stone and dirt area underneath it ends at the south line of the kitchen in a three-and-a-half-foot square cement step that is surrounded by two more steps on the east and south sides. In the latter case the steps rise to a two-by-three-foot concrete basin which holds the house water supply that is brought down a cement aqueduct, the open trough of which is only four inches wide, from a point somewhat less than a hundred feet back up the hill where the water seeps from the rocks.

Around the basin, which is approximately six feet from the south end of the kitchen, and on the flat, a focus for household activities but without any special name,* one sees such things as wood buckets, baskets of various kinds, a long plank bench and some stools to sit on, a chopping knife and board, a large Chinese type wood balance (steelyard) with its counterweight, a towel, a broom, two umbrellas, and most extraordinary

---

*Mr. Chin speaks of the flat as ti ha (ti hsia) which, in Cantonese, conveys the idea of the *ground floor* when speaking of a house. Mr. Lin says mun hau (men k'ou), the common term for *doorway* which, however, is, if relatively rarely, also used as *porch*.

[50]

Fig. 2.24. The Chin House and Vegetable Terraces

of all, a portable transistor radio hanging from a branch of the mulberry tree. To these one can add a crowbar, a pick-mattock with a piece broken off, a chicken basket, a broken funnel of a spray bucket, a pair of men's short pants, three fish trap baskets, two metal pails, and a metal dipper.

On the east side of the square concrete step previously mentioned, more concrete steps with an intervening square one continue up outside the south kitchen wall until they reach a concrete platform that is 44" above the dirt floor of the kitchen. This platform, three and a half feet wide, fronts the main Chin pig house which has a westerly exposure of a little over seventeen feet. The part adjacent to the platform consists of two open sties seven and a half feet deep, the walls being less than a yard high and only four inches thick. The principal part of the pig house is twelve feet deep and has walls to the roof. There is a window at each end and the roof, which is over seven feet above the cement floor, is a slab of reinforced concrete sloping westerly toward the sea. Technically judged, the pigs have a better shelter than their owners, but it is not evident that either set of occupants is aware of this fact.

Like the front section of the building, the rear is divided into two sections by a half wall. On the floor of the south section lies a large sow flicking her ears, while opposite to the north are seven of her offspring in the second half year of growth. These piglings are females or castrated males. In one of the front pens a young black boar has been isolated. Pig raising is not at its peak in the Chin family, but there are hopes for the future.

If we go back around the front of the Chin family house and climb to the building we passed on our arrival, we face a second pig house (Fig. 2.21). It was constructed of concrete, has a flat roof, and is in excellent condition. Somewhat smaller than the other, it is approximately thirteen feet long and nine feet deep. A wall about thirty inches high divides the building into two sections and the outer north wall itself is no higher. Both sections have front windows facing the sea, and the north section also has a window in its two other walls, besides a small door in the corner through which a pig can go in and out. Concrete food troughs are built against the inside of the west wall and there are drains to facilitate washing the floor.

At the beginning of the summer of 1960, this house built for pigs was occupied by a hired man, as well it might be without mental or physical discomfiture. A makeshift plank bed, made by placing one board and an old door on a pair of sawhorses, had been set up in the open south section, and over it a patched mosquito net had been hung on a square framework of bamboo poles, some of which were fitted through slots in the edges of the net. The rectangular top of the net frame, supported by bamboos nailed to the corners of the bed, was four feet above the bed and 70″ above the floor. The overlap on one side through which one seeks the protection of the net was closed by a patented snap clothespin and, in one place, a hole had been repaired by bunching and tying the flimsy material. By the time it was possible to make a detailed examination of this pig house, there was nothing else in it but a broom, since the hired man, suffering from the unprecedented heat of that summer, had asked for higher wages and gone back to town when the Chin family could not afford them.

When one finishes with a detailed examination of the buildings and their contents, it is not those that distinguish the Chin family from the others in Chung Nam Wan. The real difference has been obvious since the general limits of the Min and Lin property were made clear. The Chins own all of the best cultivable land which, as one can see, spreads out in a score of neatly terraced fields between their dwelling house and the sea. The fields are bisected by the tiny stream which takes a sudden bend to the north before its deep gully opens onto the beach. Standing in the shade of a palm tree and looking up toward the house, we can with reason admire the neat stone walls of the terraces and recognize the advantage of having three concrete reservoirs for water and fertilizer which have been conveniently placed and are cleverly fed by narrow concrete aqueducts from one or the other of the two available water sources (Fig. 2.25).

Fig. 2.25. Chung Nam Wan Stream Bed and Aqueduct

Turning to a consideration of the family which owns this impressive little farm, we find that the Chin household actually consists of only Mr. and Mrs. Chin and their two small children. Mr. Chin's mother climbs over the gap every afternoon from Tung Pak Wan to take care of the babies so that Mrs. Chin can devote full time to the fields, and recently her youngest son, about fifteen years of age (Ch), has come with her. Mr. Chin's mother has a pleasant, squarish face which is usually placid, and straightforward, intelligent eyes. When she smiles, she shows a gold cap on her right, upper, second incisor and most of her lower ones are similarly covered as well (Fig. 2.26). She is an inch over five feet, but her age was not so easy to discover and we can merely guess she is a slightly plump fifty-one. Invariably, she dresses in a black sam fu, either of the shiny, coated material that is so often seen, or of a lighter, textured material which is said actually to be less cool and, to local Chinese taste, less good-looking. On her feet, she usually wears black tennis shoes. Her hair is bobbed, black, and straight with a few slivers of gray. She says she should go to the barber shop in Lung Shing every two months. In each ear she wears a single baroque pearl. As mother and mother-in-law, without living in the house with her son, she unquestionably dominates it and keeps a firm hand on the purse strings.

Mr. Chin, who was born about 1936, is Cantonese like his mother. He is also exceptionally handsome, as women who know him attest (Figs. 2.27

Fig. 2.26. The Chin
Grandmother and
Grandson

Fig. 2.27. Mr. Chin on His Way to Market

Fig. 2.28. Mrs. Chin Chopping Greens

and 4.3). There is frequently a smile on his oval face with its wide but well-modeled nose. His brown eyes flash and his teeth are perfect and white. He is 65½″ tall, and his arms and legs are sinuous with muscles. His shoulders show the familiar scars common to those who regularly bear the weight of a bamboo carrying pole. In hot weather, he wears a white sleeveless undershirt as well as undershorts of European style, with faded blue outer shorts over the latter, and composition sandals with blue straps over the front of the foot. The sandals he discards when working in the fields. Sometimes he wears a T-shirt with short sleeves. On the rare occasions he goes to Hong Kong, he puts on a European style shirt and trousers.

Mr. Chin has his hair cut short, the longest strands being less than three inches. He wears a gold marriage ring on the third finger of his left hand. It represents the traditional gift of a mother-in-law. He has also owned a thirty-dollar wristwatch for four years, but it has not worked very well during the last two. Everything considered, it was probably his smile that made his wife love him at first sight.

Mrs. Chin is about a year younger than her husband. Her family is Cantonese and when she married, she could not understand Hakka which her husband and mother-in-law speak none too well themselves, but she comprehends a little now. Her face is broad and flat with a slightly up-turned nose above heavy lips (Fig. 2.28). She knows she is not beautiful,

Fig. 2.29. The Chin Children and Grandmother

but she has nice teeth except for her first upper left molar which is missing. She has a solid, powerful body which lacks an inch and a half of reaching five feet.

When first seen, she was coming home from market wearing a shiny black sam fu with a light blue undercoat showing slightly. Her jacket was fastened on her right side with loops and knotted buttons. On her feet she had Japanese style slippers and, on her head, a woven bamboo hat with a straight brim eighteen inches in diameter. Sometimes she wears a washed out blue sam fu, and at home she goes barefooted. Mrs. Chin has never owned a cheong sam.

Mrs. Chin had her ear lobes rubbed with ginger and pierced when she was seventeen (Ch). Her mother gave her a pair of gold earrings when she was married, but she later lost one of them so consequently sold the other. The holes still remain and seem large, a fact which she attributes to her children pulling on her earrings when she still had them. She never owned any other pieces of jewelry and states that if she had any, she would convert them into money.

During the early half of the summer, Mrs. Chin parted her black hair on the left side and wore it in a pony tail. Then her mother gave her money to have her hair bobbed and curled, which apparently pleased her. Usually she goes to the hairdresser only once in a year.

Like others in the community, the members of the family bathe daily, pouring water over their shoulders. In the winter, this is done in the kitchen as some hot water is needed. In summer, however, they may bathe before or after dinner in the closest of the large concrete basins that store water to be sprinkled on the vegetable garden. Mrs. Chin usually does the family laundry on a washboard in a wood tub after dinner or, less often, early in the morning. Clothing is washed every day in summer; every other day in winter.

The Chins have two small children, a girl of a little less than two, and a boy who is twelve months younger (Fig. 2.29). The older child wears a nearly-white cotton sleeveless dress which opens at the back and is almost a sheath, but has a seam encircling it at the armpits. Underneath are short, blue-striped cotton panties. The small baby seemed content wearing no more than pants with a halter and once, when the heat was at its worst, he went nude all day long.

The two younger brothers of Mr. Chin must be mentioned as members of the family. The older, who does not look forward to work on the farm, was born about 1943. In physical appearance he probably reflects the physiognomy of his Hakka father, as he does not have the round, often smiling face of his brothers and mother. The youngest of the three boys who was born about 1946 has not attained his full growth or lost his happy disposition. He is a quiet one who works with admirable consistency.

Having completed our preliminary description of Chung Nam Wan and its occupants, it is quite natural to wonder how this isolated little community came into existence. To its history we can now turn.

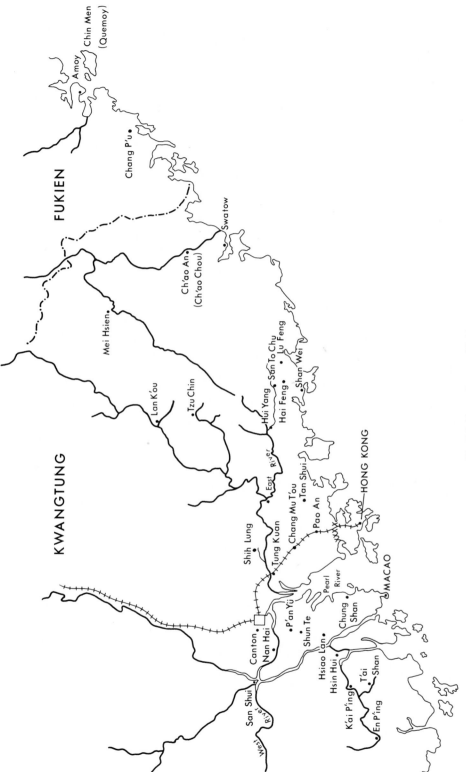

FUKIEN

KWANGTUNG

Amoy
Chin Men
(Quemoy)

Chang P'u

Swatow

Ch'ao An
(Ch'ao Chou)

Mei Hsien

Lan K'ou

Tzu Chin

Hui Yang
San To Chu
Lu Feng
Hai Feng
Shan Wei

East River

Tan Shui
Chang Mu T'ou
Pao An
HONG KONG

Shih Lung
Tung Kuan

San Shui
Canton
Nan Hai
P'an Yü
Shun Te
Hsiao Lan
Chung Shan
MACAO

Pearl River

Hsin Hui
K'ai P'ing
T'ai Shan
En P'ing

West River

Fig. 3.1. Kwangtung and Fukien

3. The Founding of Chung Nam Wan

The Chin family. To know the history of Chung Nam Wan, it is necessary to go back into the record of the Chin family for a quarter of a century or more. In 1924, the father and mother of Mr. Chin resided in Hsin Hui (Fig. 3.1) in the so-called Four Districts of Kwangtung which lie south of Canton.* Shortly thereafter they migrated to the south shore of Hong Kong where Mr. Chin was born about 1936. A few years later, his mother was married to a second husband, a Hakka whom she met in Hong Kong. This man's name was given to her son. Mr. Chin's stepfather had a bachelor cousin (father's brother's son) who drifted to Lung Chau in 1940 and not long afterward was employed by the founding family of Tung Pak Wan, the suburb of Lung Shing that lies over the hill from Chung Nam Wan. That was the first contact of the Chin family with Lung Chau.

Within a year after the Japanese occupation of Hong Kong in December, 1941, the shortage of food drove the Chins and their cousin back to their lineage town of Tzu Chin. The route is by rail from Hong Kong to Chang Mu T'ou, which normally takes only a few hours, then by road to Hui Yang. The Chin Cousin told us that he carried the six-year-old Mr. Chin most of the way from Hui Yang to Tzu Chin in a basket on one end of his carrying pole, the journey requiring seven days, although normally only four or five.

In 1947, the Chin family returned and Mr. Chin's stepfather went to work for the son of the founding widow of Tung Pak Wan. Some unoccupied government land being designated by his employer, the Chin family home was constructed on it. Mr. Chin's stepfather was ambitious and

---

*In this study, except in the case of internationally known cities, we have adopted for geographic names in China the spellings used on maps printed by the U.S. Army Map Service, Series L 500, Scale 1:250,000. These are for most part transliterations following the Wade-Giles system based on Mandarin pronunciations. They are often considerably divergent from the local pronunciations, but Mandarin is now the widely spreading official language of China, and Chinese maps are consequently printed with transliterations in Mandarin. To simplify matters, we have supplied our own maps showing our geographic references, and also geographical terms with variant spellings may be found in Appendix G. Geographic names within the Colony of Hong Kong follow the official British spellings (Cf. *Gazetteer,* 1960). Ssu I, or the Four Districts, commonly written Sz Yap in Cantonese are actually comprised of five: En Ping, Hsin Hui, Hsin Ning, K'ai P'ing, and T'ai Shan.

wanted to establish an independent farm, but unfortunately all the good cultivable land in Tung Pak Wan had been preempted by the original family and that of a sister of the founding widow who had moved in at the time of the Japanese occupation, an occupation which seems literally to have worried the first lady to death.

One holiday, Mr. Chin's stepfather, climbing over the hills of Lung Chau for pleasure, looked down upon the steep, narrow valley of Chung Nam Wan, as did the ethnographer himself a dozen years later. Chung Nam Wan offered a supply of water and, as might be expected, rich earth fronting its beach. The coomb had been dignified by name and a few graves but had no living residents as it was considered too far away from the town of Lung Shing and too difficult to reach. Mr. Chin's stepfather talked to his wife and they decided to develop a farm in the valley of Chung Nam Wan.

During the years, this cursory account was elaborated upon by other members of the family and by neighbors. Apparently another resident of Tung Pak Wan had started a garden in Chung Nam Wan after World War II, but this latter man and his wife became tired of climbing and reclimbing the hill. Even a third man was involved in the reclamation, but various reasons including the opinion that there was insufficient water and perhaps because Mr. Chin's stepfather obtained the permit for land, they sold out their interests and left him in possession.

However things may have developed, Mr. Chin's mother was pleased. It might not be a poor guess to say that she was even more ambitious and farsighted than her husband. She was a proud woman at that time with three sons, the oldest only twelve. As a child in Hsin Hui, one of the Four Districts, she did not have a happy life. Her family was poor and she had been obliged to work early and hard. Even the New Year's holiday brought no enviable memories, although she did receive the traditional red envelopes containing a present of money. She was married in a distant village at fourteen and a half to a man she had not seen until the night he took her to bed. The traditional pig was duly sent to the family and, underneath it, the red-spotted handkerchief that acknowledged the loss of her virginity. Years later she told us, "Whether you like your husband or not, it makes no difference; a blind marriage is not good." Her first husband's family were farmers and not rich, so she still had to work very hard. In due time she had a daughter who was ultimately married and bore many children in China. Then her eldest son, Mr. Chin, was born. In whatever manner she later found her second husband, we have a feeling he was her choice. It is significant that she gave his name to her first son. For the future of this child, she was willing to work hard.

Mr. Chin's stepfather, with the help of a nephew, began the terracing of the good land in Chung Nam Wan during 1948 or the year afterward, going back and forth over the gap daily. Soon he started farming and went on to construct the buildings and water system which distinguish the property. Indeed, he was still improving his holdings when he died about 1957.

Actually Mr. Chin's mother never took up residence in Chung Nam Wan. She and her husband ate lunch there regularly but preferred to sleep in their house in Tung Pak Wan which was closer to the market town. After they bought their sow in 1953, Mr. Chin's father began staying in Chung Nam Wan at night to look after it. Following the elder man's death, it was Mr. Chin himself who came to occupy the house at Chung Nam Wan permanently, with his wife of two years and their small baby daughter. The transition was gradual as they had moved in some time before in order to care for the elder Mr. Chin during his last illness which had extended over two periods of several months.

The younger Mrs. Chin's father was once a well-to-do Cantonese farmer on the south shore of Hong Kong Island who hired as many as seven men. Then he took to drinking and gambling and became poor. When the Japanese occupied the Colony (or in 1942), he sold his land and became a caddy at a golf club, earning ninety cents a game. Mrs. Chin was one of eleven children, including six sisters. Some died and some were given away; one sister, it is said, to some Occidentals who own a shop and sell beer. Mrs. Chin is an excellent worker, and it is she and her husband who will inherit the orginal Chung Nam Wan farm.

The Lin family. The Lin family was the second to take up land in Chung Nam Wan, but the first to actually live there, Mr. and Mrs. Lin having constructed a temporary shelter of reeds beside the tiny steam and moved into it in 1953. Mr. Lin confessed to having had an interesting and, we think, in some ways, an unusual life before coming to Hong Kong. At least unusual enough so that it required extended consideration and the help of his wife to get the facts straightened out. He was born in a village of about one hundred people approximately a mile from a sizable town named San To Chu in the district of Hui Yang. From it one could go by road to Swatow or by boat to Canton, although one usually walked in one day to the district town of Hui Yang, described as being thirteen blocks of roads to the westward, each block representing (but apparently less than) ten li. The area of San To Chu was occupied mostly by speakers of the Hakka and Min dialects. The members of his family were well-to-do farmers in the local sense, and the household included at his birth, his father and mother, a sister four years his senior, and his father's brother and the latter's wife who was childless. When he was two years old (Ch) his mother died and he was cared for by his aunt even after his father remarried two years later. At nine, he started school and continued until he was fifteen. Then he became the guardian of the family's water buffalo, leading it out to eat grass at five or six in the morning, and again at various intervals throughout the day. Sometimes he led it by a single line to a ring in its nose, but often he rode on its back using two lines as a bridle. He liked that and was not afraid. Once he saw a buffalo gore a person badly. He added that he had also witnessed two buffalo fight one another. When asked how they were stopped, he protested, "How can you stop them—nothing can." When not working or eating, his buffalo was put in the shade of a tree and, at dark, it was brought back to the house again. Besides the buffalo, his father's family owned an ox, and he took care of that animal also.

His stepmother had two sons. She also brought into the family a four-year-old young girl who was intended ultimately to marry her step-son, six years the senior of his future bride. When Lin was eighteen, an auspicious day was chosen and the wedding took place. His wife gave birth to no children, so after a few years, with her permission and that of his family, he took a concubine five years younger than himself.

About the same period, two things occurred which Lin remembers. His father died, and the first finger of his left hand became infected. It had scabs all over it. He lost the use of the finger permanently and, after a time, he had no feeling left in it, a fact he can demonstrate with a knife.

Mr. Lin does not claim to have ever been an ideal husband. When he became head of his family on his father's death, he hired two men to work in the fields. He also started drinking and gambling. While still young, he began trading in buffalo and pigs, and he went several times with some friends to the "flower boats" on the river near his house. A girl would row them in her sampan for three hours in the early evening and also sing songs for two dollars in silver. There were thirty or forty such craft, besides small boats which sold food, and a restaurant and a hotel on an island. Lotus grew in the river and the whole setting was particularly beautiful as Mr. Lin remembers it. There were also companionable ladies in a house, some of whom sang while others played musical instruments. One could stay with them for about sixteen dollars, but that much money Mr. Lin could never afford. Instead, he went occasionally to the movies or to the opera, which diversions were available every day. Smilingly, he described himself as the spoiled son of a rich man, such things of course being relative.

In 1949, Mr. Lin decided to emigrate to Hong Kong, avowedly because he feared Communist groups who were demanding money. His concubine did not wish to go with him so he left her and the children behind. The devoted Mrs. Lin, however, came along. Her story, told us later, added illuminating details which Mr. Lin had left out. He promptly confirmed her account in terms of the sequence of events, amplifying the description of his early marriage, and stating that we had simply confused the women in his life which, all things considered, may well have been true.

Mrs. Lin did not hesitate to admit that she was not Mr. Lin's first wife. She added the note that while Mr. Lin was preoccupied with his concubine, his wife had taken a lover. Mr. Lin's uncle discovered the wife's adulterous behavior and warned her to leave, stating that her husband would probably kill her if he found out, and that a feud might be started between their respective families. The first Mrs. Lin followed the uncle's advice. Our informant concluded her account by saying that somewhat later the concubine sold their two daughters. Then after a year, the concubine died, and the third Mrs. Lin is sure that it was the result of doing such a bad thing.

With all respect to an admirable woman, the last statements about the concubine do not seem to be a clear presentation of the truth. Later, in other contexts, Mr. Lin referred several times to the fact that his concubine would not come with him to Hong Kong and also that she later remarried. Furthermore, he asserted with good evidence that only his younger daughter was sold, admitting that this was done partly to provide money needed for his emigration to Hong Kong. It is possible that the third Mrs. Lin was mentally making room for her own entrance on the scene, circumstances which we now will relate. We should remember that, even for participants, it is often difficult to untangle the threads of a life history.

According to Mrs. Lin's statements, Mr. Lin's family wanted her because she was such a hard worker. They knew that she was not young, and at least three years older than Mr. Lin. He had seen her on various occasions over a long period as she lived in a village less than a mile away. The Lins' friend who acted as a go-between had to come several times to persuade her as she did not want a man with so many girl friends. She was also aware that people in Hui Yang laughed about the proposal. Still, she decided to live with Mr. Lin who must have had personal appeal. There was no ceremony when our informant went to Mr. Lin's home since his wife was still living. His stepmother and her children were there, but his uncle had gone. The family, which had been rich, was growing poorer.

Mrs. Lin herself was born in a village of two or three hundred persons. She was sold as a small baby and brought up in Hui Yang, a town with a population of several thousand. At fourteen, she was sold a second time. Her childhood before the age of ten when she played with other girls and boys, she remembers as the best time in her life. Then she went to work in the fields and has continued to do so almost without interruption ever since.

Mr. and Mrs. Lin lived in Lei Yue Mun for a year after coming to Hong Kong, and then moved to Shau Kei Wan where they remained until

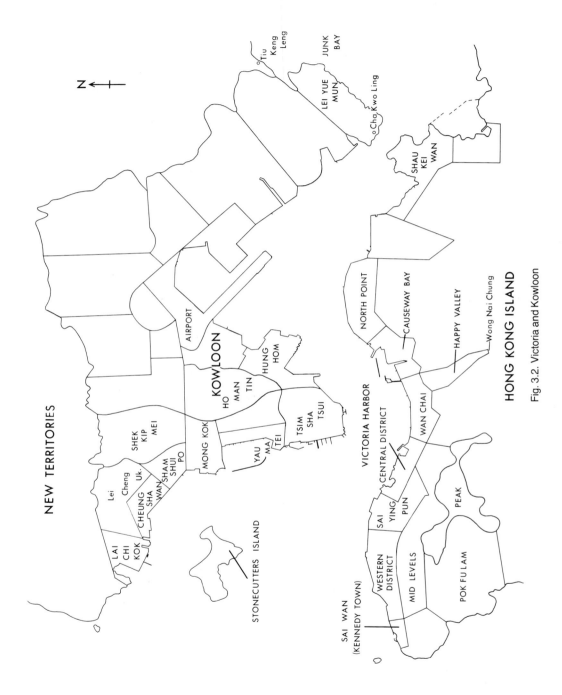

NEW TERRITORIES

LAI
CHI
KOK

Lei

Cheng

CHEUNG
SHA
WAN
Uk.

SHAM
SHUI
PO

SHEK
KIP
MEI

MONG KOK

YAU
MA
TEI

TSIM
SHA
TSUI

HO
MAN
TIN

HUNG
HOM

KOWLOON

AIRPORT

STONECUTTERS ISLAND

Tiu
Keng
Leng

LEI YUE
MUN

JUNK
BAY

Cha Kwo Ling

SHAU
KEI
WAN

NORTH POINT

CAUSEWAY BAY

HAPPY VALLEY

Wong Nai Chung

WAN CHAI

VICTORIA HARBOR

CENTRAL DISTRICT

SAI
YING
PUN

WESTERN
DISTRICT

MID LEVELS

PEAK

POK FU LAM

SAI WAN
(KENNEDY TOWN)

HONG KONG ISLAND

Fig. 3.2. Victoria and Kowloon

N

1953 (Fig. 3.2). The money he had brought with him was about gone, a thousand dollars of it having been invested in a friend's plan to sell dumplings to the boat people.* Mrs. Lin warned her husband that his partner was not honest; actually the partner expended most of the money in smoking opium, although in fairness it must be added that the dumplings did not sell well and those that were not sold would not keep.

Some fishermen friends of the Lins brought them on a visit to the Chin family. Mr. Lin was charmed by Chung Nam Wan and asked the Chins if he could build a house there. They responded that the land belonged to the government. Perhaps the Chins thought it would be a protection to have a family permanently residing near their new holding. Perhaps the two older women liked each other from the first, as they certainly did later. In any event the decision was made.

When in 1953 the Lins put together their first shelter of reeds with a tin roof, they slept on the dirt floor. The grass was very high on the hillside then, and there was not even a noticeable path until the Lins wore one bare going up and down. It was a year before their permanent house was built. They did not bother to have a geomancer determine its position. They bought wood for beams in Lung Shing, and rafters that look like driftwood from the boat people, as well as sixteen bags of cement to mix with the stones and beach sand that they collected themselves. The cement cost five and a half dollars a bag. Then they paid twelve dollars a day to a builder from town to put their home together. Piece by piece, they added the kitchen and pig houses, the last one across the tiny stream costing about $400. At first, there was profit from the pigs which helped to buy furniture, but when the partner in the food business dissipated their investment, they had to sell the pigs to pay their debts. All in all, expenditures in creating the farm amounted to about a thousand dollars.

In 1958, before the pigs were sold, Mr. and Mrs. Lin adopted a baby girl two months old. This significant event came about when Mrs. Chin was in the hospital having her first child. A woman in the same room had a daughter three days later and Mrs. Chin's mother-in-law, hearing the poor woman bemoan the fact that she had five girls already, suggested that she might give the sixth one to the Lins. Later the woman came to visit at Chung Nam Wan and decided that, as poor as the Lins were, at least the child would have food to eat. The Lins gave the mother a present of two chickens and they adored the new member of their family ever afterward.

---

*If it should seem strange that a man with a thousand dollars to invest would sell his four-year-old daughter for sixty, which was the amount he received, it may be pointed out that in such a difficult economic period as the Communist Revolution, he was also trying to safeguard a child too young to care for herself by selling her to a family who wanted a girl. Years later, we learned through letters from San To Chu that the story had a happy ending. The older daughter who had become head of the local Communist Woman's Association in about 1959 at the age of nineteen, decided to look for her sister who had been sold. She found her, took her home, and arranged a marriage for her the next year when she became sixteen, the older sister having married at that age by free choice.

The Min family. The Mins who moved to Chung Nam Wan were the second family to actually live there. Mr. Min, a Hakka, came from the district of Hui Yang in Kwangtung, as did the deceased second husband of the Chin family and the Lins, but from a different settlement. The mutual discovery of this fact when the Chins and Mins first met on Lung Chau was one reason for their friendship.

When about twenty-four years of age and working for the army in Canton, Mr. Min was introduced to his future wife and they became friends. Some time afterward they decided to marry. The ceremony seems to have taken place in 1949, and they then emigrated to Hong Kong.

Mrs. Min was a Shanghai girl purchased by a Cantonese family. Of her own parents she knows nothing. Her adoptive mother worked as a cook for foreigners in Shanghai. She also had an adoptive married brother twenty years older than herself who had a shop in which silver cups for prizes were sold. She remembers him as being very good to her. There was also a sister a little younger than the brother who was jealous because the others loved the newly-acquired little girl so much, she was so plump and white.

The future Mrs. Min had finished her first week in school in Shanghai when the Japanese came in 1937. In consequence of the invasion the whole family moved back to its home town in Kwangtung, one day's journey from Canton by small boat. Mrs. Min was reasonably happy there. Rich people gave them food to eat because she was so attractive. She did not go to school again but she learned quite a few characters from young friends who did. There were movies and operas in the place she lived and she liked to go to them whenever she could, but the family was poor. Soon after their return to Kwangtung, the brother who was the main support of the family caught cold while watching the fields and died. The future Mrs. Min had been visiting her mother's mother at the period and was called home just in time to exchange a tearful farewell. It was an unforgettable experience.

On arriving in Hong Kong, the Mins spent the first few months on the mainland opposite Lung Chau to which place they moved next and lived for five years in the west end of Lung Shing near the Kun Yam temple. Mr. Min had no trade and the first thing he did was to sell small pieces of wheat bread, which he bought on credit at a local shop, fourteen for a dollar. At ten cents each, he made forty cents profit if he sold them all; otherwise he returned them. Later, working as a laborer, he learned the mason's trade largely by watching the professionals he served. At the same time, his wife cut grass or carried water for shipbuilders in Lung Shing, receiving ten cents a trip. She thus added six or seven dollars a month to their income.

Mrs. Min did not like living in Lung Shing. Their living quarters were small and hot. Also she claimed that children could not be protected from skin infections. Her family was growing as her first three offspring were born while she lived in the town.

The solution to the problem came after Mr. Min had sold some of his cakes to one of the Chin family. They had talked, both being Hakka. Later, when one of Mr. Chin's brothers suggested they might move to Chung Nam Wan, Mrs. Min came to look and then her husband was brought and they made up their minds. The new location was nothing but a barren hill on the west side above the fields of the Chin family whose buildings had all been constructed by that time. Every day Mr. Min came with a friend and dug into the ground to create a level strip of land. Mrs. Min brought food for them. Several weeks were required just to make a place for the house. Then in 1954 they sold their old one in Lung Shing for three hundred dollars in order to get money to buy materials for the new one. The excavation for the kitchen behind it was made later, and the windows and cement floor of the house were added with money borrowed from a friend.

More significant for the development of the property was another friend, a schoolteacher of Lung Shing who entered the scene about a year or two after the Mins had settled at Chung Nam Wan. It all came about when an acquaintance of the Mins who worked in the school their daughters later attended came for a visit. He said that he could not understand why they did not raise pigs and chickens but, of course, it was simply because they had no money to buy them. This acquaintance brought a teacher from the school who fished in the bay and was charmed by the Mins who were so poor that they were faced with the necessity of giving away one of their girls. The acquaintance suggested to the teacher that he put up the money for a venture in hog raising and the latter decided to do so. Then the pig houses were built, and not only pigs and chickens appeared, but the teacher saved a place for the eldest daughter in school. The Mins owe him a few thousand dollars, for he supplied them with money for food as well, since Mr. Min had to devote all his time to the venture. In a sense, the undertaking was a failure because, after six or seven months, the six large sows and twenty-five small pigs that had been purchased became sick and died. The account of the Mins' tribulations in the raising of pigs can better be told when we come to a description of the whole economic situation at Chung Nam Wan. Suffice it to say at this point that the friendship of the teacher remained constant, and that he continued to bring presents to the family, gifts which ranged from a few chickens to clothing and playthings for the children which he obtained from the better-off parents of his pupils.

4. Domestic Life

Social structure. The demography of Chung Nam Wan cannot be considered complicated but, before giving consideration to the social structure of the hamlet, it may clarify the data to set them forth in Table 4.1.

From Table 4.1 it may be observed that twenty individuals can in some sense or another be considered residents of Chung Nam Wan at the period studied. Only three, the Mins' third and fourth daughters and the Chins' daughter, can technically be considered natives of the place. Of the twenty individuals considered, nine are adults and eleven are children. Ages, including those for whom we can only make estimates, range from one to fifty. We should add that the male laborer of the Chin family gave up his position unexpectedly during our study before he was interviewed, while Mr. Min's uncles were never even seen. Therefore we might consider the population during the period of our visit as seventeen and a half.

Chung Nam Wan comprises basically three nuclear families, each with a distinguishing surname. The Lins have one child, the Mins five, and the Chins two. At the end of the summer (the male laborer having gone), each nuclear family also constituted a household (defined as a group of individuals sleeping under the same or juxtaposed roofs). It should be noted, however, that although the Min nuclear family constituted the *de facto* household, the *de jure* household included the father's two uncles (actually sons of his father's father's brother) who were members of it, even if they seldom made use of the sleeping facilities provided them.

Next we may note that the nuclear Lin and Min families were also economic units, whereas the Chin economic family, or ka (chia), included Mr. Chin's mother (the head of it) and his two younger brothers, despite the fact that neither his mother nor brothers slept in Chung Nam Wan. To this last group, the male worker may be considered an appendage (until the middle of the summer).

The lineage, or tsuk (tsu), and clan, or sing (hsing), status of these three households appears to be almost nonfunctional because of the role of the male members, or their fathers, as immigrant refugees. Both Mrs.

TABLE 4.1
Residents of Chung Nam Wan

Name	Year of Birth (approximate)	Age (Western) in 1960
Lin Household		
Mr. Lin	1917	43
Mrs. Lin	1913	47
Lin's Daughter	1958	2
Min Household		
Mr. Min	1924	36
Mrs. Min	1930	30
Min's First Daughter	1950	10
Min's Second Daughter	1952	8
Min's First Son	1954	6
Min's Third Daughter	1957	3
Min's Fourth Daughter	1959	1
Mr. Min's Father's Father's Brother's Son (First)	1927	33
Mr. Min's Father's Father's Brother's Son (Second)	1932	28
Chin Household		
Mr. Chin	1936	24
Mrs. Chin	1937	23
Chin's Daughter	1958	2
Chin's Son	1959	1
Mr. Chin's Mother	1910	50
Mr. Chin's Younger Brother	1943	17
Mr. Chin's Youngest Brother	1946	14
Male Laborer	—	—

Min and Mrs. Chin say that no one cares about the lineage any more except a few old people. They directly attribute this state of affairs in their case to the influence of the church. Mrs. Min makes note of the time formerly consumed in her family by undertaking rituals for the dead. She also does not visit any of her maternal relatives, but then none of them are living in Hong Kong. Mr. Lin does occasionally see some patrilineal relatives in Hong Kong, but there is no evidence that his agnatic kin recognize any mutual obligations that are meaningful. The situation seems to be the same for Mr. Min apart from his grandfather's brother's sons who are both unmarried and in worse circumstances than he is. Both work in a Chinese medicine shop in Hong Kong. As for Mr. Chin, the death of his father seems to have cut the link with the past.

Names and terms of address. Each individual in Chung Nam Wan has a family name and a two-character given name, except for Mr. Lin and the Lins' Small Daughter who have only a one-character given name. Wives retain the family name of their fathers. In the Min family with five children, the first character of the given name of each, chosen by Mr. Min, is the same, or what is called a generation name, except for the youngest whose appellation was caused by an accident, thus producing a variation in the common Chinese custom of identifying one's children by a distinguishing character. The anomaly came about when Mrs. Min, somewhat drowsy from childbirth, was asked her new child's name by the nurse and she responded unthinkingly, "Fifth sister," the nurse entered those characters in the record and would not change them later on when requested to do so. The representation of the given name at birth is recognized by Mrs. Min as a new style of procedure, as distinguished from doing so at a party when the child is thirty days old. Parents, of course, may actually settle on a name for a child before it is born. She did not recognize, however, the old custom of first giving a child an animal's name to divert the attention of evil spirits during the period of greatest infant mortality.

In the case of Mr. Chin and his siblings, the situation is also somewhat exceptional. Their common generation character also was chosen by their father but put last. The practice of reversing the usual order of characters in given names is said not to be rare and is a matter of personal preference. To complicate matters, however, the second Chin brother decided to change his given name and did so in 1960 after obtaining his mother's approval. He went to the government record office in Hong Kong and legalized the substitution without trouble and at four dollars cost, one for the recording and three for the stamp tax. His reason: he simply did not like his name because the combination of characters was too common. Finally, it may be added that the two young children of Mr. and Mrs. Chin do not share a generation character in their names. Mrs. Chin does not know why they do not. Her husband and his mother were responsible for the names. She does not know the characters for either her children's names or her own. Given names of females in the village include words, such as Pearl, Happy, Jade, the mythical bird Feng (Feng-huang), and so on. Men have names such as Courage.

Terms of address used by individuals of the same sex and status vary in Chung Nam Wan. Mr. Lin, for example, calls his wife by the last character of the name of her village prefixed by the familiar particle of address a (a) and suffixed by p'o (p'o) which means "old woman." Mr. Min, on the other hand, calls his wife simply by her given name prefixed by a (a). Contrariwise, Mrs. Lin calls her husband by his full name; whereas Mrs. Min calls her husband by his surname prefixed by a (a). Mrs. Min adds simply that some individuals of either sex call their spouses by the surname, some by the given name. Mr. and Mrs. Chin call each other by their given names, and Mr. Chin's mother calls each of her sons by his given name. Children call their father pa pa (pa pa), their mothers a ma (a ma), (high tone ma), their father's mother a ma (low tone ma), and their mother's mother p'o p'o (p'o p'o).* Parents call their children by their personal given names prefixed by a (a). Mr. Lin said no nicknames were used, at least in his family.

The daily round and basic needs. In the Chin family, they say that they get up between six and seven in the morning both summer and winter which is probably a fair statement for everyone in Chung Nam Wan except perhaps for Mrs. Lin. It would take an unconscionable amount of work for a year to be empirically certain of everyone's behavior. The children who are of age and have the opportunity, soon go off to school, while the majority of residents begin their work in the fields. There is transplanting and cultivating to be done, watering and fertilizing, gathering the vegetable crops and carrying them to market. Mr. Min leaves the hamlet soon after dawn to work under contract as a mason, whereas Mr. Chin and sometimes Mr. Lin go to market in Lung Shing with vegetables for sale, the former primarily concerned with arranging for larger deliveries to the afternoon market. They each bring back two bucketsful of night soil. Mrs. Min takes care of her house and her children, while Mrs. Chin and Mrs. Lin spend a large proportion of the day in the fields, interrupted by the time required to prepare meals for their families between one and two in the afternoon. There are also children in the Chin and Lin families to be looked after. In some ways it is fortunate that Mr. Chin's mother comes over the gap every afternoon to take care of her grandchildren, and the Lins' adopted daughter is given the most devoted care by her father while her mother works in the fields. Mr. Lin tells his wife that she should rest occasionally but she replies, "There are three in the family." The Chin family, unlike the others, has sweetened water and wheat flour dumplings in the middle of the afternoon (for an honored guest, an egg may be added). At the same time, the Mesdames Lin and Min may be doing their laundry. The Min's second daughter washes her hair when she comes home from school on Saturday, but apart from school there is little distinction from one day of the week to the other. Sometimes Mr. Chin's mother goes to church on Sunday morning and, more rarely, Mrs. Min. If the latter goes, so does her family. Usually, however, Sunday is no different for adults from any other day. Certainly, Mr. Min works every day unless it rains; when it rains continuously, he cannot, and if it rains a whole week there is nothing he can do about it. Rain actually stops

---

*Actually, these four terms of address vary in Cantonese, as well as in Mandarin.

all work periodically, and provides periods of rest and conversation, if not positive recreation. Although the ideal of continuous labor is expressed, there are always intervals of relaxation. Without them, one cannot endure the heat of the sun.

Dinner often comes late, sometimes at seven, or even after eight, because the labor which must be undertaken in the fields has not been completed. Then there are children to be bathed and put to bed, and one's own bath to be taken. Mr. Lin says everyone bathes more regularly in Chung Nam Wan than the people do in Lung Shing. Mrs. Min's two younger children get to bed between eight and eight-thirty and the three older ones about nine. The last thing Mrs. Min does is to cook the pigs' food. With these things done, there follows on good days a brief period of quiet inactivity for the adults before retiring about ten, but sometimes it is later, for instance, when the Lins go hunting with a flashlight in the fields to kill the slugs (gastropods) which attack their vegetables during the summer months. Ultimately everyone in Chung Nam Wan sleeps unless there is a typhoon and water drips on their beds.

All people have basic physiological needs. First is the necessity for oxygen and, although the populace of Chung Nam Wan takes it for granted, there is no question but that the air of the south shore of Lung Chau is exceptionally pure and pleasing to the lungs. Also the water, without which human beings can survive only a relatively few days, seems to be excellent. The Chins say it is the best thing in the hamlet, and Mr. Lin insists that such good water as they have can actually make one hungry. He also says that no one ever drinks unboiled water—and a supply is prepared in a two-handled kettle every morning and put into a stoneware jar—but, despite his statement, we have seen him unthinkingly imbibe the cool liquid as it comes from the rocks and likewise offer us a cupful. The Lins obtain the water just above their house from the tiny stream. If there is no rain for three months, there is still water, but after five months of no rain there is none. Then they go to the spring flowing from the rocks just below the level of their upper east vegetable fields which never fails and is particularly clean in the winter. At times of full supply, this higher pool is used only to obtain water for the vegetables in the adjacent fields.

The Chins' independent supply of drinking water comes washing down the rocks on the east slope of the hill about fifty feet above their house. It is carried to their reservoir by a concrete aqueduct 9″ wide containing a four-inch semicircular trough. The Chins suffer no lack of water for personal use, but in dry periods, they have concern for the supply needed for their fields. The well of the Min family has already been described.

The toilet facilities of Chung Nam Wan are primitive, but cause little concern to the residents. The Min family uses the fertilizer basin at the far end of the pig houses, while the Lin family uses one nearby. The Chin family has a jar behind the house and all residents may utilize jars inside their houses if an occasion warrants. The pigs use their sties and the babies and chickens have no respect for locality at all.

The relative necessity for sleep in the life of an individual is not perfectly clear. Some individuals in the world have claimed to do without it entirely, but our own prejudice is that the importance of sleep has been underrated even by Freud. The residents of Chung Nam Wan seem to need at least seven or eight hours. Mr. Lin told us that in winter he goes to bed about eight in the evening in order to keep warm and stays there until six the next morning. He adds that he has nothing else to do. He sleeps in his underwear under a ten-catty quilt.* The cotton for such a quilt costs $4.50 a catty and the cover another $15.00. His wife, however, gets up about five. In other seasons, Mr. Lin goes to bed later and wears only an undershirt.

The beds in Chung Nam Wan are made of solid boards softened at best by a reed mat and a blanket. They also have pillows. These are of cloth—black, white, or any color, stuffed with yau kom tsz (yu kan tzu) leaves which can be stripped from the branches of trees *(Phyllanthus emblica)* that grow on the hills by running the branches through the fingers. The leaves are washed in boiling water and then dried in the sun. Packed into a ten-by-fifteen inch casing, they are said to keep the head cool and to prevent a child from developing lumps on the cranium. Both the size and shape of the pillow vary.

In discussing sleeping habits with the residents, most of them admit to resting on their sides and turning over periodically. Mrs. Chin, however, lies on her back, whereas her mother-in-law says she cannot do it. Most Chinese, it appears, would consider the supine position unusual. Mrs. Chin adds that her small daughter sleeps face downward and moves from place to place all over the bed. Before they had any children, Mr. and Mrs. Chin slept in the same bed. After their daughter was born, Mr. Chin moved onto a separate set of boards, leaving his former place to the child. When the baby had been weaned, it showed an obvious preference for sleeping with its father by crawling to his bed. They liked each other very much. Frequently he would carry his daughter fastened to his back while he worked in the fields, behavior which his wife says surprised the neighbors. When their son was born, he slept with his mother in the south bed, and the daughter with the father in the north one, and that pattern has

---

*A catty is equivalent to approximately 1⅓ English pounds.

been continued. It may be added that whereas there is special affection between father and daughter, Mrs. Chin admittedly prefers her son, as does her mother-in-law for whom the child has a noticeable resemblance (Fig. 2.26). In the extremely hot nights of 1960, the Chin family moved its beds outside of the house onto the flat under the mulberry tree. Mr. Lin also set up his bed in the open air, but all the others remained under their customary roofs. At cool periods, however, a wool blanket may be used.

The Lin family is the poorest in Chung Nam Wan. Mr. Lin states that food is served only twice a day, at noon and in the evening about seven. He and his wife drink tea very rarely as they can afford it only for guests, on which occasions they buy a small twenty-cent package. During the period of our study, we never saw them drink tea. As might be expected, they have neither coffee nor the cheap fruit-flavored bottled drinks sold in Lung Shing. Rice is their most important food, and the Lins buy a very cheap quality consisting of broken grains which cost $.33 per catty.* Mr. Lin laughs when he admits this. From the price, it would seem that this is the grade that we learned later the Chin family feeds to their pigs. Mrs. Lin cooks the rice in a flat-bottomed covered aluminum pail which has paired handles on opposite sides. Water is added to about one inch above the rice which is boiled for twenty-five to thirty minutes.

Firewood for cooking is an important item in the domestic scene. The Lins use about 300 catties per month which cost $7.50 per hundred in Lung Shing from whence Mr. Lin brings it. The wood when purchased is still green and must be spread out in the sun to dry. Sometimes they have no money for wood and are obliged to burn reeds, but this is an extravagance because a reed fire needs someone in constant attendance, besides which, in the summer, the continual feeding of the fire makes one unmercifully hot. As has been noted, a daily supply of drinking water is always boiled the first thing in the morning.

Besides rice, vegetables are eaten, but these the Lins often buy, which at first seems as strange as bringing coals to Newcastle, but they quickly explain that they can sell their fresh flowering Chinese cabbage and purchase salted cabbage which is cheaper. Salted cabbage, they add, also encourages a person to eat enough rice. Peanut oil, soy sauce, salt, and sugar are a regular part of the diet. The sugar is brown which is claimed to be sweeter than white. Fish, also, is not infrequently purchased in order to vary the diet. Noodles, pork, and eggs appear on the table more rarely.

The composition of meals varies. From observation, it is possible to give some examples of what was eaten at midday. In the last week of June, the first of three luncheons comprised boiled rice, some vegetables,

---

*All prices in Part I, unless otherwise stated, refer to the cost in 1960.

and a small fish which had been purchased in the Lung Shing market that morning.* There was also a cheap oil-fried kau kwan ü (chiu k'un yü), or lizard fish, which has such a bad smell Mrs. Lin does not like it. Finally, there was a bit of pork and salted fish to please the taste of their beloved young daughter. The following day each member of the family lunched on two bowls of rice with salty flowering cabbage, a scrambled egg with tau shih (tou ch'ih) sauce and chili, and some salted fish with soy sauce. Everyone was using black lacquered wood chopsticks with red ends, the latter rather worn. These cost $.50 for ten pairs. Formerly the family used bamboo chopsticks which cost only $.20 per ten pairs. Mr. Lin added, "If we had money, we would like ivory ones better." On the last day of June they had a big bowl of rice, some pickled bean curd, and egg soup with ginger in it, on the whole a small meal. Mrs. Lin was eating with chopsticks but Mr. Lin used a porcelain spoon, sucking noisily. Aware of his behavior, he laughed and said that he was eating like a pig. A week later, we noted them eating boiled rice, fried eggs with Chinese chives, which are considered particularly good with eggs, a soup with bean sprouts, and some tiny dried fish. All of these meals, incidentally, were eaten between one and two o'clock. After lunch, the dishes were immersed in the stream and left to wash themselves.

Feast days are special. Mrs. Lin recalled steaming two of their largest chickens during the New Year's holidays. She also made five or six catties of glutenous rice into cakes. They had pork and vegetables purchased in the market. The following 5th of the 5th month they had four dishes: (1) a steamed rabbit fish, or nai mang (ni meng), (2) winter melon with black fermented beans, (3) roast pork, and (4) bean curd.

To move on to the Mins' house, on a mid-July day Mrs. Min and her children were found eating a dish comprised of vegetables pickled in salt, taro, peanuts, and yellow beans. Taro is especially good with duck. Taro costs $.50 a catty, and the beans $.80. Two days later, with the sun so hot at one-thirty that Mrs. Min said even the chickens did not like to go outside, she and her children were eating congee (rice boiled in an excess of water), a scrambled egg with an unidentified vegetable, and water spinach. Congee, having more liquid, is especially appreciated in hot weather, as also is soup, since the people do not drink water or tea with their rice. Normally, the Min family would eat boiled rice. Third Daughter is said to be able to eat three bowls, whereas two bowls, as later verified by Mrs. Chin's mother, is the standard portion.† Very rarely is rice fried,

---

*Probably kau ü (chiao yü), or horse mackerel, but the identification is uncertain. See Appendix C.

†The common rice bowl in Chung Nam Wan is approximately eight English fluid ounces in size (full measure).

but this may be done with rice left over from the previous day. Sometimes the children have white wheat flour bread of European type that can be purchased in the market. Mrs. Min stated that there was little variance in meals between winter and summer, but there are occasional specialties. For example, Mrs. Min likes lung shat (lung shih), literally dragon lice, an insect which costs $.10 for three in the market.* In the 10th month, Mrs. Min says she can catch a sizable bowl of them in half an hour at night by dipping them out of the Chins' washing pool with a large basket tray. She kills the insects by dropping them into boiling water. Then she recovers them with a bamboo straining spoon, lets them dry, and finally fries them in peanut oil and salt. She does this eight or ten times a season. Lung shat are eaten like peanuts as a side dish. Her husband and most of her children like them. When lung shat are plentiful, she gives some to the Chin and Lin families. She knows of no other edible insects. Mr. Chin's mother also prepares lung shat on occasion.

Sometimes in the afternoon, the children are offered a drink made by mixing sweetened condensed milk with water and brown sugar. When a seven-year-old (Ch) brother tells his four-year-old sister that she is drinking more with her porcelain spoon than he is, their eleven-year-old sister gets a cup and divides the milk between them. Sometimes condensed milk is spread upon bread. It should be noted that the children will eat nothing without their mother's specific permission. When Mrs. Min and her three older children were asked what food they liked best, the mother chose duck's head, legs, and wings. She added that, of vegetables, she liked Chinese kale, garland chrysanthemum, and lettuce better than any others. First Daughter quickly decided that plain chocolate candy was the most delicious thing to eat. Second Daughter reacted to the conversation by announcing that she preferred congee, defending her choice by saying that nothing was better when one was hungry. First Son settled for chicken. At the Min house, First Daughter washes the dishes most of the time, saving the dishwater with any remnants of food to be mixed with chopped grass for the pigs.

Our impression was that the Chin family provided a better cuisine than either the Lins or the Mins, but whether true or not, Mrs. Chin complained that her mother-in-law, who controls the expenditures, provides only the poorest grade of fish. Mr. Chin's mother and her two sons

---

*We quote: "Certain species of aquatic beetles known locally in Canton as 'Lung Shih' literally meaning 'dragon lice,' are used for food by the Cantonese. Two species, namely Cybister japonicus Sharp (Dytiscidae) and Hydrous hastatus Herbst (Hydrophilidae), are commonly consumed. These beetles are boiled with salt water and sold in the market. The above mentioned two species can be purchased in any grocery in Canton, they are eaten just as watermelon seeds and peanuts are eaten by the local people. They can be purchased also in Cantonese food shops in other large cities like Peking, Shanghai and Tientsin. They may also be eaten as one of the dishes on the table. Sometimes they are fried." Bodenheimer, 1951: 276–77.

normally eat their meals in their own house in Tung Pak Wan across the gap. Certainly the Chin family has a much greater supply of garden vegetables than the others, and they admittedly use them. Otherwise the contents of meals are little different. Fish, pork, peanut oil, sugar, salt, and condensed milk for the children are purchased in Lung Shing. According to Mr. Chin's mother, who holds the purse strings, the members of the family (including dogs and cats) consume about 200 catties of rice each month (and the pigs over a hundred more). The daughter-in-law, when questioned wholly independently, said that she and her husband and their children plus the dogs, cat, and chickens consumed only about 100 catties of rice per month (3.33 catties or 4.44 lbs. per day). The difference in the estimates seems to come from the inclusion of Mr. Chin's mother and his two brothers in the former estimate. For family rice, a $.37 grade is purchased, whereas $.33 is paid for rice for the pigs.* It may be added, that for the New Year's period, the family will treat itself to fifty catties of fifty-cent rice.

Mrs. Chin says everyone in her family has congee for breakfast. Her small son likes his with salted egg. Having food regularly in the morning distinguishes the Chins from the Mins, who only sometimes have breakfast (usually congee) depending on whether the food is available, and from the Lins who normally do not eat until noon. Mrs. Lin states, however, that when her husband goes to Lung Shing in the morning he does indulge himself once in a while with yam ch'a (yin ch'a) which costs thirty cents (tea plus little cakes and dumplings). The Chin and Min families differ from the Lins in having an afternoon collation of sweet soup, usually between three o'clock and four. This consists of pieces of boiled salted wheat flour (never rice flour) in sugared water, or of noodles instead of the pieces of wheat flour. Flour is periodically distributed by the church which the Chins and Mins attend. Flour is not the most common edible material among farmers on Lung Chau, so they mix it with water and salt, knead it a little, and drop pieces in boiling water for thirty or forty minutes. Noodles come from the church also. Apparently some recipients were selling the gift flour (we may assume they had no effective way of cooking it), so the priests had it made into noodles. For sweet soup, a little less than a catty of brown sugar is put into something more than a gallon of water when about half way through the process of boiling the pieces of salted flour. The Kaifong Association in Lung Shing also periodically distributes food, the primary source being CARE, an American charitable organization. According to Mr. Lin who has participated, each family has a ticket which is shown with one's identity card when a distribution is announced.

---

*The most expensive grade of rice sold in Lung Shing is said to be $.55 per catty (1960), whereas in Hong Kong a quality as expensive as $.75 is available.

In the first six months of 1960, the Lins received twelve catties of rice on two occasions, eighteen catties of wheat flour once, and twelve catties another time. At times, the Chins will substitute noodles in beef broth for sweet soup and, in our honor, they have served chicken congee and frequently offered tea, an orange drink, 7-Up, or bananas. Guavas, which are plentifully supplied when the Chung Nam Wan trees are in season, are eaten between meals. The Chins also have papayas at times, and bananas and apples are purchased. All the families are hospitable to visitors, and Mr. Lin is not above slipping into the Chin house and pouring himself a glass or two of tea on occasion.

Before leaving this admittedly inadequate discussion of the local cuisine, something should be added on the subject of drinking and smoking. All the Chin brothers are said to drink a little when the opportunity offers, despite the fact that their mother states she does not allow it. According to one informant, the younger Chin brother becomes red in the face if he drinks even a little. Mr. Chin's mother says she does not like liquor herself. An informant in another family, however, observes that both Chin women will drink a little (the elder one very little) on feast days. Mrs. Chin later admitted to enjoying a drink which she associates with the wine given a woman recovering from childbirth.

Mrs. Min is an exception among the women of Chung Nam Wan. She frankly admits that she likes all kinds of wine (and the term is here used in the Chinese sense which includes all types of spirituous liquors). She especially likes wines that are sweet such as those made from grapes. Also I was shown a bottle of Portuguese brandy, empty alas, which friends had bought in Macao and presented to her after the birth of her last child. Spirits are considered an appropriate gift on such an occasion, and she enjoyed drinking the liquor undiluted. Mr. Min joins her in appreciating both Chinese and European alcoholic beverages.

Mr. Lin verified Mrs. Min's enjoyment of liquor, and has very clear views on the subject himself. As has already been recorded, he began drinking at an age of about twenty (Ch) and has never lost his appreciation of liquor. Asked if he would prefer a bottle of grape wine (low alcoholic content), yellow fermented wine (medium), or cognac (high), he immediately answered, "Cognac," plus the comment that a few cups of it are better than a whole bottle of the others. He then proposed that if we would buy the cognac, he would buy shrimp. One must always eat when one drinks, he insisted. Sometimes he brings liquor home. He says that he is most apt to buy a certain Chinese rose wine, but that he cannot do so very often as it costs $9.60 per catty.* Also he appreciates Shao Hsing (a

---

*Chinese wine is often sold in bulk, a container of a certain size being lowered into the large stoneware jar of liquid. The contents of each liquid container are equal, at least nominally, to a specified weight.

term originally used for a yellow Chekiang wine but more recently for any light wine made from glutenous rice) which he says his wife can make but very seldom does. Until the day of our discussion of liquor, Mr. Lin said that he had not had a drink for a month. By coincidence, it would seem, that morning at the market in Lung Shing a friend had invited him to enjoy a little very strong clear spirit which costs only $3.20 per catty. They drank three-sixteenths of a catty, later another quarter. With it, they had some pork. He showed no sign of his indulgence. He could not decide how many times he had a drink each year, which understandably may be a difficult question to answer.

Mr. Lin smokes Tarzan cigarettes, which cost forty cents for twenty. He says a package lasts him three days. Mrs. Lin does not smoke, nor do the Chin family women. Mr. Chin started to smoke in 1958. He developed the habit from one of his hired field laborers who always gave him a cigarette when he smoked one himself. Now he buys Marvels, which cost eighty cents for twenty. He also has a spirit cigarette lighter, an article which is commonplace in Hong Kong. Mr. Min uses cigarettes, and his wife sometimes will smoke one if she visits a friend and is offered one.

When I asked Mrs. Min if she had ever smoked opium, she made a face showing disgust to accompany her negative answer. Both she and Mrs. Chin said they did not even know of anyone who used the drug. No one else in Chung Nam Wan admitted to having smoked opium, nor probably had anyone done so. Opium smoking has been illegal in Hong Kong since soon after World War II, but it is still reputedly available under cover in most places that are as large as the town of Lung Shing. Mr. Lin is aware of opium because his closest relative in Hong Kong almost died of smoking too much. The latter stopped twice, but started again. In fact, certain members of the family were in the business, buying wholesale and selling retail, which made the product cheap and available to this relative.

We move on to the mention of a final physiological need which must be passed with no more than a brief mention. Under the circumstances of our study, questions concerning the frequency and character of sexual relations could not be properly dealt with. It is significant, however, that the Min and Chin families have had a child every one or two years.

Child care and family relationships. Mrs. Min stated that children begin to be weaned at six months and are not given the breast after the first year. This, we believe, is the ideal Chinese behavior and practice is certainly influenced by it. On the other hand, when Mrs. Chin was seen nursing her year-and-a-half old daughter, her reaction to our restatement of the normative practice was that she did not care about such things. From observation, babies seem to be nursed whenever the opportunity offers and the child wants the breast. When Mrs. Min's baby cries, she may jostle it and slap it gently before giving it the nipple. Crying is also the stimulus for Mrs. Chin. When sufficiently fed, the baby generally sleeps. There is clearly no regulated schedule of feeding. As Mrs. Chin says, "You do what you want." We have seen her gently slap her nursing baby seemingly in a gesture of impatience because she wanted it to stop drinking so that she could get back to her work in the fields.

All the babies in Chung Nam Wan in 1960 were over six months of age and consequently were either weaned or in the process of being weaned. Gradually rice is added to their diet, usually in the form of congee. They may also be given sweet soup or, for that matter, apparently almost anything else that can be easily swallowed. Both Mrs. Min and Mrs. Chin use a little Tiger Balm, a well-known patent medicine, on their nipples when they wish to discourage a child from sucking. A small container costs thirty cents. Mrs. Chin says one treatment is enough. After that the child is simply warned.

The Lins' adopted daughter is rather a special case. According to the statements made, she was fed from the age of two months until eight or nine months on Eagle Brand condensed milk made in the Netherlands. Then she was given congee and bits of other things. As we knew her in her second year, she was a little particular about her choice of foods, quite possibly from being pampered within the range of her parents' ability. On the other hand, she was capable of saying to her mother when her father was not home for a meal, "Don't eat so much; save some for papa." She was also bright enough to inform her mother when cautioned against eating too quickly the candy brought by her daily visitors, "Never mind, they will bring more."

Mrs. Chin uses old pieces of cloth of no special material for diapers. She holds her baby upright or lets it sit on her leg. In putting it to sleep, she neither croons nor sings any lullabies. Mrs. Min on another occasion gave the same information about herself, and added that very few Chinese mothers croon or sing to their babies. Mrs. Chin also commented that children have to be watched closely. Her daughter almost fell into one of their deep water basins. Mrs. Chin's children suck their thumbs. She says that she cannot stop them but does not worry about it. A fortnight previous to her comment, Mrs. Min, observing Mrs. Chin's daughter sucking her thumb while on a visit to the Min house, suggested to Mrs. Chin that if she would leave her children with her for three days, she would train them not to do so. Proven method as stated: she slapped her own children until they stopped thumbsucking.

Mrs. Min is also an authority on toilet training as far as her five children go. She tells a baby from the earliest possible age not to eliminate in an improper place such as a bed, someone's lap or back, or the floor of the house, but babies do not seem to understand very well for the first two years. It is easy to give verification to the last statement. Frequent are our notations, such as "Child urinates on concrete between grandmother's legs; mother wipes the concrete with a rag, using her feet to do it, then changes baby boy's pants," or "Small son has just urinated on bed—everyone laughs—grandmother wipes up the urine with a rag." Several weeks later, the record gives a case of the grandmother using her foot on a rag to clean up after the baby while mother laughed, possibly a nervous reaction to the presence of an American male visitor. Nevertheless, there is no record of Mrs. Min laughing when her baby evacuated in her lap.

When a child has not responded to verbal training after two years, Mrs. Min begins slapping. After that comes a bamboo, or a stick may be used. According to our assistant, a Chinese mother herself, the administration of physical punishment is the proper old-fashioned way of dealing with an unresponsive child. In practice, however, she opines that a mother is often too soft-hearted even to slap children much. It is almost certain that the behavior of individual mothers in Chung Nam Wan varies considerably.

Mr. Chin's mother believes that she slapped her children only occasionally and then when they were older. "What good would it do when they are too young to understand?" and she adds that it is better to use nice words. She is certainly gentle with her grandchildren, although she can speak sharply to stop one from crying, even after it has burned itself. Mrs. Min has even less toleration of her children's crying, and she is not slow to punish her children for other things, particularly the boy. For falling off the bed and accidentally making his sister cry, he was reprimanded verbally; for knocking down his younger sister, he was struck with a bamboo but not severely. He walked away and cried briefly. He was slapped for breaking a large water bottle from which he had tried to drink and scolded for drinking out of the new one the next day. When he was caught in the house squirting the visitor with a water pistol, his mother gave him a tongue lashing and then, her temper rising, she struck him with a bamboo, repeating the performance to make him stop crying, and finally ending with more verbal criticism while she hung up the washing. The whole house became silent. On the other hand, Third Daughter cries a good deal and her mother only says, "You are always crying." Third Daughter, however, seemed to be crying because she did not feel well, and she complained of being tired. Also it was notable that once when a kitten jumped from the stove onto a rice bowl which First Daughter was carrying, knocking it to the ground and breaking it, and the various animals in the vicinity ate the rice, First Daughter picked up the pieces showing no sign of disturbance, nor did anyone else in the family show any, including her mother.

Mrs. Min says, "If slapping does not make children obey, tie them." Tying itself causes no physical hurt, but it frightens the children and prevents them from playing. When my assistant tried to indicate how a child was tied, Third Daughter cried. Her mother told her to keep still, then alternately struck her on the calves of her legs with a bamboo and comforted her several times, and finally ended up by shrieking at her. The child coughed and cried more softly. Mrs. Min, in her treatment of her children, actually gives the impression of being emotionally ebullient, not neurotic. They are clearly fond of her and not obviously afraid. Other punishments, such as deprivation of food, are not practiced in Chung Nam Wan. Furthermore, Mrs. Min does not threaten her children that she will have their father punish them, and he is reported never even to slap them. Most fathers, however, are said to be nice to their small children.

The only evidence that the adopted Lin daughter is ever punished comes from a statement that she complains to her father if her mother disciplines her while he is at the market. She is still young, and the "discipline" clearly nominal. Once her mother threatened to slap her if she did not get out of the stream. She was seldom seen crying, but when she did cry, her mother fastened her onto her back, merely commenting that the child was sleepy.

The most impressive thing to the foreign observer about the play of the older children was the restriction in the space they are allowed, a limitation which seems to be characteristically Chinese. The open and seemingly harmless hills of Chung Nam Wan were terra incognita to the Min children. They were not allowed to play on the beach. When First Son climbed a small tree, his oldest sister reported to their mother, and he was made to come down. In short, children are closely looked after. For hours, they play peacefully within a small area.

A very young child like the Chin son occasionally slaps his year older sister when she takes what he has. It is claimed that she does not slap him back. The Lin daughter, however, was seen to slap the youngest Min child for a similar reason. The Chin girl, old enough to feed herself with a spoon, has been seen trying to feed her still unweaned brother with it. A puppy was the primary beneficiary. No clear evidence of sibling rivalry was recorded, and the two young mothers with more than one child did not seem to recognize such reactions. In the Min family, First Daughter takes care of her younger siblings and particularly the baby, Fourth Daughter, whom she frequently carries on her back by means of a cloth baby carrier, which cost about four dollars and has a net attached at the top to hold the infant's head up if the nurse pleases to use it (Fig. 4.1). Such a carrier, incidentally, is expected to be sent by a mother to her daughter ten days after the latter gives birth to a child, together with clothing and a chair for the infant. The baby's mother also uses the carrier if she takes the baby

Fig. 4.1. A Child Asleep in a Baby Carrier

into town. Another example showing First Daughter's maternal training appeared in her restringing of Third Daughter's beads when the latter broke them. It is less obviously maternal behavior when she tickles her brother's navel, exposed as he bends backward on the bed, and smiles at me.

Personal care of children is poignantly demonstrated by Mr. Lin's mothering of his adopted daughter. He laughingly admits that when he is in Lung Shing, he worries about what she is doing but never about his wife. The mutual affection of father and daughter has a distinct charm, and his gentle treatment of the child is matched by her intelligent concern for him. When he is at the market and it rains, she says, addressing the elements, "Don't rain so hard, papa is coming home." She can also be silly as when she presses a dollar bill over his eyes, or when she spits at him. He slaps her gently and she slaps him. In one mood she lies on the bed and sucks her thumb and pulls the blanket over her head when she sees the visitor who brings her candy. She is taught to put a thumb upward in thanks for such gifts. The inculcation of the feminine role is seen when her father straps a pillow on her back in lieu of a baby. He is also proud that she can set out the rice bowls and chopsticks for a meal. Small Daughter could eat with chopsticks at an age of about twenty-four months, which is considered bright behavior.

The Lins' daughter has a few toys including a pair of small red cymbals and a furry dog. More often she plays with boxes of matches, perhaps spilling the contents, which her father uncomplainingly picks up. Sometimes she puts a bracelet of matchboxes on her wrist. She also may play with an open pocketknife, occasionally sucking on the blade or falling into the tiny stream with it. The Min children also have a few toys. Besides the water pistol previously mentioned, First Son has a plastic whistle in the form of a pink lady, which hurts sensitive ears when he blows it. Apparently a small, red, doubled-headed Chinese drum with flowers painted on the heads also belongs to him. Mrs. Min has made him a toy balance, the pan from a piece of plastic and the yard from a rod of the same material to which a stone weight was tied with a string. The children frequently play with an incomplete mah-jongg set. They make paper boats. Second Daughter catches an insect which buzzes when imprisoned in an empty matchbox. One day we saw the girls playing jacks with a set of small stones which, of course, is the original equipment of the game.

The principal rationale for keeping dogs is to watch the house and give warning of the arrival of strangers, but they also act as pets. Small ones can be purchased in the market for four or five dollars. Mr. Lin gives as reason for their having two dogs, that one dog would be lonesome. Furthermore, it is said that without dogs someone might steal the chickens. No one ever comes, but still the Lins are afraid. One dog sleeps outside and one in the pig house. The dogs, male and female, are fed some rice and fish, but they will eat rice by itself. Ideally, they are fed two bowls of rice twice a day after the owners have eaten. As he talks, Mr. Lin gives a piece of fish with his chopsticks to the dog underfoot, perhaps because he had stepped on the animal.

Like the Lins, the Mins have a dog and a bitch. The latter, they bought very young in the market when they first moved to Chung Nam Wan. The dog is the son of the bitch. They are both simply called "Little dog," a very common designation. One is usually under the bed. Theoretically they are fed only rice which is given them in a trough in front of the house, but they get scraps elsewhere. The Lin's first dog, it is said, used to come and eat in the Min's kitchen and fight with their dog.

The Chins have two female dogs, one three years old and the offspring of the other, which is five. They are said to look after the house when no one is at home as may be the case if the whole family goes to the cinema. One is called A Ts'oi (A Ts'ai), or Rich, a common name for a dog, the other, Tao Li (from English "Dolly"). Each is said to eat two bowls of rice at lunch and dinner, just as the other members of the family do. Mrs. Chin says that their dogs and cats are fed the same rice as she eats because there is always some left over since one cannot cook the exact amount needed for people. Furthermore, these pets eat at the same time.

The Chins also have a puppy almost three months old, which is the third generation and said to be worth ten dollars. Naturally, the children like the puppies even better than the dogs, and sometimes when it rains, it

Fig. 4.2. The Lin Daughter and Friends

pours. A week before the end of July, the old Chin bitch produced five puppies, the next day the Min bitch bore six, of which one died and, four days later, the Lin bitch had four (Fig. 4.2). Mr. Chin's mother said she will sell puppies to anyone who wants them.

Cats, especially including kittens, have two functions, as do dogs. Cats are supposed to kill rats which kill the chickens, and cats, especially kittens, attract the interest of children. The Chin female cat was given to them and soon had three kittens of which two died. It is said that no one would kill kittens; instead they may be left on the street for someone to pick up. The cats have natural, short tails which twist over their backs. They are fed leftover rice and fish, or whatever the family eats. Cats have no names.

The Lins had no cats in 1959 and the chickens suffered, but they have since acquired two. They say their cats will not eat rice without some fish mixed with it. The Mins have two cats and three kittens, the last kitten recently acquired because it is hoped that it will be a better rat catcher than the others, an optimistic view no doubt. First Daughter feeds the kittens rice on the pig food stove while the cats watch and wait their turn. Kittens are not so fortunate all day long. First Son may jam the top of a thermos bottle on a kitten's head. It cries when it cannot get free and everyone laughs. Worse, Third Daughter has been observed persistently trying to stamp her foot on a kitten. Only the two of them seem concerned.

In some degree, conflict among adults is as common as the summer wind and rain. At times it is so gentle as to be barely perceptible, and then again, it breaks upon the sheltered house like the sudden typhoon. Chung Nam Wan is no exception, but it gives the visitor the impression of being a peaceful place. One is tempted to infer that the personal relationships of Mr. and Mrs. Min are seldom disturbed, if for no other reason than that he is away so much of the time. To do so might be a mistake, however, so, knowing nothing, we will write nothing. As for the Lins they seem an amicable couple, as couples go (Fig. 4.3). Mr. Lin must have rasped the soul of the hardworking Mrs. Lin sometimes, but she is a good woman. Do not demand to know too precisely what a "good" woman is. We know that the people in the hamlet recognize her as "good," and we are convinced that she loves Mr. Lin. As we observed them, they had found the common ground of friendly relations. Once when Mr. Lin was watering the fields and then came down, Mrs. Lin said that he had done a lot of work. Both of them laughed, and there was no bitterness in the sound. Still there is no doubt that sometimes they fight when no one is around. A female neighbor said, "When you look at Mr. Lin, you would think he is a nice honest man, but he spends all his money on women. Sometimes he brings them to Chung Nam Wan, and then his wife gets angry and threatens to slap them." Sexual intimacy is not necessarily implied in this criticism.

The classic and continuous case of conflict among adults in Chung Nam Wan is illustrated by Mrs. Chin and her mother-in-law. There are two points of view and each woman irritates the other. We shall first present the prejudices of Mr. Chin's mother out of respect for her age and superior position. She states that from the day of the marriage when the bride was brought home, her father-in-law did not like her. She talked too loudly. Two days later she came in from the fields with her trousers rolled above her knees. Her father-in-law objected and told her husband.* She was warned but forgot and did it again and again. Her father-in-law commented to his wife that to spend a thousand dollars for such a woman was like throwing it into the sea. Furthermore, Mrs. Chin once told her husband that she could have married a man with an automobile, but that the Chins had asked for her first. Mr. Chin did not like the remark and confided it to his mother. She told her daughter-in-law to look in the mirror and said, "Anyone who has a car would not marry a woman who looks like you" (Mother-in-law the informant). The son's wife has bad manners. Only a few months previously Mr. Chin had been eating a dish of bean curd at Mr. Lin's house, at the latter's invitation. Mrs. Chin yelled up at him, "Why do you go some place to eat when you had a good meal at home?"

---

*Women normally work in the field with their trousers rolled up, but a young woman apparently should not be so exposed in front of her father-in-law.

Fig. 4.3. Mr. and Mrs. Lin (upper); Mrs. Min, Mr. Chin (lower)

"One should not say such things so other people can hear," was her mother-in-law's reaction.* In fact, Mr. Chin's mother links her husband's distress over his daughter-in-law's behavior with his death which occurred not long after the marriage.

There is also the problem of the young Mrs. Chin's ignorance. Her mother-in-law repeated the educated, second Chin son's opinion of her. He is reported to have asked his sister-in-law "Which is more, eight ounces or half a pound?" and she reputedly answered "Half a pound is more." "See how stupid she is," he is said to have commented. "When the youngest brother asks his sister-in-law how much three plus one is, she answers, 'Five.' Then they all laugh at her," says Mr. Chin's mother and adds, "No wonder she cannot count her chickens." Mrs. Chin herself admitted that she does not know the month, day, or year of her marriage.

Finally, in her mother-in-law's opinion, Mrs. Chin does not work as hard as she should and is not properly careful in her housework. In the latter part of a cruelly hot July, Mrs. Chin was reprimanded for sitting down in front of the house and fanning herself. Her mother-in-law said, "Why are you sitting around when your husband works so hard in the fields?" (Mother-in-law the informant). Mrs. Chin became angry, packed up her children, and went home with them to her mother. The journey may have cost her a dollar.

Viewing the crisis objectively at that point, several things may be said. In defense of everyone, the weather had been painfully hot, and the fact that the hired laborer had walked off had considerably added to the physical effort required of both Mr. and Mrs. Chin. It had also added to the anxieties of Mr. Chin's mother who has constant concern for the welfare of the family and has time to worry while she takes care of her grandchildren. In her own behalf she states that Mr. and Mrs. Chin had already been having trouble and that her criticism of the moment had little to do with her daughter-in-law's departure. When the latter would return was regarded as uncertain. She had gone home to her mother before and stayed away as long as ten days.

It is obvious that the loss of one of the remaining two principal workers on the farm for ten days might be economically crucial. For the time being Mr. Chin's mother did the coooking for her whole family at Chung Nam Wan. Mr. Chin smiled, but did not feel happy. Mr. Chin's mother responded to my suggestion that her son might go and bring his wife home by indicating that he could not do that because then Mrs. Chin would feel too proud in consequence.

Mrs. Chin and her children returned after three days. She had obviously been to the hairdresser, a treat from her mother. Life seemed to go

---

*Curiously, Mrs. Lin commented on this incident the same day, a fact which suggests that she and Mr. Chin's mother had perhaps been discussing it.

smoothly as the old routine was quickly reinstated. The mother-in-law was away several days because of the death of a neighbor and Mrs. Chin had the gratification of presenting her side of the conflict. She states that she was brought into the Chin family as a wife because of her reputation for hard work and that even her mother-in-law tells her to her face, "The reason we like you is because you are strong." At first her husband did not love her and was even ashamed to be seen with her, informing strangers that she was his sister, and continuing to see other girls in Lung Shing when they went to market. When she complained to her mother-in-law, the latter did not believe her, but her father-in-law told his son, "It is not right to leave your wife, you are married now." But he continued to do so. In her own opinion, she works very hard and, since having children, her husband has come to appreciate her, but her mother-in-law complains just the same.

She also states that her mother-in-law became annoyed and protested to the priest when she asked to have a government certificate of marriage. Furthermore, she asserts that the Chin family did not carry out to the full their agreement as to what presents they would give to her family on her marriage, although she admits the prices of the things had gone up in the meantime.

Before the week was over, Mr. Chin's mother was angry with her daughter-in-law because she found water rusting the iron pan in the unused pig stove (there had been gale winds and rain). She told her she ought to be more careful. Then she said she was responsible for having let one of the young pigs die. Mrs. Chin responded that she was willing to work in the fields all the time and let her mother-in-law look after the chickens and the pigs, adding that Mrs. Min also took care of pigs and some of them died, a statement which might seem to add up correctly in anyone's opinion. And so, without mercy, the classic Chinese situation of conflict continues in Chung Nam Wan as it quite possibly does elsewhere.

Interfamily relationships. One may speak of the class situation in Chung Nam Wan and say there are three, providing one keeps a tongue in one's cheek. Mrs. Min (Fig. 4.3) seems to be unaware of classes in general and cannot correlate the idea with Chung Nam Wan families when it is explained. She says simply that one person is as good as another. Both Mr. Chin's mother and Mrs. Lin say there are two classes, the richer and the poorer. Mr. Lin when confronted with the direct question as to whether there are not three classes, answers "Yes, there is one in between." He goes on to point out that in Chung Nam Wan the Chin family has a lot of people, a lot of fields, and a lot to eat, whereas the Min family is not so well off, but better off than himself.

When the question is asked of the Chins, it is admitted that their own family appears to be richer, but then they claim that actually they are not because of their debts amounting to about two thousand dollars borrowed against the value of their pigs. They do admit that the Lins are in a different position because they have no pigs at all. Objectively viewed, it might be demonstrated that on the basis of wealth, education, and a potential for upward mobility, the Chins have a definite advantage over the Mins as do the Mins over the Lins. It is time to take the tongue out of one's cheek.

Before leaving the subject of classes, something can be recorded about slavery, more properly called mui tsai (mei tzu)* in referring to the Chinese variety. Informants in each family admitted that girls could be purchased and were owned as slaves in the Kwangtung communities from which they had originally come. No one defended the practice, and most of them condemned it. Mr. Lin, who insisted that slavery was not a good custom, pointed out that whereas some girls were well-treated, others were abused. He said that there had been many slaves in his birthplace, and that these girls of poor families who had been sold to work for others were at one extreme treated as daughters, while at another, forced to become mistresses of the men of the family. Mrs. Min stated that such girls were usually purchased between the ages of five or six (Ch) and ten or eleven as servants for the daughters of well-to-do families, and added that no one would purchase a girl at fourteen because she already knew everything. Prices varied and, in general, were cheaper the younger the girl. A ten-year-old cost from one to three hundred dollars in Chinese national currency in the decade preceding World War II.

Informants knew of no cases of slavery in Hong Kong although they stated that it formerly existed. Girls are sometimes given away but not sold, although presents may be made to seal the transaction. Usually, working girls are paid by the month. The explanation is succinct. Since slave girls can no longer be forced to be obedient because in Hong Kong they can run away, there is no use in buying them. It is more effective to hire a girl and then discharge her if she is not satisfactory than to be burdened with an irresponsible slave.

The social relationships between the three families in Chung Nam Wan seem exceptionally cordial from Chinese standards. The people all visit from one house to another, and the fact that they can make critical comments about each other at times is no contradiction. It is Mr. Lin who is the chief target of unkind words, but if there is smoke, we have no proof of the fire. When he first came to Chung Nam Wan, he is said to have referred to his wife as just a relation, while spending his money on several girl friends among the boat people. He is also purported to have sold wine on which he did not pay the tax and to have been consequently arrested.

---

*Mandarin speakers use a t'au (ya t'ou), not mui tsai (mei tzu).

5. Education, Health, Amusements, and Travel

Education. The standards of education of those identified with Chung Nam Wan are not very high, but there are indications of improvement. Mr. Lin states that he went to a private school for six or seven years in the place where he was born. The teacher was an old man and Mr. Lin admits to having been lazy as a student and to have learned little. He can read some items in a newspaper. Instead of studying, he remembers playing in the water and catching birds. He frankly states that he was spoiled, being the eldest son, and for most of his childhood the only one since his two stepbrothers were fifteen and eighteen years younger. His wife never entered school and is completely illiterate. The Lin daughter is no more than a baby, and her education is a matter for the future.

Mr. Min also went to school in his native village long enough to learn to read a newspaper which, at another time, was stated as ten years including a short period in middle school. Mrs. Min says she has seen him reading a book, but only on a few occasions. Mrs. Min herself had but a week of school before the Japanese invasion altered her life. She has learned enough characters to read the newspaper a little. First Daughter is completing her second year at School A in Lung Shing at the end of July, and Second Daughter her first.* First Daughter on several occasions was observed writing, presumably her homework, and was said to like doing it. Second Daughter was once overheard being told to do her studying and not simply play. In a Hong Kong overwhelmed by refugees, it is not possible to build schools fast enough for the new generations of children, and the opportunity to attend a school is consequently a greatly sought privilege. There is no government school in Lung Shing, but the government contributes to some of those that exist. The private school which the Min girls attend is free but costs nine dollars per term, or eighteen per year, for books, paper, and incidental materials. The girls say their school

---

*The seven schools in Lung Shing have been designated by letter. In Hong Kong, the educational system is based on six years of primary schooling and five to seven years of secondary schooling. The first three years of the latter are often termed junior middle or lower secondary schools, and some, secondary schools, high schools or colleges. University education follows thereafter. Cf. *Hong Kong 1962 Report*, 1963: 120–26.

subjects are reading, writing, arithmetic, drawing, handwork, and physical education. Another school in Lung Shing was mentioned as costing seven dollars per month (School C). The Kaifong Association has a new school built in part with contributions from local benefit performances of a Chinese opera (School D). There is also a Protestant school with a new building but it is primarily for the children of the fishing boat people (School B). The son of the Min family does not go to school, and the other Min children are too young.

Mr. Chin went to the six-year Protestant primary school in Lung Shing for three years (School B). The work seemed too difficult for him, reports a brother, so he stopped. Mrs. Chin never attended school, nor did Mr. Chin's mother, although the latter has been impelled by her church to learn a brushful of characters. The Chin daughter and son are mere babies. It is Mr. Chin's first younger brother who has distinguished himself, having finished the six-year School B in Lung Shing, which cost three dollars per month for all grades. The students at that time attended one session a day from 7:45 A.M. to 1:30 P.M., six days a week, with about twelve days of holidays at New Year's, fifty in summer, and some others, such as Christmas and Easter. Having done that, in 1960 he was just completing the course in a three-year nonsectarian junior middle school which, at sixteen dollars per month, he claimed to be the cheapest on Hong Kong Island. The school hours were from 9:00 to 12:00 and 1:30 to 3:40 five days a week, but only mornings on Saturday. The holiday periods were said to be the same as those at the primary school. This junior middle school had about three hundred students, with rather more boys than girls. He enjoys talking to the girls in school and, since seats are assigned in order of one's arrival, he has sometimes sat next to a girl. After school, boys and girls may be together, but there is little time for interpersonal activities because of the large amount of homework. The subjects taught include Chinese, English (ten hours a week for the three years), mathematics, history, geography, natural history, human physiology, music, painting, and physical education. He stated that many Chinese in Hong Kong do not try to speak English because they are afraid that they do not express themselves well. The fear is well-founded.

With so much schooling behind him, the younger Mr. Chin hopes to continue through high school, another three-year course with a similar curriculum, but his family's lack of money creates a problem. He has taken the entrance examination, however, and has been accepted at the New Method College in Hong Kong where he has paid the first month's fee of forty dollars. Because this private school is so crowded, there are two sessions a day. His, in the afternoon, is from 1:30 to 6:30. Holidays remain the same. Government middle schools, he claims cost only a little over twenty dollars a month, but they are difficult to get into. Going to high

school, he points out, is particularly expensive because of essential expenditures such as bus fare and books. Bus fare is half price for students, however. He hopes for a scholarship, but the competition makes one almost impossible to obtain, as he well knows. Sooner or later he would like to work on a ship so that he can see different places and things. He adds that men working on ships make a great deal of money but spend it on liquor and women. Asked whether he also would do that, he replies, "It is difficult to tell."

Mr. Chin's youngest brother, about fourteen, has just finished his fifth year of the same primary school in Lung Shing that his brothers attended and reputedly does not like studying too much, which is not really strange for one of his age.*

In a discussion of education, Mr. Chin's mother told her eldest son to pay attention so that he would realize and remember that if he did not start his children at the right time, they would be unable to get into school later. She also expressed the opinion with reference to her granddaughter that it would be sufficient if she could go through middle school. As she put it, "If a girl went to a university, what good would it do? It is enough to write a letter if you get married and have children." To the suggestion that a better educated girl might have a chance to marry a richer man, she replied, "Yes, but we do not have the money to send her."

Health. No one in Chung Nam Wan was notably ill during the period of our study. Mr. Min did not go to work one day because he did not feel well. The same day he went to a movie. One day the Mins' first daughter did not go to school because she did not feel well. Mrs. Min said that at the same time she herself had a chill. She knows of malaria and apparently has suffered from it periodically. Third Daughter did not impress us as being always in the best of health. One day Mr. Chin was found lying on his bed at midday. He did not feel well. He recovered in twenty-four hours. No one else in the Chin family was recorded as ill.

The attitude toward doctors varies. Mr. Lin states that if one is ill and has money, one can consult doctors in Lung Shing trained in either the Chinese or the European tradition. The Chinese doctor is described as having his medicines in small balls which are dissolved in distinctively shaped, spouted, stoneware pots. Treatment costs at least five dollars, including the medicine, whereas the doctor trained in the European tradition charges three dollars without medicine. Mr. Lin believes the latter one better, although he cannot remember when either he or his wife last went to a physician. Mrs. Min says that the Lin family does not seek out professional treatment but simply prays to Buddha.

---

*By the following year, he at least claimed that he preferred going to school to working in the fields.

Mr. Lin had an infection in his foot during the fourth month, but he had recovered by the fifth without going to a doctor. The previous year, Mrs. Lin had a large swelling on her right shoulder. She could not sleep for ten days and she suffered so much she could not even eat. They asked Kun Yam, (Kuan Yin), the Goddess of Mercy, what to do and were moved to poultice the shoulder with mulberry leaves. The shoulder became well but a scar remained. Small Daughter was ill and could not sleep for eight or ten days when about five months old. They were worried about her, but she recovered without medical treatment. Small Daughter suffers constipation at times. Mr. Lin may then rub her anus, more probably because it is sore than with the intent to induce defecation. Once we saw Mr. Lin doctoring a sore ear with a concoction he made by putting some unborn rats, together with a large centipede (reported as about seven inches long and very poisonous) which he had caught in his chicken house, into a pint bottle of Shiu Hing (Shao Hsing) wine. He applied this medicine to his ear with a little of the vane left on the end of a feather, the rest having been trimmed off. A few days later he said that the pain in his ear had gone.

Mrs. Min tells us that there is a special tonic considered very beneficial when a child is recovering from measles. It is made from fish jaws boiled with congee. Mrs. Min has taken some of her children to a doctor trained in the Western tradition to cure their eczema. She states that the Chinese style doctor always prescribes a black liquid medicine which is difficult to make the children drink, whereas her present doctor does not, and also the ultimate cost is about the same. After two treatments the children became well. She does not understand why the Chins who, she says, have money, do not take their child who suffers the same malady to a doctor. So much for the Mins' interest in health except that we may repeat our reference in another context to the "chicken-egg-flowers" which, when the whole flowers are boiled with congee, provide a tonic to make people feel better when there is a great deal of rain. One may use more or less of the flowers.

There are "chicken-egg-flowers" growing near the house of Mrs. Chin who says that she also makes a tonic from them occasionally. She reports that when her babies are sick, she sometimes goes to a Chinese medicine shop in Lung Shing and tells the symptoms of the child's complaint. The owner then prescribes and sells her the proper medicine. Also she has gone to a Western style doctor in Lung Shing, as well as to one near her former home on the main island. They charge three dollars a visit. The children's skin disease, which Mrs. Min mentioned, and which I had noted on my first visit to the Chins' home, cleared up by itself after a month. In the surrounding hills there is a plant called simply sour-sweet, or sün tim (suan-t'ien), bearing a sweet tasting, large pitted, purplish berry which ripens in June. The leaves of this plant when boiled serve as a stomach

medicine. Small Daughter ate so many of the berries, we expected her to need some of the leaves, but if so, she did not admit it.

Chinese in Lung Shing were observed drinking leung ch'a (liang ch'a) or, literally, "cooling" tea, a somewhat bitter concoction of medicinal herbs sold on the street as a tonic for those who feel that they have eaten too much "hot" food.* Mr. Chin's mother states that leung ch'a is not needed by the residents of Chung Nam Wan because their water is so good. Seeing a praying mantis on the path, she said it was reputedly eaten as a medicine for certain diseases, but that she would be afraid to eat one herself. Once she suggested that a sore throat could be cured with a dish of pig's neck cooked with almonds and dried red dates. Her second son admitted that the family patronized both doctors with Western and those with Chinese traditional training but he was not aware of why either one might be chosen rather than the other.

Cuts and abrasions are understandable occurrences. Most noticeable are Mr. Chin's scars which have resulted from years of carrying a heavily loaded bamboo pole on his bare shoulder in hot weather. Apparently the skin blistered over callouses scarifying the surface without causing bleeding. This could be avoided by using a small towel for protection, but he says it is a nuisance to carry when not actually in use and that the injury gets well by itself. His mother says that he does not use a towel because he is too lazy. Once when Mr. Chin cut his foot, it was suggested that a disinfectant might be applied. His mother produced a tube of Unguentine, which was all they had. Mr. Lin, on the other hand, owned a tube of some antiseptic reputedly containing penicillin which it was said one had to know the druggist to buy without a doctor's prescription.†

All the women show scars on the thumb side of the first finger of the left hand. These are commonly produced by errors in judgment when cutting greens with a chopping knife on a cutting board (Fig. 2.28). On first watching the process it seemed surprising they still retained the finger. Children play with knives and cut themselves. An occasion with the Chin daughter as victim produced shrieks of anguish seemingly brought on more by fright and the appearance of blood than by the actual damage caused by an unsuccessful attempt to peel an apple. Her mother simply fastened a piece of cotton over the wound with adhesive tape and then yelled explosively, but without anger, for her daughter to stop crying.

---

*"Hot" foods form a class distinguished from "cold" foods, and include particularly oily, rich and spicy foods, fried rice being an example. They are not necessarily hot in either the literal or the seasoning sense.

†Or perhaps simply because the druggist did not have the proper license to sell it.

Amusements. There are few formal amusements in Chung Nam Wan itself, one might say almost none until the Chin family purchased a small transistor radio in the spring of 1960. It is played almost continually while people are awake, most of the time hanging in the mulberry tree at the edge of the flat in front of the house and blaring a Chinese opera. With the sound turned up, it can easily be enjoyed by those working in the fields nearby and, if she is farther away, Mrs. Chin may take it with her. The radio cost $160 and was bought on the installment plan by Mr. Chin, his mother protesting at the extravagance. On it they claim to receive many stations, including especially at night those of foreign countries. Usually the radio remains tuned to one local broadcast since, as they say, it is too much nuisance to change it.* This radio has also had a definite impact on the Min family. The children, at least, are envious, but Mrs. Min has a fondness for radios as well. When she lived in Lung Shing, a neighbor had one, and both women became accustomed to listen to a storyteller everyday at one o'clock. The story was presented in installments and Mrs. Min had to be there. Her husband asked "Why don't you finish your lunch?" and she would answer, "The story might finish." The important part of the story was the end and she did not want to miss it.

Mrs. Min, with future possibilities in mind, states that a radio can be purchased from eighty to ninety dollars but that, in her opinion, it is not worth owning. For a satisfactory one, it is necessary to pay over a hundred. Her husband says that he has a sufficient income as a mason, and that she could sell her chickens on the 15th of the 8th month (the next feast day) and buy herself a radio since she wants one so much. Mrs. Min doubted that she could raise enough money. The Lins evinced no particular interest in the radio. When asked, however, they both said that they enjoyed hearing the Chin's radio and would like one themselves. Neither have ever seen television, and the instrument had to be described in order to record that fact.

Mrs. Min said that she once tried to learn to play the p'i p'a (lute) but could not. The two younger brothers of Mr. Chin have a harmonica with which they can perform modestly. The two-year-old Chin daughter has been seen trying to teach the youngest Min child how to play it but with no apparent success. The younger Chin brother looked on complacently, periodically retrieving his instrument, cleaning it affectionately, and then giving it back. Neither of the Lins can play any musical instrument.

---

*In 1961, they recognized that stock market quotations were being broadcast but disavowed any interest. In short, the radio was seemingly both ignored or enjoyed almost unconsciously. Mr. Chin's mother, who had protested the original purchase as an extravagance, had recently acquired a radio for her own house.

Opera, which is common on the radio, can periodically be seen in Lung Shing. A performance usually occurs on the 13th of the 2nd month which is the birthday of Hung Shing (Hung Sheng), the principal God of the oldest temple in Lung Shing. The shop people contribute most of the money for the performance and anyone can attend free. Mr. Lin says the performance is not very good. There are also performances of operas in the town across the harbor on the main island at the birth celebration of T'in Hau (T'ien Hou), the Queen of Heaven. They may likewise be attended without payment on the 23rd of the 3rd month. There may also be a benefit performance once a year for which tickets may cost eight dollars. Mr. Lin has also patronized that company.

Mrs. Min states that there are other opera performances in Lung Shing. For instance, one has been given on the birth of Lo Pan (Lu Pan), the patron of carpenters and masons, which occurs on the 13th of the 6th month. Mrs. Min did not attend because it was too difficult to take all the children. Mrs. Min says that she likes opera the best of any entertainment, preferring it to movies. Her husband enjoys it too. She confirms Mr. Lin's statement, however, that the performances in Lung Shing are very poor. Mrs. Min first went to the opera at the age of six. She recognizes major styles and has seen well-dressed performances in Canton where fancy silk and shiny beads of the performers remain memorable. She is critical of the Peking style operas with their different speech and singing, because the actors turn their backs on the people in order to drink tea. Cantonese opera singers drink tea also, she adds, but not while performing.

Mr. Chin's mother says that opera is only worth-while when it is performed inside a theater, rather than in the open air as in Lung Shing where her sons have only seen it. Therefore she prefers movies. Mrs. Chin confesses that she no longer understands opera because she so seldom has seen a performance, and consequently does not like it. On the other hand she goes occasionally to the movies, which she now, like her mother-in-law, prefers, but only in Lung Shing. She has seen Chinese, Japanese, European, and American pictures. She likes the Chinese best for the simple reason that she cannot understand the others as well. She pays fifty cents for her seat unless there is one left for thirty cents which a person has to go early to get. Mr. Chin attends periodically.

Mrs. Min goes very irregularly to the movies in Lung Shing, sometimes several times in a month, sometimes only once in several months. She sees mostly Chinese films and prefers them, as does Mrs. Chin, because she can understand the sound strip. She has seen few foreign productions and complains that they contained war scenes and fighting which frighten her. She added by way of free association that once an airplane crashed into the strait and everyone left the theater because of the excitement. Mrs. Min prefers films that are sad. Mrs. Min was observed

going to the single afternoon performance of the cinema in Lung Shing, taking her five children with her. She bought two thirty cent tickets. Her two youngest daughters of which only one was in her arms, and the baby on her back, were admitted free. In theory, only two children should have been admitted on one ticket, but as she says, she gets in three because they are small. It may be as accurate to say that she gets in three because of her personality and the theater in Lung Shing does not always enforce its own rules. Mrs. Min did not think highly of the Cantonese movie she saw, but the children liked it, and the baby seemed interested enough not to cry. There are two evening shows at the Lung Shing cinema, one at 7:45 and the other at 9:45.

Mr. Lin estimates that he attends the one Lung Shing movie theater six or seven times a year, sometimes not seeing a performance for several months at a time. He usually takes his small daughter who always asks for food or candy on such occasions. When he refuses to take her, Small Daughter may cry, and then he is likely to give in. Mrs. Lin seldom goes because she does not care for the films since she is a Hakka and cannot understand the singing in Cantonese which, of course, is much harder to catch than ordinary speech. Mr. Lin explains that theater tickets cost $1.00, $.70, $.50 and $.30, the last ones being too close to the screen. If not many people are in the audience, he says it is possible to sit in a seventy cent seat with a fifty cent ticket. Most of the films are Chinese (made in Hong Kong) but sometimes foreign pictures are shown. Mr. Lin can distinguish Japanese productions readily enough, but not European from American. Asked what kind he preferred, he decided European or American because he likes to see strange things and does not enjoy pictures of the Chinese type of fighting frequently depicted in historical plays. The foreign styles of fighting, he identifies with less, but he likes no kind at all. "It is no use to fight," he digresses. Movies containing singing and dancing are his favorites. The whole Lin family was recorded as going to the late show one evening. Mrs. Lin, incidentally, has never experienced airconditioning and did not know that there were cooled theaters in Hong Kong although her husband had been in them once or twice. To conclude with the information relating to the cinema, we can note that Mr. Chin's next younger brother admits that he has gone to a movie with a girl and, when he has done so he has usually paid for her ticket.

One of the most notable entertainments of the area is the Dragon Boat Festival which takes place in the harbor of Lung Chau on the 5th of the 5th month. Four boats are said to have competed in the 1960 race, each containing seventy to eighty paddlers. The boats, except for preliminary practice, are used only on that single day of the year, and each belongs to a different association. Each of the approximately three hundred participants puts up a certain amount of money, according to Mr. Lin, and the

winning boat takes all the money, which is loaned out at interest for a year to obtain funds to give the annual party for all the contestants. The boat people say that ghosts will plague them if the annual race is not performed, and a paddler is told that the ghosts will make him ill if he gives up participating. All the junks have to be cleared from the course and many Lung Chau people view the performance from in front of the temple near the ferry landing. Only the Lins' daughter and her father go to the festival, Mrs. Lin being said to have grown too old for such things. Mrs. Min does not go because, as she says, "Every year the races are the same."*

New Year's celebration may also be counted as one of the main amusements of the year and one which is characterized by feasting to the best of a family's ability and by the giving of gifts. Chicken and pork appear on the menu as well as special dishes appropriate to the season. It is the time when old clothes are replaced, if there is money to afford the new ones. Each family gives a red paper packet with a small amount of money to each child in the community including its own, the latter being traditionally placed under the pillows of the children. There are also cakes and candy for the young.

Mr. Chin's mother emphatically insists that no one has any time for sports or games in Chung Nam Wan. This is a common, idealized statement which is not far from the practice. She also adds that no one in her family even knows how to play mah-jongg, to say nothing of Hakka p'ai (p'ai). The priest has asked them not to gamble and they do not. The younger Chin brothers bring their school friends and go swimming. It is notable that the fourteen-year-old son bars the door of Chin's house when he changes into his suit, but perhaps the presence of strangers accounts for his care. Mr. Chin himself can swim a little, but it is the younger generation who are developing the sport. Mrs. Chin does not go into the water, thus exemplifying the old conservative pattern. Mrs. Min says that neither she nor any of the children can swim, but that her husband knows how, although he has not been in the water since coming to Hong Kong. Mr. Lin says that he can paddle along for perhaps twenty feet. He adds with a laugh that Mrs. Lin does her swimming in the dishwashing pool.

Mr. Lin states that Lung Shing has association football, or soccer, games, but that he does not go. He also claims that he does not understand how to play mah-jongg, but he may mean that he does not play very well. Sometimes, however, he will spend an odd hour when in town watching other people play, and this he enjoys very much. Mr. Min, on the other hand, does like to indulge in mah-jongg with his friends on a rainy day when it is not possible to work. He gambles but is said not to lose very

---

*Mr. Chin took his two older children to the Dragon Boat races in 1961, however, and did not get them home until almost bedtime. Mrs. Chin remained at home with their third child, a daughter.

much. He does not play mah-jongg with his wife, however. Mr. Min does
not attend any sports events. His wife has been to soccer games but does
not like them. She says she never gambles except perhaps on Chinese
New Year's Day. Mr. Min plays the game called Hakka p'ai occasionally
with friends in town. He claims his gambling never involves more than ten
or twenty cents, but it is not certain whether he means twenty cents an
hour or a minute. In the old days he once lost over a hundred dollars in a
single game. Hakka p'ai, he points out, has the distinct advantage, however, of allowing a player to stop anytime that he wishes. Mrs. Lin is also
inclined to place a wager when exceptional circumstances warrant it, as
we shall see when we come to the section on religion.

A comment on humor may be added as a conclusion to the discussion
of amusements. Humor is difficult to catch for an alien who does not
comprehend a language extremely well, but laughter is usually a signal.
Once Mr. Lin arrived at Mrs. Min's house during a discussion of lung shat
(lung shih), or dragon lice, which are found in pools of water. He immediately reached into his hair and said he would get a specimen for me.
Both Mr. Lin and Mrs. Min laughed, the latter with her hand over her
mouth. The same day, the two of them sitting beside each other began
to laugh because Mr. Lin commented that Mrs. Min's waist was double
the size of his. He also noted that whereas the ethnographer looked
healthy enough, the research assistant appeared thin. A week earlier, Mrs.
Min, overhearing a discussion of baby feeding at Mr. Chin's house, announced that if she herself had milk to drink, she would not be able to get
through her narrow door. This was perhaps a statement of fact thinly
disguised as humor. A fortnight afterward Mr. Chin's mother gave the
opinion that her daughter-in-law looked better than she formerly did because she was no longer so fat.*

Travel. All the residents of Chung Nam Wan visit the town of Lung
Shing with more or less regularity. It is a center of civilization, the capital
of the personally known world for most of them if one disregards the past.
Only the second brother seems to live in a world that is larger. The
amount and type of contact with Lung Shing varies. Mr. Min usually
works there and the fact that he and his wife had a house in the town for
five years before moving to Chung Nam Wan is significant. Two Min
children and the three Chin brothers go or have gone to school there for
various periods. Mr. Chin often goes to market in Lung Shing twice a day,
and Mr. Lin says he usually makes the trip once every two or three days,
but his own records show that in one twenty-two day period during our

---

*References to a person's weight seem disproportionately frequent in our notes, but this may be
because we had some anxiety about the ten pounds of her hundred that our gracefully thin interpreter
had been losing from heat and exhaustion.

study he went to market sixteen times. Mr. Lin not infrequently returns to Chung Nam Wan in the dark. He asserts that he never carries a light and never slips or falls. Scores of dogs in the town bark at him but do not bite. Mr. Lin has never climbed to the top of the surrounding hills, claiming that he has no time. He has, however, visited friends in the suburb of Sai Mi Wan at the western end of the island. Mrs. Chin carries vegetables into Lung Shing when there are many, and her mother-in-law, living across the gap, makes the trip more often still for other purposes. Mrs. Lin appears at the bottom of an imaginary list based on frequency of trips to Lung Shing. She is too tired to go when it is not absolutely necessary.

Mr. Lin sometimes visits Tung Pak Wan across the gap where he knows a lot of people, but not by name. Mr. Min occasionally works there and, of course, the Chin family owns a house in that village.

For anyone to go off the island, or at least farther than the town across the narrow strait, is extremely unusual. Rarely, Mr. Lin goes to visit a relative who is the caretaker of a temple somewhere between Wan Chai and Shau Kei Wan, districts on the far side of Victoria, the capital of Hong Kong (Fig. 3.2). Also during the 2nd month he may take the place of a cousin in watching that the pine trees and grass are not cut in a certain area of Wong Nai Chung gap where the road passes from Victoria to the south shore, the cousin apparently taking a few days off from the job at that time. Mrs. Lin does not travel on the main island of Hong Kong. Riding on the buses makes her vomit. When she first came from Shau Kei Wan on a bus, she suffered. She hardly even prefers the trains on which she rode from China, while small boats, known from experiences in transporting grass at Lei Yue Mun, she considers even worse. Mrs. Lin has never ridden in a private automobile. Very rarely does she cross the strait, and she has not been to Victoria, the capital city, since she first came to Chung Nam Wan. On the other hand, she occasionally climbs over the gap to Lung Shing early in the morning in order to buy a little food for the family.

Mrs. Min is in one sense the most traveled person in Chung Nam Wan. Born in Shanghai, she moved to Kwangtung via Singapore and then, about the time the Japanese came to Hong Kong (1942), her family took her to Annam for six months. She remembers how differently the Indo-Chinese women dressed. Mr. Min also traveled considerably as a soldier in the Chinese army during World War II. Mrs. Min stated that she had not been to Victoria since a year before the previous New Year's when she went to say kung hi (kung hsi) or literally, respectful joy (a standard form of congratulations), to some friends. She would not care to live in the city and says that, like Mrs. Lin, she also becomes nauseated riding on buses. Mrs. Min said that she has had a ride in a private automobile once or twice since coming to Hong Kong. Eight years ago, friends who had a car invited them to go to North Point (an eastern suburb of the Colony's primary metropolis) where the friends' recently married daughter lived. Mrs. Min blandly announced that she was invited because she could carry a lot of the wedding gifts being transported. Except for attending school in Lung Shing, the Min children are not allowed to go anywhere alone.

Mr. Chin seldom goes to the main island and the farthest away he has gone by himself is to visit some of his mother's nephews in Kowloon. His wife has never even been to Kowloon. Indeed, she does not remember visiting Victoria although her mother took here there as a child. She has been there at least twice since, once when she married and again on her way to the cemetery in Happy Valley, but she probably gained only a fleeting impression of the city. She was close to it when she went to the hospital where her children were born. Actually, Mrs. Chin has not been much farther away than Repulse Bay, or fifteen miles from her birthplace, in her whole life. Her mother-in-law comments, "How can she go; she cannot read and would not know how to come back." On the other hand, Mrs. Chin is not incapable of participating in the hire of a "white license" taxi when she crosses the strait to go to her mother's house. It costs her only thirty cents, and otherwise she would have to wait for a bus. She has never ridden as a guest in a private automobile, however. Mr. Chin's mother cannot read but since coming to Hong Kong she has visited Kowloon, Victoria, and Stanley, the latter place with some nuns from her church. She has not been to Kowloon for six years, but she goes to Victoria at least once a year to pay her land assessment. She insists that she immediately returns, however, as she has no time to spend in the city. Sometimes she also goes to the main island for funerals. The second Chin brother created something of a precedent in his family by making a four-day trip to Macao with other boys and girls of his middle school graduating class.

6. Birth, Marriage, Death, and Religion

Birth. No one was born in Chung Nam Wan during our study. Furthermore, the younger mothers have adopted the practice of going to maternity hospitals. Mr. Lin, however, obligingly gave his ideas of native Kwangtung custom with respect to a birth. When a woman is pregnant, she does not go to a doctor but continues to work in the fields as before. Certain snakes may not be eaten. Labor takes place in a woman's customary bed with an experienced female attending. The husband usually is not present unless there is fear that his wife is dying. The umbilical cord is cut by the person who acts as a midwife, but Mr. Lin did not know what disposal was made of it or of the placenta. The baby is washed as soon as it is born, and then clothed. The baby is fed when it is hungry, and every mother is said to know when. The mother does not work for one month after the birth and is given chicken and some yellow wine to restore her strength. When a child of either sex is one month old, it is dressed up in fine clothes for a feast at which chicken and red-dyed eggs are served and to which the family and friends of both the father and mother are invited. The guests bring presents. If a child is given a silver anklet, bracelet, or necklace to wear, it will be easier to grow up, that is, he will be more certain to survive. Mr. Lin notes this as an ancient belief, but admits that he does not know why it is so.

Mrs. Min entered the maternity hospital across the strait to have her last baby. The charge was twenty-five dollars, not including her food. Two days after the birth, Mrs. Min climbed over the gap to Chung Nam Wan carrying the baby herself. "Even if you feel tired," she says, "You must do it." She pointed out that one of the expenses of having a child results from the necessity for her husband to give up his work during the period she is away, as he has to stay home and take care of the children. She says he can cook. As previously mentioned, friends gave her an eight-dollar bottle (ca. 25 ounces) of Portuguese brandy (Patuleia) to help her recover. Mrs. Min states that her ideal family would consist of two boys and two girls. She does not know about contraceptives and has heard nothing said on the subject at her Roman Catholic church.

Mrs. Chin, who is halfway to fulfilling Mrs. Min's requirements for the ideal family, thinks two children are sufficient, and her mother-in-law, interestingly enough, is of the same opinion; in fact, the latter is worried because Mrs. Chin's two children were born only a year apart. Children cost money. Mrs. Chin also has heard nothing stated on the subject of contraception in the Roman Catholic church to which she and her mother-in-law belong, but she has been informed by the latter that there is a government doctor to whom she can apply for assistance if she states that she is very poor and does not want more children. Then he will arrange for her not to have any, but she does not understand how this is done. The idea appeals to her in theory, but she really does not want to go to the doctor, claiming that she does not know why, and then, apparently covering her fears, by pointing out that going to the doctor takes time.

Both of Mrs. Chin's children were born in a government hospital which is cheaper, if farther away, than the one Mrs. Min went to. Indeed, it costs nothing and anyone can go there. She says that she was not afraid on either occasion, although the first time she did go to the hospital a little earlier than was necessary. Actually she felt happy but, as she says, "When you give birth, you do it happy or not." She remained there a week at the time of her first accouchement, a period determined by the doctor. Someone wanted to adopt her baby girl, but her husband said that it would be a bad thing as he suspected the person of hoping to make money by obtaining the child because she was pretty. Before her second child was born, she applied to the nearer hospital, but she was asked to come every week for a checkup. She did not want to do this so she went back to the government hospital where she had her first baby. The second child arrived as a breech presentation and she suffered severe pain. Nevertheless, she was released in three days. She was given some medicine following the birth, but the delivery itself was unaided by drugs. Afterward, the nurse bathed the newborn child. Mrs. Chin volunteered the comment that anyone would know enough to give a baby a bath. She added, "Then they give it to you and you do what you want." The doctor is not paid by the patient but, if one pleases, one may give the amah a dollar or two wrapped in a red paper packet, the red paper conveying good fortune itself. After the birth, her mother brought her some wine, which she enjoyed. Also she had special food such as ginger, eggs, pig's feet, and chicken cooked with wine. Visitors presenting a red gift packet asked for a bit of the food, the eating of which is believed to bring good fortune. Mrs. Chin states that she has no preference as to sex in having her children, that she likes both, but that she does understand when people have many children of one sex, that they would like to have some of the other. Child care has made her appreciate the efforts of her own parents, but she added that she would just as soon carry her baby on her back in the fields as have her mother-in-law around.

Marriage. The subject of marriage is one about which Chinese informants, especially women, are apt to be reticent with respect to themselves. Such matters are considered too personal to disclose. Some of my questions were not answered and some were not asked. Mr. Lin, however, informed us that his marriage to his first wife who had been brought up in his house was not based upon love. His stepmother liked her and it was simply expected that he should like her too. This method of obtaining a child as a future wife for a son was a local custom adopted in order to decrease the cost of the wedding, although gifts of wine, pork, and money were made as at more customary betrothals and marriages. Mr. Lin was ten (Ch), the girl four, when she came, and the children played together for about two years. After that they did not speak to each other because, being engaged, they were too embarrassed to do so. Mr. Lin's young fiancee when she had grown older worked as an amah in the house, bringing the family food to the table and undertaking many other chores. The formal ceremony of marriage took place when Mr. Lin was eighteen and the bride twelve (in Western computation, perhaps ten and a half). Mr. Lin said that he would have been ashamed to wait longer for, if a man were over eighteen, it would seem as though the family could not afford the necessary expense. Also, it was his opinion that most girls in the district were married at twelve, although only a formal ceremony, the consummation being delayed sometimes several years (presumably until after the onset of menstruation).

The actual date of Mr. Lin's wedding was determined by a specialist in such matters. There was a feast and firecrackers. The girl's family contributed some chairs, tea, and other things. The bride wore a head-dress with a veil of pearls rented for the occasion. The young couple were given a special room (in this case, actually a small, separate house) cleaned and decorated for the occasion, and containing a new bed, but Mr. Lin did not go there at first because he believed people would laugh. Indeed he would not even speak to his child wife for a long time unless no one was looking but, having stated this fact, he reflected that they really had little to talk about anyway. He started to visit his wife at midnight, claiming it was that late before he had convinced himself that everyone was asleep and would pay no attention.* Mr. Lin insists that he was not relieved of a sense of shame with respect to sexual intimacy until his first daughter was born many years later. Furthermore, he asserts that all boys reacted with similar shyness. Mr. Lin liked his first wife because, as he says, she was not unattractive and never dared to criticize his actions as the present Mrs. Lin periodically feels compelled to do. It should be remembered with respect to Mr. Lin's account of his marriage that he is a Hakka.

---

*Since the ideal hour for sexual intercourse in Chinese culture is around midnight, one wonders if Mr. Lin was influenced unconsciously when recalling his youth. On the other hand, the psychological data indicate a realistic account.

From the beginning of the discussions in which he recounted his personal life to us, Mr. Lin did not hesitate to admit true love for his first concubine whom, it is said, he took with the approval of both his own and his wife's family in a ceremony which did not differ from that of his first marriage except that the concubine had to serve tea to his wife. He had paid a great deal of rice for the girl, who was sixteen. The two women, at least in the beginning, had different rooms in the same house and were friendly. Asked if they ever fought, he answered, "How could they, they had too much to do in order to eat and clothe themselves." Mr. Lin pointed out that in the place where he lived, many men had concubines without suffering from domestic troubles, while in other cases the wives were always slapping newcomers. Asked what would happen if a concubine slapped a wife, he said that he did not think that would happen, but if she did, people would not like it. In his opinion, a husband might tell his wife and concubine to stop fighting, but that even a husband cannot slap his wife as her family will protect her. On the other hand, if a wife did something really wrong, such as committing adultery, a husband could divorce her by inscribing his action on paper. Mr. Lin pointed out that sometimes individuals were killed because of a woman's unfaithfulness. Surprisingly, he considers it old-fashioned if a husband becomes angry because his wife simply goes to dinner or a movie with a male friend. He points out that after he came to Hong Kong, his concubine married another man, but that he himself was not disturbed by the fact. "Heaven controls such things," is his opinion, and he adds that under Communism one marries whom one likes.

Mr. Lin claims that it is disgraceful the way unmarried girls in Hong Kong have children. In his village, he says, a pregnant girl without a husband would not have been allowed to have her child in the house, and a marriage with the father would be enforced, if necessary at the point of a gun. Mr. Lin knew of an actual case. Such situations could result in a feud between the families of the girl and the boy but, at best, there was consequent shame for everyone involved. Mr. Lin also had something to say about marriage among the boat people of Lung Chau with whom he seems to be well-acquainted. He says that they both marry and divorce easily. The marriage is arranged by a go-between, and the bridegroom fetches his bride in a boat with an orchestra and brings her back to his own vessel. There, they burn candles and incense before a God. Afterward, if the husband does not find his wife to his liking, he calls in the go-between and gets rid of her. This, it is said, does not place the girl at any great disadvantage in marrying again. What Mr. Lin really does not approve of, however, is the inevitable intimacy of the boat people. He states that sometimes three couples have to sleep side by side, the men possibly being brothers. This, he says, is no good. "They don't know the shame of it. It is like the pigs."

Mrs. Chin married Mr. Chin in what has been called a "semi-blind wedding" which was arranged by a go-between, but she saw her husband once before she married him and, in theory, could have refused to accept him. She was taken by her parents to a restaurant near the ferry landing across from Lung Chau and it was there that she met her future husband and his parents. The go-between was present. She was attracted to Mr. Chin on sight, but that reaction was not wholly reciprocal. He believed she would be a good worker on the farm, as also did his mother who confided to us later that she and her husband saw that the future Mrs. Chin was a good girl and never went out with men, adding that, "These days, girls do go out with men, but they are very careful not to lose their virginity." Mrs. Chin confirmed this, saying that some boys liked her before she was married and that, although they had some good times together, her father was conservative and would not allow her to go out with them. Thus she had no choice except to marry if she wanted male companionship. On the day that the engagement was contracted, the Chin parents gave to the bride's family an engagement ring and a watch for the bride, plus $600.

The marriage took place two or three months after the single meeting with her future husband. She went to the government registry office in Victoria for a civil ceremony in the morning and to a Roman Catholic church for a religious service in the afternoon. After the last ceremony she was taken to the Chin house in Tung Pak Wan. There, the Chin family had a feast for their own family and friends, but there were neither music nor firecrackers at her wedding. She claims many people do not have them and that she herself did not miss these commonplace adjuncts of such occasions. Three days later the Chin family sent the central section of a roast pig (without head or legs) to her family. They had promised a whole pig, but the price had gone up so they apparently decided to economize. Likewise, the cakes which were sent, although correct in amount, were not very good ones, Mrs. Chin claims. About the agreed $600 that had been given her parents, no complaints are recorded. On receiving the pig, the bride's mother gave her son-in-law a gold ring, a hat, and a pair of shoes as had been promised. The bride, following custom, washed her hair at her father's home on the third day after her wedding and gave her mother a red packet containing a dollar, although she did not know the reasons for doing so. In Mrs. Chin's case there was no cloth with its token of her lost virginity under the pork which was sent to her family. As Mr. Chin's mother said, she was known to be a good girl. Mrs. Chin was married at the age of nineteen (Ch), and her mother admitted that it was an unfortunate age to have done so, later attributing the death of the bride's father, as well as the death of one of her brothers to this disregard of custom. With these losses, Mrs. Chin's maternal family became even poorer, and her mother admitted that she does not like to come to visit at Chung Nam Wan because she is afraid that, since she cannot bring adequate gifts, Mr. Chin's mother does not like her.

The marriage of Mr. and Mrs. Min, unlike the others, represents the new style of behavior. They met through friends, fell in love, and decided on the marriage themselves after he was invited to her home. When the time came, Mr. Min wore a new suit and Mrs. Min had a special dress for the occasion. They had dinner in a restaurant and many friends were invited. Mrs. Min drank grape wine, she remembers.

Mrs. Min was much more interested in talking about the custom of sending roast pig to a bride's family three days after a wedding. She says that if the bridegroom's family does not do it, even if very poor, women will say, "What a shame, no roast pig." In a small village, women may refuse to talk to a girl whose husband's family does not send the traditional gift. Even so, some people cannot afford the expenditure. If a pig is sent, the snout and tail are returned by the bride's family out of politeness. The latter act symbolizes the hope that the marriage will have a good beginning and end or, in other words, last a long time. If, however, the bridegroom's family should send a roast duck to the house of the bride, it is intended to indicate that the bride was no virgin. Such a gift will be certain to make the recipients unhappy. Mrs. Min says she herself witnessed one case. The family accepted their shame because they recognized that the implication concerning their daughter was true. Mrs. Min, after being asked, stated that she knew of no case of a duck being sent to a bride's family where the justification of the act could be questioned.

When we attempted to gain information on preferential mating, Mrs. Min averred that it would not be proper for a girl to marry either her mother's brother's son or her father's sister's son, but that a marriage with a mother's sister's son would be acceptable. Its actual desirability had apparently not occurred to her. Mrs. Lin, on the other hand, stated that all three of the relationships were socially acceptable, and that only a marriage with a person of the same surname was taboo. Marriage with a father's brother's son, of course, is unthinkable. Mrs. Chin thought that a marriage with a mother's brother's son was possible, but she was dubious about the correctness of marrying a father's sister's son. She also offered the stranger comment that she had been told that in Communist China a girl could marry her own brother. It was our impression that in this rather abstract if not abstruse matter, our kind and cooperative informants had been pushed beyond the scope of their genuine interests and knowledge.

Death. If one is born, whether one marries or not, one eventually dies, but happily none of our informants did so during the period of our study, and so no funeral was observed. Even such data as were recorded for the most part pertained to deaths which took place at other places and times. There are several old graves on the hill slopes of Chung Nam Wan, some of them clearly abandoned and only one made since the period of the first living resident. The latter grave, slightly below and to the west of the Min house, was estimated to have been made in 1952 or 1953. Mr. Chin's mother saw the geomancer select the site and she looks upon the grave with favor because, so she says, "There must be good feng-shui in the area." Asked how she knew this, she said that the fortunate character of a site can be determined by the consequent well-being of the dead person's family and that, since she sees the husband and son of the buried woman come to attend to the grave each year, the feng-shui must be good; otherwise they would not come. It may be recalled that the Chin family made a pool for washing clothes in an old grave site from which the dead person's remains had been removed because of unfavorable feng-shui.

When Mr. Lin tells us that there is an old abandoned grave at the edge of one of his fields, he means by abandoned that it is not visited. He also states that if anyone dies, he cannot be buried on the hillside and asserts that the government has not allowed such casual use of the land for interment for the last twenty or thirty years. Now poor people can obtain a plot in a government cemetery in the New Territories. Someone told him that for this, one must pay thirty dollars.* For burial, Mr. Lin says that most people use wood coffins which, being of poor quality, soon disintegrate; then what remains of the body is put into a stoneware jar. People reputedly spend a great deal of money on funerals as they are obliged to feed friends and mourners. Mr. Lin protests that some people come crying simply because they want to eat, and that as soon as the coffin is in the ground, such friends come no more.

When Mr. Chin's father died of dysentery in Tung Pak Wan, having refused to go to a hospital, Mr. Lin says the family was afraid. Mr. Lin carried the body from the bed to a cot outside the house, and later, with the Chin cousin and four other men from Hong Kong of the Chin surname, helped to carry the cot with the corpse to a sampan which took it to a government hearse across the strait. The body was buried in the Roman Catholic cemetery in Happy Valley, an area adjacent to Victoria. A priest arranged the matter for them. The cost of the grave was sixty dollars for six years.† Mrs. Chin has only been to the cemetery once but her mother-in-law has gone several times on proper occasions determined by the church. Mr. Chin's mother tells her daughter-in-law it is better that she stay at home and take care of the pigs. Mrs. Chin's father died in Queen

---

*Actually, the government fee for interment in public Chinese cemeteries seems to be either $5 or $15, depending on the section. *Hong Kong: Public Cemeteries*, 1960: 8.

†Perpetual rights are said to cost $1,500.

Mary Hospital, Hong Kong, last year and was buried in the New Territories. Friends and relatives contributed the money for the funeral. Mrs. Chin could contribute nothing herself and says that her mother-in-law would give only ten dollars wrapped in red paper to pay for some flowers.

Mrs. Min added to our modicum of data one afternoon when she encountered a newly orphaned girl of about five at the Chin house who had been brought to Chung Nam Wan by her father. Mrs. Min asked her in a loud pleasant voice where her mother was, and then answered the question herself by saying that the mother had gone to a fine country where she might do nice things for her daughter. She then confided to us that some children, as well as some old people, do not know when people are dead. They think that they are simply asleep and tell them to get up. Later, the orphaned child's married sister arrived from Kowloon in a mourning costume consisting of an unpatterned white sam fu, white shoes, and little rosettes of white wool in her hair.

Mrs. Min also gave a more or less narrative account of a rich man's funeral in the Kwangtung town of her youth. When someone dies, if a man survives, he goes weeping to obtain mai shui (mai shui), or literally "buy water," in a special bowl. Some friend follows him to make certain that he commits no desperate act. The water can be taken from any source, and the friend leaves a fan and a few coins at the place, but the informant does not know why. Should the deceased have no son, the wife will go for the mai shui. The water is used to wash the dead man's hands and feet where he lies in the visitor's room (a hopelessly ill person is removed from his own room). Relatives come with burning incense sticks held in clasped hands. New clothes are put on the body, including some extra ones, and a blanket of thin material is added. The informant said that she never heard of anything being put into a dead person's mouth.

A coffin is ordered and immediately made. The shop people deliver the box and place the body in it, covering the deceased with a white cloth. The cover is not put on the coffin, however, until after the relatives have come to see the corpse, and it may be necessary to wait quite a period until some of them can arrive. It is stated that a corpse may remain in a house from seven to twenty-four days. Many candlesticks with burning candles are placed at the head of the coffin. Relatives bring gold-silver paper money which may either be put into the coffin or burned. Women who mourn let their hair down. Musicians are employed to play whenever relatives appear. The relatives bring gifts, and one person in the family keeps a record of these. A lucky gift (perhaps ten cents) wrapped in white paper is given in return.* At the closing of the coffin, priests come from a temple to pray. Cooked pork and chicken are put on a table for the dead.

---

*Used, according to Kwangtung custom, only to buy candles for the deceased.

Relatives bow, and then take candy from a bowl. Later all the relatives gather around the stove and put some fuel under the rice which is cooking. The rice is given to the priests. The priests walk around the coffin clockwise three times.* The informant does not know of any special nails used in closing the coffin.

The procession to the grave is usually led by a nephew of the deceased who carries a long bamboo pole bearing a red pennant on which is inscribed the name and age of the deceased. Next come musicians intermingled with or followed by people employed to carry food, candles, money, and fruit. Following them is the coffin, borne by employees of the shop where it was made. After it walks the eldest son dressed in white, and other relatives follow.

When the procession reaches its destination, the coffin is lowered into the grave previously dug by the coffin shop people. The priests walk around the grave three times clockwise, praying as they go. All the relatives kowtow to the coffin once. Then everyone returns to the house of the deceased. People jump over a small fire built outside the door to prevent bringing any ghosts along with them. There is sweet soup to eat. The people wash their hands, and everyone participates in a feast, the men from the coffin shop included.

Every seven days, priests are called in to pray. After doing so on seven occasions (forty-nine days), the funeral may be said to be over. The grave itself can be made more or less imposing, depending on the wealth of the family and the amount of money they spend. If the descendants are truly rich, a stone lion may even be erected at the grave. When people are poor, of course, the expenditure may veer to the opposite extreme. Mrs. Min said that the body of her brother was put into the ground without any music save for drums.

Religion. The Lins are traditionalists in their religion, but the manifestations of the beliefs are limited, as is the case with many Chinese. There is the picture and a small figure of Kun Yam (Kuan Yin), that have been previously mentioned, in the Lin home, and the Lins ask the assistance of this Goddess of Mercy in times of great trouble. They burn one incense stick in front of their altar on the first and the fifteenth of each month. The incense sticks are purchased at the cost of fifty cents for a sizable package. Mr. Lin says that he believes in every God, and specifically mentions T'in Hau (T'ien Hou), the Queen of Heaven, whose birthday is on the 23rd of the 3rd month. He explains his attitude by saying simply that all old-time Chinese believe, and as the people believe, so does he. He admits that, unfortunately, the gods do not make one rich.

---

*A layman's memory with regard to a direction may not be trustworthy.

Mr. Lin says that there are two temples in the town of Lung Shing, and that he has visited them but made no contributions although, when they have festivals, many people bring the priests gifts of chickens, small pigs, and fish. Mrs. Lin has been in neither Lung Shing temple. The only temple with which Mr. Lin is really familiar, however, is the one on Hong Kong Island of which a male relative is caretaker. Indeed, Mr. Lin once worked there himself a few days. He describes the temple as belonging to eight people who over successive years have shared the profits which are said to have reached an annual high of $30,000 in the period of easy money following the influx of rich emigrants when the Communists conquered China. The funds were derived in part from dance hall girls who were so successful in those years that Mr. Lin's relative received tips from them sometimes totaling as much as a hundred dollars a day. The result was that the recipient was drawn into the practice of opium smoking because of this generosity. Recently, people have become much less generous as it is more difficult to earn money.

Mrs. Lin confides that her husband can talk directly to Kun Yam and that close friends, when they are ill, come to ask Mr. Lin's assistance. For such help they pay nothing. They bring only two candles, three incense sticks, and possibly some fruit for the altar, which Mr. Lin ultimately enjoys eating. In a specific case, a friend's child was ill. It was taken to a doctor and given much medicine but did not get well. After an appeal to Mr. Lin, the parents were asked to write down on a piece of paper the sick child's name, and the date and precise time of its birth, the latter being most important. Mr. Lin then placed the paper on the altar, burning the incense and candles while he sat on a stool in front of the figure of Kun Yam with his head in his arms. After a short time, Kun Yam told Mr. Lin to have the ill child eat the incense ashes. This was done and recovery followed.

Mr. Lin's more common appeals to Kun Yam are for his own family. When Small Daughter was first adopted, she was sick much of the time. Each day Mrs. Lin took care of her until midnight, and then her husband acted as nurse until morning. Finally, Kun Yam gave Mr. Lin the name of the proper medicine to buy which, having been given to Small Daughter, she recovered. Mr. Lin also learned how to cure his wife's shoulder from Kun Yam. The supernatural help extends even to the family animals. When a sow had insufficient milk for her little pigs, the Lins worried. Mr. Lin sought aid of Kun Yam and the answer was given, "Do not worry, at five o'clock there will be enough milk." Naturally, there was.

It was pointed out that it is not possible to aid the Min or Chin families because they are Roman Catholics. Once Mrs. Min wanted to ask Kun Yam something, but permission was refused because, as it is reported, "She did not belong to Kun Yam."

Mr. Lin, as is not surprising, states that he consults the almanac (or perhaps someone who understands it better than he) in order to determine an auspicious day on which to start any important construction, such as a house or a pig pen. Later he added that such advice is particularly desirable before digging a well. The almanac plays no part in his gardening, however.

In the Chin family, everyone is a member of the Roman Catholic church. Until some years ago, Mr. Chin's father and mother attended a Protestant church, he having been a member for forty years, but she only seven. Before she became a Catholic, Mr. Chin's mother says she actually had no religious beliefs. The conversion was brought about through their eldest son who was the first one in the family to recognize the new faith. She adds that the priest impressed the son with the necessity of his parents sharing his belief and that, after all, Protestants and Catholics have the same God. Since their conversion, the Chins do not eat fowl or meat on Friday, substituting fish or eggs. According to an informant in another family, when the Chins attended the Protestant church, the minister came and asked for a contribution of twenty dollars. At the time, no one in the family had accepted the Roman Catholic faith, although the eldest son attended on occasions. They then decided to change their affiliation.

Mrs. Chin, as has been indicated in writing of her marriage, became a Catholic at the time of her engagement. The priest said that otherwise he would not marry them. She acquiesced and was obliged to receive instruction. "Catholicism is good," she states, "because you are not allowed to do bad things. If you do, you have to go to confession and, since it is a bother to go to the church, you do not do bad things. Thus it is better than Protestantism." She added that eating pork on Fridays was bad because it was the same as eating God's body. "If you do not eat breakfast, however, and go to church, they will let you eat some small pieces of bread. That means that you eat part of the God and become the son or daughter of the God, but you must be careful not to chew the bread as that would break God's body." Mrs. Chin states that in her communion, she has never received wine.* Perhaps the major factor in preventing regular attendance at church is an economic one. To go costs time and money, the latter including ferry fares and offering (she usually gives ten cents) can easily amount to over a dollar for herself and her husband. She feels that she should go to church on special occasions, as for example at times of religious observances such as the Dragon Boat Festival. She took her baby to be baptized when it was a week old and reports that the priests said she should have come in three days.

---

*She did not seem to recognize the custom in Hong Kong of dipping the host into the wine.

Mrs. Chin was raised as a member of a traditional religious family, or at least her mother went to a temple in order to find out the correct time to undertake certain actions. The method consists of burning incense before the image of a God while explaining one's troubles, tossing a box of numbered sticks until one stick comes out, and having its number correlated with information in a book that fortunetellers conveniently available in the temple will undertake to explain for a small fee. Mrs. Chin no longer believes in such things, it may be presumed, and she specifically mentioned that whereas she once would have accepted her mother's interpretation of deaths in the family being caused by her being married at nineteen, since her conversion she does not. As for feng-shui, that is another matter. Even Mr. Chin's mother believes in feng-shui.

Mrs. Chin's mother-in-law wears on a silver chain a small Catholic medal bearing on one side the inscription "Carmeli-Virgo" and on the other, "Jesu-Cor" with a representation of Jesus. Mrs. Chin's daughter has a similar one on a string around her neck, but the background is colored red. Mrs. Chin herself acquired a medal when she became a Catholic, but she keeps it in the pocket of her undercoat.

The Min family are perhaps somewhat more knowledgeable in their Christianity than the Chins, and have certainly been communicants of the Roman Catholic Church for a much longer period. The fact that a complaint can be made that the Chins do not always act with a proper Christian attitude has a familiar and sophisticated ring. First Daughter says that if her mother decides to go to church, everyone goes. The principal deterrents seem to be rain and a lack of cash, the latter being thought of in connection with the cost of crossing and recrossing the strait. When they do go to church, they try to have a few cents for the collection bag also.

On the 19th of the 6th month (Kun Yam's birthday according to Mrs. Min who says the Goddess also has birthdays on the 19th of the 2nd and 9th months), Mrs. Min was stimulated to provide the information that many people belong to the Kun Yam clubs in Lung Shing. We had seen chickens and pigs and various other foods being carried down the streets on special wood carriers. One had a pink flower. According to our informant, the members of the clubs pay perhaps two dollars a month to the manager of it. Then on Kun Yam's birthday, each member shares in collectively purchased roast pig, roast chicken, eggs painted red, cakes, and oranges. The food, usually after it has been taken to the temple, is divided up and brought home by the member families and eaten. The manager is said to get an extra two catties of pork as compensation for his work.

In her religious beliefs, Mrs. Min has been affected by her church, but in some ways her ideas may have resulted from influences preceding her contacts with Christians. Mrs. Min is a firm believer in dreams, for example. One day, after a fortnight of drought, she told Mr. Chin's mother that she had seen God in her sleep and had asked Him for rain. After several days, it still had not rained and she was puzzled. This account led to another. A month or so previously, she had dreamed of a tiger, and she told Mrs. Lin about it. Between them somehow, the idea developed that it would be sensible to take advantage of the dream by wagering a small amount in a gambling game that is operated in Lung Shing to which each player contributes a few cents and chooses one of a series of animals or birds that are offered. The operator then draws a card bearing a character to determine the winner who receives all the wagers (presumably minus a commission). Mrs. Lin said she would give Mr. Lin thirty cents to give to Mrs. Min's first daughter so the latter could buy a ticket on a tiger when going to school. Mr. Lin kept the money. Then Mrs. Lin provided another thirty cents and the ticket was purchased. Mrs. Lin is said to have won sixteen dollars and, on receiving the news, was so happy that she lifted Mrs. Min off the ground.

Mr. Lin also dreams. One day he told us that the previous night he had dreamed of big snakes. He used a bamboo pole to try to kill them. Then the dream ended. Furthermore, he often dreams of two yellow tigers with which he struggles using only his hands. Then the tigers run away as though they were having a race. This pleases him because he thinks that people will come to see the tigers run. After his struggle, he enters the house and closes the door so that tigers cannot get in.

Mr. Lin on being questioned about his religious beliefs, said that an individual has only one wan ling (hun ling), or soul.* When Heaven makes a baby, it is given a wan ling. The wan ling is necessary in order to eat, breathe, and so on. It can go anywhere, and he is uncertain whether it is dangerous. The idea of reincarnation was not immediately recognized, and then Mr. Lin said he did not believe in it. He does, however, believe in ghosts (free souls or spirits). Before coming to Hong Kong, he had some experience with them. He had not believed in ghosts, however, until he did so. Although he claims to have recognized ghosts because he heard them without being able to see their bodies, he later said that if you were unlucky enough, you did see them as he had actually done. They are reported to look just like human beings. The circumstances of the encounter, he did not make clear, but he admitted to having attempted to shoot the ghosts. He apparently failed when the ghosts disappeared. Afterward, people told him that he was lucky he did not succeed, for the ghosts certainly would have killed him. It is significant that Mr. Lin states that he was ill at the time. Ghosts, he concludes, can be equated with various kinds of devils.

---

*The reverse form, ling wan (ling hun), is used by Catholics and Protestants for the word soul.

Mrs. Min stated flatly that she does not believe in ghosts. A minute later she began to tell us about the death of her adoptive father's father's brother. The old man died when Mrs. Min was a girl. When he became ill, he attributed it to the fact that his three sons did not treat him well, and for that he blamed his daughters-in-law. Each of the latter washed his clothes in turn. In his anger, he said he would wash his clothes himself. When he died, his body was kept for a week and then cremated. The day afterward, it was expected by the elders that his spirit would return to the house. The members of the family were warned to go to bed early. Those of the younger generation believed this was foolish. In anticipation of the event, food was put out for the deceased as well as his slippers and the bowl in which he customarily washed. At midnight the grandfather did come back. Mrs. Min heard the same noises as when he was alive—the swish of the slippers and the splash of the water spilling from the bowl. After that experience, she never went out alone in the dark. When Mrs. Min, who says she does not believe in ghosts, has to come back at night from Lung Shing, she always makes sure to have several of her children with her, and she carries a flashlight. Her son has inherited her fear. Mrs. Chin, on the other hand, says she is not afraid of the dark. At least she often goes to sleep alone with her babies, since her husband goes to town and returns very late.

An informant pointed out that there are individuals who give shamanistic performances in Lung Shing, most of them women, and most of them old. The charges for their services vary, and the payment is apt to be clandestine since reputedly the police may interfere if there is evidence of money being passed. The police seldom do, however, since such transactions are difficult to discover. About religion, it seems, there is never an end to what one can learn.

7. Economic Life: General

What may be written as a contribution to an understanding of the economic life of Chung Nam Wan has not been left to the end of the presentation because it has been considered less important than other aspects of the culture. Quite the contrary. From the viewpoint of the people, nothing is more vital than the activities on which they must depend for their subsistence. It also is perhaps the most complicated aspect of Chung Nam Wan life, and it has in consequence seemed best to explain it against as full a background of knowledge of the community as is possible. Consistent with this opinion, the more general aspects of the economic life will be treated first, thereafter proceeding to the exposition of vegetable gardening which constitutes the fundamental work pattern in Chung Nam Wan.

Annual round. The climate of Hong Kong, sometimes described as subtropical, produces conditions which make it possible to carry on agriculture during twelve months of the year. Mrs. Chin says she prefers autumn to all other seasons because it is neither too hot nor too cold whereas winter is sometimes uncomfortable. Mr. Lin also prefers autumn, specifically mentioning that it is good for growing vegetables since one can work more in the cool weather. As will be demonstrated later, a majority of the foods produced can be grown at all times, but for many, the difficulty of doing so in mid-summer prevents the farmers from making the effort. On the other hand, the heat and humidity, which are at their worst at that period, together with the fact that the variety of vegetables may lessen although the area cultivated need not, cause a greater drain on human energy in the hot humid season than at any other time. Secondary economic activities involving the care given to pigs or domestic fowl are as continuous as the demands made by small children. Breaks in the arduous routine are rare. There are nominal holidays, of which New Year's is the one of most significance, and then there are crises which are most often unexpected and not wanted. Among these are excessive concentrations of rain and typhoons, and less often periods of serious drought. Modern meteorological services, such as exist in Hong Kong, can only be of limited aid to the farmer. He is warned, but on behalf of his crops and his stock there is not very much that he can do. For his own safety and the psychological satisfaction of dependable predictions, however, the farmer is grateful. Traditionally, the warnings of storms were carried to Chung Nam Wan by both the school children and those going to market in Lung Shing. With the advent of the Chin family radio, weather information became direct.

It may be interpolated that the radio also makes it possible to set all the watches and clocks in the hamlet correctly, an adjustment which is desirable when there are children who are going to school. To know when the market is to open, one need not be quite so exact, and Mr. Lin still checks his timepiece by the blasting which he is convinced takes place every evening exactly at 4:55 at the Picnic Bay quarry on Pok Liu (Lamma) Island. He is usually not far off in his assumption. Mr. Chin, however, formerly preferred to set his wristwatch by the clock in the Lung Shing cinema, which he passed to and from the market.

Mr. Lin states that there is usually too much rain for the vegetables in June, and that in 1960 this was especially so. Against long, continued, excessive rain the farmer is helpless. On June 29, faced with the certainty of rain and high winds and the threat of a second typhoon that month, Mrs. Lin pulled up all her small, transplantable cabbage plants of both white and flowering varieties and put them in the house. By watering them properly, she said she could keep them out of the ground for forty-eight hours. The same day, she cooked twice as much rice as usual so that there would be food when the typhoon struck; in other words, she cooked rice four times instead of two. In the meantime, Mr. Lin put heavy rocks on the roofs to hold them down. The chickens were kept under cover. The storm proved to be less punishing than expected, but the rain leaked onto Mr. Lin's bed and he could not sleep until he had removed three of his bed boards and himself to a dry place on the floor. Except for typhoons, Mr. Lin says the only thing that worries him is that hawks will kill his chickens.

In the two other families, at least some preparations were made against the storm. Mrs. Min volunteered the information that the Chinese double-sixth month (which occurred in 1960) is always a bad one for typhoons and rain. Whether she was expressing a traditional view or her own deduction is not certain. Mr. Chin's mother said she knew of no way anyone at Chung Nam Wan could prophesy the weather. The commonplace seasonal rains, which can cause serious damage to the crops, are determined only by their obvious approach. People continue working in the fields unless the rainfall is exceptionally heavy. Lightning and thunder sometimes occur. Mr. Chin's mother was unaware of anyone being struck, but she attested that some people were frightened by loud peals of thunder.

Equal to the damage by the elements in creating crises in the annual round is the sudden and unexpected loss of man power in the labor corps. This may, of course, result from such things as sickness or death, or the sudden withdrawal of field workers. The general situation with respect to labor must consequently be reviewed.

Labor. In examining the work distribution among the residents of Chung Nam Wan, it will be convenient first to consider those who devote the largest part of their daily efforts to the production of vegetables and livestock. Mr. and Mrs. Chin and Mrs. Lin are outstanding in this respect. Mr. Lin does do some work in the fields and he also carries the produce to market. Similarly, Mrs. Min took care of her fields until the time of the typhoon which preceded our study by two weeks. Then there was the hired field laborer of the Chin family and the youngest Chin brother who succeeded him. We thus exclude only Mr. Min, his two uncles, Mr. Chin's mother and her second son plus the eight young children.

In so far as one can be said to like such hard labor as that which the fields require, perhaps Mr. Chin, his wife, and Mrs. Lin do. The real point perhaps is that they would like it if they could have more help, but for one of several reasons such desires have been frustrated. To those who have a fondness for the earth, the youngest Chin brother must be added. There is more than a suspicion at least, that he would prefer labor in the fields to going to school, and he works with a will and a smile. As for Mr. Lin, he is clearly not very fond of any type of work. He did mention once that he had been to Lung Shing to talk to friends about obtaining a job. Two months later he had not found one, nor had he evinced any anxiety in the meantime about his failure to do so. On the other hand, he does undertake considerable work on his property, especially when some new project inspires him. What he enjoys most of all domestic duties is taking care of his daughter. The case of Mrs. Min in relation to work in the fields is more difficult to judge. It may be said that she is strong, could do it, and would if she decided she should. It is difficult to believe, however, that her image of herself coincides with that of a woman trained to work in the fields. As for the hired laborer, since he worked for a salary, he could look for a different kind of employment when faced with the unusual heat of the 1960 summer.

There seems to be no question but that all those primarily devoted to horticulture, or who like it, were qualified farmers, although the youngest Chin brother was, of course, still learning. Mrs. Lin did not hesitate to affirm, for example, that she knew more about gardening than her husband, and she sometimes corrected him or, more exactly, elaborated on the empirical details of the processes of vegetable growth. Her intimacy with a cabbage or an onion was amazing, although the same familiarity presumably was shared by Mr. and Mrs. Chin. It is not intended to imply that Mr. Lin was any ignoramus on the subject. After all, he also had been a farmer most of his life. Probably the hired laborer was a qualified worker, but certainly the Mins were not in a class with these others as far as experience is concerned.

On the subject of the sexual division of labor, it would seem that such women as Mrs. Lin and Mrs. Chin can do anything in the fields that men do, and apparently as well, although perhaps not as much. Mr. Lin boasts that his wife is a very hard worker and, although thin, can carry sixty or seventy catties with her pole. Mrs. Chin has been observed to climb over the gap with over fifty catties in her baskets, but at the same time, Mr. Chin gave himself a much heavier load and it was assumed that in so doing he was apportioning the burden with consideration for their relative strength. Also Mr. Chin appears to undertake the heavier work in the fields, although no doubt Mrs. Chin could do it. To such comments we must add that the women also do the cooking, wash the clothes, tend the pigs and chickens, and basically take care of their small children notwithstanding more or less help. Child care and stock raising were the main activities of Mrs. Min, but even with five children, she seemed to have more time than the others, First Daughter playing a significant role when school was not in session. Perhaps the work of the women is harder than that of the men in Chung Nam Wan, but whether it is or is not may be regarded as a debatable matter.

Accessory workers, such as those who are hired to labor in the fields constitute a special problem. Mr. Chin's mother is the Chung Nam Wan authority on the subject as she is the one who has really employed them there. She states that in the past as many as four men have been hired to work in the Chin fields at one time. The number seems high, but possibly they were the only effective adults available on the occasion referred to. She admits that formerly everyone rested more and stopped work for short periods in the middle of very hot days. Recently she has had difficulty in keeping even one man. Without question, the reason is primarily economic. Salaries have doubled and doubled again, whereas the prices paid to farmers for vegetables have not shown a comparable advance. She added that when the prices for their crops go down, the whole family works merely to pay for help. Mr. Chin's mother recalls hiring men for as little as $30 per month plus their food and lodging. In 1960, she is said to have been paying $130 per month and offered to raise the salary to $160, but it was not accepted. Of course, the heat was almost unbearable. Her last employee, who had been with them only four months, apparently preferred to work in a factory where the physical strain would be less strenuous. It may be noted that Mr. Chin's mother reported that he had complained when lunch was a little bit late. He gave the heat as his reason for leaving, however, and also so stated to Mrs. Min.

A few minor comments on hired men may be added. Mr. Chin said that one of the family field hands had on one occasion bought himself an expensive Chinese cheong sam (long gown) in which he proudly went to a restaurant with some friends dressed in cheap Western style clothes. The waiter would pay no attention to him, and the laborer later advised Mr. Chin against making a similar error in the choice of his dress. Also Mr. Lin stated without any explanation that, when he had brought news from Lung Shing to the last Chin hired man that the latter had received a telephone message, the man had wanted to know what it was about. Mr. Lin had replied, "Lung Shing is close, go and ask."

The Chin family, on losing the last hired man, tried to find someone to replace him but was unsuccessful. Fortunately, school was just ending for the summer vacation and Mr. Chin's brothers were requested to help. The younger went to work with exemplary zeal, but the older protested. For a few days, Mr. Chin's mother persuaded a neighbor in Tung Pak Wan whose wife had just died that it would be good for him to work in the fields. His contribution, marked by tears, unfortunately proved brief. One day he simply did not come; after all, he was no farmer. Finally, Mr. and Mrs. Chin decided that they had no other choice except to work harder and to curtail their production until they could hire another man in the fall.

Turning to the activities of those who are identified with Chung Nam Wan but prefer to work elsewhere, we can begin with the second Chin brother. At the time of the family labor crisis, Mrs. Chin was not reticent about asking why her brother-in-law should not do a share of the work in the fields. He, quite as positively, responded that he did not wish to and stated explicitly, "If we all work in the fields, we will all work there all our lives." Wanting desperately to continue his studies in high school, he argued that it was necessary for him to find a position in a factory where he could earn some cash during the holiday. It was so decided. The boy found himself a position in a biscuit factory in Shau Kei Wan where he was paid $120 per month with food and a place to sleep. He developed a temporary disability but, after a few days, he returned to the factory, and apparently continued for the last four weeks of his vacation period.

Mr. Min is the outstanding case of a resident of Chung Nam Wan who works outside the community. Theoretically, he contracts himself for a nine-hour day from eight to twelve and from one to six. Ideally, his work as a mason should bring him $15.00 to $16.00 per day. For certain more difficult jobs, he may earn a little more; on the other hand, under some conditions he accepts only $10.00. The controlling factors are, in part, the location in which he works. He can earn more in the urban areas of Hong Kong, but then he has to pay for his food and lodging. Also some jobs are dangerous, as for example, the deepening of wells. Early in the year while undertaking such a task, he was hit on the head by a stone and it was necessary to pull him out of the well with a rope. He had to lie down for a while and he lost a lot of blood. On occasions, Mr. Min makes a contract to construct a building. With a helper, he can put up a small house like his own in four or five days plus two more after the concrete has dried for a week. If he figures on ten days for a job and can do it in nine, he makes an extra profit, but he may lose by estimating wrongly. Most of the time he works on Lung Chau, and after the great typhoon of 1960, he was in constant demand, working overtime almost every night. As for Mr. Min's unseen uncles, we know only that they work in a medicine shop.

Ownership. The concept of communal ownership within a family seems to be basic in Chung Nam Wan, and the economic family units or ka (chia) have been previously identified (p. 68). Pursuing the matter with respect to the most personal objects, when Mr. Lin is questioned as to the ownership of the earrings that Mrs. Lin wears he responds, "Why ask this? It is just the same (as with other things)." But then he admits with a laugh that he could not sell his wife's earrings and, furthermore, that she could without asking him. This situation also holds with respect to one's personal clothing, but that seems to be about as far as purely individual control goes. Mr. Lin states that money is common property, but to use any that is actually in the possession of a spouse, one should ask. It may be noted that Mr. Lin also claims that whatever cash they may have, they keep in their pockets. No one in Chung Nam Wan admits to having any significant amount of money, and it would be surprising indeed if more than one or two did have, although it is a commonly shared notion that even the poorest Chinese woman has her nest egg.

As to the ownership of land, the residents of Chung Nam Wan suffer from confusion, as is not strange considering the special and variable character of tenancy in the Crown Colony where all land is held in the name of a Queen who charitably tolerates squatters, and squatters all the residents of Chung Nam Wan have originally been. Everyone has recently come to recognize the value of having the government issue them a paper acknowledging the actuality of their residence, but on the other hand, there are drawbacks as well. It is a common belief that, first of all, unrecorded money must be provided in order to obtain such a paper, a fear which is not altogether unfounded. For this the residents do not blame the British, but rather the lower echelons of their Chinese assistants who come from a country historically distinguished for utilizing the indirect method of monetary payments. Then, if one does obtain the desirable paper, it is a statement of agreement that the occupant of the land may live on it for a year for a specified rental which has the character of a land tax.

Actually the wording of the paper seems to be a legalistic understatement of its true implications. Although the paper makes clear the government's right to recover the land (which is indicated on a rough survey of the property), it is not very likely that they would have reason to do so in a dingle such as Chung Nam Wan. Therefore the residents believe they have a right which can be passed on to their descendants and cannot be alienated by other individuals providing the annual payments are made. Mr. Chin's mother also assumes that if the government itself should take back the land, the family having the paper would be compensated at the rate of $.60 per square foot plus payment for fruit trees (e.g. $6.00 per papaya), buildings, and other unmovable investments. These prices would make the Chin holdings, by our computations, worth in excess of $10,000. Mr. Chin's mother, perhaps suffering a moment of frustration, expressed the wish that the government would reclaim the land because farming is such hard work.* It may be added that Mr. Chin's mother is uncertain whether the paper the family has would allow her to rent the farm to others. On the other hand she believes that if she did not pay the rental to the Crown, she would lose her present status with relation to the land, including any right to compensation were it reclaimed. Her document, incidentally, is in the joint names of herself and her eldest son. Attached to it is a sheet outlining their forty-three hundredths of an acre of land as recorded on the Crown Survey of the Colony.

Apparently the second such paper for Chung Nam Wan was taken out by the Lung Shing schoolteacher friend of the Mins for the land the latter had occupied. He apparently knew the required procedure to obtain the document and wished to safeguard his investment in pig houses. After the failure of that venture, Mrs. Min reports that he turned over his rights to her and her husband. She had previously said that he wanted to sell the property and provide them a house elsewhere, but that no one was interested in purchasing the one that they had built in Chung Nam Wan.

Mr. Lin, moved to action in turn, had not obtained his paper although he had made request for it and had received cards of acknowledgment in 1956 and 1957 stating that his land would be measured. His efforts were renewed in the late summer of 1960, but a permit was refused.

Taxes. The land rental on the Chin property was said formerly to be $120 per year, but by 1960 it had been raised to $188. They also pay $36 for a pig license. Mr. Chin's mother thinks it is unfair since it is based on neither the number of pigs nor the number of pens. Large producers pay the same, in her opinion. Our statements on the Mins' assessments are somewhat confused for reasons that are probably not their fault. Apparently at one time their land rental was $100. Mr. Lin, with no paper, pays nothing to the government for the land that he occupies.

---

*Legally, the government has no obligation to compensate squatters who are removed from the land. It was apparently the practice in 1960, however, to pay $.60 per square foot as compensation to people removed from land on which they had resided since before 1941, but only $.10 to those who had first occupied land thereafter. Some further adjustment in the practice, no doubt, has sometimes occurred.

Besides land rentals, there are also personal property taxes. According to Mrs. Min, she and her husband formerly paid $70 in taxes assessed as follows: $10 for the house, $10 for the attached kitchen, $10 for the chicken house, $20 for the pig houses, and $20 for the well. When pig raising as a major activity ended for the Mins, their taxes were reduced, and the annual payments including land rental amounted to $110. Mr. Lin pays no direct taxes at all. He states that one is supposed to have a license to raise pigs and that it costs $20 per year. He no longer has pigs. A pigeon license also costs $20 per year, but in 1960 no one had pigeons in Chung Nam Wan. There is no tax on possessing chickens or ducks. It also seems clear that when people are very poor and their holdings are minimal—whether pigs, pigeons, houses, or kitchens—the eyes of the law can become blind and the potential small tax overlooked.*

Attitude toward the government. The matter of taxes gives an opportunity to interpolate a few words on the attitude of the people toward the British government of Hong Kong. It is pleasant to report that all informants speak with genuine respect, if not actual affection, for the rule of the Queen. Even a Catholic admitting that she does not know whether Communism is good or bad says the British government is certainly better than that of the Chinese as she has known it. She says, "The British make everything nice and clean." There is universal praise for the way refugees have been accepted, and the skyscraper resettlement houses are greatly admired. No one in Chung Nam Wan wants the People's Republic of China to take over Hong Kong. In speaking of it, Mr. Lin's first thought is that the rich were forced to give up all their money. He does not like the idea. He states that the people are not free on the mainland, whereas they are on Taiwan. He does not believe that Chiang Kai-shek will ever recover China, however. Mr. Lin praises the British "for keeping thieves away." He speaks of the police in favorable terms and says that they keep watch over the people and he would not hesitate to go to them if he had any trouble. The nearest police headquarters are across the strait on the main island. To his knowledge, none of the force has ever visited Chung Nam Wan, although they are periodically seen in the town of Lung Shing. Asked what laws the police might enforce, he mentioned only those against stealing and the smoking of opium. Probed by the question, "Can you kill?" he answered, "Of course not, that is the worst thing."

Domestic fowl. Mr. Lin was not speaking of chickens of which every family in Chung Nam Wan had a score or more at the time that our study began although severe losses were said to have been suffered because of

---

*The tax situation has not been clarified. It was obviously beyond the ability of my informants to do so, and such official statements as we found time to accumulate were scarcely more comprehensible to our untutored mind.

the typhoon in June. By reason of his obvious interest in such matters, the ethnographer was probably mistaken at first for an official inspecting the results of the disaster. Consequently the early records of chicken population appear inconsistent and a little incredible. On the other hand, perhaps we are unfair. We have never experienced a typhoon in the company of chickens. There is also the fact with which to contend that the residents of Chung Nam Wan at no time seemed certain as to exactly how many chickens they owned. Chickens do not always cooperate in being counted even when food is being given them, and a few more or less seem numerically unimportant to the people, however valuable a chicken might actually be. It may suffice to say that the typhoon caused total losses for the community of approximately fifty per cent, the Mins suffering disproportionately because their chicken house was demolished. At the beginning of our study, the Lins were left with twenty-three chickens, the Mins with twenty-five, and the Chins, twenty-eight.

The attention that a family gives to chickens seems to vary. The Lins and the Mins have separate houses for their birds and special baskets containing dry grass are usually supplied for hens. Boxes or boards are also made available so that chickens can roost off the ground. In the daytime, chickens are allowed to run loose, and nowhere does one escape them except in the gardens which are more or less screened off from their meanderings. On occasion, however, they start happily eating the cabbages. This makes Mrs. Lin so annoyed that she admits to a desire to kill all her chickens. Even though they only peck the leaves a little, she points out that the plant dies. Still, no one else appears as thoughtful of chickens. At the very threat of real rain or high wind, she will round them all up and make them scurry for the hen house which she closes behind them until the weather is clement again. Perhaps the other families do the same, but I did not observe such behavior. Everyone is aware of hawks, and it is commonplace to hear the cries of wu, wu, which are made to call the chickens, and tsau, tsau (tsou, tsou), literally go away, to scare their attackers away. The hawks are not bashful and will drop on their prey a few feet from the house. More than once, a wish was expressed for a gun, but the possession of firearms is said to be forbidden, so one is reduced to the benefits of shouting. Mrs. Min notes that trees are of assistance because chicks are far less likely to be seen under them. She says when the family first came and there were no trees near their house, a hawk would come and grab four chicks at one time.* Apparently there is a considerable

---

*An ornithologist who was consulted says that it is impossible for a hawk to carry off four objects in its claws, but that four chicks might have been killed in succession and then removed at one time by a hawk using claws and beak. In 1961, however, Mrs. Min insisted that she had seen a hawk carry off two chicks in each of its claws. When Mr. Lin was asked his opinion independently he insisted that a hawk could even carry off three chicks in one set of claws, and Mrs. Lin corroborated his statement. She added by free association that the day after New Year's a hawk had carried off a chick weighing almost a catty.

loss in young chicks from various causes. One day, three of Mrs. Min's chickens died, one a hen with eggs. She attributed the deaths to their pecking on a dead chicken that one of her dogs had brought in.

Mr. Lin says that chickens are important in the economy of his family, something to fall back on, so to speak. At the time the subject was investigated, the Lins had three roosters, ten hens, and eight chicks (defined by him as birds weighing under one catty). Mr. Lin says that they do not eat their chickens except perhaps at New Year's. Chickens that are fed naturally (most on the market have been given hypodermic injections), bring almost half again the price of those that are not, but they are difficult to sell to people who cannot be sure about the feeding. Mr. Lin states that injected chickens have pinker combs. Mrs. Min does not know about the color of the combs but says she can distinguish them by the feathers; also natural feeding never makes the chickens so fat. When she has some to sell, she simply goes to the market area in Lung Shing and offers them to her friends. Mrs. Lin likes to feed her chickens four times a day, twice with uncooked rice, and twice with chaff and rice.

Mr. Lin states that chickens are important for producing eggs and laughs when he says so. Only four of his hens were laying. Some hens will brood after they lay, some will not, but he does not know why. No hen was brooding at the moment but, a few days later, he said that the event was announced by a rooster's crowing. A rooster, Mr. Lin says, also crows to call the hens when it finds food. When a hen broods, he puts any eggs that are available under it so that the total number may be sixteen to eighteen in summer, or up to twenty in winter. Eggs, he claims, can be kept for twenty-five days before being put under the brooding hen. That a hen sits on the eggs for twenty-three days in order to hatch them, he has noted by marking his calendar. He adds that the mother hen will spend about two months taking care of her chickens and after a month more may brood again. Therefore, one should take the chicks away from the hen after a month, but even a hen with chicks may lay some eggs. Ten days after laying eggs, the hen will not take care of her chickens, and unless the eggs are removed, the hen will brood. This is natural and nothing will stop her. From twenty eggs, only twelve or thirteen chicks may be hatched. From twenty eggs, none of the chicks may survive. When it was suggested that it was difficult to see how they could make a profit, he answered with a smile, "We do not see either." Mr. Lin stated that eggs were normally used for brooding, and not eaten by the family even at feasts. Except to an ethnographer it might have seemed strange when he was seen eating eggs with his lunch the next day. Ideally, eggs that cannot be expected to be hatched are sold.

Large chickens are fed cooked rice mixed with rice chaff. The rice is the same quality as the Lins eat ($.33 a catty) and the chaff costs $.28 per catty. Small chickens are said to eat uncooked rice. Full grown chickens weighing two and a half to three catties were reported to sell for $6.50 to $7. Eggs were claimed to bring $.35 each.

When a hen cackled at the Min's house, Mrs. Min sent Third Daughter to see if the hen had laid an egg. She came back and reported that she could not find one. Then First Daughter went to look and came back with an egg on which she wrote the date in Chinese characters with a pencil. In Mrs. Min's opinion, eggs cannot be kept for brooding in the heat of the summer more than ten days; in the cool season, she adds, eggs will keep fertile for a month. The Mins admit to eating some of their eggs, using up the older ones first. At the time, the Mins had nine hens (none laying), one rooster, nine half-grown chickens and fifteen chicks, twelve of which were from one brood and three left from another.

The Chin family had about twenty-eight chickens on the day we gave them particular attention. We say *about* since one was killed to make congee for us, and it was the insistence of our hosts on making this generous gesture which initiated the brief discussion. It was reported that they did not sell many chickens and seldom ate them themselves except on the three principal Chinese holidays (New Year's, 5th of the 5th month, and the 15th of the 8th month). They do, however, give them to relatives as presents. The eggs are either kept for hatching or fed to the children. On some days the hens provide three or four, on some days none. Mr. Chin's mother noted that when a hen cackled in protest, she would have no more eggs for a while. Mrs. Chin says that her husband's mother objects to the children eating so many eggs. The chickens roost in baskets placed for the most part in an unused front section of the pig house.

When Mrs. Chin's mother kills a chicken, she tucks it upside down under an arm and bends its neck back, plucking the feathers from the neck when she has it firmly in hand. Then she cuts across the throat with a small knife previously sharpened for the undertaking on a small stone. She holds the palpitating chicken for a minute as she allows the blood to drip into a rice bowl (no admixture of salt or water). Then she throws the chicken on the ground. The blood, incidentally, is allowed to solidify and is then boiled, pieces finally being cut up and put into congee or other soups. The dead chicken is ultimately plucked, washed in a bucket of water, and then boiled with rice and onion. Very tasty.

Ducks were introduced into the Chung Nam Wan economy during mid-July, 1960, by Mr. Lin. When Mr. Chin was asked if he had thought of doing likewise he replied that he had no time to take care of them. The Min family has no running stream that they could use in order to supply ducks with essential water. Mr. Lin's venture was motivated by the opportunity to buy ten ducks in Lung Shing for one dollar each, an extraordinarily low price. Happily he made a place for them beside the tiny stream below his

Fig. 7.1. The Lins' Duck Shelter

house, erecting a mat shade over the area (Fig. 7.1). A silent partner, charmed by this unexpected addition to the domestic scene, provided twenty dollars for twenty more ducks, which were greatly wanted. The next day, the lady selling ducks in the street of Lung Shing wanted $1.50 for a duck, admitting that those previously sold were sickly and not likely to live. Mr. Lin said that since the birds of his previous purchase were still alive, she was obviously mistaken. He decided to delay a further acquisition of ducks until the price was more favorable. A few days later, he had purchased twenty-five more ducks at a price of $1.30 each. Unfortunately five of the first lot had already died. A week later, only eighteen of the total thirty-five remained. One by one, the ducks continued to die until a month from the time the first purchase had been made when the situation seemed stabilized, at least temporarily, with Mr. Lin the master of twelve well-adjusted ducks. It might be added that Mrs. Lin, always dubious about the venture, was still dubious. It was she who pointed out the empirical fact that the ducks would not eat, and the inevitable fact that not eating, they died.

Mr. Lin, the more optimistic member of the family, has ambitions to raise pigeons also. The Chins have never raised pigeons, they say, because they are too difficult to keep clean. It is the Mins who have had experience since they unsuccessfully attempted to raise pigeons even before they owned pigs. Soon after their arrival, they purchased five pairs of breeding pigeons at $20 a pair. These birds and their offspring were fed green beans at $.70 to $.80 per catty, as well as some rice and corn (maize). After almost two years, their coop contained between seventy and eighty pigeons but the price had fallen and they were worth only $3.50 each. The original investment of $100 had increased to about $262.50 but the cost of the food, not to mention the labor, made the Mins regard the undertaking as unprofitable and they sold all the birds. In 1960, the price of pigeons varied from $1.00 to $4.00, depending on the age and the quality of the bird, so perhaps they were wise.

Pigs. As has been stated, all the families in Chung Nam Wan have pig houses and, in a sense, more houses than pigs since each household includes one or more which are either unused or occupied by humans. It may be interpolated that to build a pig house requires a government permit. In June, 1960, the Mins had a sow and four piglings, the Chins had a sow and eight piglings, and the Lins were pigless. For the Mins, the raising of pigs was a primary matter, so we can allow their establishment to serve as a model, indicating variations in the procedure when necessary.

Pigs are sensitive animals and require considerable care, especially with respect to the weather. Mrs. Min makes a point of the fact that sows must be kept out of the rain. It is not that they do not like water, but that they do not tolerate sudden changes in temperature very well. Also considerable effort is made to keep them clean as otherwise they will develop an infection that causes lumps on the skin (mange?). In the hot days of summer, Mrs. Min cleans the pens in the morning and again in the afternoon, using a shovel to pick up the droppings and deposit them in a gasoline can. Then she washes the floor of each pen clean with a brush using water from another gasoline can. This done, she splashes water on the sow and the piglings. The fat sow on the concrete floor, awakened from its sleep, does not move but squeals with piggish delight. In winter, when the weather is cooler, the pigs and their pens are washed only once each day.

Mrs. Min feeds her pigs about seven in the morning and six in the evening. The month before the sow farrows, she gives it an extra daily meal. The pigs are fed shu miu (shu miao), or the young growth of the sweet potato, and also ng chau ts'ing lung (wu chao ch'ing lung), or five-claw-green-dragon, a morning-glory plant, which are chopped up and cooked with rice. Mrs. Min states that a sow with piglings will eat about two cans (about twenty-eight ounces) of rice each day, a small pig half as much. Sweet potato vines can be planted anytime from seedlings and grow very fast if it rains. Once planted, they continue to increase and, if not cut, the root develops in the ground. The sweet potato, although eaten as an extra dish by members of the family, is not highly valued. The morning-glory is common in Hong Kong and easily recognized by its large lavender trumpet-shaped flower, but only the Mins have planted it at Chung Nam Wan.

Large clusters of the plants are brought to the house and bunched together like a rope of the greatest thickness that can be held in the hand. Two or three inches of the clump extending beyond the thumb and first finger are pressed down on the chopping board and cut into fine pieces by rapid blows of the razor-sharp chopping knife. The board had been laid on a burlap bag spread out on the floor of the kitchen. When a large pile of small pieces is available, the board is removed, the bag is picked up by the corners, and the pieces are dumped into the pig food drum to be boiled with about two quarts of rice and some water.

Firing the righthand burner of the Min kitchen stove for pig food is a process deserving description. First, Mrs. Min inserts an eighteen-inch length of a discarded shovel handle into the horizontal draught hole, the diameter of which is not much larger than that of the handle. Then she inserts another piece of shovel handle vertically down the middle of the fire hole and pours sawdust around it, tamping the fuel lightly. Then she withdraws the two pieces of shovel handle and cleans out the junction of the apertures by inserting a wire into the draught hole. Finally, she pours some kerosene into the vertical hole and lights it with a match. If the fire does not burn well, she adds a little more kerosene directly from the can and puts one small stick into the draught hole. The result is most satisfactory and the pig food drum is placed on the flames. Mrs. Min said she learned the process simply by seeing someone else do it. In due course, the cooked meal is poured into the cement troughs of the pig pens.

The care of the pigs at the Chin farm is essentially the same as at the Mins' except that the five-claw-green-dragon plant is used rarely, weeds or discarded remnants of vegetables being substituted and mixed with the pig vine. Indeed, at times there is so much garden refuse that Mrs. Min is invited to share it. The garden weeds fed to the pigs, a variety of purslane, are known to be edible by humans, but the Chins do not eat them. They are called kwa tsz ts'oi (kua tzu ts'ai), or melon-seed-vegetable, because the shape of the leaf is similar to that of a watermelon seed. The chopping and cooking processes were observed to be the same, but Mr. Chin's mother pointed out that it was not necessary to boil such waste vegetables as Chinese kale. This toleration for uncooked food, she attributed to the fact that their sow was not of the common Chinese breed, but one with mixed Australian ancestry. Never having had any talent for kinship studies, we did not attempt to record even the sub-lineage. Finally, in connection with feeding, it may be mentioned that Mrs. Min's sow was observed snouting into the clay where the cement had crumbled at the back of the pen. It was reported that the sow eats some clay and sometimes takes a sizable stone into its mouth.

When the Mins wish to have their sow impregnated, they usually hire a boat and take the animal to the town of Lung Shing. Of course, if there were more sows to be served, the owner of the boar would bring it to Chung Nam Wan. Four months is stated as the period of gestation. When the sow farrows, the sucklings are allowed to remain with the mother for two months. A week after the piglings have been separated from her, the sow can be taken to the boar once again. The Chins say their sow farrows every seven months. The Chins purchased one male pigling in 1960 to raise as a boar. It has a pen of its own to prevent it from fighting. The two male piglings in their sow's last litter were castrated as it would not be proper to have them inbreed.

The number of pigs in a litter is variable. Mrs. Min claims they usually have nine or ten, that they once had seventeen, but sometimes only two or three. A litter of nine or ten is said to be ideal, since, if there are many more, the piglings are too small and the sow has not enough teats to feed them. The Mins' sow's last litter was ten. The Chins' first sow which they have owned for seven years bore eight early in 1960 but one soon died leaving five females and two males. During the heat of July, one of the piglings refused to eat and it was put by itself behind the house. Mr. Chin's mother blamed her daughter-in-law for letting the pigs go unbathed several days. The pigling died shortly thereafter and the carcass was thrown away. If killed alive, it could have been eaten. In the middle of August, the sow farrowed again producing fifteen in her litter, but one died the first day. The Chins waited a few days to determine which two piglings to dispose of since the sow could feed only twelve. New-born pigs are said not to be eaten. Unfortunately the whole litter of pigs died after a month because the sow could not feed them. Next time, Mr. Chin's mother says that she will buy a tin of medicine which costs eight dollars so that the sow will have enough milk.

The financial aspects of pig raising in Chung Nam Wan are complicated by the lack of records, by the variations in prices, and by the vagaries of family credit. When Mr. Chin's mother was asked why they did not have more pigs, she replied that pigs eat too much and the eight pigs they already had cost ten dollars a day to feed. This was the beginning of the circuitous path to discovering the real problem as she saw it which basically involved the risk in having too high a percentage of investment in animals which may readily die or for which the meat price can significantly vary. Rice for the pigs is obtained on credit from a rice store in Lung Shing. When pigs are sold, the debt is paid. There is no interest charged, but the shop charges more for its food, so the transaction amounts to the same thing. At the time of the discussion, the Chin debt was stated as being approximately $2,000. Ideally, pigs are sold just before one of three outstanding holidays (New Year's, 5th of 5th month, and 15th of 8th month) when the price is high, but the 6th and 7th months are said to be usually the best, according to Mr. Chin's mother. On the other hand, Mrs. Min says there is no special time to sell pigs except when they have grown up and the price is high.

The first cost in pig raising is usually that of building the necessary shelter and that may involve more than money. When the Mins began to erect their sties, presumably some jealous person in Lung Shing told the inspector that the land did not belong to the Mins. He came and told them to pull down their pig houses. It was then that their schoolteacher partner and friend intervened to obtain a permit. At the same time the Chins' hired worker rented some of their land and had almost completed some concrete pig houses. He was obliged to abandon his building. There is an obvious difference between a farmer keeping a sow and a person who goes into the pig business.

Pigs themselves can be expensive. The six sows, or chu paw (chu p'o), which the Min family acquired about 1956, cost almost $500 each. A sow which replaced them in 1960 weighed over 200 catties and was offered at $300 by the owner, but the circumstances were unusual. Mr. Lin contributed the information that in 1960 a 100-catty sow cost about $220 and one of sixty to seventy catties, $200, the small difference being explained by the fact that pigs take on weight so fast at that stage. A pig weighing thirty to forty catties cost $120, and one two months old (capable of being separated from the parental sow), $100. All prices are admittedly approximate and they vary in time.

Impregnating a sow costs money. If the sow is taken to Lung Shing, a boat must be hired (no one suggested carrying the animal over the steep gap which isolates Chung Nam Wan as even a possibility). The boat will cost $5 and there will be the same amount for carrying the sow. Then there is the charge of from $10 to $12 for the service of the boar although, since the Mins are friends of the boar-owning family who live near the town across the strait, the charge may be reduced to $8. At best, the cost will be $18. It perhaps should be added that, according to Mr. Lin, driving a boar around for service is the lowest of all professions; indeed, one so shameful that it is done only as a last resort.

As has been mentioned in another connection (p. 67), the Mins' venture in the pig business came to an end when all their six sows and some piglings became ill and died. The disease, said to be common, was not named, but the animals were described as turning round and round in circles because of it and would not eat. The schoolteacher had advanced the necessary money, and the agreement had been to halve the profits after the original costs had been repaid.

After a period without pigs at the beginning of 1960, the Mins were loaned a pregnant sow on the condition that they would feed it and return two piglings from the litter. The sow farrowed and the Mins came into possession of eight of the ten sucklings. Fortunately or otherwise, when the sow became pregnant again, the woman who owned it said she wanted one and a half of the piglings in the next litter whereas Mrs. Min said the agreement had been for only one after the first farrowing. The owner reacted by saying that she would rather have the sow returned unless the Mins would pay $300 for it. Mrs. Min said she had no money and the owner replied that she could pay her later. Mrs. Min agreed. The owner's husband objected to the transaction, however, on the grounds that if the pig died, his wife might not get paid. Consequently a cash price of $280 payable in twenty days was agreed upon. The Mins did not have sufficient money, so they sold four of their eight piglings which weighed fifteen catties each for $3.50 a catty, thus producing $210. If they could have waited until later in the year, they would have expected to obtain $4.00 a catty.

The Lins have had no pigs for two or three years. Their one sow apparently could not feed her offspring so the animals were gradually sold. The real factors in the failure can only be guessed so it will be safer simply to record that the Lins would like to have some pigs again. Someone suggested to Mr. Lin that he take the Chins' two extra pigs and feed them himself, but he objected on the grounds that milk is expensive to buy, that the sucklings would have to be fed six times a night, and finally that such handfed pigs have to be sold when they reach a weight of seventy catties or they will die. It was added that pigs so nursed would follow their foster mother all the time. This factor, Mr. Lin did not seem to mind.

It may be appropriate to conclude this section of the study by mentioning roast pig, so important ceremonially among the Cantonese. Mr. Min, besides his activities as a mason, also assists in roasting pigs in Lung Shing. This is a special process in which a whole butchered pig is hung head down in a pit over burning wood charcoal for two hours, or perhaps a little more as Mr. Min suggested in correcting his wife's estimate of four.

Fishing. The farmers of Chung Nam Wan look askance upon fishing. Mr. Lin says that he came from an area without fishing, that he does not know how to fish, and that he does not even like to eat fish very much. His wife shares the same limitations.

The Mins do not catch fish, but they like to eat them. Mrs. Min says that to fish at Chung Nam Wan is quite difficult and that one must have patience. Their friends, such as the schoolteacher, come sometimes to fish.

Often he does not catch anything for an hour at a time. When he succeeds, he gets mostly wong fa (huang hua), or yellow croaker, or more rarely a tai ü (ta yü), or hair-tail (see Appendix C). He uses a bamboo pole with a float on the line and baits his hook with shrimp.

Mr. Chin's mother states that in her family only her children have fished and that they have done it for fun on a rainy day. When successful, the fish have been eaten. Most of the time they have had other things to do. Nonetheless, they might have been motivated to seek the benefits of the sea when they have watched fishing sampans from Lung Shing coasting off the beach, putting down basket traps in the morning and retrieving them in the afternoon with their contribution of small nai mang (ni meng). At least in 1959, Mr. Chin purchased for $30 a secondhand boat in which to go fishing and a few basket traps. Unfortunately, he did not learn the art of catching the nai mang. As they tried rice flour cakes unsuccessfully, seemingly, the proper bait was not used. The boat was not a good one anyway, so they burned it when they gave up the venture. The baskets with their stone weights can be seen at the edge of the flat in front of the house.

Fruit trees. In Chung Nam Wan grow four kinds of fruit trees —guava, papaya, banana, and peach, but the last two are relative rarities in that only one family has each type. The guava is the most common and hardiest of them all. The Chins have planted three hundred guava trees, most of them on the slope east of their house and above it, but the high winds have destroyed a good many. Few of the remainder yet bear fruit. The Mins have over thirty guavas, and the Lins own perhaps just as many or more, some of them four to seven years old. The size of the tree, of course, makes a difference in the quantity of the crop.

Guava trees are planted at any time of year from ripe fruit seeds. Mr. Lin places the seeds in earth which he had put into a broken basket that is high enough to keep chickens from eating the young shoots. The seeds are watered but not fertilized. In time the roots grow through the basket. Mr. Lin does not transplant his guava trees, whereas Mrs. Min does transplant her seedlings. In two years, the trees mature enough to bear ripe fruit. Buds appear in the 1st month and, according to Mr. Lin and Mrs. Min, the fruit ripens in the 7th. There is another type of guava which appears in the market earlier. According to the Chins, guava bear from the 6th month to the 8th, and this is verified by Mr. Lin. The fruit varies in size and quality and may be eaten with the skin or after peeling.

The Mins do not have a large enough guava crop to sell, especially since their children eat them and give them to their friends. Mr. Lin reports that he has twenty to thirty catties to sell in the 7th month despite his daughter's appetite, and that the price is about $.20 per catty. Mrs. Min reports a variation from $.20 up to $.80 depending on success or

Fig. 7.2. The Beach at Chung Nam Wan and some of the Chins' banana trees

failure in the growing season. Mr. Chin's mother says they sometimes have enough guava to market, in which case they offer them to the women who sell fruit on the streets of Lung Shing.

The papaya, known as the tree melon, or muk kwa (mu kua), is grown from seeds scattered in a seed bed where they are allowed to reach a foot in height before being transplanted to chosen spots which have been fertilized with solid pig manure. The seeds may be purchased in the market or supplied by one's own trees. As the plant grows, it must be watered each morning and evening and, when the tree is well-established, human fertilizer is added to the water. The papaya matures in six months. The fruit are green at first, then large and yellow. They continue to ripen, one above another on the branches, at every season of the year.

The papaya trees of Chung Nam Wan were almost annihilated by a strong gale (number seven signal) in 1958 and so further damaged by the typhoon of 1960 that only one tree, apparently protected by the Chin house and terrace, was observed to be bearing. The Mins claim to have had two hundred growing trees previous to 1958, including fifteen large enough to flower (perhaps three feet high). Not one of these remains. Mr.

Lin counts thirty trees as his, but these are small. He hopes to harvest forty to fifty catties from them, and points out that some large trees may individually produce as much as thirty catties in an exceptional year. There are no such trees in Chung Nam Wan, however. The Lins joke with each other about planting papaya trees, as Mr. Lin has had a bit of bad luck in raising too many fruitless male trees, the seeds of which he cannot distinguish from those of the productive female papayas. The farmers' price for green papayas was stated as approximately $.30 per catty; when ripe, the price may rise to $.80.

The Chin family alone has banana trees. We counted twenty-seven near the house, nine below the well, and fifty-one above the beach at the edge of the fields (Fig. 7.2). It is said that when one plants a single tree, it multiplies, but they need a lot of water. There are no fruitless male trees, we are happy to learn, and bananas continue to appear in all seasons but are most plentiful in the rainy season. Only those in summer are large enough to be eaten, however. Of the trees near the house, only two had bananas in the middle of June, and there were three small bunches on the trees near the shore. The Chins eat all the bananas themselves.

The Lins have two peach trees about three years old. The peach crop is negligible if only because the Lins cut branches with flowers to give to their friends in the New Year's season, a highly appreciated custom among the Cantonese.

8. Economic Life: Vegetables and Marketing

In presenting the data on gardening in Chung Nam Wan, it would be advantageous in some ways to begin with those vegetables which seem most important, such as the cabbages, but to do so involves one in value judgments which had best be avoided. Also one might proceed in the fashion of Herklots, moving from one group of vegetables to another, as from salads to roots and tubers.* All things considered, nothing seems as efficient as to take up the production of vegetables in alphabetical order as they are listed in Table 8.1. The discussion of kwa (kua), or melons (as the Chinese conceive them), however, has been left to the end. Also we should note that when we asked why farming data were given us in relationship to lunar months rather than the Chinese seasonal units, informants simply stated that in the southern climate, the variation made no significant difference and that the lunar months were the natural and easy system for them.

Beans. As will be seen from Fig. 8.1, the Lin family plants green string beans, as also the Min family did formerly, but the Chins seldom do because they say that there is an insect that eats the bean flowers all the time, also that the bamboo supports are expensive, and that the wind blows them down. In any event, they prefer to devote their fields to other vegetables. Mr. Lin states that four seed beans are planted at one time, but not too close together (not touching) and not too deeply. They should be just covered with earth or they will not grow. Mrs. Lin says bean seeds are very expensive to buy and therefore she preserves her own. The pods have to be dried in the sun in order to obtain seed. Planting may take place anytime from the 1st to the 5th month (inclusive). Beans planted after the end of the 5th month will not bear. When the beans have grown enough to need support, a bamboo tetrapod is erected over the plants to support the

---

*Herklots, 1941. This useful and difficult-to-obtain monograph was not utilized during the field season and consequently did not influence the recording of data, but it has been drawn upon afterward, particularly for terminology. The Herklots transliterations have been included as an effort to simplify identifications. A copy of the greatly enlarged second edition was not located until after the field work had been completed.

[139]

TABLE 8.1

Vegetables Grown in Chung Nam Wan

| English and Latin Names | Cantonese Names | | Mandarin Name |
	Herklots	Eitel	Giles
Bean, Green string	ts'eng tau	ts'ing tau	ch'ing tou
Vigna unguiculata (Linn.) Walp.	kok	kok	chio
Cabbage, Chinese white	paak ts'oi	pak ts'oi	pai ts'ai
Brassica chinensis var. *communis* T. and L.; *Brassica parachinensis* Bailey			
Cabbage, Flowering Chinese	paak ts'oi	pak ts'oi	pai ts'ai
Brassica chinensis var. *communis* T. and L.	sum	sam	hsin
Chinese chives	kau ts'oi	kau ts'oi	chiu ts'ai
Allium tuberosum Rottler ex Sprengel			
Chrysanthemum, Garland	t'ong ho	t'ung ho	t'ung hao
Chrysanthemum coronarium Linn.			
Garlic	suen t'au	sün t'au	suan t'ou
Allium sativum L.			
Kale, Chinese	kai laan	kai lan	chieh lan
Brassica oleracea var. *acephala* D. C.; *Brassica alboglabra* Bailey	ts'oi		
Lettuce	sang ts'oi	shang ts'oi	sheng ts'ai
Lactuca sativa Linn.			
Onion, Chinese green	siu yuk	siu yuk	hsiao yü
Allium sp.	ts'ung	ts'ung	ts'ung
Onion, Foreign	yeung	yeung	yang
Allium Cepa Linn.	ts'ung	ts'ung	ts'ung
Parsley	uen sai	ün sai	yüan sui
Petroselinum hortense Hoffm.			
Spinach, Chinese	in ts'oi	in ts'oi	hsien ts'ai
Amaranthus gangeticus L.			
Spinach, Water	ung ts'oi	ung ts'oi	weng ts'ai
Ipomoea reptans Poir.			
Tomato	faan ke'e	fan k'e	fan ch'ieh
Lycopersicum esculentum Mill.			

vines (see Fig. 11.3). Two months are required for beans to mature and thereafter a few of them can be picked from a plant every day for a little over a month. Beans sell for perhaps $1.80 a catty when they first come into the market, but the price falls to about $.60 when the supply increases.* The Lins eat the culls from their own beans; that is, the ones with short pods and with spots. In 1960, the June typhoon almost destroyed what remained of the crop.

---

*All prices are those paid to the producers, the retail prices being somewhat higher.

[140]

CHART OF THE GROWING PERIOD OF VEGETABLES

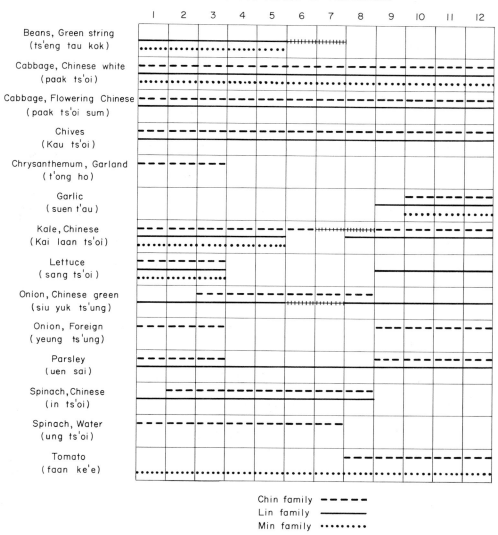

Fig. 8.1. The Growing Periods of Vegetables

The Lins are familiar with white string beans, as well as the green, but they do not grow them as the restaurants want only the latter. White beans would be grown at the same time and in the same manner. They also sell for the same price, but only in the public market. Mrs. Lin believes that the white beans actually taste better than the green, but states that they do not have such an attractive appearance.

Cabbage, Chinese white. Two varieties of this vegetable, which takes its name from its white center stems, are raised by the Lins and Chins, as they were formerly by the Mins. One has long, vertical leaves and is grown especially during the 6th, 7th, and 8th months, but may be grown all year round. The other variety has short and spreading leaves. It is grown throughout the 8th and 9th months, and during the 10th and 11th as well if there is not too much rain. The long-leaved variety can be seeded any month. It is Mrs. Min's favorite vegetable to raise, because it is so easy to plant and grows large so one can sell more of it. She did not mention the fact that the roots do not have to be cut off when it is marketed (as they do from flowering Chinese cabbage), but she did admit that it needs less water which is saving of labor in dry weather. Curiously, Mr. Lin insisted that the one kind of cabbage needed the same amount of water as the other, but the Chins gave information which corroborated Mrs. Min, pointing out not only that the Chinese white variety fared better than the flowering variety during relatively dry periods, but also that it was more difficult to grow in the rainy season. Chinese white cabbage is grown in exactly the same way as the flowering variety which will be described next, but Mr. Lin states that only ten days are required for Chinese white cabbage seedlings to be ready for transplanting, and that the crop matures in another twenty. Mrs. Lin says more than twenty. The farmer's price had been varying from $.55 a catty in the off season down to $.20 when cheap.

Cabbage, Flowering Chinese. This vegetable, also grown throughout the year by the Lins and Chins, constitutes one of the most important crops in Chung Nam Wan.* Its English name comes from the distinguishing yellow flower which, when present, increases its value. With Chinese kale, it is considered by Mr. Lin to be a specialty of Hong Kong. Mr. Lin buys his seeds in Lung Shing and keeps them in a bottle deposited in a stoneware jar in his bedroom. About once a month he or his wife spreads some of them in a small seed bed. The seedlings grow for about twenty days without weeding, but are fertilized with night soil every three days, as well as being watered regularly. When of a proper size, the cabbage seedlings are transplanted to a carefully prepared bed and set out three inches apart in transverse rows which are five to six inches apart. The first two fingers are thrust into the soil and withdrawn, after which the root of a single plant is inserted in the hole, the earth then being pressed around it with the thumb and first finger of the opposite hand. The plants are fertilized with night soil three days after transplanting and periodically thereafter. Watering takes place irregularly, depending on the weather. Flowering Chinese cabbage is sensitive to water, and the farmer must be sensitive too. It is difficult to grow in summer. If it receives too

---

*The description is more detailed because it happened to be the first crop studied and because the writer participated in the work in the fields, not because it is perhaps the most tasty of Hong Kong vegetables to foreigners as well as to some Chinese.

little water, the "heart," for which it is named, turns white. This makes the cabbage tough, but it can still be eaten. A week after transplanting, the cabbages are weeded with a three-pronged rake and the process is repeated in six or seven days if one is not too busy. The more thorough the weeding, of course, the faster the cabbage grows. The crop may be expected to mature in twenty to thirty days depending upon the individual plant as well as its care and weather. The full grown plant has thick, erect, green stems (completely unlike the European cabbage) unless the land slugs have nipped them, in which case they spread out, the growth going to the leaves rather than the stems. In harvesting the flowering cabbage, mature plants are pulled from the beds, leaving immature ones still to grow. Thus several days may be consumed in clearing a field.

According to Mr. Lin, there are five types of flowering Chinese cabbage: 40-day, 50-day, 60-day, 70-day, and 80-day. Perhaps he was infected with a feeling for a ten-day periodicity. In any event, he states that the 40-day type is difficult to grow if there is much rain, but that it has a large, fast-growing heart. The 50-day type, which he usually grows, has more leaves than the 40, whereas the 60-day kind is thicker. He offered no data on the 70-day kind, but says that the 80-day kind is seldom grown anywhere. It grows very thick, but the price is low. Finally, he points out that when people have many fields they like to mix the types because by so doing there is more variation in the time of harvesting.

Mr. Lin indicated that Mr. Chin planted the 40-day and 50-day kinds, and the latter confirmed the statement. Besides these, however, Mr. Chin knew only of the 60- and 80-day kinds. He added that the 40-day kind has longer leaves, whereas the others are of a darker color. The price paid the farmers for their flowering Chinese cabbage in July, 1960, was $.50 a catty with flowers and $.35 without (cabbages with flowers are neither old nor tough).

Chives. Both Mr. Lin and Mr. Chin grow chives throughout the year but the latter states that the plants mature very fast in the spring rainy season. The tips of chives before they flower are reputed to be especially delicious with pork and bean curd, as well as with eggs. The Lins plant this vegetable by breaking the bulbs (which are not sold with the greens) into little pieces and sowing them about six inches apart in a prepared field. This is done only once a year, usually in the 12th month, but sometimes in the 11th. If not replanted, the leaves become very thin. Also, chives may be planted by spreading the seeds over a bed, and transplanting the shoots, but this method is unnecessarily slow.

After sections of chive bulbs have been planted, they are fertilized, but one has to be careful as this vegetable is very sensitive to fertilizer, whereas it can tolerate more or less water. When the plants are a little over an inch high, the tops are cut off and the stems are splayed, which makes them produce many leaves. Periodic watering and fertilizing continue. Chives mature in fifteen days. The crop is then cut and sold, this process being repeated every fifteen days. The price for chives varied from $.50 to $.60, but can drop to $.20 or $.30. Immediately after the June typhoon, the price skyrocketed to $.80 a catty.

Chrysanthemum. The Chins raise garland chrysanthemum only during the 1st, 2nd, and 3rd months although, as Mr. Lin points out, it can be planted after the 9th month through the 3rd if the latter is cool. The procedure is said by both Mr. and Mrs. Lin to be identical with that followed in raising cabbages. Approximately a month is required for the seedlings to grow tall enough to transplant them, and an equal period for the vegetable to mature. The Lins and the Mins do not grow it and, since it is a winter crop it was not possible to observe the procedure during the summer. Garland chrysanthemum is said to have sold in 1960 at between $.20 and $.30 per catty.

Garlic. All the families in Chung Nam Wan plant garlic, the Lins commencing in the 9th month, and the Mins and the Chins in the 10th, all continuing through the 12th. Natural sections of the bulb are inserted in the ground and immediately fertilized with pig manure. This done, the area is covered over with the dried stems of a plant (each of which has about forty small leaves) that grows wild around the houses. Stones are placed on top to prevent them from blowing away. This cover is left in place for about two months until the garlic matures, this treatment being said to make the bulbs grow large. After the first twenty days have passed, any kind of liquid manure may be used, and it is applied every three days. When the sun shines warmly, garlic should be watered early. This smelly vegetable is said not to be bothered by insects. It is pulled up to harvest and tied in bunches with sea grass. Once the harvesting is begun, no part of the crop can be left in the ground more than ten days. Garlic is said to bring as much as $1.30 per catty in the market and to be always salable.

Kale. This specialty of Hong Kong is grown by all three families, although only the Chins attempt to do so continuously through the hottest season of the summer. Insects and heat are both hazards. Actually, according to Mr. Chin, kale causes problems from the 5th month through the 8th. Mr. Lin said there were two types of kale, but that only one kind was planted in Chung Nam Wan and that it bears curved and more delicious tasting leaves. Mrs. Lin says it is one of the two or three vegetables that she likes most to grow. The raising of kale follows the pattern of the cabbages and garland chrysanthemum. The plant takes two months to mature after transplanting.

Helping Mr. Chin, we pulled kale seedlings from his field under the bank closest to the beach. It was too hot a location for chives and for us, but all right for flowering cabbage and kale when well-watered. The seedlings had to be watered before transplanting in order to loosen the roots from the baked earth, but no serious damage is done if half of the roots break off. We selected as many seedlings as left hands would hold; then deposited the green plants in a basket. The planting immediately followed in a bed already watered to prepare it for the seedlings. Slight furrows about six inches apart were made across the bed to mark the rows for planting. Six seedlings were placed six to a row, which made them about five inches apart. The first finger of the right hand was pushed into the damp earth to make a hole, a seedling picked up and inserted, and then firmed down by pinching the surrounding soil between the thumb and first finger of the left hand. Kale usually was selling between $.40 and $.50 per catty, but at times it had gone up to $.80 or $1. It is always in demand.

Lettuce. Like garland chrysanthemum and garlic, lettuce is essentially a cool weather crop in Chung Nam Wan. Mr. Chin claims that it can be grown in summer, but that he does not attempt to do so because of the difficulty. All the families may grow it in winter. According to Mr. Lin, the seeds are spread over a bed anytime beginning in the 9th month continuing through the 3rd. After a month he transplants the seedlings, and in about two months more they mature. Lettuce requires a great deal of water and fertilizer; the water is supplied twice a day as to other plants, but more water is sprinkled, while the fertilizer is spread every three days, but again, somewhat more lavishly. When mature, the lettuce is cut, and only once. A plant may weigh two or three catties and sell for $.20 a catty or sometimes more. There is always a demand. Mr. Lin admits to eating lettuce uncooked.

Onion, Chinese green. Nothing is more easily recognized in the fields than the distinctively green tubular shoots of the common Hong Kong onion. The Chins grow them beginning in the 3rd month through the 8th and the Lins do so all year. Mr. Lin says the most care is needed in the 6th and 7th months, but that is the best time to get the highest price for the crop. These onions may be planted from seed, the shoots being transplanted when they are about six inches high (Mrs. Lin says after a month, or about four inches high), or the seedlings may be purchased in the market, which saves time. Mr. Lin purchases his, which he admits is the more expensive procedure, but he says that he can get all the seedlings he needs for a planting at a cost of $3. It may be added that the latter are said to grow more to stem and less to bulb, besides having a better flavor, factors which make them preferred by most restaurants. The seedlings are fertilized lightly, weeded with a fork after a rain, and take a month to mature. The farmer's price early in July, 1960, was about $.40 per catty. It was said that the price fluctuates readily and may drop to as low as $.30. On the other hand, it can rise to $1.20 a catty.

Onion, Foreign. Between the 9th month and the 3rd the Chins grow foreign onions which are presumably the Bermuda white variety. These are grown from pieces of the bulb and are not transplanted. Mrs. Lin says they taste better than the other variety, but are much more difficult to grow ("they die easily").

Parsley. This green vegetable is usually grown by the Chins and Lins, but the latter did not do so in 1960 because Mr. Lin failed to go to the large supply house in Victoria where the seeds can be purchased. He planted some in 1959, however. Parsley is difficult to raise in the summer heat and Mr. Chin does not attempt it then. The Mins have not grown it at all. According to Mr. Lin, the seeds are thrown over the bed to be used and there is no transplanting. It takes three months to mature and the summer is the best time to sell it, but the price is unstable. In July, 1960, parsley, used for garnishing as in the West, brought $3.20 per catty, but it is known to go as high as $10 or more. On the other hand, it may not even be wanted, whereas other vegetables are. Parlsey, like lettuce, is said not to be cooked, or at least only lightly.

Spinach, Chinese. All the families of Chung Nam Wan grow Chinese spinach, or at least the green-leaved type. Mr. Chin raises some of the red also, which has heavy, red-streaked leaves. Mr. Lin, who restricts himself to the green, says that it is planted from the 1st month to the 7th or 8th by throwing out the seeds, as is done with parsley, and not transplanting the shoots. He says that spinach is not so sensitive to water or fertilizer and consequently can be grown when other vegetables are failing. Furthermore, it can always be sold. The price offered in July was $.30 per catty but it can go up to $1 early in the season.

Spinach, water. This green vegetable which has a hollow base, sometimes known as swamp cabbage, is grown only by the Chins. Mrs. Lin says she does not like to raise it because her fields are particularly susceptible to land slugs which have a great fondness for the plant. She also says it is host to a green insect which gets into the base and is considered dangerous by many people if eaten. Since the spinach is always cooked, she is uncertain as to whether the insect could have any effect on a person. Ordinarily, water spinach is planted in a seed bed and then transplanted after a little over two months, according to Mrs. Chin. It then matures in a month. Mr. Chin points out that if there is too much of this spinach in a field, it may be transplanted from cuttings, or by pulling it out by the roots. Even when cut, it will continue to grow. The shoots are broken off to harvest them for a period of two months but afterward, in the 8th month, what remains is used as food for the pigs. In the middle of July, 1960, the price was only $.06 a catty, so low that it was not worth the trouble to carry water spinach to market from Chung Nam Wan. The pigs thus benefited sooner than usual.

Tomato. This distinctive vegetable is favored by the Mins, Mr. Chin seldom plants them, while Mrs. Lin grew some in 1959 but did not continue doing so. She says they require too much attention as the tomatoes have to be harvested green and allowed to ripen from yellow to red which she considers troublesome. Mr. Chin says he plants tomatoes only for home consumption in the 8th or 9th month, and that they last until the end of the year. They may be planted at any time, however. Mrs. Min, our authority, buys small plants in Lung Shing. She says it is just as easy to grow them from seeds, but the seeds themselves are not as available. She replants her seedlings when about eight inches high as they would be too close together otherwise. The plant takes about a month to mature. If well fertilized, the leaves will be thick. Some are removed as better flowers (and tomatoes) result. The tomatoes are harvested several times; then the plants are removed and one starts over again. Most of the crop is eaten at home, but if there is an excess, it is sold. The price may be as low as $.20 a catty.

Eggplant. The Chins have planted purple eggplant in the past, although they did not do so in 1960 (there are said to be green and also white eggplant). The seeds can be sown in any unused place. After a month, the seedlings are transplanted, and in another month the eggplants mature. They are said to be easy to grow.

Melons (kwa). The Chinese word kwa embraces melons, gourds, and the papaya, or muk kwa (mu kua), among plants at Chung Nam Wan. The latter having been discussed as a fruit, we can conclude by describing the others. All the families grow gourds, but the Mins do so only rarely. Mr. Lin plants them from seeds which his own gourds supply. Sometimes his daughter helps him wash the seeds and lay them out on a board so they will dry. Planting may take place anytime from the beginning of the year until the 7th or 8th months. Twenty days after putting the seeds into the ground, the shoots are transplanted and, with periodic fertilizing and watering, they mature in about two months. The Lins use some and sell the rest, for gourds are always in demand. The price in 1960 was about $.35 a catty.

Mr. Lin grows tung kwa (tung kua), or winter melons, rarely, but Mr. Chin plants them quite regularly in the 3rd or 4th month, harvesting his crop in the 7th or 8th. Mrs. Min says she sometimes grows winter melons, and that they are easy to raise.

Only the Mins grow nam kwa (nan kua), or southern melons. Mrs. Min says that she plants the seeds individually by pushing them into the earth without bothering to cover them over. This is usually done in the 2nd month. With proper watering and fertilizing, the first of the crop matures in the 5th month and, about a month later, the plants will dry up. Some of the melons are sold, the price being remembered as $.15 or $.20 per catty. Mr. Lin says they have tried to grow southern melons, but that theirs have spoiled inside, so they have given up the attempt.

Only the Chins grow shui kwa (shui kua), or water melons, not to be confused with American watermelon called western melon, or sai kwa (hsi kua). The Chinese water melon is green, perhaps a foot long and two inches in diameter, with dark lateral lines and rough greenish spots. The growing season corresponds with that of the winter melon. Mrs. Min adds the note that water melons are usually cooked with ginger.

Vegetable fields. The planted areas of Chung Nam Wan have been roughly mapped as shown in Figs. 8.2, 8.3 and 8.5. It may be observed that the Lins have three cultivated areas above their house and one below it. Each area is divided into from two to five terraces, and each terrace into from two to seven beds. The distribution and disassociation of the areas result from the fact that the fields have had to be cut from the steep hillside. Constructing the supporting rock walls of the terraces when they are several feet high is a special art, and experts are employed for the work at a cost of ten dollars or more a day (Fig. 2.24). Such a man, if supplied with stones, may lay up perhaps twelve feet of low wall in one day. Fortunately, stones are plentifully available at Chung Nam Wan and Mr. Lin has a homemade pair of wire baskets with which he conveys them to the site using a carrying pole over his shoulder. The heights of the Lin terraces one above another vary from a simple step to ten feet, the average for all rises being thirty-eight inches. The area of the Lin fields varies between 636 and 772 square feet, the total being 2815 square feet or about one-fifteenth of an acre.* The thirty-seven beds themselves vary from only seven square feet in area up to 189, the average being sixty square

---

*The measurements of each bed, terrace, and field were recorded crudely, by tape or pacing, and to that extent must be considered only approximations.

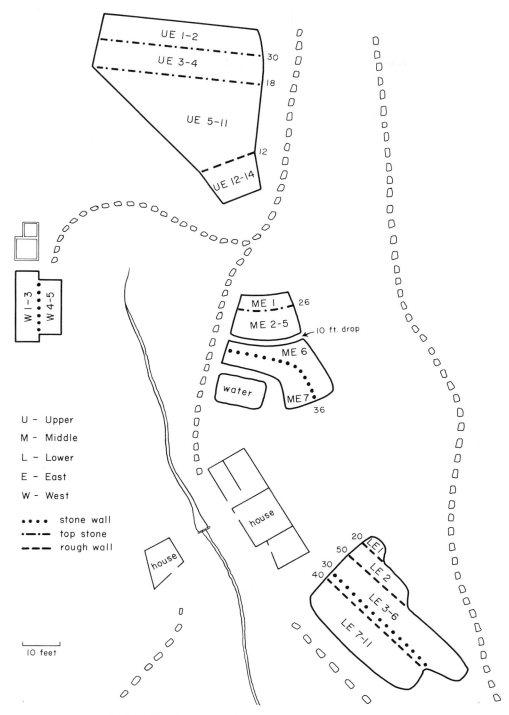

UE 1-2

UE 3-4   30

UE 5-11   18

                          12

UE 12-14

W 1-3
W 4-5

ME 1   26
ME 2-5
            ← 10 ft. drop
ME 6
water
    ME 7
         36

U – Upper

M – Middle

L – Lower

E – East

W – West

• • • •   stone wall
-·-·-   top stone
- - -   rough wall

house

house

                    20
            50   LE 1
        30   LE 2
        40
                    LE 3-6
        LE 7-11

house

⌐ 10 feet

Fig. 8.2. Lin Fields. Figures at ends of walls indicate heights of walls in inches

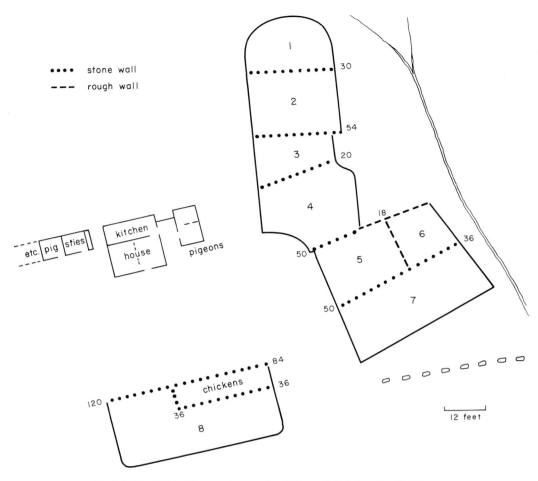

Fig. 8.3. Min Fields. Figures at ends of walls indicate heights of walls in inches

feet.* The width of a bed is usually a reachable two to three feet, but it may be narrower or, in exceptional cases, much wider.

The Mins' garden consists of two fields, one east and above their house, the other below it. Mr. Min constructed the terraces, but his wife has done all the cultivation. The east field is divided into seven terraces with walls from eighteen to 54″ high and ground areas between 169 and 624 square feet, comprising all together 2755 square feet. The field below the house is a single terrace with an area of 744 square feet, giving the Mins a total garden area of 3499 square feet or about one-twelfth of an acre.

The Chins have two cultivated areas, one below their house east of the tiny stream, and the other below their house and west of the stream

_____

*The narrow paths around the beds account for the difference between the total area for beds and for terraces.

(Figs. 8.4 and 8.5). The Chin terrace walls, often beautifully laid, vary from a mere 8″ in height to an imposing 92″, the average being almost two feet. The east field has fourteen terraces totaling 15,232 square feet, and the west one has nine with 7,632 square feet, the whole cultivated area amounting to 22,864 square feet or slightly more than half of an acre. The contents of the specific beds of Chung Nam Wan fields on certain days are given in Fig. 8.5.

Vegetable cultivation. To prepare a field, the remnants of the previous crops are removed with a three-pronged rake, the lumps of earth are broken up, and the ground is smoothed over with a six-pronged rake. When possible, it is considered beneficial to allow the earth to dry after cultivating, but if there are seedlings which must be transplanted, this may not be possible. The final smoothing of a bed is more difficult than it appears since a slight ridge must be raised completely around the edge of each bed with the six-pronged rake. Then when the bed is otherwise level, water may be sprayed on without any loss of dirt or liquid which, without the ridge, would be dispersed onto the foot paths.

Nothing is more time-consuming for the Chung Nam Wan farmer than watering his vegetables, and the arrangement and construction of water basins is an important consideration. The Chins planned wisely in this respect and have three concrete basins well-spaced with respect to their fields. These are fed by low, concrete aqueducts from their two sources of water. One basin on the east side below the house is 52″ wide and 130″ long with a water depth capacity of about 35″. Another in the lower center of the property is 62″ wide, 113″ long, and 36″ deep. Across the tiny stream and farther down is a third basin 84″ wide, 144″ long, and 26″ deep. Besides these, a reservoir pool about ten by twenty feet in area has been created by erecting a cement wall close to where the tiny stream enters the garden. It holds water to a depth of only about twenty inches ordinarily but has a potential of perhaps eighty. It is not fed from the tiny stream but from seepage through the rocks.

To utilize a water basin or reservoir, one balances two empty spray buckets from the ends of a carrying pole on the shoulders and walks down the two or three concrete steps provided in each basin. Actually, the 144-inch-long basin has two sets of stairs. Normally, the farmer is barefoot and has his trousers rolled above the knees. With hands on the cross bars of the buckets that have their long spouts stretching forward, the containers are swung upward and then drawn toward one to fill (Fig. 8.6). The double discharge of spray should fall evenly within the bed to be watered from one end to the other (Fig. 8.7). Such calculated distribution is a minor art. Mr. Chin reports that it requires 130 trips, or 260 bucketsful, of water to spray all of his terraces.

Fig. 8.4 The Chin Fields

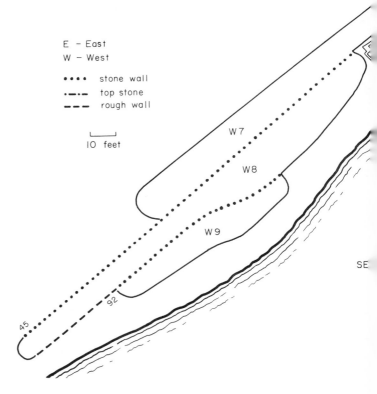

E — East
W — West

•••• stone wall
-•-•- top stone
--- rough wall

⊢—⊣
10 feet

W 7

W 8

W 9

SE

45

92

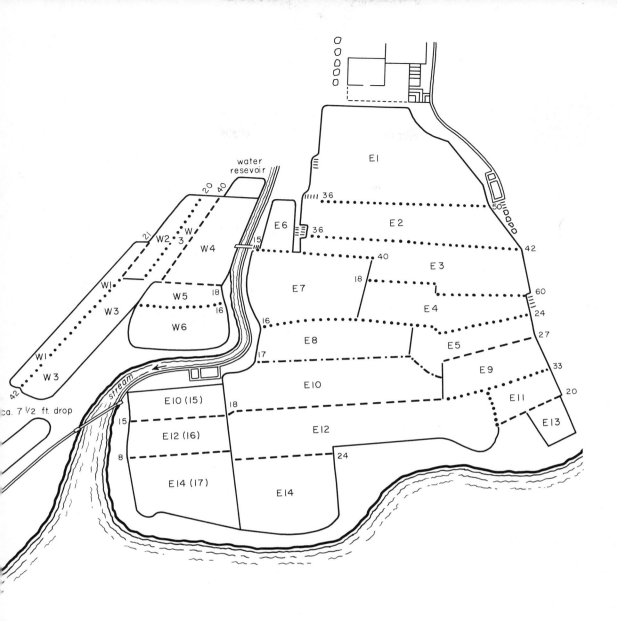

water resevoir

E1

E6

E2

E7

E3

E4

E5

E8

E9

E10

E11

E13

E12

E14

W2
W
3

W4

W1

W5

W3

W6

W1

W3

ca. 7 1/2 ft. drop

stream

E10 (15)

E12 (16)

E14 (17)

SEA

Fig. 8.5 Chin Crops, July 29, 1960. E1—Fallow, to be weeded; E2—cleared of Chinese white cabbage, to be hoed and raked; E3, 11, 13—Chinese green onions (medium to large); E4—Chives (too old for use) and small Chinese green onions; E5—Part fallow, part red Chinese spinach and Chinese green onions for seeds; E6, W2—Chinese kale and flowering Chinese cabbage; E7, 8—Flowering Chinese cabbage planted July 27; E9, 10, W4—Flowering Chinese cabbage; E12—Chinese green onions, red Chinese spinach, and flowering Chinese cabbage; E14—Chives and flowering Chinese cabbage (some cut); W1—Young Chinese kale; W3—Young Chinese kale in east end, west end hoed and ready for planting; W5, 6—Flowering Chinese cabbage seedlings and chive seedlings; W7—Chinese green onions plus a few papaya and water melon; W8—Water spinach in east end, Chinese green onions in west end; W9—Weeds replacing seedlings. Figures at ends of walls indicate heights of walls in inches.

[153]

Fig. 8.6. Dipping Water from a
Chin Reservoir

Fig. 8.7. Watering the Chin Vegetables

Mr. Lin says that beds require sprinkling three times a day if it is hot weather, whereas normally twice will suffice. A light rain is a blessing, for nothing is more common at Chung Nam Wan than to hear someone asking if the fields have been watered, or if they should not be. Mr. Lin first used a pool cut close to the bed of the tiny stream where there is a spring just above his house. It is about ten feet across and half surrounded by one of his terraces. About 1958, he had a concrete basin about 78″ square with three steps constructed at the upper end of his west field. It catches the surface rainwater of the hill to a maximum depth of 26″, but in dry weather it fails, and he has to carry up water from the pool.

Fertilizing is practically as important as watering, and basins for liquid manure adjoin all the concrete basins for water. The depth of the basins in each location is the same. The one in the east side below the Chin house is 36″ wide and 44″ long; that in the lower center of the property is divided into two parts, one of which is 21″ wide, the other 26″, both being 32″ long. The third water basin has an adjoining fertilizer section 36″ wide by 50″ long. Mr. Lin also has a basin for fertilizer attached to his concrete water basin. It is about four feet square at the top level of the liquid but the sides slope slightly inward. The Mins have a fertilizer basin 48″ by 52″ at the end of their row of pig houses. Concrete basins are used for pig manure. Mrs. Lin says night soil is not put in the basins or mixed with pig manure, and that this is true at the Chin farm as well. Mr. Chin says he uses his basins for mixed fertilizers of any kind even including chicken droppings. The confusion in this matter was unfortunately not noticed in time to resolve it. Mr. Chin did make clear that there is an advantage in having a fertilizer basin divided into two parts as that makes it possible to store fresh manure while some other is maturing. Fertilizer buckets are the same as watering buckets, but the pairs used for one purpose are not used for the other. The liquid manure is transferred from the concrete basins to the buckets by a dipper 10″ in diameter and 6″ deep.

Fertilizer is primarily of three types—human, pig, and commercial, the first being the most common. Mr. Lin obtains his from friends who remove Lung Shing night soil from the public toilets for eventual disposal in the sea. He usually brings back two bucketsful (14″ diameter, 13″ height) a day, occasionally giving the disposers a couple of dollars or a little flowering cabbage and sometimes inviting them to tea. Mr. Lin says he has never fallen with a load of night soil despite the steep descent into Chung Nam Wan. Mr. Chin also brings two bucketsful every morning which he derives from a large jar that he has placed near the Tung Pak Wan Path in Lung Shing where it is convenient for people to dispose of their waste. In Chung Nam Wan, the night soil is poured into stoneware jars kept for the purpose. The families also use their own waste. When fertilizer is needed, twenty ounces of night soil is mixed into a five gallon

(160 ounce) can of water, or in the proportion of one to eight.* The age of the fertilizer does not matter once it is diluted. It is sprayed on the beds as is water. Young plants must have liquid fertilizer. Cabbages are sensitive to it, however, and can be treated only in the early morning or after four in the afternoon because in the middle of the day everything is too hot. Chinese spinach, on the other hand, may be fertilized anytime.

Pig manure is available to the Mins and Chins. Mr. Lin obtains his from certain families in Lung Shing who keep pigs illegally. This heavier manure is used on partly grown vegetables. Mr. Lin states that crops fertilized with night soil taste better than those treated with other kinds of material.

Occasionally commercial fertilizers are used in Chung Nam Wan, but these are believed to be more expensive. At least, money has to be paid for them. The Chins have a type that comes in circular flat cakes a foot in diameter and three-quarters of an inch thick which costs $.40 per catty. The cakes are dissolved in water in a basin for fifteen or twenty days. Mr. Chin's mother affirms that this type is cleaner than night soil, and that the vegetables taste better and are softer when cooked. The market price for such vegetables is no higher, but they grow faster and look better, which is economically advantageous. The Mins sometimes purchase peanut chip fertilizer—the residue of peanuts which have been pressed for oil—in Lung Shing. The material usually costs only $.30 per catty, but it is not often available.

Insects which eat vegetables are a problem, and only a few vegetables, such as garlic, escape. The Lins spend a considerable amount of time at night searching for ground slugs with a flashlight. They say the Chins have an advantage over them in this undertaking as there are more people in the family. They have already taught their daughter to smash up snails, which are large and plentiful. Mrs. Lin also spreads a white powder just before transplanting and works it into the ground with a three-pronged rake. This insecticide costs $.15 a catty.

Mr. Chin, for a period, was using an insecticide called Lindane Emulsion which he pumped onto the beds with a Japanese sprayer borrowed from someone in Lung Shing. He could not afford to buy such a tool as one cost $50. Also the insecticide costs $3 (a quart or fifth gallon?). It is mixed with twenty buckets of water. Mr. Chin can spray all of his fields for $6 and claims that it should be done twice a month, which was what he was doing.

---

*Proportions were determined by measurement, but farmers only estimate. The five gallon can is equal to four imperial gallons.

Marketing. Some vegetables require special preparation to sell them. This is true of flowering Chinese cabbage in particular. In the Chin family, the vegetable is pulled from the beds and brought to the flat in front of the house and deposited in a pile. The workers cut off the roots from the green stalks by pushing on the back of a short-bladed sharp knife. The frayed outside leaves fall away leaving the few heavy ones in the middle if one is precise. The clipped cabbages are put on another pile from which another person, for example Mr. Chin, selects piece after piece, laying them fan-wise on the palm of his right hand beginning at the little finger. With the stem of one plant interlocking with the next, he places them base outward very evenly until they form an arc all the way to his arm. This done, he lays the cabbage in one of the large baskets nearby and returns to start over again. If these fifteen-inch wedges of cabbage are well formed, they may be tossed in the air without entirely coming apart since the leaves intertwine. The cabbage in the basket after a weighing is periodically separated by a leaf torn from a banana tree, thus dividing the contents into sections of five or more catties. The same treatment may be accorded to Chinese white cabbage and kale, although Mrs. Min said it was not necessary to cut the roots off the former. Mrs. Lin, on the other hand, prefers to cut off her flowering cabbage in the fields as she harvests it, since it has to be cut for the market anyway. By so doing, the stalks remain cleaner. She adds that it is easy to rake up the roots.

Chinese onions are pulled up and trimmed of all brown leaves, then bundled in a strip of dried palm leaf if the latter is available. Mr. Lin uses sea grass which he purchases in Lung Shing. Mr. Chin wets a palm leaf in a bucket of water, splits it, and ties the onions using a granny knot with the end slipped. Once bundled, the onions are washed in one of the concrete field basins. This also increases the weight by approximately twenty per cent. The wetting of vegetables is looked at askance by the retailers who wish to take advantage of the practice for themselves. Mr. Chin, however, points out that carrying the produce over the hill dries it out.

Going to market consumes time. It is one of the real drawbacks of living in Chung Nam Wan. Mr. Chin's mother says there is not time enough left for work in the fields. Mr. Chin usually goes to Lung Shing in the morning to get fertilizer and to obtain orders for vegetables from retailers in the street market, taking a little of his crop with him, and returns to town again in the early afternoon so as to arrive with the requested vegetables before the market opens for its second session about three. Mr. Lin usually goes only in the morning with his vegetables. Sometimes he sells them to a restaurant, sometimes as does Mr. Chin to women who retail them in the street. Not infrequently several individuals in the Chin household go to town together. Also there are days when no

TABLE 8.2
Sales of Flowering Chinese Cabbage

Day	Amount Sold (Catties)	Price Received
1	3	$1.50
2	4	2.00
3	3½	1.75
5	6¼	3.10
7	6	3.00
8	3	1.50*
9	3	1.50
10	3½	1.75
11	3½	1.75
12	2½	1.25*
13	3	1.50
14	2½	1.25
15	2	1.00
18	5	2.50
19	2	1.00
22	4	2.00

*Paid in full.

TABLE 8.3
Price Range for Produce from Chung Nam Wan, July, 1960

Vegetable	July	Mr. Chin		Mr. Lin	
		High	Low	High	Low
Beans, Green	?	$1.30	$.35	$ 1.80	$ .60
Cabbage, Chinese white	$.20	.55	.20	.50	.20
Cabbage, Flowering Chinese	.55	.90	.20	.60	.20
Chives	.20	.60	.20	.80	.20
Chrysanthemum, Garland	?	?	?	1.30	.20
Garlic	?	?	?	1.30	?
Kale	?	.60	.40	1.00	.40
Lettuce	?	.30?	.05?	?	.20
Onions, Chinese green	.20	.60	.20	1.20	.30
Parsley	?	?	?	10.00	3.20
Spinach, Chinese	?	?	?	1.00	.30
Spinach, water	.06	.30	.06	?	.60
Tomato	?	?	?	?	.20

vegetables are ready to be sold. Men transport fifty catties (twenty-five in each basket), and women about forty, although both Mrs. Chin and Mrs. Lin can carry more. This is a heavy load when, as has been observed, the temperature is ninety-five degrees, and Mr. Chin swings over fifty catties up the precipitous hill.

Prices are difficult to deal with in Hong Kong because they vary so rapidly and because the small farmer may have a more or less favorable outlet. At least an example of sales can be demonstrated from Mr. Lin's account book (Table 8.2). He was selling flowering Chinese cabbage at $.50 a catty to a restaurant in Lung Shing during the second 6th month and put down the record which ended on the day before it was copied. The 23rd of the second 6th month (double 6th) was July 15, 1960.

As can readily be computed, the Lins' income from selling flowering Chinese cabbage alone during a twenty-two day period was $28.35 or, if extended, would be about $40 a month. Time is also consumed in collecting one's payment for vegetables, although there was no indication of any trouble in doing so.

The price range per catty paid the farmer for produce is listed in Table 8.3, as given by Mr. Chin. The prices of some of the vegetables he did not know for one reason or another. Also it is not certain, as he admitted himself, that he could remember the range. Mr. Lin's information has been added.

Discrepancies are notable in a few cases, such as the beans, but Mr. Chin does not grow beans. The difference in the high price of onions must be an error which had best be attributed to the ethnographer. Mrs. Min gave evidence of the difficult situation when she pointed out that in 1958, flowering Chinese cabbage sold for as little as $.05 per catty, whereas water spinach found no buyers at all. Even the pigs would not eat it, she insisted, laughing somewhat ironically.

Although for various reasons—including a lack of family records and remarkable shifts in prices that may occur monthly, seasonally, or annually—we do not have precise data on the incomes and expenses of the three families, we dare to say that the Lin family has an average income of about $200 a month, while the Mins have $300, and the Chins perhaps $400. In each case, expenses leave little opportunity for savings.

9. Reflections

In presenting the purposes of this study, a description of culture as replete in its detail as possible was given the primary place. To expose the insufficiencies of the account as now perceived by the author would savor of masochism, since the really significant weaknesses of the work must undoubtedly be those to which he is blind. The reader, however, will already have drawn his own conclusions, no doubt having been wearied at moments by the maze of minutiae regarded as essential for the creation of a durable image of a few typical Chinese residents of Hong Kong and of their modest estates in the precipitous valley of Chung Nam Wan. If there be value or comfort in the thought, it may safely be assumed that these slivers and chips of a culture have been even more difficult to record than to read. As was anticipated, no claim can be made to a significant refinement of concepts, but it is now possible with the objectivity bestowed upon alien eyes to see a brief moment of history passing by. With some degree of thoroughness we can dissolve a small culture complex into its component parts and with this, once done, consider the source of these elements and the probable time of their introduction into the complex. Some of these elements were born in China's distant past, while a few can be recognized as coming from other parts of Asia. Many more had their geneses in Western civilization, particularly in Great Britain or America. Also, in a general way, we can distinguish these traits as they appear in Chung Nam Wan on a time scale of three periods. Some have characterized Chinese culture for over a thousand years, while others have been introduced into it during the twentieth century. Among these we can attempt to ascertain the elements that were adopted before the Japanese invasion of Hong Kong, and those since 1941. We reiterate that these are the author's reflections for which in some cases historical support may be added in Part V.

Historical Considerations

Chung Nam Wan is a settlement that has been created by population pressure, and more specifically, by a need for land on which to grow vegetables. This need was felt by certain residents of the community of Tung Pak Wan from which Chung Nam Wan is an offshoot reached only through a gap several hundred feet high in the hilly crest of the island. It is significant that the first settlers—except two of the women—were Hakka, a people considered by the Kwangtung Chinese as "guest families," and a group traditionally accustomed to converting unused and somewhat inaccessible hill areas to agriculture. The fact that two of the men married non-Hakka women may possibly be conceived as a sign of upward social mobility, or at least as an indication that the families involved were not the most culturally conservative to be found. On the other hand, there is no reason to believe that the practice of mixed marriages is not old, especially when the husband is Hakka. Linguistically, there is a tendency to replace Hakka speech by the use of the Cantonese dialect that has long been the lingua franca of the Hong Kong Chinese.

Food. Reviewing the culture at Chung Nam Wan, we find that a great part of the food, either grown or eaten, has a long history in Asia. One naturally thinks of rice, and most of the vegetables and fruits, as well as all of the domestic animals, including chickens and pigs, the latter being almost ubiquitous in China. Also in connection with the eating of food, two traits stand out as preeminently indigenous—chopsticks and the concave iron pan in which fried dishes, larger portions of rice, and pig food are cooked. Equally oriental is the utilization of night soil in fertilizing the gardens, as well as the terraces themselves.

Intrusive traits connected with food are, with one or two exceptions, more obvious than fundamental. Wheat and wheat noodles, although ancient in north and west China, have been imported into the southeast of the country. Furthermore, the wheat eaten in Chung Nam Wan is a non-Asiatic acquisition which seems to have come almost entirely from America. The related bread and biscuits, which are appreciated when they can be afforded, are baked commercially in the British manner. Among vegetables occasionally grown is the tomato, a South American plant that has been highly improved by the Italians. Also, one should mention candy concocted in the Western form, which is much appreciated by the children. Perhaps one of the most significant innovations is condensed milk from the Netherlands or America, a most useful food for small children, and sometimes truly a life saver. The same can only be said figuratively of the bottled soft drinks made in Hong Kong, which are obvious, and often licensed, copies of the American originals. Cognac, needless to say, harks back to France, but from some of the brands sold in Lung Shing, one would not be likely to know the historical source. Tobacco in cigarette form is greatly appreciated by the men in Chung Nam Wan and, of course, was indigenous to America. No one could tell now in what countries the tobacco in the cheapest cigarettes originated as it is allegedly composed of the remnants of other cigarettes more expensive to buy. Packaging is available in both the British and American styles. Insecticides and chemical fertilizers are also non-Chinese in cultural origin, although the modern source of some of them is apparently Japan. One of the few clearly recognizable pieces of Japanese merchandise in Chung Nam Wan is a borrowed insecticide sprayer.

Dress. Only the dress of adult women remains essentially Chinese, and even those costumes have European intrusions. Silk cloth and the sam fu are purely oriental, and the straw hats are probably ancient. To these elements, we can add only the typical Chinese earrings plus Mrs. Lin's long fingernail, the latter surely a symbol of customs that are passing away.

Western influence shows itself in the machine-made cotton prints with designs borrowed from many countries including India and Japan. The use of the Japanese style rubber or composition slippers is probably the most conspicuous contribution of the island empire to Chung Nam Wan and, by the cord slipped between the toes, they are easily distinguished from those with a single strap, a local form so simple that the origin is not easy to place. Some of the women wear tennis shoes of British style, and then there is that non-Chinese garment, the brassiere. The Chinese, of course, have traditionally bound the breasts in circumstances where they would otherwise be conspicuous. The modern brassiere appears to include a contrary function, however.

Men's clothing, from hat to shoes, is almost exclusively in the English tradition, although sometimes mixed with the American. The same is true of the dress of the children. Bobbed hair can be added to the list of alien traits, a style that has finally seduced all the women in Chung Nam Wan, and the permanent wave is proving hardly less popular. Gold-capped teeth can be added to the traits of personal adornment, as well as the toothbrush and concomitant paste in occidental form. Finally with reference to dress we can note that wristwatches are Swiss, whereas that most English of accessories, the black umbrella, is, in its automatic manifestation, an export of West Germany.

Shelter. The form of the Chung Nam Wan buildings is Chinese enough, as are most of the heavier fixtures, such as the beds and the stoves, plus brush fuel for the latter. On the other hand, the concrete from which they are made is composed of Portland cement and reinforced where needed with iron rods, a technique which is European in origin. Also, the use of corrugated galvanized iron roofing on secondary structures, and the adoption of masonite for interior finishing is western. Kerosene used for lighting results from American promotion, or at least the oil first flowed freely from United States wells. Its use on sawdust for firing pig stoves, however, is a quite secondary contribution. As for the double deck bed, it could have been copied in Hong Kong from the accommodations on Western ships, but that is a guess.

Travel. Concerning travel or transportation, there seems little that directly involves the inhabitants of Chung Nam Wan that is new or intrusive. The inhabitants customarily walk wherever they go, rarely making use of the ferry, a bus, or an automobile. Indeed, there seems to be negative—and frequently quite positive—resistance to the utilization of such modern machines. The females cannot swim, and only a few of the younger males indulge when they can. Most common and most Chinese of all traits is the carrying pole with its pendent paired baskets or buckets. We may also mention the baby carrier.

Tools and implements. Clearly, the basic tools in Chung Nam Wan are still Chinese as one may conclude from the following list in which the plural forms indicate different varieties: hoe, rakes, sickle, dippers, gourd, buckets, tubs, stoneware jars, porcelain dishes, baskets, mats, brooms, palm fiber string, sharpening stones, knives, kitchen cleaver, scissors, and steelyard. In the Western tradition—on the basis of form, material, or both—one finds a comparable list: pick-mattock, trowel, insecticide sprayer, gasoline can, tin cans (actually, steel), enamel and aluminum kitchen wares, glass bottles, thermos bottle, kerosene stove, kerosene lamp and lantern, flashlight, patented clothespin, and chicken wire. Money, in notes and coins, is, of course, British, but the tradition is equally Chinese. The washboard, we suspect, was originally European.

Arts and amusements. In this category, Western influence is predominant. It is true that the adult women have suffered from the traditional Confucian disregard for female education, and the oldest male in the Chung Nam Wan group was not much better rewarded, although an abacus in his house remains as a symbol of the ancient pedagogical methods. It is also true that there is recourse to Chinese medicine periodically. Mah-jongg, a few other gambling games, an occasional opera, and attendance during the celebration of one or more of the principal annual festivals in Lung Shing is about all that remains of traditional formal amusements.

European type education has encompassed all the younger generation of Chung Nam Wan, and with it, pencils, calendars, and alarm clocks. Doctors with Western type training are more popular than their predecessors. As for amusements, the cinema and the radio have become the principal attractions, while soccer, a harmonica, and plastic toys represent less sensational impacts from the Occident.

Social and political organization. Chinese traits retained in the social and political areas of culture are most noticeable with reference to the position of women. The dominant role of the Chinese male is acknowledged by the females, even by those among them who in traditional fashion dominate. Any political consciousness seems lacking, however. Also the prominent function of women as field laborers is no European introduction. The concept of ownership of property is still Chinese, with control in the hands of males unless there is a strong-minded female as the surviving representative of the ascendant generation. We can also mention the special kit pai (chieh pai) relationship between close friends, an old Chinese institution.

Contrariwise, we see the breakdown of the ancient lineage tsuk (tsu) organization and a new emphasis on the nuclear family as the result of occidental influences. Whether changed political conditions in China or Hong Kong might restore the traditional lineage structure cannot be predicted. Possibly stable conditions may induce a new emphasis on clan (sing [hsing], or surname group) affiliations, or perhaps a British-like social system may evolve. For the moment, the struggle for existence seems to set aside any realistic new development in such matters apart from securing and extending the existing nuclear groups. The employment of farm labor is directly affected by the demands of modern industrial developments. Finally, the government is British which, despite certain similarities to that which long characterized the Middle Kingdom, is free of oppression, fiscal or physical, and leaves the guests of the Queen in full possession of their personal liberties, a condition greatly to be respected in these times.

Life cycle. As in other aspects of culture, the crises of life as known by the residents of Chung Nam Wan run the gamut of East-West alternatives. Most of the residents entered a world that was strictly Chinese. Several of the females were sold or otherwise alienated from the families into which they were born because their parents apparently could not afford to rear them. Now children are kept and watched over with typically Chinese restraints. Concubines we have in Chung Nam Wan, and also wives who have experienced blind marriage in the old-fashioned ceremonial manner of Kwangtung. The pattern of strong daughter-in-law mother-in-law discord did not have to be borrowed. This complex of customs, however, seems certain of change.

Nowhere does European influence show itself more obviously than in the institution of the hospital. There go the mothers of today to have their babies, and the children are now born into a world of doctors and nurses and aseptic smells. The younger women include those who have experienced semi-blind marriage and that of free choice. There is high probability that death, unless it comes suddenly, will be experienced in a hospital. Then the body will be removed for burial in conformity with British law, if not of the Christian church.

Religion. Chung Nam Wan still includes a traditional faith which combines elements of Confucianism, Taoism, and Buddhism. Incense burns, and there is communication direct with the deities. Even more widespread is the belief in ghostly spirits, and the acceptance of feng-shui is strong. Also, the principal holidays of the year have not lost their ancient Chinese flavor. Actually, the Roman Catholic Church is the great promulgator of spiritual change in Chung Nam Wan. Two of the three families belong to this Western religion and espouse its tenets to the degree which their comprehension allows.

The Temporal Sequence of Change

Without assuming responsibility for the detailed accuracy of a complete ethno-historical study, we can now divide our complex of traits into three groups. The first we can characterize as containing elements that have been typical of China for over a thousand years. For economy of presentation, we place them in a list following the order of our previous discussion.

Food

Rice	Peanut oil (16th century)
Vegetables	Bean curd
Terraced fields	Soy sauce
Fruit	Salted fish
Pigs	Insects
Chickens	Dogs
Ducks	Cats
Salted duck eggs	Night soil

Dress

Straw hats	Earrings
Silk	Long nails

Shelter

House style	Plank bed
Pig stove	Stools
Brush fuel	

Travel

Foot transport	Baby carrier
Carrying pole	Non-swimming

Tools and Implements

Hoe	Mats
Rakes	Brooms
Sickle	Palm fiber string
Dippers	Sharpening stones
Gourd	Knives
Buckets	Kitchen cleaver
Tubs	Lens-shaped cooking pan
Stoneware jars	Scissors
Porcelain dishes	Steelyard
Chopsticks	Money
Baskets	

Arts and Amusements

Females not educated	Opera
Abacus	Dragon Boat Festival
Chinese doctors	Gambling games

Social and Political Organization

Dominance of men	Chia concept
Female servants bought and sold	Yam ch'a (yin ch'a) at teahouse
Women working in fields	Kit pai (chieh pai) relationship

Life Cycle

Generation names	Concubinage
Selling of children	Blind marriage
Children closely watched	Mother-in-law— daughter-in-law conflict

Religion

Confucianism-Taoism-Buddhism	Belief in feng-shui
Incense	Almanac
Belief in ghosts	Annual festivals
	Belief in dreams

Another sizable group of traits includes those which were probably adopted before 1941 and, if not after 1900, then relatively recently.

Food

Wheat noodles	Cognac
Canned milk	Western type cigarettes
European style candy	

Dress

Men's dress clothing
Men's underclothes
Rubbers
Umbrella
Brassiere
Bobbed hair

Men's raincoat
Rubber sandals
Gold tooth crowns
Toothbrushes
Toothpaste
Western style soap

Shelter

Cement
Kerosene lighting

Double deck bed

Tools

Pick-mattock
Gasoline can
Tin cans
Thermos bottle
Glass bottles

Kerosene stove
Kerosene lantern
Flashlight
Chicken wire
Washboard

Arts and Amusements

Western calendar
Pencil
Alarm clock

Harmonica
Photographs
Soccer

Social and Political Organization

Hong Kong British Political system

Life Cycle

Semi-blind marriage

Finally, we conclude with a group of traits that can most safely be attributed to the period since the time of the Japanese invasion, or 1941.

Food

Wheat flour
Bread
Biscuits
Tomatoes

Soft drinks (U.S. type)
Chemical fertilizer
Insecticides

Dress

Plastic sandals
Tennis shoes
Children's clothes

Modern barbering
Permanent wave
Wristwatches

Shelter

Reinforced concrete
Kerosene-sawdust fuel

Masonite

Tools and Implements

Trowel   Aluminum wares
Sprayer   Patented clothespin
Enamelwares

Arts and Amusements

Western education   Movies
Western doctors   Radio
                                Plastic toys

Social and Political Organization

Breakdown of lineages   Modern labor system
Identity cards   Private ownership dominant

Life Cycle

Hospital births   Hospital death
Modern marriage   Modern burial

Religion

Roman Catholicism   Denial of old superstitions

As will quickly be realized, a considerable potentiality of error is involved in allocating the traits of the last two groups. Whereas the traits themselves are taken from the record of occurrences in Chung Nam Wan, since the population is made up of individuals not living there in the period of 1900 to 1941, it has been inferred that the adoption of certain traits known in the Chinese culture of Hong Kong would have affected the populace of Lung Chau. Then there are specific cases of uncertainty. Whether the brassiere was adopted before or after 1941 involves research which has not been undertaken. The same may be said of the kerosene stove and the alarm clock. Also, non-material traits are subject to a judgment of degree. The lineage system was certainly losing strength before World War II, but the real breakdown of the social organization is regarded as a post-Communist phenomenon.

Comments on Cultural Change

The cultural complex of Chung Nam Wan deserves further examination to see whether it is possible to explain and evaluate the changes which have occurred. If we consider the food habits of the people, we can safely say that they have changed fundamentally very little from the old Chinese pattern. The villagers appreciate their comestibles, as well as the manner in which they cook them. The problem for them is only to obtain a sufficiency of these desirable things to eat. The most valuable innovation, canned milk, has unquestionably been adopted because it compensates uniquely for a necessary food which may be in short supply. In the old days, a mother's lack of milk often caused the death of her child.

Changes in dress, on the other hand, have been significant, and especially for men who, moving about easily and perhaps spending money more freely than women, have apparently reacted less slowly to the status differences which one's dress can confer. Practicality is perhaps no less important, especially with regard to the clothing that males wear when they wish to dress up. The cheong sam is not an ideal costume for men of the modern world. Even the men's sam fu is not as functional as the T-shirt and shorts for summer work in the fields.* Women, with an excellent costume in the sam fu, have concentrated their modernization on fixing their hair. The impetus comes partly from the practicality of bobbed hair, and partly from the intangible impact of style. Of specific material objects, plastic shoes must be mentioned as an innovation which has clearly resulted from the cheapness and effectiveness of the material.

The Chung Nam Wan homes and their primary furnishings, like the food of the people, have also changed little. The significant contribution has been the use of reinforced concrete which enables one to build effectively in an area which has a serious shortage of timber and frequent strong winds. Travel is the least affected subdivision of culture, probably because of the isolation of the island, which does not even have a road to its suburbs. In the houses of Chung Nam Wan, light is furnished by kerosene lamps and by flashlights; glass, aluminum, and enamelware provide containers. The reasons for these adoptions are obvious enough: an old-fashioned oil lamp supplies very poor illumination compared to the kerosene equivalent and, with some important exceptions, pottery vessels prove fragile containers when they have to be cleaned.

Whereas change appears to be of minor importance with respect to material objects, there have been revolutionary disruptions in other aspects of culture. The impact of modern education in the Western tradition cannot be underestimated, and the effect of European hospitals and medicine is of complementary importance. The Chinese have been taught to value education since the days of Confucius, and it is consequently no surprise that they reach out to take advantage of the opportunity to send their children to school. The Western concern with health exerts its almost universal appeal by demonstrating empirical results that are superior to those in any other system.

Even more revolutionary is the social change resulting from the disregard of the old lineage or clan system which, especially in southeastern China, held groups of families together in a powerful political and economic organization. Emigration to Hong Kong by either individuals or nuclear families at all periods was disruptive of patrilineal bonds, but as

---

*An informant who I gave a light pair of Western trousers told me several years later that he could not go back to wearing fu as the latter chafed and no longer felt comfortable.

long as it was possible to visit or even communicate with one's relatives who still functioned as members of an extended family, the separation could be conceived of as a temporary affair, no matter how irrevocable one's isolation proved ultimately to be. With the Communist attack on the tsuk (tsu) system, and with communications discouraged, the young people know that they can no longer depend on the extended family. Therefore, even as a symbol, on Lung Chau it is rapidly disappearing down the river of time.

From the social decay of the family, a new orientation of the individual has logically followed. Women are becoming relatively free. Absolute mother-in-law control does not survive the dissolution of the group of older and dominant males who gave the sanction of classical authority to the tyranny exerted over the girls. Girls with education work outside the community. They are choosing their own husbands. They go to the government hospitals to give birth while their husbands take their place and care for the other children. When they feel abused, they go home to their mothers, and their husbands are appreciative when they return. In illness and death, the new generation goes back to the hospital, a great social institution. The connection between this overall pattern of life and that of old China soon may not be easy to discern.

Finally, in that most abstract segment of culture, religion, we see the impact of Christianity. Evaluate it as we will, there is no escaping the fact that its power in changing an alien culture proves great. This is particularly so in a situation such as Chung Nam Wan where the inherited social structure has disintegrated, leaving little formal resistance to new ideas. Priests from the West come bearing gifts, a great ethical system, and God's promise of paradise for the good and the faithful. The church also provides a new sense of belonging, a strengthened security, and a social group which is a solace to individuals who may have found their recently-acquired freedom a little bit frightening.

The World Beyond

The community of Chung Nam Wan has been in existence almost ten years. The younger generation of children know it as their only home, and even from the viewpoint of their parents, it is the center of the world. Tradition and nearness connect the hamlet with Tung Pak Wan, a settlement of a hundred people across the gap. In it, for two of the children, is their grandmother's house. All the men of Chung Nam Wan not infrequently go to the neighboring community either to work or to visit. Tung Pak Wan has the reputation of being dominated by Communists, or at least the older and richer families demonstrate their attachment to the People's Republic, but there are Christian Hakkas in the village as well. The path down to Tung Pak Wan is much steeper, however, than that to the busy town of Lung Shing, and the ancestral suburb is only rarely not bypassed by the residents of Chung Nam Wan.

It is Lung Shing that has the market, the stores and the restaurants, the schools, and the amusements. There one hears the whining lathes and whistling torches of the men who work on diesel engines which lie spread out in pieces along the sidewalks. Hidden behind the maze of structures lining the shore are the slipways of the boat builders with their sea-roving junks wedged squatly in the air. This is the island civilization of Lung Chau, ten thousand people on a few acres which have great meaning for the three families of Chung Nam Wan. To this larger world we must now turn.

The Growth of a Settlement

Preface to Part II

The settlement which we shall call Tung Pak Wan was technically a more difficult place from which to obtain and organize ethnographic data than was Chung Nam Wan. A veteran field worker would know that fact intuitively from only casual contact with the village. From a high place on the north side of the island, one could see that this community was more closely tied to the town, which meant that a great number of involvements could not be disregarded, to whatever degree they might be minimized. Indeed, at first viewing, it did not appear that a physical separation really existed between the two areas. The downward vista blended out the topographical irregularity that would later record itself unmistakably in clear kinesthetic images when one climbed back and forth over the ridge between Tung Pak Wan and Lung Shing.

Not only did the suburban character of Tung Pak Wan conflict with the simple cultural unity of a more isolated place, but also the condition and relative newness of many of the buildings themselves indicated that Tung Pak Wan was a settlement encumbered with the processes of growth, a warning of cultural complications which would not easily be fitted into established patterns already known. A few visits to the people themselves not only emphasized a lack of social integration in the village, but evoked intimations of what threatened to be fundamental conflicts. A small community in which the members do not know each other or share a preponderance of basic values, is a community of unease and insecurity. Insecure people tend to have fears and do not greet investigators with pleasure. An ethnographer had to be strongly motivated to choose Tung Pak Wan as an area for study.

That Tung Pak Wan would ultimately seduce us, however, became more and more apparent as we skirted its northwest rim on our daily visits to Chung Nam Wan. Nestling in the deep gully of the hills, with its extremities stretching out as an elliptical beach touched by the blue sea, no one could deny a physical attraction to the larger settlement. Coming and going, we were stimulated to discover what an acceptance of intimacy would really contribute to our understanding of the island. Then, when we learned that Tung Pak Wan had given birth to Chung Nam Wan—that one village, so to speak, was the parent cf the other—the lure of this fecundity

[175]

overwhelmed us and we turned irresistibly to the historical problem raised by this relationship. The contrasts that at first had been regarded as disruption assumed the new and intriguing form of a continuous growth, the processes of village formation foreshortened in time. Thus with admiration and excitement we accepted the challenge of Tung Pak Wan.

Although the simplicity of the accounts of the eighteen households might suggest a casual acquaintance, the distillation of data into comparable units resulted only from seemingly endless visits. What has been written was chosen for the symbolic value of the traits as one will realize as a knowledge of the island in its entirety is achieved. Cheong sams denote class as do earrings, a radio indicates an awareness of a larger world, Chinese doctors indicate conservatism, and the universe can be divided on the basis of political and religious prejudices.

10. Tung Pak Wan: Introduction

The Physical Setting

One might be very familiar with Lung Shing without ever becoming aware of the existence of Tung Pak Wan. Lung Shing, itself, comprises a narrow margin of flat land along a half mile of shore backed by a steep rising hill which leaves a gap at each end where projections stretch out into the sea. One must ascend toward the eastern of these gaps and then push on beyond the immediate conjunction of houses and over a ridge to discover the settlement of Tung Pak Wan in a valley (Fig. 10.1). The ridge is perhaps only eighty feet high, but the ascent is more abrupt when approaching it from town, where one climbs a series of concrete steps that lead to narrow passages between closely huddled houses. From the gap, it is only a short distance down the inclined path to the low middle point of Tung Pak Wan (Fig. 10.2).

Seen from the beach, the village lies in a narrow, steep valley marked at the northeast by a distinct promontory as well as deeply cleft rocks which make an attempt to walk to town along the adjacent shore much too difficult for any but an adventurous purpose. To the southeast, the shoreland rises again, which impediment being passed, one comes to a cove sometimes made use of by boat people to whom it gives access by sea. When one turns back, one looks northeasterly toward Lung Shing (Fig. 10.3).

The bay at Tung Pak Wan is too open to constitute an ideal harbor for small boats, although being part of the strait, fishing craft often anchor offshore as though in temporary escape from the thousands of craft that block the sight of the water closer to the town. The contact of the people on these boats with the people on shore is negligible, although some boats take on fresh water from their wells.

The view of Tung Pak Wan from the sea is the most comprehensive one. It shows a narrow stretch of land, perhaps a hundred feet wide, almost flat at first, and then rapidly rising between the gullies of two small rivulets, only the southerly of which carries any noticeable water after a few days of fair weather. This latter rivulet disappears into the rocks from which it springs at a height of about two hundred feet on the steep hillside, whereas its unidentical twin is lost among dry stones and bushes in a direct line to the pass of Chung Nam Wan. Westerly of this latter rivulet and

[177]

Fig. 10.1. View Easterly over Tung Pak Wan

Fig. 10.2. View South over Tung Pak Wan

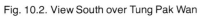

Fig. 10.3. View Northeasterly over Tung Pak Wan

above the two hundred foot line, are jagged cuts where torrential rains have furrowed the steep slope leaving completely exposed clays of brilliant color varying through shades of tan to those of yellow and orange.

As one looks down from this height, the valley appears narrower than it actually is for, as one descends, two wings are seen stretching north and south. It is on these that a great number of the Tung Pak Wan houses lie, many shaded by trees, but many more stark under the semi-tropical sun.

Purpose of the Research

As has already been indicated in the preface, it was the realization that the founding family of Chung Nam Wan had come from Tung Pak Wan and the consequent recognition of the processes of historical growth which were being compressed into a short space of time that was the most important of the several impulses which initiated the field work. It was decided to visit each household in order to discover the date and causes of its establishment. Almost unconsciously simple questions about selected aspects of the culture that would emphasize change were brought into our interviews which were made in as an informal and unhurried a manner as was possible. More intensive portrayals of family life did not seem necessary since they had been the essence of our approach in Chung Nam Wan, but in any event, all such decisions had to conform to the limitations of time. As the work progressed and the overall character of the settlement appeared, more effort was devoted on the one hand to the elements which obviously bound various of the households together, and on the other, to those aspects of the culture that caused a clear split in the unity of the village. Withal, the essential purpose of this segment of our study has been to illuminate the historical development of a village with emphasis on factors of both unification and dissension.

Problems of Field Work

Perhaps because research in Tung Pak Wan had complicating factors, it was not undertaken intensively and continuously; instead we conducted our interviews in the village a few days at a time leaving shorter or longer intervals between periods of contact. Ultimately this procedure became part of a conscious technique in de-emphasizing the investigatory aspects of our visits. Fortunately, the Chinese have a great tolerance for intellectual curiosity as we asked questions almost continuously.

The initial advantage of working through the Chin family of Chung Nam Wan, as it turned out, rebounded against us. They represented the principal household of the minority faction in Tung Pak Wan, and identification with them did not help our status with the majority. The first few days, we had hoped that we could employ the second Chin son as an assistant. At the age of seventeen, having lived almost his entire life in Tung Pak Wan, it seemed that his knowledge of the people in the community would be invaluable, and that he could quickly be trained to obtain more. Instead, we not only found that his knowledge of the village was consistently unreliable, but discovered that he had been conditioned to an avoidance of many of his neighbors, while he had not even met a number of the newcomers in the settlement. In these characteristics, however, he proved only to be like most of the residents of Tung Pak Wan.

One difficulty of working in the village was the attitude of some individuals in households said to be Communist. To them, an American was symbolically an anti-Communist and Christian. These are pre-ordained conditions from which it is difficult to maneuver into a favorable position. Contrariwise, among individuals who were not nominally pro-Communist or who were Christians, there was a theoretical advantage. Both reputations would gladly have been sacrificed for an unprejudiced character.

While on the subject of informants, one piece of good fortune may be mentioned. The house high on the hillside nearest the trail from Lung Shing to Chung Nam Wan was occupied by an elderly widow related to the richest family in Tung Pak Wan. Because of its proximity, we occasionally stopped at her house before we began our regular visits to the village, and she always welcomed us thereafter. Best of all, however, was the fact that most people are hospitable in small communities, and we must report in tribute to the villagers of Tung Pak Wan, that even among those whose welcome was least cordial, none closed the door in our face and none refused a reasonable minimum of answers to our multiplicity of questions.

One result of these complications was the necessity of using one after another interpreters. All preferred to work in other parts of the island. As for the ethnographer himself, having perhaps a modicum of oppositional tendencies, there was some provocation in the delicate operation of drawing a few bucketfuls of data from the cultural wells of Tung Pak Wan.

With regard to the information that we did succeed in obtaining, certain objective facts should be noted. First, a date line at the year 1960 may be assumed for our statements unless some other year is specifically indicated. Since we continued the study in 1961, there may be areas of inexactitude, but this being noted, it is assumed that the variation should not greatly matter in research which is primarily concerned with larger units of time, insofar as time is considered at all.

Secondly, dates given for a preceding decade are not always reliable, although considerable effort was made to check them. The Chinese system of noting chronology is not one that simplifies for illiterate persons the art of remembering some past point in time. It should be recalled that even in the West with a continuous serial system of numbering years, rather than counting them in cycles, few people can give accurately the significant dates in their lives. As one control on this problem, when a preliminary list of the temporal order of the establishment of households in Tung Pak Wan had been made, return visits were undertaken to ask whether the family had arrived before or after the others nearest on the list. On occasions it seemed that there would be no resolution of the problems since they became involved with such questions as whether a husband or a wife was married at the time of his or her first residence in Tung Pak Wan, whether they lived with either employers or relatives or in their own house, and if the latter, when it was built, and so on. Irrespective of the absolute validity of details, however, the pattern of historical development seems unquestionably to have been set.

Thirdly, we should specifically reiterate the near impossibility of converting into the Western system the Chinese ages of village people who do not know the day of their birth or have had it accidentally confused on their identity cards. The problem has been greatly simplified by not attempting to resolve it. Therefore one may subtract the average year and a half from those ages given, remembering that a Chinese is spoken of as one year old when born and two years old the next New Year's Day, even if he was born the previous evening.

Fourthly, in speaking of marriage customs, we have used the terms blind, semi-blind, and modern to denote the three approaches to marriage. Blind marriage, a translation of the Chinese expression refers to a union established without either husband or wife having seen each other (at least with any anticipation of such a relationship) before the ceremony. Semi-blind marriage refers to a union before which the principal parties had been given the opportunity to look at each other with at least the nominal right to refuse the chosen partner. Modern marriage simply implies free choice on the part of the marriage partners.

It should be noted that references concerning an ability to read or to write refer to the traditional Chinese characters. With these preliminary guideposts established, we can now proceed to a consideration of the households of Tung Pak Wan, which for reasons of convenience and anonymity, have been indicated by number rather than by name. In dealing with them we have first located the residence, then surveyed the physical establishment, and finally moved on to an introduction of the family members. A general range of cultural characteristics is then surveyed for each household in the order suggested by the table of contents under Chapter 12, a section in which the selected aspects of culture have been reviewed. Finally, at the end of each description of a household, there is a paragraph which is in large measure an ethnographer's commentary. These paragraphs have been specifically designated, not because they might not be distinguished as such, but because of the importance of setting apart data that at least approximate empirical fact from those that represent opinion, however scholarly. Such epistemological niceties have always been the principal theoretical concern of the writer[1] and will be more significantly stressed in later sections of this work.

---

1. See, for example, Osgood, 1951a.

11. The Eighteen Households

Household One

The house of the first family of Tung Pak Wan is close to the shore a short distance south of the larger of the two rivulets which drain the area, and it is consequently one of the more distant establishments from the viewpoint of a person approaching from town (Fig. 11.1). One reaches the door by walking between a long, double line of pigpens which, to the unprejudiced visitor, are more interesting than unpleasant (Fig. 11.2).

The living quarters of the family consist of a two-story, basically concrete structure with somewhat decrepit solid wood shutters which are swung outward in pairs from the iron barred windows. Most unusual is a small wood balcony on the front facing the sea. When admired, it was said never to be used, or at least this was intimated by the response, "We go to bed at nine o'clock," which statement, of course, was meant to imply that everyone had to work too hard for any such relaxation. Members of the family certainly enjoyed their periods of ease, but they were apparently not taken on the balcony. At the far edge of the flat in front of the house—or directly across from the door—was the kitchen, open except for the back side and a gable roof. In it was an excellent stove with three fire pits, and a collection of the complementary utensils distinguished by the shine on the aluminum potlids. The family is also notable in having three wells, which were dug to provide an adequate water supply, and in having electric lines, not only for light but also for power. There are two cats in Household One and they are said to have done a great deal to decrease the population of rats. Two dogs defy visitors with bark and fang so vicious that even the most sympathetic newcomer is pleased to see their owners restrain them quickly.

The head of the household is a man of approximately forty-two.* On the holiday that we found him at home, it was extremely hot, and he was dressed in an undershirt and shorts, which made his wristwatch the more evident. His wife, whom we saw more frequently, typically wears a sam fu with a bluish-gray top over a light colored under sam and black silk

---

*This was indirectly computed from data supplied by his wife; by the same method his later data give forty-five.

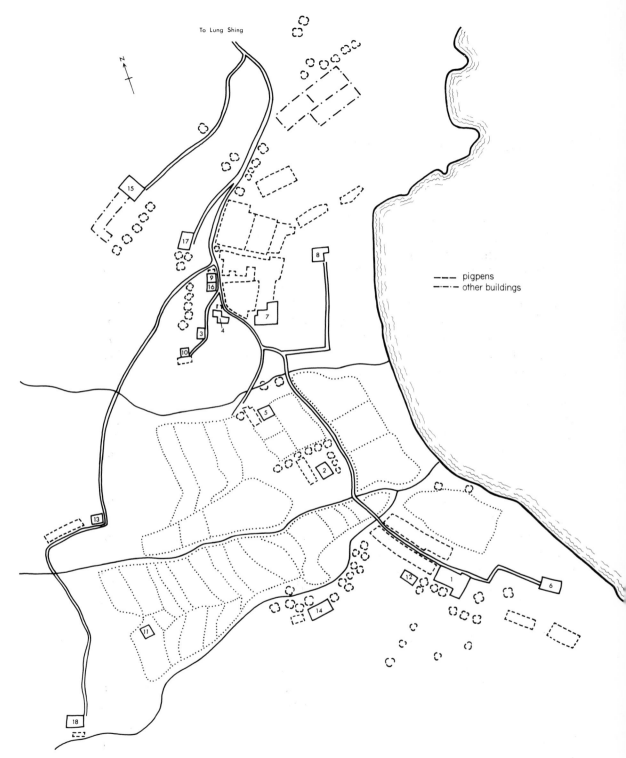

To Lung Shing

pigpens
other buildings

Fig. 11.1. Tung Pak Wan Showing Location of Houses by Household Number

Fig. 11.2. Pigpens at Entrance of Household One

trousers.* On her feet are slippers held in place by a plastic band over the flat top of the foot. She, likewise, has a wristwatch, and her bobbed black hair is set in a permanent wave. She is probably a few years younger than her husband.

There are seven children in the family, six of whom are daughters aged seventeen, twelve, nine, seven, five, and three; the son is fourteen. The oldest daughter was not seen, but the other children wear European style clothing, the boy favoring shorts. There are also two men employed to care for the pigs, as well as an amah to whom we can attribute the shine on the potlids. The amah wears the characteristic costume of black trousers (fu) and white jacket, although the latter has a very small greenish blue stripe. When needed, she dons a dark blue apron with a protective bib. She is not a member of the well-known coterie of amahs who use the single long pigtail as an insignia but rather wears a straight black bob.

The father of the family evinces no feeling about the problem of population increase and says it is no concern of his. He does favor modern

---

*The sam fu is the most common costume of the Chinese of Kwangtung, and by no means restricted to that province. The sam consists of a loose coat or jacket with a soft vertical collar and long sleeves. The woman's sam opens down the right side and lacks pockets; the man's down the middle of the front and has two or more pockets. The fu of both sexes consists of loose trousers like pajama bottoms reaching to between the knees and ankles. The material is usually cotton or silk, the latter often coated (see Fig. 2.8).

procedures in choosing a marriage partner, however, as opposed to the traditional or semi-traditional methods. He also believes in education for his children, although he himself did not finish primary school. He had attended a private school in Lung Shing (School C)* and also another primary school in the town across the strait. Several of his children now go to school in Lung Shing, but he hopes to send them to Canton, where his eldest daughter is in school, when they have finished their elementary education. He states that to do so will save him a great deal of money.

There is a radio in Household One, but no one plays any musical instrument. The father indulges in mah-jongg which is the principal gambling game of Hong Kong, the younger children swim, and everyone likes to go to the movies. Since he works in the city, the father sometimes attends a cinema in Victoria. For medical assistance, a doctor with Western type training is the one usually turned to, although the services of a Chinese style doctor may be called upon. But, as the father says, "for cholera, of course, what could a Chinese style doctor do?"

If religion plays any role in the household, it is a quiescent one. Political matters are not discussed with comparative strangers, although the head of the household does not hesitate to say that the British do very well in their government of Hong Kong. Indirectly, it may be inferred that the household has a Communist orientation by the fact that its head works for a monthly salary as a caterer who supplies food for the staff of a newspaper which is generally known to be Communist, and by the fact that Canton is selected as the place for the advanced education of his children. The head of the family does not belong to the Lung Chau Kaifong Association. It is certain that the family pays taxes on its land, but its status as the Queen's tenants—always something of a mystery—is not clear, especially in so far as it relates to the question of the extent of the land under its control.

Household One produces enough vegetables for home consumption and, in season, to sell in the Lung Shing market. In the winter, vegetables are taken to Victoria, but this outlet may be related to the owner's position as caterer. In any event, vegetable growing, although probably the largest of such undertakings on Lung Chau, is a minor activity compared to pig raising. On our first visit, the mistress of the family stated that they had between 130 to 140 animals, which is too many pigs to verify by casual glances. Also there is said to be more than 4000 square feet of pens. Water is pumped by means of an electric motor and piped to the sties where the pigs are given a bath twice a day in hot weather by the two hired men. Although some greens are grown for the pigs, their main food is lees, eight buckets of which are bought daily at a distillery across the strait for a little over fifty cents per bucket. Rice chaff is also purchased for the same purpose. The

---

*School designations by letter refer to Lung Shing schools. They are described in Chapter 42.

pigs are sold in the Hong Kong market, ideally only when the price is favorable. It is said that the profit has been small in the past two years, but that the price improved in 1960. There are also "a few tens of chickens" belonging to Household One, but not pigeons. Pigeon raising has been considered, but there is said not to be enough help to take care of them. At times, they do have a few ducks to supply the table. The papaya and guava trees around the house are incidental to the economy. If there is fruit, the family eats it, but they do not pay attention otherwise as the trees are said to be more trouble than they are worth.

It appears obvious that there is no lack of food for the family. As is customary, when pork is to be eaten, a few catties are purchased from one of the butchers in Lung Shing. The head of the family states that he usually orders shrimp and pork dumplings for breakfast at a teahouse. Also, like most men, he likes to drink. He smokes only periodically, however, and admits that he cannot tell which brand of cigarette is superior if he tries.

Household One was established in Tung Pak Wan about 1930 by the widowed mother of the present head of the family when the latter was twelve to fifteen years old. He was born in the town across the strait. His father is reliably reported as having been a Hakka from Lan K'ou which is north of Tzu Chin, but the mother who founded the settlement was a Cantonese* from Hsiao Lan in the Chung Shan district (hsien) of Kwangtung (Fig. 3.1) and, for various reasons, the family is generally regarded as now belonging to the latter group. The move was made on the advice and help of the widow's relatives who pointed out that it would be more economical to acquire some land on Lung Chau than to continue to pay rent in the town across the narrow strait where she then lived and had borne her two sons and a daughter. Presumably the small valley of Tung Pak Wan was selected for her residence because the land was available, but the details are no longer clear to the family. It is reported that the original stone and cement house—which was replaced by the present residence in 1953—was built on a hard, smooth area indicating previous use. Also a lot of broken brick and tile were found suggesting that the site had once been used for a kiln. Of this, no corroborating evidence has been found. The founding widow died soon after the Japanese invasion, an event which worried her greatly, and her eldest son remained on the property. His younger brother and sister are both married and live in Kwangtung. Another sister lives in Lung Shing.

Members of Household One claim to have shown consideration for their neighbors, although to do so at times has not always been easy. There is

---

*The word *Cantonese* is used in this monograph to refer to a native of Kwangtung Province (or Hong Kong) whose family speech is of the standard Hong Kong Cantonese in contrast, for example, to that of other districts, such as Ch'ao An, and to other groups, such as Hakka, Hoklo, or Tanka.

evidence that they are speaking the truth. Some time ago, government agents told them they were holding more land than they were entitled to on the basis of the tax which they paid. Given a choice of paying more, they refused, and the beach area in front of the house was then assigned to a company. There was a dispute over the amount of land which the assignee marked off as his own, and the latter won. Then the owners of the company decided they did not want to use the land and offered to return it all to Household One, but the annual tax, said to be $300, was deemed prohibitive. Recently, the land was rented to people in the fish drying and sauce-making business, which smells. This is not a happy situation, but Household One hospitably supplies drinking water to the workers on the basis that the unpleasantness is no fault of theirs. Also other neighbors and sometimes boat people come for water, which is perhaps explainable on the basis that the present mistress of Household One came from a boat family.

Commentary. The people of Household One were not an easy family with whom to make contact. Their dogs were ferocious. When we had the courage to disregard them, we found the lady of the house hospitable, as also was the husband when we discovered him at home some time later. Furthermore, on other visits, and on the innumerable occasions over the years when we entered the premises, we never suffered any unpleasantness. Nevertheless our contacts were more restricted than we would have liked. This was basically because the head of the household worked regularly in Hong Kong while his older children have recently spent most of their time in schools in Canton where their mother periodically visits them. All in all, the intelligible universe of the members of Household One seems large from the viewpoint of Tung Pak Wan. Their knowledge of a metropolis such as modern Canton as well as that of Hong Kong, their obvious identification with the People's Republic of China, the scale of their pig raising and general economic level, even the recent diversity of language and origins, are all factors which broaden their world and set them apart from most families on the island. It was not surprising to find that the head of the family not only has visited the most distant settlement of Sai Mi Wan, although he knows none of its residents, but has even climbed over to Chung Nam Wan for a few hours of pleasure in being alone.

Household Two

The second family in Tung Pak Wan has a two-room single-story concrete house set back a short way from the beach between the two rivulets in approximately the central line of the settlement. One passes directly in front of it when going to town from Household One. The gable roof paralleling the sea is of tiles and there is a definite yard protected from the path by high bamboos and a fence. All in all, the aspect is one of the pleasantest in the community, but at times there is a positive plague of flies that enamel dishes laden with poison do not noticeably diminish. The head of the house says the flies came when refuse brought in baskets from Lung Shing began to be buried on the beach, but there is also some reason to suspect the extensive piggeries which have been developed on both sides of his domain.

The interior of the house with its concrete floor appears to be unusually well-furnished, a circumstance attributed to the fact that when the head of the house became engaged, his fiancée's family asked that various articles be supplied as part of the marriage agreement. This was admittedly an unusual request, but no one suggested that it may have been a compensatory reaction since the girl's family were boat people. In any event, the house contains, among other things, an elaborate chest of drawers, on which has been placed a small aquarium. In one of the rooms is a spring bed with a pleasant mat on top, as well as a second bed made with the customary boards stretched on wood horses. Besides these exceptional items, there are a folding wood chair, a typical wood stool, three thermos bottles, a miscellaneous collection of medicines, a large supply of stacked boxwood for cooking, some cockroaches, and a spider of extraordinary size on a roof beam. There are also many less conspicuous rats and four cats to chase them away, but the latter are reported to do their task poorly. A bitch offers little assistance, her attention being directed to six puppies which the owners will gladly sell. We should add that for two years Household Two has been provided with electricity having meters for both lighting and power (power costing less). When there is a storm, the wires sometimes sparkle from short circuits and the women become frightened. They have a well in which there is said to be always sufficent water.

The head of the house is a man of twenty-eight, and his pretty young wife is only twenty. They have been married three years and have an eight-month old son whose elaborate blue "walker" with casters in Western style is a conspicuous addition to child training equipment in Tung Pak Wan. The father's mother, aged fifty-seven, lives with them. She has rheumatism in her hands and can no longer work, but she looks after her grandson. In dress, the family is not distinctive. The old lady typically wears a black sam fu as does her daughter-in-law but, whereas the older woman uses slippers with straps across the upper part of the foot, the younger has adopted the Japanese style with a thong between the first and second toe. She also sometimes wears a light-colored sam fu, or at least a light-colored sam. Both women have straight bobbed hair and gold wedding rings, and the wife wears a wristwatch. The grandmother has a gold crown on her second right upper incisor. More notable is the silver anklet with bell which adorns the baby above his left foot.

The head of the house was married semi-blind. His wife said they were simply introduced to each other beforehand and she agreed to her parents' decision. Even the grandmother says that blind marriage is doomed and that most people are marrying partners of their own choice. She states that the marriage of a girl either to her father's sister's or mother's brother's son is not proper, but that one to a mother's sister's son is acceptable. The family view about having children seems to be that if one is rich, a large number are desirable but, if one is poor, they are not. The members of Household Two have enjoyed only limited opportunities for education. The head of the house did attend School B for three years after World War II when it was still conducted in the Mission. His wife went to a private school in Lung Shing but only for a few months.

Like many other residents of Lung Chau, the head of Household Two, when asked about amusements, immediately replied that they have no time to do such things as attend a cinema. This is not quite true (the rest of the family came home from the cinema a half hour later), but for various reasons they may enjoy institutionalized recreations less than some other families. They do not indulge in mah-jongg. No one swims or plays a musical instrument, but there is a radio in the house. The people seem healthy but, when necessary, a doctor with Western type training is chosen as he reputedly cures a disease more quickly. In religion, the family is conservative, or at least there are several altars to ancient deities in the house including the Stove God. Another seemed to be a God who looks after children. They did not know that the birthday of the Earth God had just been celebrated although his altar was at the right bottom of the door, but they did offer the gratuitous comment that most families in Tung Pak Wan burned incense on the 1st and 15th of each month.

Politics is a sensitive area for the head of the house. He states flatly that he does not care whether the British ever leave Hong Kong or not, claiming that the members of his family will have to work anyway, which is the important matter. He has never belonged to a Kaifong Association. The economic situation is what really occupies his mind. Living expenses for the family approximate $400 a month which he says he is not making (August) but, if the price of vegetables is high enough in the winter, it will compensate for the summer losses. Although basically a farmer, the head of Household Two devotes much of his time to a business in the town across the strait. This organization, of which he is a partner, is engaged in buying refuse from a factory which bottles a soy bean drink (which looks like milk) and selling it to pig raisers. They pay $1.75 to $2.00 a bucket for the refuse and sometimes have to sell at a loss, as they were doing at the time, or dump it in the sea as they had to do later. The partners are said to have invested several thousand dollars in the business at the start.

Fig. 11.3. String Beans on Bamboos at Household Two (upper); Home of Household Three (lower)

The vegetable business at home is taken care of by a hired man who is paid $120 a month plus his meals. The task is made easier than for most farmers by the utilization of an electrically powered pump which discharges water from the excellent well through a plastic hose. In August, the crop comprised green string beans and sz kwa (ssu kua), or angled luffa, a common Cantonese vegetable which looks like a long, hairy cucumber. Flowering Chinese cabbage was eventually to be substituted for the beans. The beans, growing on bamboo frames (Fig. 11.3) give a distinctive and verdurous character to the immediate surroundings of Household Two, and the owner only regrets that the rats eat so many of them.

There are also over twenty pigs to be taken care of, and as many chickens. This labor falls on the wife, who also does the housework. She splashes water on the pigs three times a day in the hot summer weather. They seldom become ill, and her husband knows which medicine to buy if they do. The family does not bother with either pigeons or ducks. Their papaya trees were blown down by the typhoon of 1960, and they have not planted any more because they take so long to mature and the fruit sells for so little. This same disinterest applies to their few remaining guava trees.

Apparently, the family eats fairly well. It is said that the expenditure for purchased food supplying two meals for four adults is $3.50 per day. The master of the house admits to drinking on occasion, but only beer. He also smokes, and his mother is attached to her new metal water pipe of the type commonplace in south China, which friends bought for her in Canton at a cost of $20.00. She added that such a pipe cost only $3.00 in her village when she was young.

The paternal home of the grandmother in Household Two was in Hsiao Lan, Chung Shan (hsien), Kwangtung, a district distinguished as that in which Sun Yat Sen was born. She came to Tung Pak Wan in 1942 as a widow bringing two sons, the elder of whom now works in Hong Kong, while the younger, who was then eleven or twelve, has taken over the homestead. The opportunity which attracted the widow was not hard to discover: she is the sister of the widow who established Household One and was apparently happy to share the then plentiful land. "Why don't you come?" the latter is reported as saying. "I'll give you some land. It is safe." So it proved, but not pleasantly so. When bombs fell in the sea nearby, they hid under the beds. Before long, only her elder sister (of Household One), herself, and her younger son remained in the settlement, the others including her elder son having returned to their native village. The grandmother reports that she and her sister threw stones at the fishermen who came from their boats to steal their sweet potatoes and taro. Vegetables sold for as much as $15 to $18 a catty during the Japanese occupation, and rice reached $340 a catty. There is also another parallel between these first two households as the young wife comes from the boat people and was born on the water. Her parents now have a small fishing vessel which operates from Lung Chau.

Commentary. Although the members of the family are clearly more restricted in movement than those of Household One, the head does have a business off the island, while to his mother, Kwantung is still very real. Both have been to Chung Nam Wan once, and both have visited the most distant settlement of Lung Chau, while even the world of the new mother embraces the life of the fishermen who go daily to sea. This younger woman showed herself exceptional in Tung Pak Wan by an overt graciousness with which she seemed to approach people in general. Without being forward, she would smile when an occasion offered as does a happy person who naturally likes other human beings. Youth, good health, and probably the background of lesser retraints, which characterize the boat people, must have contributed to her personality. Unfortunately her husband gave almost the opposite impression, and he has the reputation of being unfriendly and saturnine. Often he would not look at us, or even voice a greeting. From the ordinary Chinese viewpoint he was rude, but to us he had a quality that was endearing. Perhaps he had been somewhat put upon by his mother, a strong character, and certainly he had growing economic problems. When we forced a package of cigarettes on him, he could not keep himself from returning us a smile. Later, we heard that he had been seriously ill.

Household Three

As one comes from town, Household Three occupies the third of four homes on a narrow strip cut into the hillside. It is reached by turning up off the main path as it descends to the base of the valley toward the houses previously described. Given a first house beyond the rivulets and a second between them, it was probably the most logical place for the third if the builder wished neither to encroach on his neighbors nor to climb up the hill behind them. The gable-roofed structure has one room and was made of concrete with a cement floor by the present owner (Fig. 11.3). The windows are slightly larger than in some houses. In one corner is a bed with an enclosing mosquito net. On top of the bed is a folded cot. Bags, baskets, and numerous blackened kettles hang from the ceiling. On the floor stands a large brown stoneware jar decorated with a buff-colored dragon. There is also a small tub for bathing the baby and a kerosene stove. Numerous flies walk on the cement. Above a round folding table is a calendar with a sheet to be pulled off for each day. Also on the wall is a crucifix with a colored picture of the Virgin Mary below it. There is no electricity in the house. Nor is there a dog or cat. Water is drawn from the well of a neighbor.

In the house live a husband and wife with five children, four of whom are daughters aged ten, seven, four, and one. The only son is two. The father, a rather gaunt man with a striking, pock-marked face and hair sprinkled with gray, is forty-six, while his wife, a sweet-faced woman with fine white teeth is thirty-six. She characteristically wears a black sam fu and wood sandals with a black plastic strap across the top of the foot. Not unfrequently she goes barefoot and, on occasion, she puts on a pair of painted wood shoes with red plastic straps. She annually visits a barber shop in Lung Shing just before New Year's where she is given a haircut and a permanent wave. If she owns any jewelry, there is no sign of it, and she said that her generation of girls did not have their ears pierced as their mothers and grandmothers did. The children wear a miscellany of European type clothing.

The head of the house said that he married his wife by free choice in 1945, and that he had been introduced to her in their native village of Tzu Chin by her brother. Interestingly enough, on an earlier occasion, his wife had told us that she was married blind. Obviously the evolution of a situation in which blind marriage is normal to one of free choice is not quite as simple as we had once thought. The wife had told us that she believed that the modern procedure is better, but that she does not comprehend how young people arrange it. Pursuing the subject further, she said that she did not think a girl should marry her father's sister's son, but that to marry one's mother's brother's son is a fairly common practice. Later she added that it is all right to marry one's mother's sister's son.

The last baby was born in the house, rather than in the hospital across the strait as is more usual among the islanders, but a nurse did come for the delivery. The mother states that she has too many children and would like to give the little one away so that she can go out to work, but she knows of no one who wants it. Of the possibility of contraception, she is ignorant.

No one in the household has ever attended school except the eldest daughter who in the summer of 1960 had finished second grade in School D in Lung Shing. This cost six or seven dollars a month. With the birth of the last daughter, no further education can be afforded. According to his wife, the head of the household can read and write a little. He also has a general comprehension of how to play mah-jongg, but has no time to do so. She says they go to the movies about once a year. They have no radio. The two eldest girls sometimes go bathing in the bay which is only a few hundred feet distant, and the older one can swim about twenty feet. The members of Household Three seldom go to a doctor. Sometimes leung ch'a (liang ch'a)* is purchased at a Chinese medicine shop for the children or, if the latter are not well, the shopkeeper is told the symptoms and he sells them medicine.

In China, the family was traditionalist in religion, but after coming to Hong Kong, religious activities ceased until about 1958 when one of the daughters became seriously ill. A Catholic priest arranged for the child to be sent to the government hospital across the strait and the mother promised that they would become Christians if the child was cured. This being the case, the whole family is now Catholic and attends church on Sunday. In their native village, everyone worshipped their ancestors, our infor-

---

*Perhaps we should state again that leung ch'a means "cool tea," an herb drink taken periodically as a tonic. It is sold by street vendors, in groceries, and various shops.

mant said, but now as Catholics, they are not allowed to have ancestral tablets. They are also forbidden to make extra money by pasting tinfoil for the gold-silver paper factories. The priest comes once or twice a year to bless the house and put holy water on it; also if the family fails to go to mass a few times, someone comes to find out why. The head of the house says that now, as a Catholic, he has no belief in feng-shui; on the other hand, he adds that he paid no attention to it when he built his house before he became a Catholic. They see no contradiction, however, in celebrating five of the traditional Chinese feasts: the Dragon Boat Festival on the 5th of the 5th Month, others on the 14th of the 7th and 15th of the 8th, as well as the Winter Arriving Festival and New Year's itself. They added that in their home village of Tzu Chin, only three festivals were celebrated: the 5th of the 5th month, the 14th of the 7th, and New Year's. At the latter time, they try to give a red paper packet containing ten cents to all the children in Tung Pak Wan. Also it may be added that when the head of the house is presented with extra money by his employer to have a feast in honor of the Earth God on the 2nd and 16th of the month, he does so.

According to the mother in the family, the British govern the Colony better than would the Chinese. Having no permit for their land, they apparently pay no taxes on it. Also, they are not members of a Kaifong Association. Economically, the household is one of the poorer ones in Tung Pak Wan. At the time of our first interview, the father of the family was working as a coolie on the mainland where he was paid five to seven dollars a day or sometimes less. He returned home only on the weekends. Later, he obtained a job taking care of pigs in Sai Mi Wan at the other end of Lung Chau. This allows him to sleep at home every night, but he leaves at five in the morning and does not return until the evening at eight. For his labor he receives $100 a month, which his wife points out is too little income on which to raise five children. Additional money, however, is supplied by his employer for food so that he and his one or two co-workers may eat two or three meals during the day which they cook for themselves. On a feast day he has been observed to buy a chicken from a farmer, and then return a few minutes later to trade it for a fatter one. Furthermore, his employer has recently given him two little pigs which his wife takes care of along with about twenty chickens. Any eggs are sold for about thirty cents each (summer price), the money being preferred to the extravagance of eating such expensive food. There are no ducks, pigeons, fruit trees, or garden belonging to the family of Household Three. Their relative and neighbor, Mrs. Chin, provided them with a place to plant vegetables in Chung Nam Wan, but they gave it up as they could not make the undertaking profitable. It may be added that the head of the house smokes and also likes to drink wine very much, whereas his wife does neither.

The family of Household Three has its patrilineal origin in Tzu Chin, Hui Yang hsien, Kwangtung, as do those of One and Four and, more significantly, the deceased head of Household Four and the present head of Household Three were the sons of two Hakka brothers. The Mr. Chin of Household Three first came to Hong Kong about 1940 because he thought he could earn more money. He settled in Lung Shing simply by chance. Through friends from Hui Yang he met the family of Household One and went to work for them building a shack on the site of his later house. Not long after the Japanese invasion, he returned to his native town of Tzu Chin with the family of his cousin, the stepfather of Mr. Chin of Chung Nam Wan, as has been mentioned in our account of that hamlet.

During our conversations, one facet of special interest was the descriptions of Tzu Chin, a town in the center of a Hakka area. It was claimed that one could walk five days in any direction without coming upon a predominance of people who spoke any other language. When asked, our informant said that he could walk one hundred li in a day, although with his wife, only seventy. We were particularly interested in the wai lung (wei lung), or fence-cage houses, known to be built by the Hakka, and fascinated by his explanation that, at least recently, they were not constructed for defense but to obtain the proper feng-shui in their relation to the hills.[1] Some wai lung in Tzu Chin provided a home for over a thousand individuals of the same tsuk (tsu), or lineage. These three-story circular apartment houses were built of brick, kiln dried on the outside and sun dried on the inside where the rain does not strike them. Further data were not forthcoming as our informant had not lived in one of these communal dwellings himself, nor had he returned to Tzu Chin since World War II.

When he resettled in Tung Pak Wan in 1946, he brought his wife of a few months with him and they enlarged his original dwelling. She told us that she cried periodically for the first years because she was so lonesome, a condition aggravated by the fact that, although there were numerous people around, she could speak no Cantonese. Also she was accustomed to urban surroundings of a traditional type while the path into Lung Shing was bordered by graves (Fig. 11.4). Perhaps that was one reason the husband wrote to the cousin in Tzu Chin who later founded the hamlet of Chung Nam Wan, asking him to join them. The head of Household Three went back to work for Household One, but only at intervals.

Commentary. As friends of the Chin family, we were pleasantly received in Household Three on our first visit although there did not seem to be the intimacy between the two families that we expected. Our expectation was naive as we had assumed the relationship to be closer; in Chinese

---

1. See Boyd, 1962: 103–08; 127–32.

Fig. 11.4. Graves on Path to Tung Pak Wan

terms of reference, one can speak of paternal cousins as brothers. Apart from the educational deficiencies of the members of Household Three, it must also be recognized that although nominally these were two Hakka and Catholic families of the same lineage, the three adults of the one were all born as Cantonese, not Hakka, and between the two heads, cultural and personality differences were clearly discernible. From our point of view, this was chiefly significant in so far as it might effect lineage cooperation between families of immigrants. We knew the young mother of five children better than we knew her husband. She was still sufficiently attractive as a female to perhaps think of herself with ego satisfaction and, other things being equal, as having at least that slight superiority over her husband which he most of all may have appreciated. Good people we found them with an intelligible universe which threatened to close in around them. The husband knows the physical terrain of the island better than most residents, while his wife is so tied down that she almost never leaves home except for her daily visits to the Lung Shing market. She has not been to Victoria in ten years, and her eldest daughter, who has lived that long, has never been to the great metropolis at all.

Household Four

The house borders the present-day path which runs from the town. It is pocketed on a small artificial flat area directly below House Three and near the bottom of the land rising to the ridge which separates Tung Pak Wan from the town of Lung Shing. The basic structure, including the floors, is of stone and cement like the homes previously described, but whereas House One has a flat concrete roof and House Two one that is gabled and tiled, the roofs of House Four, like that of House Three, are of less durable material. The plan of House Four shows a typical rectangular building with a smaller one adjoined at the southerly end near the eastern corner (Fig. 11.5). The main northerly building is distinguished by a corrugated metal shed roof that slopes easterly down toward the sea, while the smaller addition has an east-west gable roof of boards covered with tarpaper. There is a crudely constructed kitchen shed across a small courtyard, facing the door of the main building. Unfortunately, an off-island visitor, if not distracted by the stench from the large number of pigs raised by a neighbor, is sure to be disturbed by the myriad flies.

Two typical plank beds used by two adolescent boys stand end to end in the main room, while the most notable thing in the southern, occupied by their mother, is a large, wood encased pendulum clock of a type which has been popular in Hong Kong as it was several generations ago in the

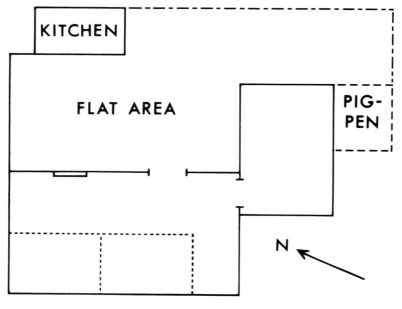

Fig. 11.5. House Four

United States. It was received as a wedding present when her eldest son married. The water for the household is brought from the well of a neighbor, and electricity is still something seriously hoped for.

Household Four is the residence of the widow Chin and her two younger sons, all of whom have appeared in the account of Chung Nam Wan, in which place the eldest son and his wife now reside with their children on the family farm. Therefore there is no need to elaborate on the dress or domestic life of this group. It should be recorded, however, that Mrs. Chin has no government paper for her house site. Also, she belongs to the Kaifong Association of the town across the strait rather than to that of Lung Chau. She says that the officers of the latter group would not let her join because they viewed her as a Communist due to the reputation which has been gained by Tung Pak Wan's most prominent citizens.* "How can I be a Communist?" asks Mrs. Chin. "I am a Catholic and go to church." Her membership dues consist of $2.20 per month, and she states that in the few years she has belonged to the Association, she has not received any of the aid which sometimes passes through the hands of such organizations. This, she admits, may be due to the fact that, living so far away, she does not hear of any distribution that is scheduled. The main advantage of the Association from her point of view is burial insurance, $500 being paid on the death of a member in her category of payment.

Since the economic activities of the Chin family center on farming in Chung Nam Wan, they have no vegetable garden in Tung Pak Wan. Neither are there pigs, chickens, pigeons, ducks, or pets of any kind. There are not even fruit trees. Lately the widow has joined in the common activity of making paper for the dead for a Lung Shing factory. The paper, tinfoil, and paste are supplied her. She places a piece of the straw-colored paper in front of her, adds two inch-square pieces of tinfoil and sweeps them with paste so that they will adhere to the next piece of paper, and so on ad infinitum. She completes three piles two feet high of these pasted papers for $1.60. Sometimes she gets a neighbor's little girl to help her. "A whole family could not make twenty cents if they worked all day," she comments sardonically. Then she adds, "Of course, I have nothing else to do."

The history of the Chin family has been recorded in our study of Chung Nam Wan, and it is necessary only to mention once again that the widow herself is a Cantonese from Chung Shan as was her first husband, while her deceased second spouse was a Hakka from Tzu Chin in the Hui Yang hsien of Kwangtung, as was his cousin in Household Three. Also her

---

*Her assumption, however firmly believed, is probably not correct. If the Lung Chau Kaifong Association refused her application for membership, it was most likely because of either the restriction on the number of members at that time or her age.

two younger sons who share the house were born in the Tzu Chin home of their Hakka father. Soon after World War II, the head of Household Four was working for the family of Household One, and his widow says that the position was found through friends, not through his cousin. She also denies the cousin's priority in other respects such as who was the earlier resident, but we have had to adjudicate against her in this instance.

On one thing there seems to be unanimity of opinion. It was their employer in Household One who indicated the area where the Chin cousins might build, pointing out that it was government land. Later, perhaps disturbed by the development in this area of the valley, the same employer obtained a crown permit for the land which reached from his original holding around that of Household Two, thus making the rights of the newcomers even less tenable than they were in the first place.* If insecurity has resulted, no occupant of Household Three or Four has said so to us. The Widow Chin does state that she prefers Chung Nam Wan because it is quiet. On the other hand, she does not like to climb over the hill. It is perhaps surprising that she has visited Sai Mi Wan at the other end of the island a few times as she does not like walking at all. As we expected, she has not climbed to the top of any of Lung Chau's several hills.

Commentary. We admired the mistress of Household Four from our first meeting and came to know her well, despite an understandable reticence, and occasional contradictions about her early life. Her marriages provided contact with more than one language and culture, and she may well have been the dominant partner in one of the relationships if not both. Some of her ambition and intelligence has passed on to her sons, although it is not clear how far it will carry them beyond the sphere of their local cultural environment. Perhaps her greatest misfortune has been that she has lived most of her life in a society in which women have been at a disadvantage when without the strong personal backing of men.

Household Five

One reaches the residence of Household Five by going up from the main lower path before coming to House Two. The house is like the others in having concrete walls and floor, the latter rough but tidy (Fig. 11.6). Overhead is a wood gable roof, and there is no electricity to light the interior. Notable is the presence of a double-decked bed. Water is carried

---

*Problems involving land tenure have been difficult to solve because we often could not verify the data presented. For various reasons, householders may not be really cooperative. On several occasions we were privileged to see sections of the map records kept by the Crown Lands and Survey Office but, although given help in other ways, we were refused a copy of a map showing the distribution of permitted holdings even when we offered to cover the expenses of duplication with the names and payment data deleted. Apart from the question of legality, the draftsmen were described as too busy. There was always the question of time, and if we had possessed more of it ourselves, cooperative friends might well have resolved our difficulties.

Fig. 11.6. Home of Household Five

up from a neighbor's well. As around other houses in Tung Pak Wan, there are many rats on which two cats and a bitch have declared ineffective war. It struck us as unusual that although the bitch had given birth to four offspring a short time before, the family had recently purchased a puppy a month or two old. We were told, however, that the owners did not eat dogs. In fact, the dogs were all in evidence a year later and the family simply stated that no one wanted them.

The family consists of a husband aged thirty-seven, a wife of forty-five (an older wife is not uncommon among the Chinese), and two sons, one thirteen and the other eleven. The males of Household Five during the hot season wear a T-shirt, blue shorts, and blue Japanese style slippers which the boys, at least, frequently discard. The woman was always dressed in a black gummed silk sam fu. Sometimes she uses Japanese slippers but we have also seen her in painted wood sandals with black straps, which she says are the coolest footwear in summer and especially good in the house. They are also much cheaper than the composition ones, and cost only seventy or eighty cents. More unusual were her pearl earrings showing clearly against her curled and bobbed hair.

The mistress of the house admitted with disarming frankness that she quarreled a lot with her husband and that probably they were not ideally suited to each other. When asked what form of marriage she preferred, one of her sons demonstrated his precocity by answering before she could that it is better to know one's future spouse beforehand. It seemed clear whose viewpoint he was reflecting. She herself was married semi-blind.* In answer to our query, she said that to marry a father's sister's son was wrong, but that a mother's brother's son was an acceptable mate.

About having children, the mother in Household Five stated that the number does not matter if one is rich; but if one is poor, a few are enough. Only her younger son was born after she and her husband had moved to Tung Pak Wan. At that time nurses did not come to the island to serve as midwives, so an old woman who was merely a friend had helped her. The elder son attends School D in Lung Shing where he is in his second year. This is said to cost $3.40 each month. There was no room for the other boy and he attends a class given by one of the teachers with a fee of $7 for the same period or, in other words, the unregistered section of a private school.

The boys seem to enjoy life. They swim every day in summer and the older one is quite competent. There is a radio in the house and they go to the movies on occasions. Their mother takes in one boy free on a thirty cent ticket (the cheapest), and if their father goes too, he takes in the other. No one plays mah-jongg; it is said there is no time. When necessary, a doctor with Western training is called upon on the assumption that cures brought about in the traditional Chinese manner take too long.

The mistress of the house says the family has no religion. There are no ancestral tablets such as existed in her father's home. Although any belief in superior beings is denied, she once in a while burns incense on Buddha's birthday, to which statement a dusty bag of incense sticks on the wall gives support. Her son in School D reports that every Thursday afternoon a priest comes from the Catholic church across the strait and his class has to stay and study the Bible. The boy says that he does not know what to believe because each person says his God is better than anyone else's.

The family evinces little or no interest in political matters. The quick-spoken boy says he does not care who runs the government, which is not surprising. His mother thinks the British do better than would the Chinese, referring to the Chinese in general. Of the government of the People's Republic of China she knows nothing, although from letters which she receives, she shares in the general knowledge of the food shortages in Kwangtung. Recently the family received a permit for the house

---

*Perhaps it should be repeated at this point that a semi-blind marriage refers to one arranged wholly by the parents, but one before which the major participants view each other and have a nominal right to halt the procedure.

site. The members of Household Five do not belong to a Kaifong Association.

Numerous statements setting forth the economic difficulties of the family, although not without foundation, probably were motivated by the hope that some advantage might be gained through our sympathetic interest. On the other hand, Household Five is extraordinary in Tung Pak Wan in being dependent for its subsistence primarily on farming undertaken at home by the head of the family. Behind the house are three small fields in which flowering Chinese cabbage and Chinese white cabbage are grown as the principal crop. They also have melons used for soup but, curiously enough, the location is said to be too wet for the green string beans that are so characteristic of the household below them. Also the family has owned one sow for three years, a remarkable creature which once produced twenty-three pigs in a single litter. Since the sow has only fourteen functional teats, only that number could be raised, but one does not easily forget an occasion of such gratuitous fertility. The young pigs are said to be sold when they are only eighty days old because cash is necessary to pay food bills, the credit having been given on the security of the pigs. The latter weigh seventeen or eighteen catties when sold and were bringing $3.50 per catty or about $60 each.

The family owns over thirty chickens including fourteen or fifteen hens, also a pair of pigeons which have four squabs. There are one guava and one papaya tree on their land. The mistress of the family says over a hundred dollars a month is spent on food, which is inadequate. She and her husband eat no breakfast but may give the boys ten to twenty cents for some food in town. Recently, after being in the hospital for a period, she did not feel they could afford to kill a chicken for soup although convalescents are expected to have such meals. She and her husband both smoke, and, during one visit, she admitted that both she and her husband enjoy clear, strong Chinese wine.

All the members of Household Five are Cantonese. Before they came to Tung Pak Wan, they lived in a rented house in Hong Kong where the head of the family worked in a metal shop. They were acquainted with people on the island as the mother of the head of Household Two is the sister of the father of the head of Household Five, as was the mother of the head of Household One. It was the mistress of Household One, however, who suggested that they join in the new community, and the move was made in 1949. The head of Household Two let them build on his land, however.

Like many other of the older villagers in Tung Pak Wan, the parents of Household Five have a remembered background in their native Kwangtung. Also they lived in Hong Kong and when the father worked for a while in Kowloon a few years ago, his older son went there with him. The same child has also been to Deep Water Bay on a school picnic (Fig. 1.1). It is notable also that the father, in about 1955 or 1956, worked on the farm of the Chin family in Chung Nam Wan. In taking up farming, he has become more and more sedentary, although he still occasionally takes a trip to Hong Kong if, for example, he needs disinfectant. His wife and children, on the other hand, go to Lung Shing almost every day to do the marketing or to attend school. It impressed us that the elder son knew the name of Sai Mi Wan at the other end of the island, which his mother did not and, when asked how that happened, he said that he had been there to play.

Commentary. There is an element of excitement in Household Five as though the brushes of a motor were ill-adjusted and giving off a furtive odor that might be interpreted as prognostications of trouble. Nevertheless, it appears that the family might continue intact for as long in the future as it has in the past. The husband-wife relationship is perhaps stabilized, and we would suspect that conflict, if conflict arises, will focus around the boys, one of whom has taken the lead by his independence and intelligence, a circumstance which may direct the other into trouble to obtain ego distinction. None of these factors may be of sufficient significance to affect the development of the community; indeed, they may be merely one sign of its growing maturity.

Household Six

The sixth family to identify with Tung Pak Wan is a special case as it does not live in its one-room concrete house, which is occupied periodically during the day by a caretaker and his wife. It is located a stone's throw beyond the residence of Household One and thus marks the extreme southern limit of the settlement. Electric light is available, wires having been extended from the house of the above-mentioned neighbor. The numerous more or less broken-down concrete pigpens hugging the slope of the hill are the most conspicuous aspects of the establishment, which is essentially a pig farm with terraces, built in tiers above the pens, on which to grow sweet potato vines for pig food. At the time of our first visit, there were seven sows and a total of about forty-five pigs altogether, but the number seemed to increase during the period of our study.

The establishment has its own well which affords water with which to bathe the pigs twice a day in summer. In the winter, a few vegetables are grown, and there is also a flock of fifteen to twenty chickens.

The history of Household Six in relationship to Tung Pak Wan, once discovered, seemed perfectly simple. The mistress of the house is said to be a daughter of the widow who established Household One and consequently a sister of its present head. She knew that the land was available, and took possession in 1950 because she and her husband wanted to raise pigs to increase their income.

The head of Household Six came with his father and mother to Lung Chau from Canton about 1920 at the age of seven. He and his wife have had nine children, seven of whom are boys, and the oldest is nineteen. His mother who is over eighty years of age also lives with them. Even with the trade of a carpenter at which he can make ten dollars a day and as owner of a pig farm, it is understandable that he is pressed to care for such a large family. Since the family is not regularly resident in Tung Pak Wan, we shall not consider its economic problems here.

Commentary. Even without any real personal knowledge of this family, it took on a significance because of the statement of a neighboring relative. It should be recognized that the verbalization, which came without any suspicion or probing on our part, is probably more important than the information conveyed, which may well be considered by some other residents as slander, albeit against an anonymous woman in an anonymous household of an anonymous island. The simple but illuminating remark was that the mistress of Household Six had not been the daughter of the Founding Widow in the strict sense, but rather her daughter-in-law and her son's first wife. As can so easily happen in a traditional Chinese marriage, the husband and wife found they were not suited to each other and, being intelligently wordly in such matters, amicably parted company and eventually found more satisfactory spouses. We were told that the head of Household One said that if she would leave, she could assume the role of his sister. Under such circumstances, obviously an unusual factor entered into the growth of the settlement.

Household Seven

Without doubt, the establishment to be described as that of Household Seven is the most impressive in Tung Pak Wan. As one walks from the town of Lung Shing, its buildings on one's left are the first to be seen after surmounting the crest of the hill which sets the village apart. First appear extensive pigeon houses bordering the ridge, then terrace upon terrace of pigpens as one follows the path beside them down past the home of the Chin family which has been referred to as Household Four. The large two-story, flat-roofed, concrete residence of Household Seven lies across the path just below the Chin widow's residence, and the land occupied includes not only all the north slope of the village between the main path and the sea (excluding the beach area itself), but another tract high on the hill in the northwest section above Household Three. If one looks up from the shore near the middle of Tung Pak Wan, the piggery of Household Seven vaguely suggests the monastic architecture of Tibet.

The house itself, which faces in a southerly direction, is set slightly apart on a flat area at the bottom of the property. Its square front yard is closed off with a pipe-framed wire fence that reaches high above one's head, conveying the aspect of a prison yard, an impression that is only partly relieved when it is colored by lines of blue or white laundry (Fig. 11.7). Also, unused materials overflow into the yard from seemingly constant expansion and improvement activities, and these give it a desultory appearance to eyes not dulled by familiarity. Inside the house, from casual observation, one sees little to differentiate it from others in Tung Pak Wan. There are the customary concrete floors and the cluttering which might well be expected in an active household with half a dozen children. The adoption of folding chairs seemed a point worth noting.

The utilities that have been provided for Household Seven are unmatched in Tung Pak Wan. There are three wells. Electricity, which was installed about 1957, provides not only light but also power for pumps, for a machine for grinding pig food, and for such appliances as the radio, refrigerator, clock, and iron. They have not considered a washing machine, Rediffusion*, or television, but they have had a telephone for eighteen months. It not infrequently fails to function and costs, including the island surcharge, over $300 a year, we were told.† Of more commonplace luxuries, there are three bitches with numerous puppies and uncounted cats.

The people who live in the house include a husband and wife and an amah. The couple has three daughters (now aged sixteen, fourteen, and twelve) and then three sons (aged ten, eight, and six). There were also six or more male workers or dependents at the time of our inventory, including a woman who comes in to care for the pigeons. One of the male workers has a house nearby, one dependent lives in a shed adjoining the pigeon coop, and the sleeping places of the others, who comprise a shifting population, are not certain.

As might be expected in such an affluent family, the dress of its members is of superior grade. The mistress of the household once attracted my attention by the blue-flowered sam fu and blue raincoat which she wore going into town. One of her several distinctions in Tung Pak Wan is that she also owns a cheong sam. She is not unattractive with her bobbed hair and permanent wave. Besides her wristwatch, a large jade ring is noticeable. Her eldest daughter dresses in sam fu, while another

---

*Rediffusion (Hong Kong) Limited is a company which provides a wired broadcast service between 7:00 A.M. and midnight throughout the Colony. *Hong Kong 1962 Report*, 1963: 282–84.

†Business telephones cost $300 per year in Hong Kong; residential , $225. These are flat rates for all calls in Hong Kong and Kowloon area. Calls to the New Territories have a surcharge. There is also an annual surcharge on Lung Chau of $80.

Fig. 11.7. Home of Household Seven

was seen in blouse and fu. In summer the boys usually wear T-shirts and shorts, either white or blue.

The parents of the six children knew each other from an early age as they grew up in adjacent houses in Lung Shing. The mother's father was a Cantonese who operated a slipway, an old established industry on the island. The young couple married by free choice and they unhesitatingly agree that the modern method of choosing a spouse is the best. Interestingly enough, it is reported that when first married the hardworking young husband, as well as his mother, moved into his wife's home, while her father went to live at his slipway, which now belongs to her brother.

The head of Household Seven left school about the age of fourteen to help his father who had a meat stall in Lung Shing. Having little of his own, education is highly valued for the children, the two younger of whom attend primary school in Lung Shing while the four older go to various schools in Hong Kong. This effort to raise the scholastic level of the family is said to cost about five hundred dollars a month including tuition, books, bus fares, lunches, and miscellaneous items.

As for pleasures, it is claimed that everyone in the family swims, but that the father goes into the water very rarely. They see movies once in a while, but no one admits to playing mah-jongg. A radio has already been mentioned. In matters of health, the head of the family said that he would consult a Chinese-style doctor for a disease that involved coughing, whereas if injections were needed, he would certainly go to a physician who had Western training.

On some matters, it was difficult to obtain information from the parents in Household Seven. On one occasion it was stated that the family was traditionalist in religion, and later the head affirmed flatly that he believed in God, but then refused to say another word on the subject. He also claimed to have no interest in who governs Hong Kong, and evaded further questioning. He does belong to a Kaifong Association, however, and it was taken for granted that he has a permit for his elaborate establishment.

In Household Seven there is an obvious devotion to economic advancement, which has been fostered by success. Pig raising has been developed into a major business which seems to be expanding by the month (Fig. 11.8). The best estimate of the number of animals seems to be between six and seven hundred, including about fifty breeding sows. One of the serious problems is to keep enough workers to take care of them, and labor is sometimes hired by the day at a wage of from five to six dollars. The head of Household Seven owns a sampan for the express purpose of transporting pigs and bringing in feed. The pigs are sold in Hong Kong and are said to be of superior quality to those which reach the public market in Lung Shing. In the latter place, Household Seven has a butcher stall presided over by the mistress of the family (she is reported to receive a regular salary for this undertaking), and the pork which is sold in the stall is purchased in Hong Kong, where the head of the household seems to spend most of his time. The telephone, it may be added, is really an adjunct of the pig business.

Apart from the piggery, a second considerable undertaking is the raising of squabs which are sold to representatives of the Central Market in Hong Kong who come once or twice a week to purchase thirty or forty at one time from the approximately seven hundred on hand. The price ranges from one to four dollars according to the size of the birds and the seasonal value. The pigeons are stated to be all of one variety despite the variation in color. They are kept almost immobilized on tiers in eight large cages, laying eggs in a 40-day cycle, a half of which time is spent in brooding. Brooding pigeons coo in the daylight. Presumably, the squabs are sold when they are about four weeks old and weigh perhaps three-quarters of a pound. There seems to be little problem in raising the pigeons except for feeding them and cleaning the cages. The schedule of feeding is seven and eleven in the morning, and again at four in the afternoon. They are given a mixture of sweet corn, sorghum (kaoliang), beans, and other things, not to mention sand and earth. The pigeons in one room eat from a series of

Fig. 11.8. Pigpens of Household Seven

drawers. Once the feedings are over, the cages are given their daily clean-ing. The head of the household has medicine for the pigeons but they are seldom ill. A woman from Household Eighteen comes in to take care of them from seven to twelve and from two to five. She also cooks for the other employees. For her eight-hour day she is paid $120 per month. A re-tired seventy-year-old man who, if not a close cousin, at least bears the same surname as the master of the family, sleeps in the shed at the end of the pigeon cages, thereby serving as a watchman. His are not uncomfort-able quarters as he has a metal single bed with springs, and also an electric light. He eats with the family, but says that he does not get paid. Occa-sionally he asks the head of the house for some money, although it hurts him to do so, and the latter gives him a few dollars.

Chicken raising and vegetable growing are relatively minor activities in Household Seven. They have about thirty chickens but these with their eggs provide provender only for the family. Various vegetables are grown, but not in the summer as it has been too difficult to obtain labor-ers, and the latter must be utilized primarily to care for the pigs. Usually, however, two men work in the fields. It seems almost peculiar that Household Seven has no fruit trees.

Notwithstanding that fact, the members probably eat as well as anyone in Tung Pak Wan. The family is stated to have two meals a day, whereas all the workers have three. The head of the family smilingly admits to liking beer and all types of wine. At least, as he puts it, there are few kinds he won't drink, and a lot that he will. He was observed smoking Abdullah cigarettes, while his cousin who watches over the pigeons is devoted to a worn-out bamboo water pipe.

The members of Household Seven are Cantonese. As seems consistent with the history of the family, pigs were the cause of their moving to Tung Pak Wan in 1950. The father of the present head of Household Seven is said to have come to Lung Chau in 1909 from Chung Shan (hsien) in Kwangtung. There he established himself by selling food to the boat people. The family also raised pigs in Lung Shing for many years, but not very many. Finally, the father died in Lung Shing. After World War II when there was a tremendous rise in the population, pig raising was banned from the town and the present head looked for a place to remove them. Tung Pak Wan seemed most convenient and when his good friend, the head of Household One, invited him to share his land, the family moved.

Commentary. It is clear that the world view of the members of Household Seven is a broad one from the standard of Tung Pak Wan. The head of the family and four of the children spend much of their time in Hong Kong. Historically, they represent an old family on the island in the sense of one that has been there fifty years or more. Lung Chau has been home for two or more generations and the father, at least, knows it well. Twice a year, he climbs over the pass to visit his ancestral graves on the slope of Chung Nam Wan. Of whatever the family's orientation toward Communist China consists, it indicates a range of consciousness that is not entirely local. Because of their multiple activities and affluence, the members of Household Seven have become the object of more comments than those of any other family in the settlement. Gossip, however, is not an outstanding characteristic of the people in Tung Pak Wan; indeed, their detachment from neighbors can be phenomenal. Perhaps we stimulated talk about Household Seven because of its significance in the community; perhaps they themselves also created some of the stimulus for gossip.

In any event we were frequently told that the family was Communist. We were told that at a time previous to our arrival, the flag of the People's Republic of China was flown at the house and that it attracted so much attention that the police came several times, after which the flag was no longer seen. We were told that the head of the house once sent six big pigs to China as a congratulatory gift on the occasion of a national holiday. We were told that he reads a Communist newspaper. We were told that he became a Communist because he could buy pigs cheaper in China. We were told that he was not a real Communist at all. We were told that he and the other members of his family do not talk to many people who are not Communists.

They talked to us, but on each occasion only after considerable effort. The head of the house impressed us favorably, but we had been previously biased by evidence that he had tried to be helpful to various of his workers and other people most closely associated with him. He also proved himself sensitive enough to refuse any answer to statements with political implications. From direct evidence, we know only that he is greatly interested in pigs.

And as hundreds of pigs no doubt must deserve, there has been gossip about pigs. There is the story that Household Seven once won one of the lesser tickets on the Royal Hong Kong Jockey Club Sweepstakes which produced thousands of dollars with which they bought pigs. Moreover, these pigs did not often get sick, apparently because of the magical principle. "Once lucky, everything is lucky," as they say on Lung Chau. Also significant is the belief that the wife of the head of the household obtained the money from her mother with which to buy pigs. Or perhaps from her father, as there is some reason to believe that her mother never emigrated to Hong Kong. The informant added that the husband is afraid of his wife because of her role as a provider of money. Gossip is gossip, and there is no real evidence that internal relations in the family are not excellent.

Whatever the effect of the wife on the husband, there is no question of her effect on other women. Periodically, females annoy other females in a particularly feminine way, and so many women expressed unfavorable opinions of the wife of the head of Household Seven that we were puzzled. Rarely was any factual support offered for the attitude, except that the woman was not gracious in the expected Chinese manner. This we could verify. She passed neighbors without seeing them. Her face was consistently dour and repelling, and although we observed her many times over a period of six years, we never saw her smile, not even a preoccupied smile.

Household Eight

The composition of Household Eight confused us at the beginning since no one belonging to it was in the village at the time of our first visits. Furthermore the identities of two men of the same name from Fukien, whom we shall call Fei, were confused. Finally, the establishment—or perhaps we should use the plural—is essentially an ink factory, and while we were working in Tung Pak Wan, we did not want to become entangled in the study of factories. The next year, however, when we purposefully did so at Sai Mi Wan, we finally obtained fairly clear impressions of the role and history of these inkmakers.

The structures appurtenant to Household Eight spread along the west edge of the beach line below the property of Household Seven and are conspicuously distinguished by rows of concrete ink vats which fairly blaze with purple color in the hot summer sun. Behind the vats at each end are boilers with adjacent buildings including a compact chicken house at the western end. On the property are two good wells, the older of which in ordinary seasons has supplied water for at least four or five Tung Pak Wan families. The water is claimed to be unsurpassed in quality by any well on Lung Chau where such water is often more or less saline. There is also electricity with meters for both light and power, the latter being used for pumps and for supplying heat to a chicken house in winter.

The legal status of the property on which the Fei men have their ink plants and other buildings was not quickly made clear for various reasons. Originally, the area is said to have been beach. Later, it became obvious that someone held a permit for the land, as there is a tax on the combined holdings, which one of the Fei men reports as $600 a year. Later we discovered that the property is not in the name of the original inkmaker, and finally it was attributed to Household One whose second encircling permit has been previously mentioned.

The Mr. Fei who came last (and whom we shall identify as the chicken raiser) lives in the building next to the chicken house. He is a lithe, busy man who states that he is not married and never has been. On being asked, he even asserts that he does not want a son. His specificity suggests that he has been embittered by the opposite sex. This attitude may have given rise to the gossip that he has been married and divorced. Away from home, Mr. Fei is what might be called a smart dresser, but on a hot day, we found him wearing blue shorts, the lower parts colored with purple ink which also showed on his hands and feet, the latter protected by flat strap composition slippers. Mr. Fei employs two men, one Cantonese and the other Fukienese, to assist him, and they all take turns in doing the cooking. Only the Fukienese sleeps regularly in Tung Pak Wan, however. Each is paid something over $100 a month plus two daily meals. They follow the Cantonese custom in eating two meals a day, but the first is not until one in the afternoon or a little later and the second about five, as he points out that it gets dark early. In the mornings, however, he and the workers may go out for yam ch'a (yin ch'a), or perhaps eat some congee.* Mr. Fei will not eat chicken. He says that he looks at them all day. Consequently he prefers fish with his rice. Periodically he smokes a mentholated cigarette which costs seventy cents a package and brushes his teeth with fluoride toothpaste. He has one dog, but dispenses with cats as his chicken coops are all adequately protected from rats.

---

*Breakfasts, or yam ch'a (yin ch'a), are irregular and are not technically considered a meal on Lung Chau.

Mr. Fei admits to only one year of schooling but claims to have taught himself to read newspapers by learning some characters, then remembering the implied meaning of intervening ones. He can also write a little and keeps simple business records. Mr. Fei looks and feels healthy, but says that if he had to go to a doctor, it would be one with Western type training. He has no radio but he does go swimming frequently, the water being only a few feet away. Formerly he played soccer. It was noted that he attended the Dragon Boat races. He seldom goes to the movies and takes a positive pride in stating that he does not play mah-jongg or otherwise gamble and has none of the usual and expensive bad habits, such as consorting with dancing girls or using narcotics. He admitted that he is afraid of strong wine and only occasionally drinks a glass of beer. His friends go to nightclubs and feasts, but he says he cannot afford them. Actually, he does not want to spend his capital and also does not have the time as he must be back in Tung Pak Wan when his worker's day ends at nine.

Mr. Fei does not belong to a Kaifong Association and believes there is no advantage for him to do so. After disclaiming any interest in politics, he said that the change in government in China has made him pessimistic. His basic complaint seems to be that the Chinese officials are untrustworthy and will shift from one viewpoint to another all too easily.

As for religion, more than once he told us that he had none. He says that he does not even believe in the Earth God as most farmers do. "If burning incense would cure chickens, who wouldn't believe?" he asks.

Mr. Fei, lacking pigeons and pigs, is now devoted to chickens which he looks to as his primary source of income, especially when the market for purple ink is not good. He proudly announced that he has about two thousand, which we interpreted momentarily as boasting, but on pursuing the subject when he insisted more conservatively that he had over a thousand, we came to the conclusion that he spoke modestly. In a relatively small structure were chickens beyond counting, the smaller ones in cage above cage only a few inches high, while the larger ones perched on wire over boxes which serve to collect the droppings that are removed twice during each day. Seldom does a structure have such concentrated utilization, for with bags of feed piled adjacent to the cages, it was difficult to squeeze into the building. A thermometer inside registered 93 degrees Fahrenheit. We were impressed by Mr. Fei's modern approach to the raising of poultry. A medicinal drop is applied to the nose of the small chicks soon after birth. Then the chickens are fattened abnormally through the medium of an injection of about 1 cc. of vitamin B in the breast when they weigh approximately a catty and a half. Also a hormone drug is injected into the head a month before they are sold. These chemicals are of American origin. Mr. Fei informed us that he sells about three hundred chickens a month, most of them to restaurants in Lung Shing. Neither of the Fei men grows any vegetables.

The distinction of the two Fei men is that they are both Fukienese from Amoy. Despite their common surname, however, they are not related. The first Mr. Fei, whom we shall now describe, left China with empty pockets soon after the Japanese had departed (ca. 1945). There were already quite a few Fukienese on Lung Chau and he knew some of them. Friends suggested that he go into the purple ink business and he did so about 1948. Shortly thereafter, or about 1950, he expanded and set up another plant in Tung Pak Wan on land apparently obtained from the family of Household One. He continued to live in Lung Shing, however. Since the first Mr. Fei suffered from some disease that prevented the use of his hands and did not know the ink business empirically, he always depended on employees who did, among whom was the second Mr. Fei.

The second Mr. Fei, who raises chickens, states that he was born about 1930 in a town perhaps as large as Lung Shing about six hours north by fast motorboat from Amoy. He does not remember it as his father left the ancestral home and settled in Amoy when Mr. Fei was a boy. Even when his rich grandfather invited all the grandsons to gather for a division of the property, Mr. Fei did not go although, through his father as eldest son, he was entitled to two shares. His reluctance was accounted for by the simple statement that his father who died about 1938 was not a nice man. Since the Communists came, none of his relatives remain in his ancestral village. His mother died during the revolution and although she had eleven other children, not one of them has survived. He came from Amoy about 1949 with a well-to-do man for whom he worked as a cook. This employer set up a gold-silver paper business in Lung Shing because it was known as an inexpensive place in which to live. After a year and a half, the second Mr. Fei went to work for the first Mr. Fei whose branch factory in Tung Pak Wan had been built the previous year. Actually, the second Mr. Fei did not live in Tung Pak Wan until five or six years later when, having become an expert inkmaker, he set up his own plant there adjacent to that of his employer. Later, with competition affecting the ink business, the second Mr. Fei was motivated to raise chickens, an endeavor he has recently expanded.

Commentary. As should be clear, the orientation of both of the Fei men is not centered at Tung Pak Wan, although the second Mr. Fei, because of his chickens, is moving closer. Their traditional homeland is farther away and different linguistically and culturally from that of the majority of the islanders. In that sense one might say that the world of the two Fei men is larger than that of the typical Tung Pak Wan resident.

Household Nine

One comes upon Household Nine just before reaching the home of the Chin family of Household Four in walking from town. It is a modest two-room single-story concrete structure with a gable roof which was built by the owner and wholly occupied by his family until 1958 when he disposed of the southerly of the two rooms to a maiden lady from Lung Shing who wanted to raise chickens in Tung Pak Wan (see Household Sixteen). The decor of the interior of the house lacks distinction, but it does have a pendulum clock on the wall which strikes the hours. There is no electricity. On a hot day the smell from the adjacent pigpens of Household Seven is as strong as the sun. It is something one seems to grow accustomed to, however, and it is possible that the bitch named Tao Li ("Dolly") who lies on the small flat area outside the door may even enjoy it. Water for the house is drawn from a neighbor's well.

The sad-faced man associated with the establishment is fifty years old, and his long-sleeved shirt, deep blue shorts, and Japanese style composition sandals scarcely suggest that his own personal qualities are as exceptional in Tung Pak Wan as those of his house are meager. Unfortunately, his unhappiness was increased by the death of his wife in July, 1960, as was his responsibility in caring for their six-year-old child. An elder daughter, married and living in Kowloon, was not in a position to assist him. At first he was impelled to try to place the child in an orphanage, but he was persuaded to keep her at home.

It is understandable when this widower makes a clear statement that having many children leads to serious problems among the villagers. He states flatly that blind marriage is not good, although there is no indication that his own was especially unhappy. He is pleased, however, that a free choice in selecting a spouse is becoming more and more common. Most of all, he is concerned about the shortage of schools with respect to the burgeoning population. This is logical as his own education is far superior to that of anyone in his age group in Tung Pak Wan. Before leaving China, he had been a teacher in both primary and middle schools, and taught Chinese and history in a normal school. He not only speaks Hakka and Cantonese, but his Mandarin is reasonably adequate. He can even write his name and a little bit more in English. In the fall after the death of his wife, his daughter was admitted to School D, and he tutored her in the evening. He claims that his only pleasure is reading books and newspapers, but he does have a radio. He seldom goes to the movies, and he never plays mah-jongg. He says that he knows how to swim a little, but has not attempted to do so since coming to Tung Pak Wan. He cannot play any musical instrument. As for doctors, he prefers them to be trained in the Western tradition as he believes that the latter can cure a disease much more quickly.

The former teacher professes to have had no religious beliefs in his youth, even at the age he started to school. He accounts for his agnosticism by stating that his father did not worship his ancestors, although he suspects that his grandfather did. Neither was there any acceptance of Buddhism in his father's house. His disregard of religion continued until a year or two before his wife died. Finally, under the influence of his neighbors and friends, he went to the Catholic church where he was impressed by both the preaching and the sincerity of the priest. Shortly thereafter he became a convert. Later it was the priest who persuaded him to keep his child at home, pointing out otherwise he would be lonely and that the little girl would soon be old enough to stay alone when he went out to work.

The former teacher appears to have stronger political feelings than most of the residents in Tung Pak Wan. Coming from a class which he calls "masters of the land," a relatively rich segment of the pre-revolution population, he believes that he would be killed by the Communists if he returned to China. Until about 1958, he communicated with his mother who remained in the family home. She instructed him that if he could possibly stay alive in Hong Kong not to come back. Then she asked him not to write any more letters. He approves of the British Government and does not think the Chinese have the political skills to rule so well. He speaks of the Government owning the house which he built since he does not have a permit for it. Membership in a Kaifong Association, he says he cannot afford.

The past decade has been one of desperate economic struggle for the former schoolteacher as he was not accustomed to the physical effort necessary to obtain a meager subsistence. In recent years, his principal income has been derived from hiring himself out as a common laborer, usually as mason's assistant, for which his salary has been as low as five or six dollars a day. When we knew him, he did no farming as he had no land, but he did manage to grow some greens on the hillside in order to supply food to his remaining sow which in her proper time produces sizable litters. Until his wife's last illness, he had several other pigs, but he was forced to sell them to meet the expenses which resulted from their misfortune. There are also about twenty chickens in a wire cage, and he regrets that he has not money for the feed which would enable him to keep more. Pigeons and ducks are beyond the capacities of his establishment.

He cooks the meals for his little family using purchased wood for fuel. Tobacco he regards as essential, adding that "when one works hard, one must drink a little wine when it is finished."

This former schoolteacher, a Hakka, came to Hong Kong in 1948 from Tzu Chin (Hui Yang hsien) in Kwangtung in order to escape the Communists. He did not expect to remain in the Colony permanently, but having considerable money, he went into partnership with a man and opened a store in Kowloon for the purpose of selling chairs. After some initial success, the partner absconded with all their cash and fled to Macao. The schoolteacher followed, but he could not ferret out the man who had fleeced him. His remaining resources were gradually exhausted in the purchase of food.

The removal of his family to the island of Lung Chau was an act of desperation which occurred in 1951 or shortly thereafter. The choice resulted from the fact that his wife was the sister of the Mr. Chin who had established Household Four in Tung Pak Wan and a native of Tzu Chin. After settling on the island, the former schoolteacher and his wife made a meager living by cutting grass and selling it to boatmen who burned it under their beached boats to clean the bottoms. His condition is exemplified by the fact that his wife had to teach him how to bundle the grass.

Commentary. Financial problems have largely immobilized the master of Household Nine. He goes into Lung Shing every second and third day, and occasionally as far as Sai Mi Wan where he has a friend. On Sunday, he crosses the strait in order to attend church. Because of his predilection for reading, it must be presumed that his intelligible universe is larger than many of the residents of Tung Pak Wan. On the other hand, tragedy and sorrow may be walling him in.

Household Ten

The house is above, and a little southerly of Household Four. It is approximately on the same level as the homes of Households Three and Nine and reached by the same path. It differs from these others, however, in having only its lower walls of concrete, the upper sections being built of wood. The overall impression is of a one-story building that is small and flimsy. There is no electricity, and water is drawn from a neighbor's well. We recorded a small kerosene stove and the absence of dogs and cats.

The head of the household, we never saw in his home, as he leaves very early and comes home very late. His wife is an obliging woman, somewhat simple but not stupid, who was usually dressed in a sam fu with black trousers and a blue coat. She is in her late twenties and her husband is a bit older. They have three children aged five, four, and three of which the oldest is a boy. He was born in the Tung Hua hospital on Hong Kong Island across the strait. The two younger, she gave birth to at home with a nurse from the maternity hospital across the strait to assist in the delivery. This is an economical procedure, and one can pay the nurse what one likes.

The husband and wife are unusual in that they met in Tung Pak Wan where they were working in different households, and the decision to marry was wholly theirs. Quite reasonably, the mother says children should be allowed to choose their own mates, and quickly adds the rationalization that children will not obey their parents any more anyway.

The master of the house reputedly went through primary school in China; indeed he was a student of the schoolteacher of Household Nine. His son started his education in the kindergarten of School E in Lung

Shing in 1960, paying six dollars a month or half the standard tuition. It is safe to say that his father is the only member of the family who reads and writes. His mother states that no one in the house knows how to play mah-jongg, that no one swims, and no one has time to go to the cinema. It is certain that they do not own a radio. Sometimes a doctor trained in the Chinese tradition is consulted, sometimes one in the Western; the former when the latter is not available.

The head of the house is a Protestant and has been since before his marriage. He has fastened a picture of Jesus on the wall above the calendar. On Sunday, he goes to the Baptist Church of Lung Shing with his employer. Occasionally he takes his family. The head of the house also celebrates five festivals: those on the 5th of the 5th month, the 14th of the 7th month, the 15th of the 8th month, at New Year's, and one preceding it which is almost certainly the Winter Arriving Festival. Recognition consists of killing a chicken or buying a little extra food. As for the lady of the house, she was an agnostic when she married, and remains one. She is also one of the residents of Tung Pak Wan who definitely prefers that the British continue to govern Hong Kong. She says that if the Chinese had the responsibility, they would not be obeyed and everything would soon be in a mess.

The head of the family has no permit for their house, but he has recently joined the Lung Chau Kaifong Association, paying $1.70 per month for which $300 will be given in case he dies. The comment heard elsewhere was repeated that the Association does not distribute food in Tung Pak Wan when an opportunity offers because there are Communists in the village.

The head of the house works in a store in Lung Shing, a position he has held only a short time. He leaves his home at seven in the morning and returns at about ten at night. For his services he receives $100 per month plus his meals. The family has neither a vegetable garden nor fruit trees, but did acquire a sow in 1960, which may make the smell of the neighbor's pigsties more bearable, although not the excess of flies which they say results from the manure that is dumped on the hill. They also have over twenty chickens of various ages. The eggs are sold, but on occasion, a chicken is eaten. Breakfast is not a regular meal. The head of the family smokes, but his wife does not. She says that he drinks once in a while when he is very tired.

The members of Household Ten are both Hakka. The man came to Kowloon from Tzu Chin (Hui Yang hsien), Kwangtung, as did the former schoolteacher of Household Nine. The head of the house was brought to Lung Chau itself about 1950, however, by the Mr. Chin of Household Four who needed a worker on his Chung Nam Wan farm. They had met through a mutual acquaintance. Unmarried, and living in Household Four, it was natural that the newcomer met the young woman employed as a servant in neighboring Household Seven. She had been born in a town near Yuen Long in the New Territories, as was her father before her. Perhaps with marriage in mind, the future head of Household Ten went to work for Household One, the latter supplying him a place on which to build his house. After this had been done he transferred his services to the pig raising Household Seven in whose employ he continued for about six years, having married soon after he began it.

Commentary. Poverty and meager education have limited the outlook of the head of Household Ten. That of his wife is even more restricted. She goes into town almost every day to buy food, but she has never been to Sai Mi Wan at the other end of the island, and a few years have passed since she visited Chung Nam Wan which is only fifteen minutes' walk over the hill. Unlike most people of her age group who live in Tung Pak Wan, she has never been out of the Colony.

Household Eleven

If one stands on the beach at the central point of Tung Pak Wan and looks straight up the hill between two of the drainage gullies, one sees about half way to the top an unusual house standing on a terrace. It is an almost cubical story-and-a-half box with a flat roof. The walls are concrete for the first three feet of their height, and on this foundation is a superstructure of evenly placed clapboards. Doors exist in the easterly and southerly walls, while the south wall is distinguished by a most unusual window. In the first place, it is taller than average and has two vertical sashes glazed with diamond-shaped panes in the center and with four panes both above and below, four of the latter being notched for the window bar edgings of the diamond (Fig. 11.9). No explanation of this artistry was forthcoming because the man for or by whom the house was originally built was not interviewed: he and his family left Lung Chau four or five years previous to our visit.

Inside there is a further distinction in that the house is floored with red cement in a manner that gives the appearance of tile. The building, which is essentially one room, does have an upper half-story, set off by a layer of bamboo rods on stringers, which provides a storage area for light objects. There is no electricity supplied to Household Eleven, but there is a well. The present lone occupant keeps a cat to curtail the population of rats which attack his chickens. He says he is so poor that he cannot afford a chair on which to sit, and there is no sign of one. Also his bed lacks the expected straw mat. He wears blue shorts, his feet are bare, and there is a hole in the shoulder of his shirt. It is poverty with a dash of disdain, however, for this sixty-one-year-old resident of Tung Pak Wan is a man of strong and forthright opinions.

The occupant of Household Eleven has a wife in China to whom he was married semi-blind and whom he has not seen in over a decade. He also has six children—three boys and three girls—in China. He says he does not care in what style they marry, but that he himself thinks the modern method of choosing a partner is best. On being asked about preferential mating, he stated that in the old days he did not believe that it would have been proper for a man to marry either his father's sister's daughter or his mother's brother's daughter. Then he added that under the Communist regime, perhaps a man can marry his sister.

Our informant admits to knowing only a few Chinese characters, the remnants from four or five years of school attendance. He claims that he does not go to the cinema because he does not have enough money, at the same time affirming that everyone would like to attend. When it was pointed out that he has a predilection for an expensive kind of beer, he retorted logically enough that it is natural to satisfy one's stomach first. There is no radio in Household Eleven and the occupant insists that he does not even know how to play mah-jongg. He can swim, however, but seldom goes into the water, an admission which must be considered along with the fact that he is growing old. He prefers doctors to have had Western training because he believes that they can cure people much faster.

In his attitude toward religious matters, our informant was positive and sometimes scornful. Having stated that he had no religion, on being questioned directly about traditional beliefs, he replied that he accepted none of them. "I have a cat," he said. His reaction to the value of feng-shui was: "Even if you believe it, so what?" Moving to the role of ancestral tablets in family life, it became clear that he did not identify this aspect of Confucianism as religious. He stated that there had been "tablets" in his home, and reflected that "it would be nice to have them" in Tung Pak Wan. Of Christianity, his summary comment was: "To be a Catholic or Protestant you must either have money or know someone."

On political matters, our discussions led to conclusions no less certain. The master of Household Eleven would like to have the British turn over the government of Hong Kong to the Chinese, but only under the conditions that the latter were not Communists. His view of the latter is explicit. "I don't care what anyone else thinks. I don't want Communism. I will not get enough to eat." He admitted that some of the residents of Tung Pak Wan were Communists (a term loosely used to include anyone avowedly sympathetic with the Communist regime), and then went on: "I fight with them, as old as I am. I'm not afraid to die." It did not seem inconsistent when he stated that he had never belonged to a Kaifong Association.

Our informant in Household Eleven was clearly in a prejudiced condition about his economic affairs when we interviewed him the first time.

Fig. 11.9. Home of Household Eleven Showing Unusual Window

His livelihood depends on his raising of chickens and vegetables. The four previous days of tropical rain had left him seven out of 120 chickens. He had spent thirty dollars on his crop of green string-beans and it was a total loss. His two papaya trees had barely survived. With no pigs, pigeons, or ducks, there was little left to live on. It was a ruinous season, and even in a later one, when asked if he owned a dog, he answered quickly, "Why have one? There is nothing to steal."

During the winter, he normally plants Chinese white and flowering Chinese cabbage as well as green string beans as a cash crop which brings him about seventy dollars a month. In his straitened circumstances, more often than not he can afford only one meal a day, which he cooks on a clay pot stove. He does spend ten or fifteen cents daily for tobacco which he smokes in an old bamboo water pipe. Also he asserts his fondness for clear strong wine, as well as the aforementioned "Three Horse" beer which he brings home one bottle at a time, a restraint which is understandable since his favored brand costs over a dollar.

This Cantonese old man of Household Eleven—who looks twenty years younger than the sixty-one years inscribed on his identity card—left his home in Hsiao Lan (Chung Shan hsien), Kwangtung, about 1948 to escape the Communists. He thought they would be gone in a few months so he did not bring his wife and six children whom he has not seen since.

With a hundred dollars for his expenses, he came directly to his relatives in Household One where he lived for some time without being gainfully employed. The founding widow of Tung Pak Wan was his father's brother's daughter, as is also the old mother of Household Two, while the head of Household Five is his father's brother's grandson. In desperation, he finally went to work cutting grass and selling it to the boat people, as did the former schoolteacher of Household Nine. In this way he earned two or three dollars a day. In time he became a good friend of the owner of his present home, a man with the same surname as the family in Household One but unrelated to them. When his friend's family went back to China about 1955, our informant was given the establishment to occupy and care for. His friend who works in a store in the town across the strait also has supplied him with fifty or sixty dollars to buy chickens, an investment which unfortunately has been largely wiped out by riotous storms. Others also have helped him with periodic gifts of money. Although his head was bloodied by fate at the period we met him, his spirit remained unbowed.

Commentary. The master of Household Eleven has never really traveled except on his trip from Chung Shan to Hong Kong. Occasionally he visits relatives in other parts of the Colony. He has also climbed over to Chung Nam Wan several times, and he walks into Lung Shing frequently for supplies, but his economic condition and, to some degree, his age have tended to immobilize him. He is one of the few residents living in Tung Pak Wan who have survived since the end of the nineteenth century, and his outlook has at least the perspective of an unusually long life. This span has more meaning because he still acts and interacts in the community with independence and considerable vigor.

Household Twelve

The home of Household Twelve is directly behind and above the pigpens of Household One and no more than a hundred feet away. It is thus one of the four establishments south of the southerly drainage rivulet which it faces. It is also one of the two houses which are almost hidden by trees. Built entirely of wood above a low concrete wall on a concrete platform, it gives the impression of being run down. The gable roof is covered with tarpaper, and the clapboards are gray and uneven. A ramshackle shed kitchen has been built up at one end of the house with the aid of large pieces of tin, an effect that is partly relieved by a row of green bamboo outside its large open window. Inside the house, which is divided into two rooms with a half second-story providing additional space for sleeping, the contents overwhelm the observer by their conspicuous disarray. The numerous inconsequential small things contrast with the large and solid objects associated with the kitchen, such as the stove, baskets of fuel, a stand painted green, and great stones around which wires are so arranged as to hold down the roof in a storm. With a large family, except for beds, there is no room for big things in the house. The residents have no cat or dog to add to the confusion. An electric line from Household One feeds an incandescent bulb, while water is also obtained from the latter establishment.

Although the family consists of a husband and wife plus five sons aged twenty-one, nineteen, fifteen, eleven, and seven, it is not easy to find anyone at home in the daytime, or to communicate with them when two or three are. Our data, in consequence, are not as complete as they might be.

Four of the boys have attended primary school in Lung Shing and the fifth is just about to start. The eldest completed fourth grade at School D and the second boy all six grades at School B. The third son is in fifth grade in School B, and the fourth son is three grades behind him. Putting so many sons through school is an obvious achievement, and their mother told us frankly that she considered education to be the most important thing in life, whereupon she was contradicted by one of the boys who asserted that experience and influential friends could be even more significant. Secure in her opinion, the mother did not reply.

It was said that the chief amusement of the boys was swimming in the nearby bay, although they also go to the cinema occasionally. They have not been able to afford a radio, and according to one of the sons, no one in the house knows how to play mah-jongg.

Two of the sons have been ill in recent years and one has not fully recovered. They have gone to a doctor with Western type training because they believe he is more economical and cures faster than those with traditional Chinese medical learning. The attitude does not preclude placing value on leung ch'a (liang ch'a), which we saw one of the boys drinking in the house because, as he says, he feels tired and lacks spirit.

The head of the house says he has no religion, nor do the two elder sons. His wife and the three younger sons are Protestants, however, and it was asserted that they were influenced in becoming so because of the educational advantages which were offered. The principal feast days of the Chinese calendar are celebrated, but only New Year's with firecrackers. It was pointed out that families who visit each other on that occasion present the younger unmarried children with red packets containing money.

The land on which the house is built belongs to Household One, which may or may not have any bearing on a reticence to discuss even the most simple facts about politics and government. It is quite possible, on the other hand, that a personal interest is negligible. The boys with whom we talked, said they know nothing about government. No one in Household Twelve has a membership in the Kaifong Association.

The family grows no vegetables and owns no pigs, although it has periodically raised two or three. They claim no more than ten chickens of various sizes and have never had pigeons or ducks, nor have they planted fruit trees. The mother of the boys works periodically in the fish drying business nearby, while the father, who returns for a night only occasionally, is a professional caretaker of costumes at the Chinese opera. He is paid five dollars a day for folding the costumes, but unfortunately has employment only about seven days a month. The union to which he belongs supplies him with a place to sleep and lets him know when work is available. In between times, he earns a few dollars as an assistant on construction jobs. He is said to be the only one in the family who smokes. The two elder sons are studying in Lung Shing to be metal workers. During their apprenticeship they receive only "small" money and food.

The family is Cantonese speaking. The father came from Nan Hai near Canton before the Communists occupied the latter city in October, 1949, the mother a little later having given birth to her fourth son there. After living in Lung Shing for a period, their house fell apart, whereupon they moved about 1956 to their present abode in Tung Pak Wan. They were obviously invited to do so by the mistress of Household One who is sister to the mother of the five sons.

Commentary. The general outlook of the woman of Household Twelve, apart from suggesting a certain exhaustion, remains unclear, as does that of her husband, although the latter's association with the theater may hide a knowledge of a world quite strange to the residents of Tung Pak Wan. We learned, for example, that the three elder sons were born in Singapore where the family had settled for a few years with a theatrical troupe. It may also prove significant that an exposure to Christianity shows a definite effect on one of the sons, and that his interest seems not to be jeopardized by any opposing views among his closest associates. Perhaps the most obvious distinction of Household Twelve, however, is simply the fact that a mother has been raising five boys in her small poor house, a unique achievement in Tung Pak Wan.

Household Thirteen

The buildings of Household Thirteen are located on the northwesterly slope of Tung Pak Wan high above those of Two and Five. Viewed from the south, the establishment is one of the most conspicuous in the village because of the concrete pigpens which make a white dash along the yellow clay of the hills (Fig. 11.10). The house, a good two stories in height, is built on a concrete floor with walls of the same material rising 17″ on three sides and 38″ at the back. On top of these rest wood frames about two feet square faced with sheets of flat metal. This single-room building has an almost flat gable roof made of a corrugated composition material which

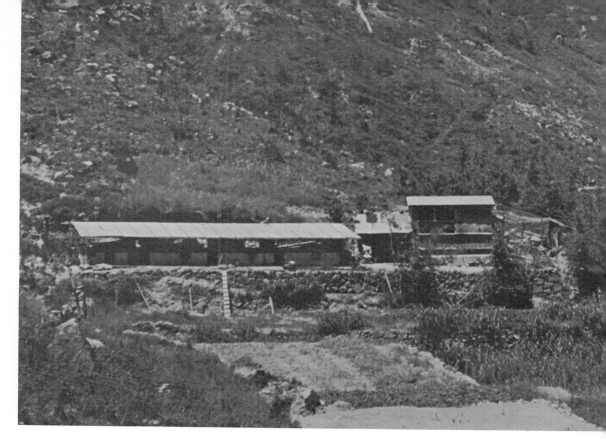

Fig. 11.10. Home and Pigpens of Household Thirteen

wire and large stones help to hold in place. The windows have no sashes but are covered by single shutters of light metal that swing out and up to open.

Inside the house there is a low gallery with a wood floor over the north half of the room providing an area for storage. It can be reached by a ladder made from two-by-two inch wood. The furnishings of this residence are quite typical of rural Lung Chau as one can see by comparison with Chung Nam Wan. The to-be-expected large table for family dining is missing, however. There is the usual bed of planks on a pair of wood horses with a covering pad protected by a piece of patterned green oilcloth that doubles as a table instead. On it are pillows and blankets; above it is a mosquito net. There are also two low chairs of modern style upholstered with green plastic covering. On the walls we noticed a straw hat with painted decoration, a large round wood-framed clock with one hand and its pendulum missing, a white and red plastic basket with a dish inside it, and a calendar with the familiar day pad. On the floor stood one large stoneware jar, a large basket, and numerous gasoline cans with the tops cut out; on a table, a thermos bottle and an aluminum kettle.

The customary built-on shed kitchen extends west of the house between it and the receding line of pigpens. In it, apart from a large pig food stove, we observed two stoneware jars, half a dozen assorted baskets, a gasoline can with the top cut out, a carrying pole, a metal pail, and an enamel wash basin. The establishment has its own meter for electricity, which supplies the single, unprotected bulb hanging in the middle of the room. The cost for light is a little over a dollar a month. Water reaches the house by conveying it from a nearby pipe faucet to which it is pumped up the hill from a well of Household Seven in order to water the gardens belonging to the latter. Residing in Household Thirteen at the time of our first visit was a small brown bitch and a cat. Not long afterward the cat met its demise in the mouth of a neighbor's dog, a tragedy which has been welcomed by the rats that have noticeably increased. Vaguely compensatory is the fact that the bitch has been blessed with five little puppies. These will eventually be sold, but when the dog buyer comes to take them, it is arranged that the soft-hearted owner is not at home.

The mistress and sole human resident of Household Thirteen is a widow of sixty-two. Her face is wrinkled, but her lower teeth are still sound. In the course of her life, she says she has borne two daughters and a son who are still living, as well as three or four children who died. We thought it more likely that only three had died since they came between the older living daughter who is forty and the second who is thirty-four, but later we learned that two of the daughters were twins. The only son is thirty-three. None of her children live in Tung Pak Wan, but the youngest has a family in Lung Shing. This old lady invariably wears a sam fu of the common glossy black gummed silk material, brown on its inner surface. At home in the extreme heat, she hangs up the sam exposing a patched and much washed, blue polka dot undercoat with pockets. Noticeable are the small gold circlets in the lobes of her ears which were pierced when she was a child. The earrings, however, she purchased herself a quarter of a century before we first knew her. She has never owned a cheong sam. One distinction in her dress is the fact that she often appears, even in town, in her bare feet.

The lady of Household Thirteen is exceptional among the married women of Tung Pak Wan since she herself was a concubine. It is not surprising that she could not remember which of one's cousins it would be proper to marry or not marry. She never went to school and states that no girls did when she was young. Indeed, she does not know even the characters of her name which are commonplace ones. She has never owned a radio and cannot play a musical instrument. She never gambles and does not know how to play mah-jongg. Once in a while she goes to the cinema in Lung Shing, purchasing the cheapest, or thirty-cent, ticket. When she is ill, she visits a doctor with Western type training, but then, if she is no better after five treatments, she turns to one whose learning is purely Chinese.

Religion seems to have little place in Household Thirteen. Its mistress never visits a temple or church. Asked about spirits, she laughs and says that she never hears any. When queried on the possibility of their existence she responds reflectively, "You cannot believe, but you cannot not believe." Of feng-shui, she not only states that she knows nothing, but that she does not "ask for any knowledge." When her husband was alive, he talked about feng-shui a great deal, and there is the intimation that his concubine perhaps wearied of the subject.

The head of Household Thirteen claims with all sincerity that she does not care what kind of government Hong Kong has as long as there is food to eat. To this summary statement she added the gratuitous comment that in China it seems that many people do not have enough food. She has a permit for her property in Tung Pak Wan and says that her annual tax on it is two hundred dollars, adding that the assessment has recently been raised. The lady does not belong to the Kaifong Association, and indeed, it might be said that she does not understand what kind of institution it is.*

The main economic activity in Household Thirteen is pig raising. At the time of our first visit there were only two sows and five young pigs for the four concrete stalls, but one of the sows had been loaned out for feeding to a poor old man in Lung Shing at the cost of all save one of its litter, although she said it was customary to receive two. He was miserable and she felt sorry for him. A short time before, her other sow had produced twelve young pigs which made everyone happy, but most of the offspring had died. When her older pigs become ill, she calls on the head of Household Seven to help her, and he knows what to do, sometimes giving the sick animal an injection. To feed her pigs, she brings two buckets of bean curd refuse from Lung Shing every day.

Raising chickens is a supplementary form of economic support. She estimated her flock at twenty-eight and the daily production of eggs as between four or five. For these she claims that she can obtain from twenty-five to seventy cents each, depending on the season and supply, but the latter figure seems unbelievably high. Later she explained that it was the price chicken raisers paid only when chickens were in great demand at the end of the Chinese year. She either retails the eggs herself near the Lung Shing Market, or sells them to individuals who come to her house to buy. Curiously, she would rather sell her own chickens than eat them for, after she takes care of them, she will not kill them or cook them. Even when she has to part with a pig, she cries and tells herself it is only an animal. She says she is not unique in her sensitivity. When she first

---

*In fairness, it might be added that we had some difficulty in comprehending it ourselves.

moved to Tung Pak Wan, thieves came sometimes and stole her chickens. She was afraid of being alone, and when it grew dark, she locked herself in. Asked about the safety of her pigs, she affirmed that thieves cannot steal them because a pig would make too much noise. Recently, she has become more secure, and there has been no more thieving, which is a change to reflect upon. On the other hand, one day when we called on her, she had just been frightened by a snake, as were her dogs. She reported it as being about six feet long and possibly poisonous. She had wanted to stone it as it went off down the path but was afraid it might turn on her.

No gardening is undertaken by the lady of Household Thirteen. She formerly had about thirty papaya trees, but they were felled by the great storm of 1960 which, however, did little harm to the thin row of slender bamboos in front of her house. Of guava trees, she has never had any. To add to her income, she has sometimes taken home work from the gold-silver paper factories. If she works all the time, she can make a dollar a day but, because of other duties, such as caring for her grandchildren in Lung Shing, to earn a dollar usually takes two or three days. We were not surprised when she told us that from her various economic activities she could sometimes help out her son with a few hundred dollars. Normally, she eats two meals a day. If she goes into Lung Shing in the morning, she eats ten or twenty cents worth of food there, and then does not have another meal until night, the remnants of which are given to her dog. She does not smoke or drink.

The owner of Household Thirteen says she was born near Canton, but she is not absolutely certain just where as she does not remember the China which she left more than forty years ago. Furthermore, when she was very young she was given away by her parents to another family, the members of which fell into straitened circumstances and likewise gave her away. Consequently she never really knew her own parents, but she speaks Cantonese. When she was still a girl, she was picked up by a soldier and followed him to the city of Canton. Later he died and she came to Hong Kong to work as a servant. At the age of about twenty or about 1919, she reached Lung Shing, the settlement then comprising only two or three hundred people as she remembers it. There she met the father of the head of the Household Seven who, appreciating her good qualities, suggested that she leave her position and live with him as his concubine. She did.

They lived in a rented house on Church Street paying $8 a month, and raised pigs in an open area nearby. Her husband was relatively poor at the time (it was his first wife's only son who was destined to become the rich man of Tung Pak Wan). She bore twin daughters in Lung Shing and gave them both away to some people in the next street. One died, but the other lived to marry by free choice and now has seven children. Recently this daughter has recognized and been nice to her consanguineal mother.

Another daughter whom she brought up herself also married by free choice and has four children in the town across the strait. Her only son, however, was married blind, a girl having been selected from her husband's village in Chung Shan.

The concubine, after being widowed, might never have moved from her home, in which she had resided for over thirty-five years, had not part of the Lung Shing property been needed to make room for a new church building. The government had offered to exchange her land for that in another village, but the latter location was too far away. Also she wanted to raise some pigs. Then the first wife's only son suggested that she take up land in Tung Pak Wan and, with his help, she did so in 1956.

Commentary. The world view of the mistress of Household Thirteen is limited almost exclusively to the island on which she lives. She has not been to Victoria since the Japanese occupation (twenty years almost) and says she has nothing to do there. She does not mind riding the buses, but she is afraid of being hit by a car. Actually, she thinks she has only been in the city five or six times in her life, and she has not been as far as Kowloon since she came from China. Crossing the strait from Lung Shing is another matter because of her married daughter living on the far side. Still she seldom visits her since, as she explains, she would have to spend a dollar on presents for her grandchildren, and that she cannot afford to do. In her whole life, she had never had a pleasure trip on a sampan. She does know the island itself relatively well but has seldom visited its other recently developed out of the way settlements. She is close to Chung Nam Wan but points out the obvious fact that the path is too difficult for her to go there often. She frequently visits her son in Lung Shing who works as a butcher at a stall in the Market and still rents their same old home for $50 a month. His mother says he liked to play and was not industrious like his half brother when young. Also, when there is a great wind threatening she moves into town. She told us the last typhoon was particularly bad because people spoke of it as a p'ut fu (p'o fu), or shrew, rather than politely. Most of her days, however, are spent in Tung Pak Wan and, considering this fact, it did seem a little surprising at the time, that it was we who introduced her to her newest and closest neighbor. We shall always remember the mistress of Household Thirteen, the first person we met in Tung Pak Wan, as she easily gained our continuing respect and affection.

Household Fourteen

There is an unusual attraction about the residence of Household Fourteen because it nestles in behind a grove of bamboos which have slender stems rising well above its story-and-a-half height (Fig. 11.11). Also, the rivulet breaks out of a hidden ravine just above and spreads over

Fig. 11.11 Home of Household Fourteen

a stony stream bed a yard or two wide in front of the house. The latter is reached by turning up a well-made path that begins near the shore between Households One and Two. Climbing stone steps at intervals, one passes Household Twelve half hidden back among the trees, and continues for some distance above the latter. The newer house is set into a niche on the slope and is reached by a wide concrete flight of stairs with nine steps leading to a concrete flooring. The construction of both frame and siding is of the simplest kind: wide board slabs that look as though at one time they had been burned are nailed against studding and topped by a nearly flat gabled roof of corrugated composition material. As the builder, who is head of the house, confided, it is legally a little too high. According to his statement, no wood house over ten feet is allowed, and his posts were a few inches longer. There was an objection at first, but the inspector generously did not make an issue of the matter. The house rests on the usual concrete base. The window openings are large and unglazed. Above the area set off as a bedroom, there is an inside gallery reached by a ladder.

Electricity was obtained by 1961 by extending the necessary wires from Household One. Cobwebs stretching between the wires are especially conspicuous as the house is otherwise clean. It was not surprising to be told that this utility is not used when there are storms, for there is obviously some fear of the lines that convey electrical current. Household One is likewise the source of water, the latter being conveyed from a well in buckets. Guarding this establishment is a small dog named Ho Ts'oi (Hao Ts'ai), or Lucky, and two cats.

The head of the house is a man forty-four years old. When we first talked to him, he was wearing a dirty green sweat shirt over a clean white undershirt; also gray trousers, striped red socks, and old composition-soled canvas shoes. On his wrist was a watch. His wife is a year younger. In the course of her life she has borne five children, two of whom died. The eldest survivor is a girl of twenty-four. Then there is a boy of thirteen and a second girl of twelve, the youngest in the series of offspring. The mother, when first seen, was dressed in a black gummed silk sam fu over a white undercoat. No rings were visible on her fingers and none in her ears. Her feet were bare and she wore her hair in a long straight bob. From her point of view, she should have a permanent wave twice a year which would make her hair easier to care for, but she does not have the five or six dollars to spare that each visit to the hairdresser would cost. Later she was seen in a sam fu of unmatched cotton material and typical slippers with single green straps. No one in the house owned a cheong sam at the time of our first visit, but the next year when the elder sister was married by her own choice to a man among the boat people, she managed to buy a cheong sam, and the younger sister now thinks she would like one. She also says that a blind marriage kills a lot of people; that is to say, they feel as though life had gone out of them. She is firmly convinced that people should decide for themselves. An inquiry about her parents led to the point that she did not actually know how they had been married.

The mother in the family did not attend school. Her husband had a few years of primary education and can read or write a little. The elder daughter, however, attended school for five years, and the younger two both graduated from School B in Lung Shing in 1961 (the girl went seven years instead of the normal six as she had to repeat one of the grades). Both children have applied for entrance in a Middle School across the strait, but do not know whether they will be admitted.

The mistress of the house says that she attends the cinema rarely, and that she prefers Cantonese pictures when she does go for the simple reason that she can understand the sound-strip. She reports that no one in the family can play mah-jongg, but that everyone except herself goes swimming. The younger daughter admits that her maximum distance is only about twenty feet. They have a radio that someone recently gave them, but she is not certain who it was. She also is uncertain why the family prefers doctors with Western type training unless it is because the Chinese medicines taste awful.

There is quite an elaborate altar shelf in the outer room of the house with two pictures of Taoist deities above it. The father says he has no religion, and no interest in feng-shui, protesting with a laugh that he did not use it in building his house. He admits, however, that his wife honors the gods. The mother says the family has no religion, at the same time conceding that incense is burned on the occasion of some festivals. The younger daughter refers to the family as Buddhists which in her mind seems to mean only that they do burn incense. She herself sometimes likes to go to the Pentecostal Holiness Church in Lung Shing on Saturday night and Sunday morning, but she could not explain what it is that has attracted her.

The parental attitudes on politics were not specifically obtained. The younger daughter, for whom the term Communist seems to have no meaning, does think it would be nice to be governed by Chinese. The family does not belong to a Kaifong Association.

Although basically the family has been dependent on relatives since coming to Tung Pak Wan, its economic situation has apparently been improving. Having started by borrowing ten young pigs from Household One, they have repaid the debt and by 1960 owned four sows and about fifty pigs altogether. By the same procedure, the family has accumulated five hens and about twice as many chickens. These are raised to eat and not to sell. Besides its bamboo trees, another appealing aspect of Household Fourteen is the ducks that swim in a small pool formed in the rivulet near the front of the dwelling. Only one of the ducks of 1960 survived, but nine more were purchased to replace them the following year. The family has no pigeons, nor any fruit trees, nor do they cultivate a vegetable garden, land for which is apparently not available.

Although only two meals a day are eaten, breakfast being passed over, there was no complaint about the shortage of food. Some help was contributed by the elder daughter who came home once a week until she married. She earned $100 a month in a factory off the island sewing gloves and managed to save something for the family despite her expenses for room, food, and clothing. Also, there is the small amount that can be earned by pasting the tinfoil squares on paper for the Lung Shing manufacturers of gold-silver money for the dead. The father smokes and also drinks a little, but he is the only one who does in the family.

Both patrilineal and matrilineal ancestral lines of Household Fourteen are boat people from Lung Chau. The head of the family passes his father's mother's grave whenever he goes to town. It lies on the crest of ground which sets off Tung Pak Wan from the nearby population center. Both he and his wife were actually born on boats. She remembers being told that her father found a midwife for her mother when she came into the world, a lucky thing because if her mother had been the only female on the boat at childbirth, no man would have helped her. Afterward she and her mother were allowed to rest for a month on a relative's boat that was permanently moored in the harbor. This was the usual custom forty years ago. Now a pregnant woman is not so likely to risk being away from the harbor and seeks an anchored vessel reasonably in advance of the date of her expected parturition.

In 1956, the shrimp boat of the head of the house, on which all the children were born, broke down. It was too old to repair. To resolve the problem, they were invited by the mistress of Household One to put up a house and raise pigs on the rear hillside area of her land. The suggestion is understandable as the one who invited them is a sister of the head of the former shrimp boat family. Between the two households, we were told, "there is no talk of rent," nor do the newcomers pay the fee for the land.

Commentary. The head of the house was not very successful as a fisherman, however much he may have traveled on the sea. We asked him what he knew of Tung Pak Wan as a boy. He said that people never came to the little valley because poor boat people deposited their dead children among the rocks of the area and only stopped doing so after World War II. Now he seldom goes off the island, although he occasionally goes to the city. We did not find it surprising that the young daughter of Household Fourteen had never been to Chung Nam Wan and did not even know where Sai Mi Wan is. The father has no interest in returning to sea. He seems to have economic problems that he cannot resolve, and his burden lies like a cloud over his family.

Household Fifteen

After climbing over the crest which sets off Tung Pak Wan from the urban center of Lung Chau one may take a path which, instead of descending to the older residences of the community, rises to an artificial shelf cut into the hill. One then proceeds past a series of wire chicken houses and comes upon a two-story wood house with considerable additions of metal sheathing, including a corrugated gable roof of uncertain material. There is also a one-story wing the full width of the house, its shed roof sloping off to the northwest. One somehow gets the impression that the building is a factory before one has proof of that surmise by noting the professional equipment for the making of vermicelli. Beyond the house is a more extensive building devoted to the raising of pigeons. In 1960, there was no electric current, but lines were installed early the next year and the establishment became distinguished in having a fluorescent light. An electric iron had also been acquired, while an electric pump to bring water from the household well was an anticipated goal. Four dogs including a well-grown puppy have the responsibility of chasing away rats since there are no cats in the family.

In the house live a man of forty, his wife who is thirty-nine, and six children. These comprise a daughter thirteen, a son eleven, a daughter eight, a son six, another son four, and a daughter three. There are also four male workers and an apprentice who likewise engages in the manufacture of vermicelli and a sixth male worker who cares for the pigeons.

Nothing unusual was noted about the clothing of the various members of the household unless it is a tendency to dress slightly better than the average resident of Tung Pak Wan. We observed the mother in a gray fu and black sam, while the eldest daughter wore a gray sam fu with some black patterning in it. The latter also sometimes wears a skirt and blouse. Also she wears red or green slippers indicating an awareness of colors. The mother has solid gold button earrings, and both women have wristwatches and bobbed, curled hair. Neither owns a cheong sam. When it is cool, the father wears a nice gray cardigan over his cotton undershirt, plus commonplace trousers and slippers.

The parents were married by free choice, having met each other in a vermicelli factory where they both worked in Lung Shing. The young lady of the family is also unhesitatingly of the opinion that modern marriage is best. She is a bright girl who was graduated from School D in 1961 and expected to enter Middle School across the strait that fall. She knows some English but is hesitant about speaking it. Her second younger brother attends the afternoon session of the same school, but the elder one goes to a Catholic parochial school across the strait, having been accepted on the basis of an examination, while the second daughter in the family is enrolled in School B. The two youngest members of the family have their education ahead of them. According to the same informant, both parents can read a little. In due course, however, we learned that the mother had one year of schooling in Lung Shing while the father had no education at all.

Nearly every day in hot weather, all the children go down the hill to play in the sea. The two eldest know how to swim and so does their father, but their mother does not. The family owns a portable radio and periodically various members attend the cinema, although the parents least often. The eldest daughter prefers Mandarin pictures to Cantonese, as the former are more sophisticated, while the father likes Peking opera. The head of the house is the only one who understands how to play mah-jongg, but is said not to play it. When anyone is ill in the family, a doctor trained in the Western tradition is consulted.

The household is traditionalist in religion, and despite indications of Christian contact through the schooling of one of the sons, no one had accepted Catholicism up to the time of our last visit, according to the eldest daughter. She, however, expressed disfavor of Communism and believes that, if the British left Hong Kong, Chinese administration would prove inferior. No one in the family belongs to a Kaifong Association, although the father did once.

No family in Tung Pak Wan gives such an impression of economic activity as do the members of Household Fifteen. This is because the mother, the father, and several workers are primarily engaged in making vermicelli, and when they make vermicelli, they have little time to do anything else, even talk. They normally produce over two hundred catties of wheat vermicelli a day and sell their product for $.90 a catty. When nothing goes wrong, it would seem that the business is profitable. The family neither grows vegetables nor raises pigs, which is understandable as there would hardly be time for such additional undertakings, especially as they do care for sixty to seventy chickens. In 1960, they also owned two ducks and one goose (another had died), but they ate all three on the following New Year's. Except for a mulberry tree, there are no fruit trees on the property. The family has a regular morning breakfast of congee with various complementary dishes. Both parents smoke, the mother rolling her own cigarettes from mild shuk in (shu yen) tobacco, and the father favoring Abdullahs. On occasion, they drink a little.

The family is of Fukienese lineage, but Cantonese, the native tongue of the mother, who was born in Lung Shing of parents from Tung Kuan, is the common language since only the elder daughter among the children can understand Fukienese, and that only a little. The mother has learned Fukienese well, however, and she and her husband usually converse in that language. The patrilineal home of the head of Household Fifteen was in a suburb of Amoy where the making of vermicelli was commonplace because of cheap rents and good transportation to a large market. His father died when he was a small boy after which he was apprenticed to a vermicelli maker at the age of eleven and has continued in the business ever since. About 1937, he emigrated to Lung Shing, a vermicelli making center of Hong Kong. Having fallen in love with a fellow worker, their marriage was arranged for late 1941. To celebrate the occasion his mother, his brother, and the latter's wife came from Amoy for the ceremony. The Japanese attack immediately followed as did personal tragedy. His sister-in-law was killed by a Japanese bomb dropped on remnants of the defenders who fell back on Lung Shing after the British surrender. The mother and brother returned to Amoy alone.

After sixteen years of married life, the family found the chance to start a business of its own. A well-to-do friend and native of Amoy wanted to raise pigeons and obtained a permit for the area on the upper edge of the Tung Pak Wan settlement. He offered to pay the head of Household Fifteen to take care of them and at the same time provide a place to make vermicelli. The head of the family has been getting up at four in the morning and working very hard ever since.

The pigeon raiser owns a gold-silver paper factory in Lung Shing and has also invested in a concern making plastic beads at the west end of town. He told us that he started raising pigeons more or less for fun, but that it has turned into a passable business. The unusual aspect of the venture is that he has paid very high prices for select pairs of American and English pigeons. The latter, which have unusual beaks, he purchased out of curiosity as he says they are too small to be bred profitably. His large American pigeons, he crosses with ordinary Chinese ones to increase the size of the more commonplace offspring. Sales are principally confined to birds one month old, which are supplied to some of the more expensive restaurants in Hong Kong for half again as much as ordinary pigeons will bring on the market. As the birds breed little after six years of age, they are then sold to people who stew them. He uses a mixture of corn, rice, beans, and oats as feed three times a day for the breeding pigeons, which themselves feed the squabs. Also water is piped to each cage and kept available to the birds at a certain depth by a system cleverly devised from the ball and valve fixture of a flush toilet. Each cage also has a separate box containing earth, sand, and shell. The almost feather-less baby pigeons sit on special boxes containing excelsior which they seek out when they want to be warm. The pigeon raiser also has medicines for the birds' various ailments. As a final note on the undertaking, it may be recorded that the pigeon droppings are considered too strong for use on growing vegetables and are consigned to the sea.

Not content with his bird farm, the extraordinary Fukienese pigeon raiser (who is apt to be seen on the street of Lung Shing in a costume that looks exactly like a striped cotton suit of Western pajamas) has also taken to raising fine breeds of dogs, which he keeps in cages near those of the pigeons. If this latter venture ever becomes profitable, it will not contradict the fact that he finds obvious satisfaction from the possession of these animals.

Commentary. Returning to the family of Household Fifteen, they give the impression of representing that half of the Tung Pak Wan population that shows a wider world of consciousness, but this judgment may be prejudiced by both the activity of the parents and the avidity of the eldest daughter. Obviously, the children are well acquainted with Lung Shing. They have also visited cousins in Kowloon. On the other hand, our young lady informant who had been to Repulse Bay had visited neither Chung Nam Wan only ten minutes away nor Sai Mi Wan at the other end of the island. Her parents and their friend, the pigeon raiser, seem to exemplify the qualities of integrity and steadfast devotion to their special interests which characterize so many of the Fukienese on Lung Chau.

Household Sixteen

The residence we shall refer to as Household Sixteen consists only of the southerly of two rooms in the single-story building which has been previously mentioned as occupied by Household Nine. The house, which is neat and clean, has the usual plank bed with addition of a mosquito net over it. There is no electricity in this abode, which the owner shares with her cat that she says catches a great many rats.

Water was brought from the well of Household Eight until the summer of 1961, when the owner of the well did not have enough water for his hundreds of chickens. This was not really surprising as Households Three, Four, Nine, and Ten, as well as Sixteen, were diminishing the supply. In the face of this crisis, the five families cut off from water banded together and had a new well dug at a cost of almost $400. It required over one week of the well-digger's labor. The well is thirty feet deep and the water is very clear. The five families wanted the well in front of Household Ten, but the well-digger persuaded them that his choice of locations between Households Three and Sixteen was better, and they agreed, conceding that he was the expert. The well is directly behind and at the roof level of Household Four. There is a wood cross piece mounted above the well which supports a single block pulley with a one-inch rope attached to a pail. There is also a locked cover on the opening, but nonetheless, the mother in Household Three is afraid her babies may fall into it as the cover is left open when someone is making continuous trips for water. The fact that the well does save the labor of carrying water a considerable distance up the hill is appreciated, however.

The sole member of Household Sixteen is a maiden lady who gave her age as forty when asked. She usually wears either a pleasant appearing light blue striped sam fu or a black one. There are white tennis shoes on her feet. She has never owned a cheong sam and commented that the women of her parental family dress only in black gummed silk sam fu, not fancy ones. Our informant has straight bobbed hair which has grown quite long. In her ears are small gold earrings of a shape suggesting the letter A. They are of a type that could cost about twenty dollars. She has neither bracelets nor rings, but then her hands are in some degree crippled.

Illness has been a dominant factor in this lady's life. At about twenty years of age she began to suffer from a disease of the bone characterized by swelling and fever which has left her hands and feet more or less weakened ever since, and for five years off and on she resided in one or another government hospital. She states that she consistently patronizes doctors trained in the Western tradition of medicine but gives as the reason that they are cheaper.

There is little activity in her life that might be classed as amusement. She no longer goes to the cinema although she states that she used to attend sometimes. She does not own a radio. When the opportunity offers, she watches others play mah-jongg. She understands the game but does not play it herself. Also she does not have the benefit of books, as does her neighbor, never having been to school. She does claim the knowledge, however, of a few of the most significant characters in the Chinese translation of the Bible.

The lady of Household Sixteen is a Catholic and her conversion goes back to the period of her hospitalization when she was befriended by a nursing Sister. She is still helped by her church, receiving periodic gifts of rice and flour. She does not belong to a Kaifong Association.

The economic structure of the Household is not too clear. Understandingly enough, our informant invariably stresses how poor she is, sometimes demeaning herself in the process, an approach which is not typical of people in the community who are in straitened circumstances. On the other hand, she appears to be in a position to obtain limited sums of money. She admitted to paying more than three hundred dollars for her half of the house, which was first lived in by the sister of the head of Household Nine. Her most obvious income is derived from selling eggs. She has about thirty chickens of which half are hens. According to her own statement, however, her chickens provide so little income that she has been losing money on them. She has no fruit trees, grows no vegetables and, in 1960, she had no pigs. In the spring of 1961, deciding that chickens die too easily, she obtained two small pigs on credit and hopes for some improvement in her financial affairs. When asked how she acquires money for food, she states that she also gets that on credit. It would seem that her own diet is a limited one. She eats two meals, usually of rice with fish and vegetables, one shortly before noon and the other at six in the evening. She added that she would eat a lot of other things if she could afford them. Furthermore, she neither drinks nor smokes. Sometimes she prints gold-silver paper by which means, if she works to the end of her strength, she can make a little over a dollar in a day. Also, despite her crippled hands she spends a great deal of time knitting socks, which she turns over to a Sister in her church through whom she obtained orders. Several years later she informed us that for a half dozen years after she left the hospital, or until about 1956, she received $15 a month from the church. Then she was told those who have been in trouble more recently should have their chance for support.

The maiden lady of Household Sixteen comes from a Hakka family, although she now speaks comprehensible Cantonese. She was born in Tan Shui which is southwest of Hui Yang (Hui Yang hsien) in Kwangtung Province. She had some cousins living in the New Territories and came to

Hong Kong originally to seek a cure for her disease. Ultimately, a nursing Sister in one of the hospitals helped her to obtain a cigarette vendor's license, which cost $60, when she was finally released. With a close friend she had made in the hospital and who was also released, she sold wood slippers in Sai Ying Pun. Then they tried Kowloon and added food to their offerings. Business was poor so they settled on Lung Chau because friends suggested that it would be a good place. She herself lived in Lung Shing for some years, as her friend still does, but she says that people were unkind to her. When asked how they were unkind, she commented that the established families of Lung Shing are not friendly to newcomers and demand that the latter make a good appearance and have money if they are going to do business with them. In any event, she was unsuccessful in the cigarette business and she finally gave up her license, having persuaded her present Hakka neighbor in 1958 to sell her half of his house so that she could have a little more space and raise chickens.

Commentary. The lady of Household Sixteen has been more or less restricted in movement by her disease since coming to Hong Kong. She nonetheless usually walks into Lung Shing once every few days, but sometimes she does not go for a week and her neighbors do her shopping for her. Despite her years of residence on the island, she knows nothing of Sai Mi Wan at its far end; indeed, she has not even knowledge of that or the other names by which that settlement may be designated. Consequently it was more unexpected to discover that she has twice made the difficult climb up and down to Chung Nam Wan where lives the Lin family whose native villages are in the same general area as her own. On the whole, illness and penury have been a heavy weight on the spirit of the lady of Household Sixteen, and one that may well never be lifted.

Household Seventeen

The residence of Household Seventeen is a one-story wood structure built on the usual base of concrete with low side walls of the same material. The walls are clapboard and the gable roof is wired down with large stones on the flat places. A chicken coop is attached at the north end and there is a kitchen shed to the south (Fig. 11.12). It is the home one reaches first when one descends by the main path into Tung Pak Wan, it having been set on a niche cut into the steep side of the hill across from the pigpens of Household Seven. Fortunately, its height not only provides a pleasant vista, but also the exposure allows breezes to disperse the strong porcine smell of the area. Only the graveyard to the north might be considered objectionable (Fig. 11.4).

The main structure is divided in two, and there is a gallery over the bedroom. Water is piped to the kitchen area from the well of Household

Fig. 11.12. Home of Household Seventeen

Seven. It is said to be "sweet and cool," thus preventing people from becoming "hot," a condition which may result in a sore throat, toothache, or some other unpleasant disease. From the same household come the wires to one incandescent light. There is a small dog called Tao Li ("Dolly") which looks out for the family, but there are no cats.

The family consists of a husband who is a little over thirty years of age, a wife who is thirty, one son of eleven, another of four, and a baby daughter. Two days before our first visit another son aged seven had died from causes unknown in a hospital across the strait. The younger son seems to be suffering from some mental or physical defect as he is unable to talk.

The mother of the house dresses usually in a black gummed silk sam fu, but she has been seen in a blue print sam and black trousers (fu). She has never owned a cheong sam. At the time we first made specific note of her costume, her feet were bare as they usually are, and her hair was done in a permanent bob. She said that she goes to a hairdresser in Lung Shing before each New Year's and is charged five dollars. In her ears, she wore small gold rings.

The mistress of Household Seventeen was married blind, and she expressed no dissatisfaction with this traditional procedure which perhaps was a correlate of her general diseregard for speculation. Asked about marriage to cousins, she did not know which ones it might be proper or improper to marry. She herself has never attended school and does not know the character for either her husband's or her father's surname. Her husband did have three or four years of schooling, whereas their elder son is only in his second year under a private teacher who charges ten dollars a month. His mother admits that the boy is not bright and that he could not get into any of the regular schools.

There is no radio in the house and no one in the family plays mah-jongg. If they did, they would have nothing to eat, says the wife. The older boy goes swimming. When there is sickness, a doctor with Western type training is visited. His charge is three dollars including medicine. The mother adds that she is influenced by the fact that she would not like to make her children drink Chinese medicine. She also says that the members of the family have no religion unless one includes the Confucianism indicated by the paper above a shelf containing ancestral names. Incense is burned before this "tablet" every morning—when she does not forget to do it. Our informant did not seem to comprehend the simplest political questions, to say nothing of having any political opinions. The family has no membership in a Kaifong Association.

The head of the household works from early morning until evening taking care of the numberless pigs of Household Seven, and when a sow gives birth, he may have to be on hand at any time during the night. For his labors he is paid $120 a month plus three daily meals. The house, including water and more recently electricity, may properly be added as part of his recompense. The family has no pigs of its own, nor any pigeons, ducks, or fruit trees. They also grow no vegetables. On the other hand, they do raise chickens and in 1960 had fourteen hens in a coop that adjoins the bedroom. A year later the total number of chickens had increased to over a hundred, the birds being confined to small cages and supplied with injections to fatten them. We watched the eldest son mix corn flour, wheat chaff, and olive oil in the center of the bedroom floor to feed them. Then he added some pulverized dried fish and some grass powder. No regular breakfast is served in the house, two meals a day being considered normal for the mother and children at home. The baby is breast fed because, as the mother says, she cannot afford canned milk. We were told that about a dollar is spent on dishes for each meal. The husband sometimes buys ten cents worth of congee in the morning, as does the son going to school. The cooking is usually done in a pot-stove. Sawdust, in order to use it as fuel, is packed around a vertical bottle which, when withdrawn, leaves the essential draught opening, later connected to another at the bottom made from the front of the stove with a stick. The mother does not smoke, but the father likes his tobacco; also he drinks a little on occasions.

The family is comprised of Cantonese speakers who came originally from the so-called Four Districts of Kwangtung (the wife is from Hsin Hui). They first moved to Macao where all of their children were born except the baby. The father came from Macao to Hong Kong in 1955 and went to work for Household Seven, a friend having introduced him to its head. In 1958, his employer built a house for him and he was able to bring his wife and children to live in Tung Pak Wan. The latter stayed with his employer's mother in Lung Shing for a few months, however, before the house was completed.

The head of the house has seldom had time to go anywhere, although his knowledge of Macao presumably gives him a type of experience not shared by many residents of Tung Pak Wan. His wife has a few relatives in Hong Kong whom she visits periodically, and she also has been to Kowloon. The mistress of Household Seventeen usually goes shopping in Lung Shing every morning and, although she has not climbed over to either Chung Nam Wan or Sai Mi Wan, she knows where both settlements are.

Commentary. Despite its travels, it would seem that this family is cognizant of a smaller world than most of its neighbors in Tung Pak Wan. It is significant that the mistress of Household Seventeen had never met Mrs. Chin of Household Four until we introduced her, and that the latter, along with other neighbors, only knew of this family by the nickname given her husband because of a supernumerary finger on one of his hands. Curiously, the wife did not recognize the nickname. If she is the least educated woman in Tung Pak Wan, she at least has the intelligence to point out to us that most Americans are known for their habit of giving away things.

Household Eighteen

As might be anticipated, the last house to be erected before the period of our study is the highest, and consequently for that reason, perhaps the most conspicuous in Tung Pak Wan. The members of Household Eighteen normally reach their home by taking the second subsidiary path to the right after crossing the crest which separates the village from Lung Shing, and following it past the widow's home referred to as Household Thirteen, gradually climbing as they do so, then crossing the westerly gully and continuing to the place where the easterly rivulet comes out of the rocks. It is there that they have cut out of the hill a flat terrace supported by two tiers of well laid rock, each more or less six feet in height (Fig. 11.13).

As the path approaches the site, one first comes upon a series of wire chicken coops sloping back up the hill and in another few feet the rectangu-

Fig. 11.13. Home of Household Eighteen

lar, clapboard-sided house a story and a half high, its nearly flat roof slanting down to the north. One has to go around to the far side to reach the door which opens onto a generous-sized intervening area separating the house from a row of three concrete pigpens bordering the rivulet. A little above and beyond the pigpens is a shady little pool in the rocks in which float three large ducks. Nearby is a well.

Despite the fact that the concrete of pigpens, which cost almost a thousand dollars, has already cracked because the earth of the terrace has settled, no home of Tung Pak Wan has such a pleasant aspect. First of all, the view from the height is magnificent and cannot be disregarded on a first visit. It is more surprising to be greeted affectionately on the path by a small bitch that seems to convey in advance the friendly welcome of its owners. The house itself, on which also almost a thousand dollars have been spent, is divided into two small rooms on the first floor and has an interior gallery above that is reached by a ladder. Without doubt, it is unsurpassed in cleanliness by any residence on Lung Chau. This is not altogether due to the fact that the building is only a year old, but rather to a certain compulsiveness on the part of those who take care of it.

The house could hardly contain more plain wood furniture, and there is the usual complement of thermos jugs, bottles, clocks, calendars, and lamps (electricity is not available) that gives a Chinese village home a cluttered appearance. Also on the walls are scores of photographs of various sizes (Fig. 11.14). In this house live eight people including three children, yet it gives the impression one could happily eat on the smooth concrete floor. Indeed, the occupants take off their shoes when they enter, but the dog, named A Ts'oi (A Ts'ai), or Mrs. Rich, is not excluded. It is uncertain what the family attitude was about her two puppies the next year, or about the pair of small cats that had been obtained to prey on the rats.

The people of Household Eighteen first of all comprise a widow of sixty-two and her son of twenty-nine who works as a butcher in the town across the strait and seldom comes home. His mother says that he does not make enough money to get married. Then there is the widow's husband's brother's son, aged fifty-one, who also works in the large public market of the town across the strait, his wife who is thirty-seven, and their fifteen-year-old son. The latter is serving his second year of a four-year apprenticeship to a plumber in Wanchai. He receives his meals and room plus a little over ten dollars a month. In consequence, he practically never comes home, preferring the company of his friends in the Colony's metropolis.

Besides this lineage group, there is another nuclear family composed of the widow's daughter who is thirty-three years of age, her husband, forty-four, and their three children, a son twelve, a daughter ten, and another son of eight. Thus ten people are technically members of Household Eighteen, and of them, eight sleep at home regularly. It was reported that the father and mother with three children sleep in the half-story, the others on the ground floor.

The dress of the members of Household Eighteen did not attract special attention. The women all wear sam fu and none owns a cheong sam. When the small daughter was asked if she would like a cheong sam, her grandmother laughed and answered for her saying that if she had money, she would like one when she grew up. The widowed grandmother wears gold earrings with a large bottom part the size of a finger ring, but no bracelets.

It was the butcher's wife who expressed herself most freely about marriage and children. She herself was married blind, as was the widow in the family, at a time when there was no other method in China. Now she believes that individuals should choose their own mates. Curiously, in speaking of preferential marriage, she thinks that one may marry neither a father's sister's nor a mother's brother's son. As for children, in her judgment three or four are enough. "How can you feed more?" she asks, and then adds, "But what can you do about it." Obviously, contraception is not within her ken. The widow's daughter was married semi-blind, and while we were discussing the matter, her daughter spoke up and said that free marriage is best. "Of course she will choose," added her grandmother.

Fig. 11.14. Interior of Home of Household Eighteen

All three of the children attend school. The elder boy is in fourth grade in School D in Lung Shing and his sister has attained grade three. The cost is $3.40 per month for each. The younger boy goes to the afternoon session of the government school across the strait for which the fee is $5 per month. The two oldest women in the household had no schooling whatever, but the widow's married daughter had three years, while the widow's son had two. Although the married butcher had only two or three years of schooling in his native village, he is said to read quite well as he has practiced considerably since that time.

During summer vacation and when out of school at other times, the children usually play close to the house, although they do occasionally go swimming. None of the adults can swim. In the course of our visits, we noticed that some roses and other flowers had been planted on the banks of the rivulet above the pigpens. We learned that the children had been given the seedlings at a house conspicuous for its flowers which they pass in Lung Shing when coming from school. The children also enjoy an American transistor radio. It is notable that two of the female members of the household sometimes play mah-jongg. The widow plays in the Lung Shing market with her former neighbors, but only for small stakes, such as ten or twenty cents a game.

The butcher's wife says everyone believes that doctors with Western type training cure faster. She prefers them, emphasizing her opinion that Chinese medicine is not only slow in producing results, but that the children are afraid to drink it. A doctor with Western type training is available to them through the Lung Chau Kaifong Association. His charge is $3, a fee that is cut to $2 for the members. She has belonged to the Association for eight or nine years, the family paying $1.70 a month for the various benefits. The widow also has a membership but none of the men in the house belong.

The individuals in Household Eighteen are traditionalist in religion. Our informant claims that she knows the difference between Buddhist and Taoist temples, but that no one in the family visits either. There is a pair of pictures of gate gods pasted onto the double doors of the house. In the front room, there is an altar to T'o Ti (T'u Ti), the Earth God, with numerous candles and incense sticks which attest to the respect paid him. Incense is burned on the God's birthdays—they were reported as five, occurring on the 10th of the 1st, 2nd, 3rd, 4th, and 5th months—and sometimes on other days, both in the morning and at night. The butcher's wife said there were no ancestral tablets in the house, and that there were none in her father's, back of whose time she could not go. We learned somewhat later, however, that there is an ancestor's tablet in the house. Also two red plaques with gold letters are placed outside the front door with incense cans beneath. On one is written "God of Heaven grant us happiness," on the other simply "Door God, Earth God, Money God."

There is a crown permit for the land in the name of the widow's unmarried son, and an annual assessment of about $135 is paid on it. The house, however, was spoken of as though it belonged to the widow's son-in-law. Politics did not prove to be a rewarding subject of discussion, the butcher's wife, for example, claiming that she does not understand such things and has no interest in which government runs Hong Kong.

The economic situation of the family is obviously better than most in Tung Pak Wan. To begin with, the widow's son-in-law works as a boat builder in Lung Shing, which provides a regular cash income, and his wife works for Household Seven feeding the pigeons and cleaning their cages from seven to twelve and two to five for which she earns $120 per month as has been previously mentioned. She formerly worked as an earth coolie. The widow's son may also contribute. The married butcher likewise earns a salary. We can compute that the combined incomes might well run to over $750 a month.

Besides these sources of cash, there are the pigs. In 1960, the family had three sows. A year later, one sow had been sold, but there was an addition of five offspring eight months old and six that were two months making a total of thirteen pigs. In 1960, there were about thirty chickens and these have increased. There is no vegetable garden but east of the rivulet new terracing at the same level as the house is being carried out and corn (maize) is being grown for pig food. A few guava and papaya trees were also planted, but these unfortunately died. The family has no pigeons and ate up its three ducks at New Year's.

The adults do not eat breakfast except once in a while if they go to market. The children, on the other hand, are given twenty cents each with which to buy food and they spend it for cakes and similar items at the stands near their schools. They are said to prefer this to eating rice at home; it was asserted that they did not spend the money for candy. One day just before noon we saw the widow, her granddaughter, and the butcher's wife having lunch. They had prepared a large bowl of boiled flowering Chinese cabbage (first quick-fried in oil, then water and salt are added, the soup being brought to a boil), three Chinese sausages, a small dish of cut up salted fish, and a goodly supply of well-cooked rice. The butcher's wife ate three bowls of the latter, and the others, two. The older women were using ivory chopsticks that had turned brown from age. Neither of the children's parents smoke, but the butcher's wife enjoys tobacco, rolling her own cigarettes from mild tobacco, shuk in (shu yen). The widow uses the same brand but smokes it in a man's curved-bowl brier pipe of Western origin. The elder lady is also known to drink a little sheung ching (shuang cheng), or Double Distilled, a spirit of about sixty proof, when the opportunity offers, and her eyes light up at the mention of wine. On feast days, however, all the adults drink.

The occupants of Household Eighteen are Cantonese speaking, and all have lived on Lung Chau for many years. The lineage home of the husband of the widow's daughter is in Tung Kuan, whereas that of the married butcher, and consequently of the widow's husband and their children is in San Shui west of Canton. The widow herself was born in a village near that of her husband. The married butcher wanted to raise pigs to increase his income and about 1957 a permit for the land was obtained on which a house was built two years later. In fact, the full complement of the household had not moved into its new home until the third month of 1960.

Commentary. The regular contacts of the family obviously extend beyond the island with one husband working and one child going to school on the other side of the strait. The elderly widow who seems in some ways to be the dominant person on the scene, told us that she had been in Macao over twenty years earlier. When we asked about her husband on the day we first met, she explained that he had been selling preserved eggs in Kam Shan (Chin Shan), or Gold Hill, i.e., California, for the last twenty years. We answered, "That's good." and she replied "What is good about it?" We had not immediately caught the significance of the Cantonese statement, for she was telling us that her husband was dead (preserved eggs are coated with earth) and had gone to a good place (Gold Hill). Our friend in Household Thirteen discovered the error after we introduced her to the widow whose husband we had said was in the United States. Most of the shopping for the family is done by the widow who says she has to purchase things in the market in Lung Shing twice a day or otherwise the food would go bad. The mother of the only son, on the other hand, says that she seldom walks into town and has not been to the metropolis of Hong Kong in ten years because she becomes car sick. If a trip is necessary, she goes on an empty stomach and does not eat until some time after her return. She does not seem to even know of Sai Mi Wan, and she has not visited Chung Nam Wan which is only a few minutes away, although the children in the family have been there. She says everyone is too busy to go visiting. The final impression one gains of the occupants of Household Eighteen is that if their world is relatively large, it at least has not yet really encompassed their new village, the growing settlement of Tung Pak Wan.

12. Analysis and Comment

The People

The population of Tung Pak Wan will be stated as approximately ninety-eight for our date line of 1960. The number first of all represents those who sleep in the village most of the time, as otherwise the uncertainty would be even greater and the population smaller since, from a Chinese point of view, some of the men must be considered as still residents of China. This is because they have wives and children living in their ancestral homes and thus the men may be said to be absent merely to gain a living. On the other hand, we have reasonably included fathers and children of Tung Pak Wan families who work and more often sleep outside of the village. Then there are individuals who spend most of their working hours in the settlement but are neither members of Tung Pak Wan families nor regularly sleep there. All these we have added together, obtaining the total of ninety-eight. We have excluded, however, members of three families who have property and undertake business or farming in Tung Pak Wan but whose residences are in Lung Shing. These three families are associated with Households Six, Eight, and Fifteen.

To make matters clear, we have listed the ninety-eight individuals associated with the eighteen households by relationship symbols, which in the more common cases we can abbreviate. Thus we will have husband (Hu), wife (Wi), son (So), daughter (Da), and combinations of the same symbols with father (Fa), mother (Mo), and brother (Br), as for instance a wife's father's brother's son's wife (WiFaBrSoWi). We shall also find need to include symbols both for male (Ma) and female (Fe) heads of households who are not known to have been married. To these designations we can add the age of the individual in parentheses when known. This list gives the composition of the eighteen households:

1. Hu(42 or 45), Wi(40?), Da(17), So(14), Da(12), Da(9), Da(7), Da(5), Da(3), plus three employees.
2. Hu(28), Wi(20), So(1), FaMo(57), plus one employee.
3. Hu(46), Wi(36), Da(10), Da(8), Da(4), Da(2), So(1).
4. Wi(51), So(18), So(15).
5. Hu(37), Wi(45), So(13), So(11).

6. One employee.
7. Hu, Wi, Da(16), Da(14), Da(12), So(10), So(8), So(6), plus six employees.
8. Ma(31), plus two employees.
9. Hu(50), Da(6).
10. Hu(30?), Wi(30), So(5), Da(4), Da(3).
11. Hu(61).
12. Hu, Wi, So(21), So(19), So(15), So(11), So(7).
13. Wi(62).
14. Hu(44), Wi(43), Da(24), So(13), Da(12).
15. Hu(40), Wi(39), Da(13), So(11), Da(8), So(6), So(4), Da(3), plus six employees.
16. Fe(40).
17. Hu(30?), Wi(30), So(11), So(4), Da(1).
18. Wi(62), So(29), WiHuBrSo(51), WiHuBrSoWi(37), WiHuBrSoSo(15), WiDaHu(44), WiDa(33), WiDaSo(12), WiDaDa(10), WiDaSo(8).

One of the things we can see first from our list is that in the eighteen households, eleven families are nuclear (conjugal) consisting of only parents and children insofar as relatives are concerned (1, 3, 4, 5, 7, 9, 10, 12, 14, 15, 17), although two of these are broken in that only one parent survives (4, 9). Approaching our data from another point of view, we see that only two of the households contain relatives beyond the range of one generation of parents and children (2, 18). Actually, a third household falls within this group as the husband's mother lives in it, but the members are not included as they live in Lung Shing (6). This leaves four households, which do not in the strict sense comprise families. There is the inkmaker (8) who claims he has never been married, the old man who left his wife and children in China (11), the concubine who has her own home (13), and the crippled spinster (16).

Turning back for a moment to the two families with individuals of more extended relationship, we can first note that one falls into the common Chinese pattern of a stem family, in this case broken, in which a son and his wife reside with his parents (2). The other represents what would be an unusual conglomeration of relatives in any society except perhaps one burdened with refugees (18). Theoretically, one can construe it to be a joint family which has taken in a son-in-law (Fig. 12.1). With the benefit of hindsight in this latter case, we conceive of the household as comprising a widow who is something of a matriarch, her son, and her brother's son and his wife and child. Thus we have a patrilineal group with the addition of the widow's daughter and family. In fact, shortly after the date line of our study, the daughter and her husband moved into Lung Shing, leaving their three children with the widowed grandmother whom we have judged to be the head of the household.

We must note that nineteen employees are also listed. Of these, two are women, one an amah who lives in Household One and the other a member of Household Eighteen who works for Household Seven. We should note that, as the last is listed twice, the total household members (80) plus the total employees (19) must be reduced by one to give ninety-eight. Also, perhaps inconsistently, we did not list the head of Household Seventeen who works for Household Seven as an employee. The remainder of the employees are men, most of whom are employed either in taking care of pigs or in making vermicelli. Since these employees arrive and leave Tung Pak Wan, both permanently and periodically, with confusing irregularity and in most cases have little bearing on our historical study, we shall dispense with any further consideration of them save in exceptional instances.

A simple calculation indicates that of the eighty individuals in our population disregarding employees, thirty are at present, or have been, married, and fifty single, only three of the latter being over twenty-one years of age. One of these is the slightly suspect case of the inkmaker (8), another the crippled spinster (16), and the third, a young man in Household Eighteen. Clearly, the Chinese tradition of expecting all individuals to marry is borne out in Tung Pak Wan.

The preponderance of children in the population is demonstrated in Table 12.1, which suffers from the fact that the ages of four adults could not be obtained.

We might emphasize the fact that there are only eight individuals between the ages of sixteen and twenty-five (fourteen and a half to twenty-three and a half in Western computation).

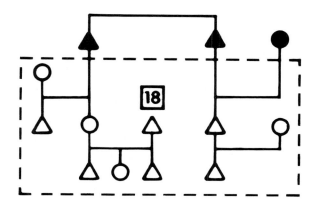

Fig. 12.1. Relationships of Members of Household Eighteen

Age Classes in Tung Pak Wan

Age*	Male	Female	Total
0-5	5	8	13
6-10	6	6	12
11-15	11	5	16
16-20	3	3	6
21-25	1	1	2
26-30	4	2	6
31-35	0	1	1
36-40	2	4	6
41-45	3	2	5
46-50	2	1	3
51-55	1	1	2
56-60	0	1	1
61-65	1	2	3
Total	39	37	76

*The ages are both approximate and European, as explained in the section on the problems of field work.

The Homes

The houses of the eighteen households indicate a definite change in building practices between 1951 and 1954. All existing houses constructed before 1954 in Tung Pak Wan were made of reinforced concrete, usually with flat roofs, although one has a gable roof covered with tile. This group includes the residences of ten households (1-9, 16). It should be noted that the dates at which the houses existing in 1960 were built do not always conform to the establishment of the household. For example, the present residence of Household One, the founding family, was constructed in 1953; that of Household Sixteen, in 1951, although the present occupant did not come until 1958. After 1951 to 1956, four houses (10-13), were built with the lower walls of reinforced concrete and the upper parts of wood or metal.* From 1956 on, with the exception of one house with low concrete sidewalls (17), only wood houses were put up (14, 15, 18). Why wood gradually replaced concrete as a building material is not absolutely certain but it is assumed that the costs of concrete construction greatly increased during the past decade. Three of the eighteen homes in Tung Pak Wan are two-story buildings (1, 7, 15). These include some of the wealthier families and represent local status in at least two instances (1,7). Four homes are

*The date when one house (11) was constructed is uncertain as the builder and first occupant had departed. It may have been before 1951.

story-and-a-half structures, which in most instances represent later buildings (11, 13, 14, 18). Curiously, a pressing demand for space is obvious only in the last (18). As a final note on the houses, it is said that none has ever been destroyed by fire, and that about this danger, the people are careful.

In connection with the houses we find that in 1960, eight households had wells (1, 2, 6-8, 11, 15, 18) and ten did not (3-5, 9, 10, 12-14, 16, 17). The correlation is based on economic factors, since wells are expensive, plus factors of dependence. Employers and relatives supply water. It is also interesting to note that all the Hakka families were without wells in 1960, but that in 1961 the five (3, 4, 9, 10, 16) banded together to have one dug. It should be noted, however, that Household Four formerly had a shallow well in which the originally clear water ultimately became dirty and undrinkable. Apparently there have been some other wells in the village which have become unusable for one reason or another.

Factors of wealth and relationship also seem to have determined the acquisition of electricity which came in later and is not as essential as water. Nine households had this utility in 1960 (1, 2, 6-8, 12-14, 17) and one more acquired it in 1961 (15), but among these, two households supply current to four others (1 to 6, 12, and 14; 7 to 17). We might add that where there is light, there is usually power. As for a telephone, only Household Seven has one, and it is rationalized as an adjunct to the requirements of conducting an extensive pig raising business.

Before leaving the matter of utilities, we should mention the possession of cats and dogs which seem to function as one. Their prime purpose is as rat diminishers or discouragers. No one claims they function with a high degree of efficiency and four families (3, 4, 10, 12) do without them altogether. Seven households have both dogs and cats (1, 2, 5, 7, 13, 14, 18) and six more either one or the other. The inkmaker Fei has only a dog. The old man of Household Eleven and the crippled spinster of Household Sixteen have only cats. Cats one may assume are less of a responsibility than dogs and go nameless. Dogs are usually called A Ts'oi (A Ts'ai), or Rich; Ho Ts'oi (Hao Ts'ai), or Lucky; or Tao Li (from Dolly).

Dress

Our notes on the dress of the people of Tung Pak Wan indicate that the women are more conservative than men and that the older people are more conservative than the younger, which is no epochal discovery. Most of the men and almost all of the younger children wore costumes which impressed one as more Western than Chinese. The outstanding conservative element appeared in the sam fu, the pajama-like coat and trousers traditional in most areas of China. This type of clothing was retained by a few of the poorer males and by almost all of the females of about twelve years of age or older. In approximately half of the households which included women, the sam fu that was worn in all but the coldest weather, was made of the relatively expensive gum-coated silk cloth with a shiny black surface. These black, gummed silk sam fu were certainly the choice of older women and poorer women (most Hakka females were in one of the two groups). We can now suggest that the poor tend to be more conservative than the rich, for wearing a black gummed silk sam fu is certainly a conservative trait.

Younger and better off women have adopted modern lightweight printed materials for their sam fu, some of which can be very expensive and none of which can equal the extraordinary wearing quality of the shiny black cloth which in the long run proves cheap. After decades of wearing such black sam fu, it is difficult to change. As one woman said, "In our family, it is what women wear." Thus we see custom fortified by the value of tradition.

The role of the cheong sam, the gown with a high collar and split skirt which is commonplace in Hong Kong, has been clearly established in the city. It has been the dress of the middle and upper class woman outside the home, and varies greatly in cost according to the quality of material and tailoring. If we were to look for it in Tung Pak Wan we would seek out the richest family, and that is where we find the one occurrence in the village. Only the mistress of Household Seven owns one. In asking if there were others, we found two cases of anticipation with respect to unmarried girls (14, 18). No adult woman indicated a desire to have a long gown and it seemed certain that the women would feel out of place wearing one. The class associations of the cheong sam are based on the substitution of its esthetic attractiveness for the practicality of the sam fu which is surely appreciated as a most excellent costume in its own right as is demonstrated by the fact that Chinese women of any class often choose this type of dress to wear within the home.

It was thought that an observation of footwear might be indicative of values in the process of change, but this is not demonstrable if it is so. Most residents of Tung Pak Wan in warm weather wear slippers of an old Chinese style—simple soles with a broad strap over the foot—or the Japanese equivalent with diagonal straps joining the sole between the first and second toes. These, it is assumed became popular since the Japanese invasion. Our survey indicates no preference for one kind of slipper or the other by age, sex, or economic condition. Various members of the same family choose different types. Technically, it may be argued that the Japanese variety are superior in that they do not slip off the foot so easily when they are old, being controlled by the toes, whereas when the flat strap of the Chinese type stretches, one's foot can slip too far forward, which is annoying. Two of the adult women more or less frequently go barefoot.

Most noticeable is the popularity of bobbed hair which has the advantages of being easier to wash, less warm in summer, and providing opportunities for popular styling. Only a few of the older and poorer women retain the traditional long hair done up into a bun at the back of the head. Once cut, most women have a permanent wave at least once during the year and usually a hairdresser in Lung Shing is visited just before the New Year's holidays.

Jewelry is not conspicuous on the people of Tung Pak Wan, although earrings are not uncommon among the married women, five of whom were noted wearing them on ordinary occasions. It is interesting that none of these instances were found among the four or five families presumed to be the richer ones in the village. Furthermore, four of the five women with earrings were wearing small circles of gold, which represents a conservative style. Presumably, wealthier women have more modern earrings worn only on dress occasions. The fifth woman referred to above wore single pearls in her ears, and I would judge them to be imitation.

With wristwatches, the situation was reversed. They were noted being worn only by the mistresses of well-to-do households (1, 2, 7). No attempt was made to check the ownership of wristwatches among men as it may be assumed that the majority of adult males own them.

Birth and Marriage

The traditional Chinese pattern was for a woman to give birth in her husband's home. During the past decade it has been commonplace for wives living on Lung Chau to cross the strait to bear their children in hospitals on the island of Hong Kong. In Tung Pak Wan, there seems to be a reversion to the custom of remaining in one's house, at least among the poorer families, since midwife service has recently been available, nurses coming from the hospitals and clinics across the strait to aid at parturitions.

Planned parenthood, insofar as attitudes were expressed, was favored by women. Too many children—by which more than three or four seems to have been meant—are considered a great burden for the poor. There seems to be no uncertainty about this. One mother with five small children was trying to give away her youngest child, so difficult was her economic condition. To say that she was unhappy about the situation is not exaggerating the meaning of her emotional restraint in discussing the matter.

Although only a few fathers were interviewed on the question of contraception, the impression was gained that they were less concerned with the problem than were their wives. Perhaps we can conclude that they are one degree more removed from the burden of numerous children? In any event, we hazard the opinion that it is the potential fathers who should be educated about the values of planned parenthood by those in favor of it, not simply the men's wives who are less likely to act without connubial approval and encouragement.

As for the method of arranging a marriage, we found no one who does not favor the modern method of free choice and the trend has been clearly in that direction. In our relatively few cases, we find individuals as young as thirty-three who were married blind (i.e. ca. 1948) and as old as sixty who were married semi-blind many years ago. Only two cases of modern marriage among residents of Tung Pak Wan were recorded. One occurred in 1941 (15) and the other about 1955 (10). It may be added that the latter couple was the latest to be married among Tung Pak Wan household heads.

Collecting opinions about preferential mates was only rewarding from older people, or at least the younger seemed uncertain as to rules. Where clear statements were made, all informants agreed that not only was the marriage of a boy to his father's brother's daughter improper, but also one to his mother's brother's daughter. On the other hand, no objection was recorded to a boy marrying his mother's sister's daughter, but neither was any special desirability recorded. As to a boy marrying his father's sister's daughter, three out of five informants said such a marriage was improper, whereas the other indicated such marriages were acceptable or common. The split in viewpoint was not based on difference of provenience, however.

These data, insofar as they have been correctly recorded, perhaps indicate little more than that even the older people are now confused about traditional values except the seemingly universal Chinese notion that one does not marry a paternal parallel cousin (the child of a father's brother) who would be a classificatory brother or sister. Certainly the marriage of a boy to his mother's brother's daughter is one widely preferred in China.[1]

Education

The most striking thing about the educational data on Tung Pak Wan is the consistent desire of the people to give their children education and the sacrifices they make to do so. If the motivation conforms to Chinese ideals, the effort has been clearly stimulated by the recognition of economic rewards to be gained through the westernized educational system of Hong Kong. Perhaps the competitive aspect of the struggle brought about by the over-crowded school facilities also plays a part. The refugee society is highly competitive.

Only two or three of the married men in the village completed primary school and only one has finished secondary school. We have no

1. Cf. Osgood, 1963: 360.

record of a married woman doing either (although one of our less cooperative informants may have). Almost all of the older women and many of the
older men are practically illiterate. This is the traditional state of affairs.

The children of school age, contrariwise, are almost all in school. One
boy who finished middle school in 1960 was said to be the first individual to
do so while residing in Tung Pak Wan, but others are pressing on behind
him. Obviously, the richer families have a great advantage. We have
noted one household (1) from which children will be sent to Canton for
middle school. For most of the younger generation, the goal will be to
finish primary school, for to obtain more education a student must leave
the island and that increases the cost. More and better schools are one of
the most wished for developments expressed by parents in Tung Pak
Wan.

Three boys between the ages of fifteen and twenty-one are apprenticed to learn trades in Lung Shing or other parts of Hong Kong, leaving
only one other youth in that range who is not.

Amusements

One of the commonest answers to questions concerning participation
in various forms of amusements is "There is no time," which statement
having been made and recorded, one may proceed to a consideration of the
limited diversions which the people enjoy. Since the settlement borders
the sea, as do all on Lung Chau, it seemed inevitable that some people
would swim at least during the hotter seasons of the year. Inquiry among
the various households indicated that almost all children apparently go
into the water on occasion but few have learned to swim more than a few
yards. As for the adults, only one or two women ever go into the water
and hardly more men, although several others claimed that they could
swim. Two factors appear to have militated against this form of amusement. There is little leisure time, even for children, and most of the
families have come from parts of Kwangtung which are not on the sea. The
households directly on the beach take more enjoyment from the water,
and it may be significant that they are the oldest residents and economically more secure.

It would seem that going to the cinema is the major formal amusement of Lung Chau people. Although many informants have stated they
are too busy to go, it is demonstrable that everyone attends more or less
often. In this activity, the economic position of the family is very important, for with many children, attendance at the movies can be expensive.
In the poorest households, it was claimed that movies were seen only once
or twice a year, but people tend to go more often than they remember.

The radio has become an increasingly popular source of pleasure and
the ownership of instruments was not difficult to determine. Of the

eighteen households in Tung Pak Wan, there were radios in nine including one acquired in 1961 (1, 2, 4[1961], 5, 7, 9, 14, 15, 18). On the other hand, eight had none, (3, 8, 10, 11, 12, 13, 16, 17), leaving the one case in which the family lives in town (6). Almost without exception, the families lacking radios simply cannot afford them.

The fourth source of amusement which attracted our attention was the playing of mah-jongg which at first seemed ubiquitous in the Colony of Hong Kong. Certainly the repetitive slapping down of the domino-like pieces produces one of the most characteristic sounds of the city and town. In Tung Pak Wan, however, only one man and two women admitted that they actually played mah-jongg, although two other persons said they knew how. Otherwise the answers were consistent; the people could not afford either the time or the money and did not even know how to play. Mah-jongg is essentially a gambling game, and allowing for the fact that some individuals would avoid admission of a weakness for the game, it is clearly not a common form of indulgence in the village. Even those who admit to playing say that they do so in town. One thing that seems remarkable is the fact that there seems to be no occasion—social, religious, or economic—in which all the residents of Tung Pak Wan, or any large group of them come together, unless one wishes to see the case of the five households that joined together in digging a well as disproving the rule.

Health

Medical attention is needed periodically by most families in Tung Pak Wan. There are many children. In the seventeen households from which we obtained information, sixteen, with a few reservations, preferred physicians in the Western tradition. In four of these households (4, 7, 10, 13), however, doctors with traditional Chinese training may sometimes be consulted. The other family (3) said that medicine was simply purchased from a Chinese medicine store whose owner, on hearing the symptoms, advised them which drug to buy. It was added that seldom had anyone been ill in the house.

One or more of three reasons are regularly given for favoring the doctor with Western type training. First and most commonly, he is said to cure quicker. Secondly, the cost is less, and this is especially true if one belongs to a Kaifong Association. Finally, and by no means unimportant, children protest so much about the bad taste of Chinese medicines that their mothers hate to force it on them.

Some comments were made by those who took exception to the general rule of favoring doctors who know Western medicine. The man presumed to be the richest in Tung Pak Wan announced that whereas he would prefer the former type of physician for injections, he would go to a traditionally-trained Chinese for treatment of a disease involving coughing. Perhaps he was unconsciously drawing a parallel from the effectiveness with which he could doctor his own pigs. Another and clearer exception involved the notion of using traditionally-trained physicians if the exponent of Western medicine did not produce satisfactory results quickly enough.

Apart from the pragmatic reasons given for the preference in the type of medical treatment, the general recognition of the power of Western drugs seems to have seeped into the unconscious of the people. The many new hospitals in Hong Kong with their out-patient services, the sanitation controls, and the quick dissemination of immunization in the face of epidemics has surely not been without a strong educational effect on the population.

Religion

The religious aspect of Tung Pak Wan culture is predominantly traditional with an obviously increasing encroachment of Christianity and especially Catholicism in the last few years. Traditional religion in China—referring to the last few hundred years—is a mixture of Confucianism, Taoism, and Buddhism, a compound which is often difficult to analyze, and also one which, at least on Lung Chau, frequently produces households of agnostic or atheistic people. In the larger sense, all but four Catholic households may be considered traditional in their beliefs. Among these, however, six households are described by members as having either no religion or none shared in common by the family (5, 8, 10-13). This may not exclude the occasional burning of incense on feast days, however. Also, one of these households has a Confucianist coloration not thought of as religious (11). Furthermore, of the traditionally religious households, one places an emphasis on Confucianism, unusual in Tung Pak Wan (17). Finally, with regard to the household self-categorized as non-religious, two contain members who are Protestant Christians (10, 12).

Of the four Catholic households (3, 4, 9, 16), at least it may be said that there are no obvious signs which remain of the traditional religion, these having been replaced by the sacred pictures and crucifixes of the new one. It is certainly significant that these families comprise four of the five Hakka households in the settlement, to which we may add that the head of the fifth Hakka family is a Protestant (10). Coincidentally, three of the Catholic families are among the poorest households in Tung Pak Wan. They have certainly needed help.

Our evidence for a belief in feng-shui is limited to one household (13) in which the deceased husband is reputed to have devoted a great deal of interest to the subject.

Political Considerations

Government does not make its weight felt in many areas of life in Tung Pak Wan. Police were only mentioned with respect to one occasion, and we never saw any in the settlement. No postal service is provided to the area. More significant, as far as our evidence shows, perhaps three-quarters of the households have no legal status with reference to the land, being either squatters on the Queen's domain or occupying ground assigned to a relative, a friend, or an employer. With no crown permit for the house, as the matter is locally expressed, no annual payment is made into the royal exchequer. For such poor and landless families, the most common attitude is expressed by the statement, "We don't care who runs the government as long as we get enough to eat."

On the other hand, when questions are put which tend to force a judgment on whether a British or Chinese government in Hong Kong would be preferred, the majority admit that the British do very well and a minority further insists that any Chinese group of administrators would do worse. Inevitably this line of inquiry leads into positions of preference with regard to Communist versus anti-Communist administrations, and then sides are taken. The Hakka households are most definitely pro-British and anti-Communist which does not seem to follow simply because they are largely Christian and Catholic. Indeed, it may be the other way around. Some were anti-Communist before they were Christian as are some of the non-Christian households, an attitude going back to the disruption of their homelife in China following the revolution in the late nineteen-forties.

Interestingly enough, it is the earliest and richest families in Tung Pak Wan that must be regarded as pro-Communist, although not necessarily anti-British. Since these people, if their relatives and employees are included, comprise the majority of households in the village, the settlement understandably has a reputation for a Communist bias. As far as we could tell, however, many individuals in this group have no real political feelings, and one or more are even outspokenly anti-Communist. Of the more genuine sympathizers with Communism, we noted certain characteristics. Descending from individuals who came to Hong Kong before the war, they have not been injured personally by the disturbances resulting from the revolution. Indeed, some of their neighbors say they are only pro-Communist because of the advantages to be gained. Obviously they would be in a most favorable position if the People's Republic of China took over the Colony, an idea which inevitably ripples through the minds of many people in Hong Kong. One family has been able to enroll its older children in an advanced school in Canton which it might well not have been able to do at home. The head of the same family is employed by what is said to be a Communist firm, but since he himself did not admit to being a Communist, it is difficult to say whether his job or his political sympathies came first.

The man presumed to be the richest in Tung Pak Wan, as has been said, was reported by his neighbors to have flown the flag of the People's Republic of China over his house and to have been moved to take it down by the police (the only instance of police ever coming to Tung Pak Wan). It is not clear how his sympathies have helped his pig business, but they are reputed to have done so. Personally, this man has an excellent reputation among his fellow villagers and from our limited conversations with him, he is something of an idealist and perhaps of the kind to which simplified facts about Communism reasonably appeal. As far as could be discovered, his real knowledge of both the history and doctrines of Communism is very limited. It should be repeated in this connection that his household is frankly traditionalist in religion and that he himself stated specifically that he believed in Shan (Shen), apparently using the word in the sense of a superior being.*

One result of the reputation for Communism borne by the village is reputedly the restriction on admitting its residents into the Kaifong Association of Lung Chau. At least this is the explanation originated by one woman who claims in consequence that she was thereby forced to become a member of the association in the town across the strait. There is also the possibility, however, that there was a waiting list at the time of her application.

In any event, only three households contain members belonging to the Lung Chau association and, of these, one household (18) has two women who were members before moving to Tung Pak Wan, while in another (10) a membership was obtained very recently. The third is that of the aforementioned rich family, which also may antedate its residence in Tung Pak Wan or possibly may not even be in the Lung Chau association. Finally, the widow of Household Four belongs to the association in the town across the strait.

Economic Activities

In half of the households in Tung Pak Wan, some member of the family, and usually its head, works outside the community for a cash income, and their undertakings are shown in the following list:

Food caterer (1)
Pig feed supplier (2)
Laborer (3)

---

*Shan (Shen) is one of the words used to translate God, especially by Protestants.

Meat market (7, 18)
Mason's assistant (9)
Store assistant (10)
Costume caretaker (12)
Glove maker (daughter) (14)
Boat builder (18)

We should also note that two households (17, 18) derive a small cash income through employment by another family (7) in Tung Pak Wan. Some of the above households also do significant farming or pig raising in Tung Pak Wan as well (1, 2, 7). Eight households survive without regular sources of earned income outside Tung Pak Wan by either conducting factories, such as for ink (8) or for vermicelli (15), or doing some farming (5, 11), or raising chickens or pigs (5, 8, 11-16), or undertaking odd jobs, such as working on gold-silver paper at home for the manufacturers in Lung Shing (3, 4, 13, 14, 16) and knitting socks (16). Mrs. Chin (4) should be specially noted as living largely off the income from her farm in Chung Nam Wan, which is run by her eldest son and his wife.

Farming and pig raising deserve special attention. The latter is so important that Tung Pak Wan can be called a pig raising village. It is doubtful that any other settlement in the Colony has such a high percentage of these animals for each resident. Of the eighteen households, eleven raise pigs (1, 2, 4-7, 9, 10, 13, 14, 18), and in five cases these are more than casual undertakings (1, 2, 6, 7, 14). In a village of eighty people (disregarding employees), there are more than nine hundred pigs, nine-tenths of which belong to four households, and two-thirds of these being owned by one. It is a wonder that the smell is no greater and the flies are so few. To obtain a very rough idea of the investment we can figure one hundred sows with a value of $300 each and eight hundred pigs at $150 each, which gives us a total of $15,000. It is an uncertain estimate of the village wealth in pigs, especially as it does not include the cost of pigpens and we cannot compute how much credit (which is suspected to be considerable) has been advanced on the animals.

Farming, in the sense of growing vegetables for sale, is a much more restricted activity in Tung Pak Wan because of the shortage of arable land. Many of the households are crowded together and have little space outside their homes. Consequently we find that of the eighteen households, only five engage in farming (1, 2, 5, 6, 11), and of these, only three in an economically basic way (1, 2, 5). It is Household Two, one of the first to be established in the village that perhaps has the largest farm, green string beans and cabbages being the principal crops. The others who grow vegetables raise cabbages primarily. Clearly, Tung Pak Wan is not what we would think of as a farming community.

Every family owns chickens, although Mrs. Chin of Household Four has hers over the hill in Chung Nam Wan. If we except four households that seem to specialize in raising these fowl, the others own an average of two dozen each, the flocks ranging from about ten to forty. One household (15) has over sixty chickens and another more than a hundred (17). We should also mention the special case of the old man of Household Eleven who recently lost over a hundred of his chickens in a tropical storm. Finally, and most important, there is the inkmaker (8) who has gone into the chicken raising business in a serious way and who owns about two thousand or four-fifths of the total in Tung Pak Wan.

The total value of the chickens is difficult to estimate because of their varying sizes. The great majority were certainly too young to be eaten. Except for the four households actually in the chicken business, the effort means only a few eggs or birds to eat or sell. Inevitably, the richer the family, the more of this food is consumed at home. The two largest producers (8, 17) restrict their birds to close quarters in tiers of cages, giving them injections to fatten them for market. In both cases, the undertakings are still too new for one to be certain of their economic success. If all goes well, large-scale chicken raising will undoubtedly spread, however.

Pigeon raising is associated with three households (5, 7, 15). The half dozen birds belonging to one of the families (5) hardly count against the total, but the rich pig raiser (7) has about seven hundred birds. Of these he sells perhaps fifty a week for an average price of $2.50 each which gives him a gross of $125.

Associated with Household Fifteen is the pigeon raising establishment of a man who resides in Lung Shing. He is said to have about four hundred birds including some valuable types for breeding. Since they are neither owned nor tended by residents of Tung Pak Wan, they can be passed over with a notice.

Three households have ducks (14, 15, 18), and another has had them occasionally (1), but except for Household Fourteen which has about ten, the other ducks merely waddle unconsciously toward holiday meals. The same may be said of the lone goose surviving in Tung Pak Wan (15). Actually, there is insufficient water in Tung Pak Wan to raise many of these birds.

Only four households have any guava or papaya trees (1, 2, 5, 11). For the most part these belong to those families longest in residence and those with the most land. Several households, especially those higher on the hill, lost their few fruit trees in recent tropical storms. The local fruit is enjoyed for family consumption, but everyone agrees that its production has little or no economic value.

One of the ideal images of Tung Pak Wan life is that the people eat two meals a day, skipping breakfast. At least that was the statement from almost every family. As it turns out, men who work hard and children who go to school usually spend a little money in Lung Shing for food in the morning. That leaves the women and small children who often find something to eat as well, we suspect. It is definitely said that in Tung Pak Wan, nobody starves.

Almost every adult male smokes tobacco in the village, usually cigarettes. Indeed, only one non-smoking male was found. On the other hand, only three females admitted to smoking, one of them using a water pipe. It is possibly significant that they were among the older women, aged thirty-nine, forty-five, and fifty-seven.

The situation is almost identical with respect to drinking alcoholic beverages, except that the pleasure is indulged in much less often. Only one male is reported to be completely abstemious, while only three women were found who admitted a taste for wine. Two were among those who smoked, and the average ages of the three were no younger.

Of the total population of ninety-eight, including employees, we should report that two men are said to be opium smokers while two others quite certainly take heroin. For various reasons, our data on narcotics will be consolidated in our report on Lung Shing, the population center of the island.

In concluding our summary of economic activities in Tung Pak Wan, we should recall that one household (8) is engaged in the inkmaking business and another in the manufacture of vermicelli (15). There is also the fish drying and shrimp sauce factory on the beach which belongs to people who live elsewhere. Since such small business will be taken up in detail in the studies of the suburban settlement of Sai Mi Wan and of Lung Shing, the urban center of the island, we shall not attempt to explain them here, a procedure which would unnecessarily complicate the picture of the small village of Tung Pak Wan.

Historical Considerations

One of the most interesting things about the eighteen households of Tung Pak Wan is the representation of linguistic groups. Two are Fukienese (8, 15) and five are Hakka (3, 4, 9, 10, 16), the remaining eleven being Cantonese. Two of the wives, however, are Cantonese (4, 15), a fact of historically little importance for Tung Pak Wan. The remaining eleven households (1, 2, 5-7, 11-14, 17, 18) have been considered Cantonese, although one family might technically be claimed as Hakka (1) since the husband was Hakka. He died before his widow settled in Tung Pak Wan, however, and she being Cantonese, the sons seem to have identified with her. Nevertheless, the dual linguistic group origin of the founding family is very significant in the florescence of the new settlement, as we shall now see. First, it may be helpful to summarize the establishment of the eighteen households by listing them in order of the dates when they were set up in Tung Pak Wan.

1—1930	7—1950	13—1956
2—1942	8—1950	14—1957
3—1946	9—1951	15—1957
4—1947	10—1954	16—1958
5—1949	11—1955	17—1958
6—1950	12—1956	18—1959

The settlement began about 1930 when the widowed mother of the present head of Household One was helped to establish a home in the little valley so that she could avoid paying rent. With the coming of the Japanese at the end of 1941, it is easy to understand why the worried old lady would welcome her sister's family who were interested in finding a place to raise food, and considering the disruptions of the period, the more isolated the better. Even so, the founding widow is said to have practically worried herself to death over the Japanese occupation. In 1945, at the end of the war, there were still only two households in Tung Pak Wan.

Shortly thereafter, however, two more households (3, 4) were set up, both representative of Hakka families from Tzu Chin (Hui Yang hsien), Kwangtung, the original home of the founding widow's husband. These two new families had both come as employees of Household One. Then in 1949, a family arrived from Hsiao Lan (Chung Shan hsien). They were descendants of the founding widow's brother. Thus up until 1950, five households had been settled in Tung Pak Wan, including two from the village of the founding widow's husband (3, 4), and two from her own (2, 5). A dual pattern of historical growth had already been established; place of origin and relationship had proved to be important in the early development of the village.

Beginning in 1950, a notable period of growth began stimulated basically by the great influx of refugees from Communist China. More specifically, as the village of Lung Shing expanded into a sizable town, pig raising was prohibited in the urban area and we find established families looking to the suburbs. First of all, the founding widow's daughter-in-law (or daughter ?) and her husband set up a pig raising establishment (6) which was ultimately to be overshadowed along with all others by that of Household Seven. This latter family seems to represent the first Cantonese household unrelated to the founding widow, but theirs was a lineage also from Chung Shan (hsien), Kwangtung. Much greater was the break with tradition introduced by the two inkmaking Fei men of Fukien (8).

In 1951, the Hakka schoolteacher arrived in desperate circumstances, his wife a sister of the head of Household Four, and consequently also tied to Tzu Chin in Hui Yang hsien. Then in 1954 came another Hakka man as laborer, no relative of the others but also from Hui Yang hsien. Thus in that year, of the ten households with which we are dealing, eight had connections with one ancestral home and four were indisputably Hakka.

Then a son of the founding widow's father's brother came in 1955, hoping to better himself economically in the British colony. He was followed the next year by a man whose sister is the present mistress of Household One. Household Thirteen was also established in 1956, in this case for the concubine of the father of the present head of Household Seven because her home in Lung Shing was needed for a church site and she wanted to raise pigs. The next year another family came because they wanted to raise pigs and again there was a relationship to the founding family as the wife of the head of Household Fourteen was sister to the mistress of Household One.

A second family came in 1957 at first to care for pigeons and then to manufacture vermicelli. This was only the fourth household in which there was no one related to other people in Tung Pak Wan or having any connection with the two districts from which most of the others came. The crippled Hakka spinster who settled in 1958 was also unrelated, but at least she came from Hui Yang hsien. The families who comprised Household Seventeen and Household Eighteen, were also unrelated to any other by blood or place of origin. Clearly, the period in which family relationship or place of origin was the primary determinant of settlement had passed.

Our pertinent data are summarized in the lists below, as well as in Fig. 12.2.

Interhousehold relationships

Hu(1) is Hu(2) MoSiSo
Hu(1) is Hu(5) FaSiSo
Hu(1) is Hu(6) WiBr
Hu(1) is Hu(11)FaBrDaSo
Wi(1) is Hu(12)WiSi
Wi(1) is Hu(14)Si
Hu(2) is Hu(1) MoSiSo
Hu(3) was Wi(4) HuFaBrSo
Wi(4) Hu was Hu(3) FaBrSo
Wi(4) Hu was Hu(9) WiBr
Hu(5) is Hu(1) MoFaSoSo
Hu(5) is Hu(11) FaBrSoSo
Hu(6) Wi is Hu(1) Si
Hu(7) is Wi(13) HuSo
Hu(9) Wi was Wi(4) HuSi
Hu(11) is Hu(1) MoFaBrSo
Hu(11) is Hu(5) FaFaBrSo
Hu(12) is Wi(1) SiHu
Wi(13) is Hu(7) FaWi
Hu(14) is Wi(1) Br

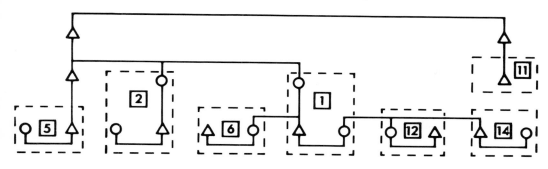

Fig. 12.2. Diagram Showing Interrelationships Among Certain Households

Linguistic affiliations by households
Hakka-Cantonese: 1, 4
Cantonese: 2, 5, 6, 7, 11, 12, 13, 14, 17, 18
Hakka: 3, 9, 10, 16
Fukienese: 8
Fukienese-Cantonese: 15

Theoretically, we should perhaps distinguish the members of Household Seventeen from the other Cantonese, as their Four Districts dialect can hardly be considered in the same group as those which are mutually intelligible from the viewpoint of standard Hong Kong Cantonese. We have not done so in the summary listing, however, as the fact seems to have little historical significance.

Provenience affiliations
with Hui Yang hsien (by Households)
1. Founding widow (through husband)
3. Husband and wife
4. Husband
6. Wife (through father)
9. Husband and wife
10. Husband
16. Female

Provenience affiliations
with Chung Shan hsien (by Households)

1. Founding widow
2. Husband and mother
5. Husband
7. Husband
11. Husband

Notable is the fact that although Household One is linked to six others by relationships with its members, there are only two families in the group with the same surnames (5, 11). The connections are all through the female line, and not only by way of the founding widow but also through her daughter-in-law. The contrast with the growth of the traditional clan (lineage) village with patrilocal residence is clear and sharp. Apart from this linked group of seven families, there are only two other groups of two households each with the same surnames (3 and 4; 7 and 13). In these, the relationships are patrilineal, however. Finally, we should perhaps remember that the boat people, or Tanka, are represented in Tung Pak Wan by women in four households (1, 2, 12, 14).

Reasons for settling, according to
households, may be summarized as follows:

1. To avoid rent (founder).
2. To farm (related to 1).
3. To work for 1.
4. To work for 1 (related to 3).
5. To farm (related to 1).
6. To raise pigs (related to 1).
7. To raise pigs.
8. As an employee and to make ink.
9. To survive (related to 4).
10. To work for 4.
11. To farm (related to 1).
12. To survive (related to 1).
13. To raise pigs (related to 7).
14. To raise pigs (related to 1).
15. As an employee and to make vermicelli.
16. To raise chickens.
17. To work for 7.
18. To raise pigs.

Interestingly enough, five households (6, 7, 13, 14, 18) were established specifically to raise pigs and six resulted from individuals who came as employees (3, 4, 8, 10, 15, 17).

Comment

In our study of the eighteen households of Tung Pak Wan we have come upon what appears to be a fairly typical group of Hong Kong residents, many of whom came to the Colony after 1945. Most interesting is the not altogether casual manner in which they developed a new community with clear cut historical antecedents and distinctive values involving religion, politics, and class. To summarize that history, we would say that originally a widow and her children arrived in Tung Pak Wan almost completely by chance. A lesser element of chance appears in the fact that the second household established was that of her sister, rather than that of a member of her children's and deceased husband's lineage. Nonetheless, chance probably was predominant as we have no reason to believe that any members of her husband's lineage were available and willing to live in the then desolate locality of Tung Pak Wan. Still, there may have been some tendency for a relict in a mixed marriage to turn toward the Cantonese side of the family, if only because of Cantonese dominance in the local scene.

The second branch of the historical tree appears when the technically Hakka son hired a Hakka laborer to help on the farm. For the next ten years, the addition of new households was largely either by the matrilineal relatives and friends of the founding household, or by the relatives of the first Hakka employee. Furthermore, each of the two branches ultimately became associated with certain religious, political, and economic values which seem to be directed toward the evolution of a class structure.

If we return for another look at the present head of the original household, we see a hardworking, ambitious man. Three factors in his life may be linked together as not altogether coincidental, although any relation of one to the other could be chance. First of all, we see an individual of mixed parentage, half Hakka, half Cantonese. Although it is easy to discount the disadvantages of such a background when the individual is a member of the lower class, there is a long tradition of opposition to mixed marriages in Kwangtung. The second factor appears when we discover this man married to a woman of the boat people, formerly an outcast group to whom a poor Hakka farmer, such as Mr. Lin of Chung Nam Wan, feels superior. Now, it would be foolish to argue that, in the middle of the twentieth century, a Hong Kong man, simply because of mixed parentage, should seek out a wife from a formerly outcast group when he might even more likely be influenced by the fact that the girls among the boat people are often exceptionally attractive. The third factor appears in this man's association with a Communist group. It is not clear, of course, whether his sympathies came before or after that fact. In the view of the ordinary Lung Chau Chinese, a man is more likely to become a Communist sympathizer—or a church member—for the advantages it may bring him, but it is possible that in this case the chance of obtaining work was the primary influence. Whatever the direction of stimulus, however, the result is of consequence.

What we do see in the linkage of the three factors is motivation and struggle for personal distinction. For some people of strong will, the circumstance of being born in an unusual position is best fortified by making it even more unusual, and when one can turn a wheel, it is easier to keep it turning. Clearly, it was of the greatest significance when he welcomed his Cantonese friend—also in the hog raising business—to Tung Pak Wan. The latter man was also a Communist sympathizer and perhaps even more ambitious than himself. By 1950, the leaders of Tung Pak Wan society had given a recognizable color to their bid for upward mobility, and it was only a matter of time before they had—however unconsciously— geographically pocketed and contained the poorer Hakka families who did not even have permits for the land.

The second or true Hakka branch in the genealogical tree of Tung Pak Wan has become anti-Communist and Christian. The anti-Communism arose out of the fact that one or more members actually suffered because of Communism. Surely, when one family in the group became Christian, others were influenced, and certainly when they became Christian, they had reason not to be sympathetic toward Communism if they were diffident before. With one Hakka family pushed to form a new settlement in Chung Nam Wan, and a spinster and widower left in two others, the Hakka branch seems to be dying with a great likelihood of soon being cut off.

A third branch, so to speak, of the historical tree is now flourishing however. It perhaps may be said to have started with the pig raising friend of the head of the founding household, but its main characteristic is its independence, although the majority have a connection of employment, if not actual relationship, which presupposes a unity that perhaps is more apparent than real. Others in this group are linked only by friendship to one and by language to another, but in a small way they are carrying on a tradition of business and industry which began with the man in Tung Pak Wan who learned to raise pigs by the hundreds.

It is highly doubtful that any other settlement would originate and develop exactly as Tung Pak Wan has done, but at least we have the record of one way that a settlement has come into being. Certainly family relationships and friendships are factors that can be important in the growth of a community.

13. Appendix. Notes on Little Tung Pak Wan

In 1961, during the second summer of our research on Lung Chau, we became aware of a small but deep little valley between high rocky points extending out from Forelegs Hill marking the southerly edge of Lung Shing and the northerly boundary of Tung Pak Wan (Fig. 13.1). Since we had already become more or less acquainted with every other aggregate of houses on the island, we were impelled to visit this newly found unit that was also clearly set apart from the rest. Indeed, as we looked down over this defile with its central farm, a garden of various colored greens surrounded by a rising border of small houses hidden among trees, its esthetic appeal made us hope that it would prove to be a segment of Lung Chau on which we might find it rewarding to concentrate our attention for a few weeks. Unfortunately, we discovered that working conditions in this valley were as repelling as the physical scene was beguiling (Fig. 13.2).

In the first place, this aggregate of fourteen households seemed to be about as socially uncoordinated as a community could be; in fact, it appeared to be unjustifiable to consider it a unit except by the chance circumstances of its physical contours. The preliminary survey which was necessary to reach any judgment provided evidence that the members of the five households which seemed outstanding for various reasons had little or nothing to do with each other, and the nothing at times verged on positive antagonism. If such relationships had grown up as a result of natural, though unfortunate, social interaction, it would have been interesting, though unpleasant. In this case, however, the situation seemed to have derived from the fact that the social orientation of each of these five families was outside the valley and for them, the presence of the others was merely a regrettable correlate of the excessive immigration that burdened all of Hong Kong. What made things worse was that a few of these families who did not speak to each other would hardly speak to us which, since it was a case of first contact, could only be attributed to the spirit of the place, and some places are simply like that. The majority who proved more hospitable, however, also had conditions complicating research, such as internal conflicts and, in one case, the heads of the family were absent. The remaining households, although nearly double in number, were almost entirely poor and peripheral. Their reception was

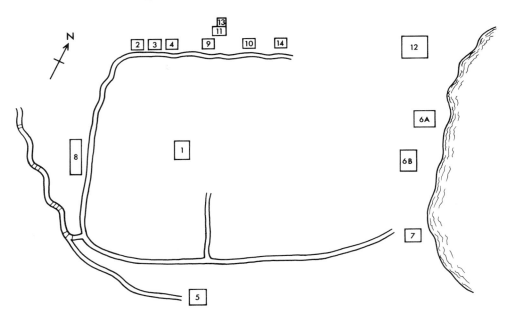

Fig. 13.1. Little Tung Pak Wan

Fig. 13.2. View of Little Tung Pak Wan

friendly and normal, but they too were unrelated families and, as such, not unlike those we had studied elsewhere.

In view of these factors, we would not have considered it worth recording such data as we have, were it not for the contrast between the historical development of Little Tung Pak Wan and its larger and wholly unrelated neighbor, Tung Pak Wan itself. We shall therefore set forth our few facts in a parallel order, concluding with some analytical and comparative comments.

Household One. The original family to settle in Little Tung Pak Wan found the isolated valley soon after the Japanese left Hong Kong at the end of 1945. The couple was young and had come from a small village near Tung Kuan which, as the reader may already have learned, lies between the Colony and Canton. They were farmers and immediately saw the possibilities of the acre or two of nearly flat land in this verdurous pocket so they built a house on it. Their first child, a son, was born a few years later and by 1961 they had four more boys and a daughter, the latter being their third child. When we knew them, two of the farmer's brothers were also living on their land. Besides their vegetables, they had two pigs and a few chickens. They told us that about two years after they arrived, a second family came, but the latter sold its house after three years although to whom is not clear. Soon after the second family, came a third, and later many more, but just how many, the founders of the settlement did not know, although they reiterated that they themselves were the only farmers, well aware of their role in the great Chinese tradition.

Household Two. When all our data were reviewed, we found that the second oldest household was that of a Ch'ao-Fu-Hui* speaking widow with an eight-year-old son. With her lives an old man, a relative of her husband's, thus making three in the family. Her husband had found the site on the hillside to the northwest of the previously mentioned farm in 1947. Her sole income is a little over a dollar a day which she earns by printing gold-silver paper plus $15 the old man pays her as rent. Making a difficult situation worse, she suffers from tuberculosis.

Household Three. About 1951, another young couple settled in a second shack beside the first on the hill. The father of the family said that he came to Lung Chau to learn to make paper for the gold-silver money producers, and this trade he still follows, working in the smallest factory on the island and spreading the rough paper he produces over any open area he can still find. The papermaker and his wife were natives of Hai

---

*For the definition of Ch'ao-Fu-Hui, see Appendix F and p. 462.

Feng and consequently speak the Ch'ao-Fu-Hui language as do their three children, a daughter of eight and two sons aged five and three. It was from this family that we learned that a fire which occurred about 1954 destroyed the three shacks on the hill northwest of the farm and that the government made an exception and allowed the occupants to rebuild them.

Household Four. The third shack on the hill had been built almost at the same time as the second one. When we visited it, only a widow remained. Her son who had also been a papermaker recently had moved with his wife and children to another part of Hong Kong where he had found work in a plastics factory.

Household Five. In 1953, Lung Chau gained one of its more unusual residents, a man from Amoy who walked over the hill as did we and, looking down on the almost hidden valley of Little Tung Pak Wan, decided it was the place where he would like to have a house. Turning off the path before it reached the bottom, he took over the unoccupied slope for himself, erecting a two-story concrete building on a leveled off shelf. Eight years later when we visited the owner, we considered it the most attractive residence we had seen on the island. Influencing our judgment was the arbor near the entrance of the house and at the edge of the slope where one could look out over the valley and bay. In the center of this viewing place, the head of the household had constructed a table, the top of which consisted of a flat stone about one foot thick and perhaps three in diameter. Around it were four very solid stone seats, they and the table resting on a pebble-in-cement floor. Except at the front and rear, the arbor was enclosed by a border of bamboo and flowers.

Pleased as we were with this expression of a feeling for beauty on Lung Chau, we were equally surprised to find near the other outside corner of the yard, the Chinese characters representing the name of the house contrived in an eight-foot medallion of a meticulously trained plant. This, with a sizable papaya tree besides another with an apple-sized fruit bearing a tuft at the end added charm to the scene.

Our host, who served us tea in English type cups with handles, explained in somewhat rusty but still fairly coherent English that he had come with his family from Amoy where he had worked for a European firm. He described hmself as a farmer, which in his case must be ascribed to a somewhat subtle Chinese evaluation that lies along the road between conceit and modesty. We must admit, however, after he told us that from the first he intended to raise pigs, pigeons, and chickens, we became conscious following a second and third surveillance that there were animals and poultry in the buildings against the hill and that various practical matters had caused considerable encroachment upon the artistry lavished on the front of the house. Also, seaward along the flat was a vegetable garden. Considering that, besides our host, there were two adult women in the family and ten children including seven boys, the oldest child being a girl of sixteen (Ch), it seemed improbable that any vegetables were sold. Before we left, our host informed us that when he had arrived there were only three families in Little Tung Pak Wan, but we later suspected that he failed to distinguish one more in the shack settlement on the opposite side of the valley, an area he may well never have visited.

Household Six. The next arrivals in the valley came a year or two later and comprised a family also not without distinction. Its head, a Cantonese boat builder who in a later place we shall refer to as Mao, had operated a rented slipway in the New Territories for ten years when the owner wanted it back. In the search for a new location, some friends pointed out the isolated cove which marked the little valley from the sea. He decided it suited him although it was then nothing but mud and rocks, a condition that was remedied over the years by the addition of considerable amounts of concrete.

At the northerly end of the cove, the shipwright likewise built an imposing concrete house for his wife, but in this case it was the inside of the dwelling that was surprising. First of all, there was red cement tile on the floor; then a couch ran around two sides of the wall which, considering the sufficiency of windows, suggested a modern, or international, type of decor. In addition there were curved arm chairs with upholstered seats, several large electric fans bringing in sea air and, in clear view on the back wall, a telephone.

The lady who served us tea was certainly no ordinary woman of Lung Chau and we suspected that her background might be one of considerable more cultivation and wealth than her husband's, an opinion we report as the impression given unconsciously by our hostess rather than one confirmed by any facts. From her we learned that she had one son twelve years of age who attended a Catholic school in Hong Kong. She also had a source of great sorrow in her life. Back of the slipways was a second house in which lived a woman whose charm was of a different kind. She had not been introduced into the family menage as a concubine in the proper way, or until recently, but the fact remained that she was the mother of three daughters and a son by the master of the household, the oldest being a girl of fourteen whose existence came as a sudden surprise to her father's wife.

Household Seven. Having admired the ships that the boat builder had on the ways, we stopped at the blacksmith shop at the corner of the cove which was run by a man as an independent financial venture, although obviously one in close association with the maker of junks. In fact, the blacksmith is the son of the latter's wife's sister, and he told us that he had settled in Little Tung Pak Wan at the same time as his uncle and aunt which was in 1954 or the year afterward. His wife, a Cantonese like himself and obviously pregnant, had borne him a daughter of five and a son of two. Also in their household, was a man who worked with him at the forge.

Household Eight. The blacksmith told us that he had settled in the valley before the members of the household which we later calculated was probably the eighth to have been continuously established, and the members of the latter confirmed they lived in Little Tung Pak Wan for five years, which gave us the date of 1956. They came from the western coastal area of Fukien and said that they had settled on Lung Chau in order to raise pigeons of which there seemed to be large numbers in narrow cages extending along the lower edge of the steep back hill of the valley. Their hospitality was not to be imposed upon as five barking dogs rushed to within a few inches of any visitor coming to their entrance or passing beyond it to the collection of homes on the northerly hill. We were happy to discover, however, that the wire fence of their yard was reinforced in such a manner that the dogs, one a fierce German shepherd and another a competitively ferocious coach dog, could not effectively use their mouths when they pushed them through holes in the wire. From this family we learned little beyond the fact that there were eight in the household including four children, all of them sons. We also had the ridiculous feeling that if we pressed a little more, we might learn what would be unfair to report.

Household Nine. With the beach on one side and the steep end of the valley seemingly cut off from further encroachments, newcomers were practically limited to the northerly slopes already marked by temporary structures, and that is where they settled. In 1956, a Cantonese brought his wife and year-old son from Shih Lung to live in a small, crudely constructed house just easterly of the others. Two years later his mother joined them. He is a cook at one of the great floating restaurants in the strait and, wanting to live nearby, he pushed beyond the edge of Lung Shing which he said even then was already too crowded. This will also be the destiny of Little Tung Pak Wan, apparently, for when we visited his home, a daughter of five and son of three had been added to the family.

Household Ten. Adjacent to the east on the northerly slope is the home of the second papermaker in the community. He came the same year as the Cantonese cook, basing his choice of the site on the fact that there is a little open ground beside his shack so that, as he said, if he makes a mess with his papermaking, at least he can clean it up. His factory is possibly a few feet larger than that of Household Four and, as might be expected, he also came from the Ch'ao-Fu-Hui area. This papermaker had a wife, two daughters aged five and three, and a son of five months when we knew him.

Household Eleven. In 1958, a Cantonese from Tung Kuan moved his wife and one-year-old daughter into a rented half concrete, half clapboard house directly behind and above that of Household Nine. It was reported that he came because the owner who lived in Hong Kong charged only $20 a month which was cheaper than he could find a place in Lung Shing where he works. Curiously, he too is a cook, but for the Joyful Elegance Restaurant (p. 552). With no evidence to the contrary, we assume the fact that one cook lives behind the other as simply coincidence. Since their arrival, the second cook's wife has also added two children to her family, a son of three and another of five months.

Household Twelve. That same year of 1958, a most unusual family came to Little Tung Pak Wan and built a sizable two-story concrete house with outbuildings at the shore edge of the northerly slope of the settlement slightly removed from the line of shacks. We did not see the owner as he had left for England the week previous to our first visit but, after having been given some intimations of the facts by neighbors, we returned to the house and talked to his two sons, both of whom spoke English well. They were both living in the house at the time, and both were looking for jobs.

The master of this exceptional family was born in K'ai P'ing, one of the so-called Four Districts of Kwangtung, and educated at a university in Shanghai where he obtained his degree in medicine. His wife, however, belongs to the Ch'ao-Fu-Hui group. Wishing to escape from the congestion of Hong Kong, where he practices, he found the location on Lung Chau on which he has built what might be described as a villa or gentleman's farm, spending the night there when his practice permits. Water has been piped in from Lung Shing at a cost of $600, and a telephone was to be installed when lines became available. Above the house, the doctor has an extensive chicken house with about 2000 birds cared for by two servants who live on the property.

That the doctor has little to do with the local community is demonstrated by the fact that when the shipbuilder arranged to have a concrete sidewalk leading out of the settlement cooperatively constructed by the wealthier residents, the doctor refused to join in the venture, stating that the sidewalk had no value for his family, an assertion which suggests that the members may enter the property either by boat or by coming down the hill from School D.

Household Thirteen. In what was formerly used as a kitchen by the members of Household Eleven now lives a family from T'ai Shan, another of the so-called Four Districts. This husband and wife with two sons and three daughters arrived in 1960. The man works in a machine shop in Lung Shing while his wife and eldest son wash dishes in a restaurant there when needed.

Household Fourteen. The last family at the time of our visits to have settled in Little Tung Pak Wan arrived about the first month of 1961, and moved into the most easterly of the shacks on the northerly hill, which actually belongs to a friend of the present occupants. The young husband who speaks the Ch'ao-Fu-Hui language works in a plastics factory in Hong Kong. His wife, however, who bore her first child, a daughter, only two weeks before our visit, is a Cantonese.

Analysis and comment. In the fourteen households of Little Tung Pak Wan we found eighty-one persons, including forty-seven children and three workers, but there are a few more uncounted in the latter category, a number of whom certainly come to the settlement only during the day. In eleven cases the families in these households are clearly nuclear, and in the three others they are probably so, although the data do not make the matter perfectly clear. In one instance, a man has had children by two women in the household.* It is possible that concubines also exist in at least two other families.

From the standpoint of their visible establishments, it would seem that five households (1, 5, 6, 8, 12) are financially much better off than the others but, although there is additional evidence in most of the cases, appearances can readily be invalid. We have also compiled the following list of the principal economic activities of the heads of the households (with the household numbers in parentheses):

2 Farmers (1, 5)
2 Papermakers (3, 10)
2 Cooks (6, 11)
1 Paper money printer (2)
1 Paper money factory worker (4)
1 Pigeon raiser (8)
1 Shipbuilder (6)
1 Blacksmith (7)
1 Doctor (12)
1 Machinist (13)
1 Plastics worker (14)

---

*It is a question as to whether there are not two households in this case, but we did not so record it.

In the matter of provenience, if we consider both husbands and wives, we find that exactly half are from the Ch'ao-Fu-Hui area and half from other parts of Kwangtung. This includes two families where the marriages are mixed. We should also note that one of the Cantonese families, as well as the father in another, are from the linguistically distinct region of the so-called Four Districts.

The reasons given for settling in Little Tung Pak Wan are the usual ones of trying to find space in which to build a house where one could farm or carry out other special occupations, or to be near one's place of employment. In two cases, some rationalization, or at least consideration of retirement, may have been involved. Most of the people were recent immigrants from mainland China as one might conclude from the fact that the first settlement of the cove did not begin until after the end of World War II and, except in two cases, until after the Communist revolution as the following list shows:

1—1946	4—1951	7—1954 or '55	10—1956	13—1960
2—1947	5—1953	8—1956	11—1958	14—1961
3—1951	6—1954 or '55	9—1956	12—1958	

In our consideration of these few data, probably nothing recorded is more significant than the chance character of the settlement for, to the best of our knowledge only two of the households contain relatives and, furthermore, it is unlikely that more than one or two of the other families knew each other before their arrival. This is a quite different pattern of development than that in Tung Pak Wan itself, and at first it struck us as quite incredible. We now regard it as a somewhat fortuitous example of the anonymity of urban growth in that it happened to occur in an isolable geographic unit.

A Suburb with Small Industries

Preface to Part III

On the day that we first visited the island called Lung Chau, after climbing above the town and skirting the crest of the main hill clockwise we had seen Tung Pak Wan and decided that it was simply the eastern end of the populous center we had left and thus not a logical segment to be cut off for study. Then stumbling on, we looked down on the hamlet of Chung Nam Wan almost hidden in its lonely defile. Chung Nam Wan, we concluded, was too limited a settlement to satisfy our purposes of learning. Cautiously making our pathless way, we rounded the south slope of the island and beheld the blue finger of water named Sai Mi Wan. Its immediate appeal was soon diluted by the realization that, although in many ways an ideal social segment for research, it had the specialized and complicating features which characterize an area with numerous small industries. Furthermore, earlier in that month of June, the typhoon brashly called Mary had created havoc among the buildings. Clearly, the occupants needed time to recover, and for an adequate anthropological analysis, certainly more time was needed than we ourselves had.

As has been explained elsewhere, the study of Chung Nam Wan was started that summer of 1960, almost in last resort as a kind of an experiment. The work went better than expected and before the season was over, we were nibbling at a knowledge of Tung Pak Wan. The second summer, 1961, work was continued at Chung Nam Wan during a few days each week while on the other days we introduced a new interpreter-assistant to the simplicities of ethnographical research in the town of Lung Shing. Our assistant, quite understandably, found the procedure somewhat uncomprehensible and completely exhausting. It occurred to us that Sai Mi Wan might give her the illusion of being an easier place to work or at least one that had visible confines. We moved there and things suddenly went well enabling us to establish friendly relations with many of the residents and to record a great deal of data that season.

Once involved in the local industries of Sai Mi Wan, however, we also became more and more tied to the town and the ultimate plan of our study began to take form. It seemed that we could perhaps make the Chinese culture of Lung Chau clear by gradually enlarging the picture in a natural way, just as it had expanded and was growing clearer for us. We had begun by spending parts of a summer with three families, and then gone on to achieve some historical perspective by reviewing the development of the parent community from which their hamlet had grown. Now we would turn to the study of an even more complex segment of suburban life, the logical prelude to a cultural comprehension of the crowded and noise-filled town. By analyzing the one, we could move on and ultimately encompass the other. With this goal in mind, we now turn to our suburb with its various small industries.

14. Sai Mi Wan: Introduction

The place. Sai Mi Wan, as we call it, is not often visited by casual visitors to the island of Lung Chau; indeed, the people of Lung Shing seldom visit it either. The town has no automobiles so it is not surprising that there is no road leading to this suburb. In truth, Sai Mi Wan is not a place that one is likely to come upon accidentally but only by intent (Fig. 1.2). Following the narrowing main street of Lung Shing in a westerly direction, near its end one reaches the Kun Yam (Kuan Yin) Temple and the waterfront (Fig. 31.2). About seventy-five feet short of that point, on the hill side of the street is an alleyway so narrow that two adults may have to turn sidewise in passing. There one begins climbing steps and traversing stretches of path to reach a break in the hills. Once started there is no way to get lost and the altitude of the divide is actually some-what less than a hundred feet. Pausing to recover one's breath, the view down over Sai Mi Wan is a pleasant surprise.

At the bottom of a more precipitous path interspersed with stretches of concrete stairs is the foot of a narrow bay that retains its constricted form for perhaps a quarter of a mile before merging with one of the sea lanes south of Hong Kong. On both sides of this bay, the hills rise high, but more steeply to the southeast where the central peak of the island is formed. The northwesterly ridge does not go up much more than the pass itself until one reaches its end. Before the period of the Japanese invasion, it was marked by a myriad of gravestones of people brought from Hong Kong for burial. Soon after the war when the great wave of immigration reached Lung Chau, however, the stones could be noticed in new buildings and on the street where they constitute a considerable portion of the paving. Few remain on the hill. Even a more basic displacement occurred when the sand was removed from the beach of Sai Mi Wan and flat areas were created around most of its foot by the building of sizable stone sea walls. Even before, as now, there was a long stretch of mud flat when the tide was out (Fig. 14.1). Once in a long while, strangers still sail into the blue bay for a boat picnic, while fishermen who have beached their vessels temporarily near the mouth are a commonplace sight, but what only a dozen years ago in 1949 was an unoccupied inlet has now become a community of groups of juxtaposed houses, farm buildings, and small

Fig. 14.1. A View of Sai Mi Wan

Fig. 14.2. Sai Mi Wan. 1—Inkmaker; 2—Hotel Man; 3—Papermaker; 4—Farmer; 5—Caretaker; 6—Carpenter; 7—Seagoing Tailors; 8—Shipbuilder's Son; 9—Retired Man; 10—The Friend; 11—Duck Raisers; 12—Bean Curd Maker; 13—Fish Dryers; 14—Noodle Cake Maker.

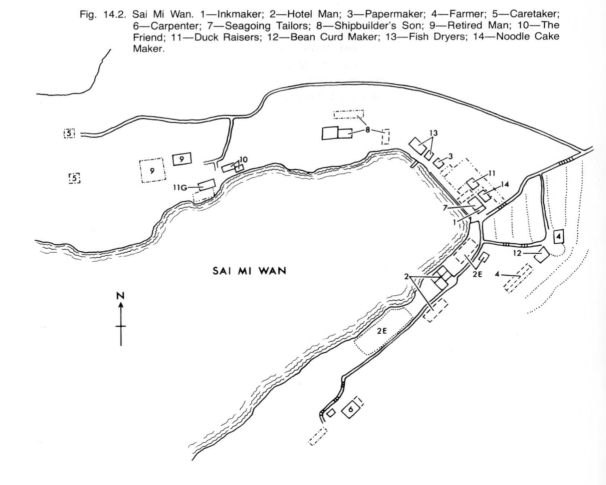

commercial structures integrated by a walkway close to the beach and paths going up from it (Fig. 14.2).

Sai Mi Wan is set off topographically and socially from a series of shack houses reached from the same pass by turning off at a right angle and gradually climbing the slope of the southerly hill. This area is sometimes spoken of as the Peak by the residents, and perhaps with a bit of humor in imitating an expression used by the rich who live on the mountain above the city of Hong Kong. The dwellers in the heights relate directly with the town and are much poorer than those around the edge of the bay with whom they have no contact at all. Thus set apart, they will not be included in our report on the suburb of Sai Mi Wan.

A bushy undergrowth and tall grass grow over the slopes surrounding the bay. What trees existed in the wild state of the area have long been removed for timber and firewood. Today one finds clusters of trees only around the houses. These are mostly papaya, guava, or bamboo, but there are occasionally some others that have been planted such as mulberry and banana trees, and even some rarer ornamentals. The beach line as it moves out toward the mouth of the bay is marked by large rock formations and at high water there are places where it is impossible to walk along the shore.

The people. The residents of Sai Mi Wan are affable human beings, by and large, and we were received with that combination of self-restraint and courtesy which distinguishes the long-civilized Chinese. Inevitably, some individuals were better informants than others, being endowed by personalities in which frankness and honesty were natural constituents. Some also had that intellectual curiosity which quickens from the excitement of a mutual interest in the experiences of living, in the struggles of the past, and in the challenges of the future. One distinction of Sai Mi Wan is the multiple geographic and linguistic origin of its people. Fundamentally Fukienese in its beginnings, inevitably Cantonese speakers from the nearby districts of Kwangtung moved into the settlement but have never dominated the area. Quite as important are the Ch'ao-An speakers from the eastern coast of Kwangtung who linguistically and culturally are more closely related to their Fukien neighbors than they are to the farmers from districts surrounding Canton. Actually Sai Mi Wan has one-fifth to two-fifths of its establishments peopled by each group.

The method. Our procedure of field work consisted of introducing ourselves to a family or group of factory workers, talking a while, and then returning to talk again when our fast schedule of recording and mood concurred with the opportunity. It was not surprising that we spoke with the earlier residents first since their property is closest to the town. No one introduced us to neighbors, but naturally the latter had observed and heard some gossip about the visiting American. It may be interpolated that during the period of our study we never saw another non-Chinese in Sai Mi Wan, so the presence of a barbarian naturally inspired more or less curiosity. Inevitably, in certain instances, our first visits were largely confined to watching what was going on as busy people tend to keep their minds on their business. As the days went by, however, we were more and more welcomed, smiles lighting the faces of our hosts, while in certain cases we were actually put to some effort in order not to cause a work stoppage. Such developing cordiality may naturally be attributed more to the charm and good character of the young woman who acted as interpreter-assistant than to any appeal by a strange white-haired man who smiled and asked questions.

No routine set of queries or questionnaires was used, key bits of information simply being accumulated whenever it proved timely to do so. This is no implication, however, that with our study once completed, questionnaires could not be satisfactorily used in copying the approach elsewhere, since essential differences in the results would be apparent and readily checked. A variant method of describing a community has to be originated before it can be improved upon. In a case where hindsight becomes professional skill, foresight would be genius.

In the evening, our mass of notes was sorted and checked against the data desired. A recording of the technical processes of certain industries, of course, could not be undertaken even that casually, and in each case the manufacturers were persuasively inculcated with a willingness to cooperate. Out of mutual respect, this was done mentally, not materially, on a basis of good friendship. No one in Sai Mi Wan refused to assist us, although the only explanation offered for our study was that it might help Americans to understand better the Chinese way of life, at least on Lung Chau. Complex technical descriptions, we might add, were transposed from notes into manuscript and then re-written in the field as additional points needing explanation had to be discovered in order to be understood. No other method will suffice, as recorders of technology all know.

In historical matters involving dates, we have emphasized order over exactness of year. Even so, relatively too much time was probably expended on dating. Some older people, particularly women, seem to regard the delving for the exact times that events have occurred as a form of masochism. In truth, one can be overly compulsive. Even to establish the chronological order of the various families and factories in Sai Mi Wan was frustrating. It seems impossible to be certain of the exact year in the earliest cases. When a number of arrivals occurred in the same year, as in 1958, one was faced with confusion. Was the claimed priority based on the first visit, the application for a permit, the granting of a permit, the erection of a building, its temporary or permanent occupancy, or something else? In the end, we were content if A said B's house was there when he came, and B said A's house was not there when he came. In the permutations of at least five people's opinions, however, the result was not perfect.

Some informants are intrinsically less reliable than others because their personalities contain less ingrained regard for accuracy. To the experienced ethnographer, this creates an expected difficulty, and when it involves purely personal matters there may be nothing one can do about it. Even when it is possible, checking through third parties is at best time-consuming and often unreliable.

Finally, there are areas of discussion which, if not actually taboo, are difficult to approach. Sickness is an example, unless the informant himself is ill. There is a feeling among some Chinese that talking about sickness may cause it. Since few people that we encountered were ill, we tried to deal with sickness indirectly by discussing doctors. Death is an even more sensitive area to explore.

Where personal prejudice was suspected, we tried to compensate. When an individual praises the British Government only because he thinks the inquirer will approve, he is apt to display a change in attitude if a contrary point of view is presented. Observation cannot be dispensed with and we pried with our eyes. Non-smokers seldom own pipes nor do Christians have red incense cans. Still it is difficult to know how much jewelry a woman hides.

Actually, in Sai Mi Wan, our interest centered on the special activities of people, whereas in Chung Nam Wan we had tried to present the basic and intimate life of the family and especially that of a farmer. No detail had been too trivial for attention. In Tung Pak Wan, we had shifted to a larger suburban group and paid particular attention to the historical growth of the community and those cultural features symptomatic of changes in time. Here the focus of attention turned to the most commonplace technical developments that characterize the island's economy, thus emphasizing the cultural links to the town of Lung Shing which had inevitably entered each previous presentation and had proved most significant in tying the whole populace of the island together. Pursuing this purpose, we shall now present our descriptive data from Sai Mi Wan under sectional headings which are descriptive of the families or are symbolic of the particular cultural activities which distinguish the fifteen establishments of that settlement.

15. The Enterprising Woman

The history of the suburban community of Sai Mi Wan begins with the economic ambitions of an Enterprising Woman who lives high on the Lung Shing side of the pass, which separates the town from its suburb. Undoubtedly the new settlement would have sprung up without her, considering the pressing need for land created by a million refugees spreading over every available acre near the population center of the Colony, but it was she who set the special character of the place and no one more typically represents the class of people who own and operate the various commercial undertakings that distinguish Sai Mi Wan. To know the place, one must know her, and therefore we shall not only formally introduce her but give an account of her life.

In 1961, our date line for information on this community, the Enterprising Woman was sixty-four years old but still demonstrating relentless strength and energy.* The daughter of farmers living near Fuchou, she had been given in marriage to a manufacturer of rice vermicelli from Amoy (Fig. 3.1) who had been practicing his trade in her native city for seven years. Rice vermicelli, or mai fan (mi fen), incidentally, should not be confused with ordinary vermicelli, or min sin (mien hsien), which is made of wheat flour. She was only fourteen at the time of this important event and he twenty-six. Their first son was born when she was eighteen and two years after they had moved to Amoy where she was to give birth to eight of her ten children, of whom eight grew to maturity and seven still survive. During this period, she went home once each year to visit her parents in Fuchou, but she never saw them again after moving from Amoy. Her later reaction was that too much money is spent on such formalities. About 1934, their vermicelli business which consisted largely in supplying this food to Chinese in Southeast Asia became unprofitable because the customs duty on exports from Amoy was increased $3 per

---

*All ages, unless otherwise noted, are given according to Chinese computation.

hundred catties in local currency in order to raise money to support the resistance to Japanese attacks that were already reaching Shanghai. With their financial security threatened, it was decided that her husband should proceed to Hong Kong and find a suitable locality for a rice vermicelli factory there. Accordingly he set out with their eighteen-year-old son, leaving his pregnant wife in Amoy. It was two years before she was able to follow with the other children; she says he was never too intelligent in business matters, unconsciously accounting for the delay. He had established himself in Lung Shing for no other reason than that it was one of the places in Hong Kong that Fukienese people live, for there was the inevitable language problem. Cantonese, the lingua franca of the British Colony, is unintelligible to the Fukienese, as indeed it is even to Chinese from the eastern part of the province of Kwangtung, of which Canton is the capital. The Enterprising Woman said that it took her ten years after coming to Lung Chau before she could speak Cantonese well, while her husband never really learned the language but, fortunately, the children did quickly. In Lung Shing, they lived at the east end of Main Street and it was there that the Enterprising Woman bore her last child, a son, the next year.

Vermicelli-making did not suddenly bring wealth, and the independence-minded eldest son insisted on going into the gold-silver paper business, one of the core industries of Lung Chau. His father was perhaps somewhat offended and decided that the family should look for a better location for vermicelli making—or perhaps it was the Enterprising Woman. In any event, they located a large building at cheap rent with an adjacent empty hillside on Tsing Yi Island which is opposite the settlement of Tsuen Wan in the New Territories on the west shore above Kowloon (Fig. 1.1). They moved to that island in the summer of 1941.

It could hardly have been predictable that the Japanese would occupy Hong Kong in December of the same year, and the occupation put a stop to vermicelli making temporarily. In twenty days there was no rice. Seeking means to sustain life for the family, the Enterprising Woman noticed crowds of people buying kerosene at a high price. Knowing this commodity was produced on Tsing Yi Island, she inquired at the refinery where she was advised to buy up a stock as the price was still rising. She purchased twenty of the twenty-five-catty cans. On further investigation she learned that whereas she had paid $40 per twenty-five catties* (it had cost about $5 before the war), it could be sold in Yuen Long, a population center some fifteen miles to the northwest of Tsuen Wan, for $80. The Enterprising Woman and her husband, each with a carrying pole, transported four cans at a fast walk and made $160 a day, the round trip

---

*The U.S. five-gallon cans hold twenty-seven catties, but the wholesalers took some out.

requiring twelve hours. With the business quickly established, some men were hired to do the portering, but this profitable undertaking survived only two months as the kerosene was hijacked making carriers fear for their lives.

Fortunately, soon after the demise of this kerosene trade, rice was rationed by the Japanese, and it was possible to begin making vermicelli again. The premises which the family had found on Tsing Yi Island had been a soy sauce factory. Included were a large building and a smaller one plus a considerable yard at the back with many great jars, decorated with dragons, of the kind that at one time were sent from China filled with preserved eggs. For this establishment they paid only $40 a month.

The vermicelli business flourished, rice being purchased from people to whom it had been rationed. Without electricity on the island, a water buffalo was used to supply power until that worthy animal was forcibly taken from them by a band of thieves. People were starving, and the Enterprising Woman lived constantly fearful of robbers. Within a year after the Japanese occupation, her first son who had insisted on going into the gold-silver paper business in Lung Shing joined the family on Tsing Yi Island. He had not done well before the Japanese came, and afterward they confiscated his property. At twenty-six years of age, he was strong and healthy and he started cutting the trees on the hillside for fuel, which was bringing the inflated price of $30 per hundred catties (133 pounds), the amount he could accumulate in a day. Then, in the summer of 1942, the husband of the Enterprising Woman died. She remembers the event clearly because just previously he had complained that he was tired and had no money. Annoyed, she took their capital which she had in her possession wrapped up in a handkerchief and threw it on the floor. He picked up the bundle and hid it, then died suddenly a few days later. She could not find the money afterward and presumed that he had buried it in a jar somewhere as was the custom during the occupation days. When the house was torn down several years later, however, a daughter said she saw a workman washing the handkerchief.

As the war progressed, so did the rice vermicelli sales which were only limited by the fact that with the human power of seven workers they could produce only 270 catties a day. This required 300 catties of rice, the only raw material used besides water and fuel for the fires. The vermicelli sold for at least double the cost of the rice. They only stopped working when it rained (vermicelli must be dried) or, occasionally, out of sheer weariness. The workers were paid a mere $12 a day, but what interested them more was the food they received, and that cost as much as $2,000 a day for the household. The Japanese circulated money which was at first valued at two to one, then four to one, and the inflation continued. At its peak, rice was $130 a catty, peanut oil $1,200 a catty, and even grass $32 a hundred. The maximum profits under the Japanese were $8,000 a day.

In the early spring of 1945, the Enterprising Woman was forced to give up the rented property in Tsing Yi Island as the owners wanted to sell it, so she moved her rice vermicelli factory across the strait to Tsuen Wan. Soon the war was over and business did so well that she did not leave for about two years despite the lack of hill space for drying the vermicelli and her continued fear of thieves. Rice could be purchased at that period for $30 per hundred catties and the rice vermicelli, greatly in demand by the Chinese in Southeast Asia, sold for $100 per hundred.

The Enterprising Woman was in her fiftieth year when she finally returned to Lung Chau with her six children. By that time the first three sons were thirty-one, twenty-five, and sixteen; the two daughters fifteen and twelve; leaving a boy of ten. The family was relatively well off and the mother was ambitious to be even more secure. Their rice vermicelli machines were set up in a rented factory at the west end of Main Street, but again the first son wanted to be independent and he re-established his gold-silver paper business, while the rest of the family produced vermicelli. Then, with an eye to greater profits and opportunities for the younger sons, the Enterprising Woman decided on extending their activities to the Portugese colony of Macao where rice was considerably cheaper than in Hong Kong. Consequently more machines were purchased and her second son went with her to establish a factory in a building that she had obtained very cheaply on a five-year lease. It was near the barracks in Macao where there was plenty of space for drying the vermicelli. Thereafter, for a period of three years, the Enterprising Woman spent more or less time in Macao with her third son, the second son having returned to continue the production of vermicelli in Lung Shing.

It was not long after the start of the Macao venture that the first son once more failed in the gold-silver paper business, whereupon his mother gave him the new Macao factory to manage. Things went well for a time, but again the first son wished to demonstrate his independence and early in 1950 insisted on moving the vermicelli machinery to nearby Chung Shan on the mainland of China. His shrewd mother visited the plant for one day soon afterward, pointing out that it was a risk for Fukienese like themselves to do business among rural Chinese of a different tongue, quite apart from the fact that the Communists had recently taken Canton. The first son was more impressed by the cheapness of the rice than possible dangers. Within a few months, however, his business was nationalized. His wife and children were allowed to return to Macao, where she knitted stockings to support herself and children, but he was held until his mother obtained permission for his release through officials in his native Amoy.

In the meantime, new machinery was obtained to replace that lost in Chung Shan, and the third son continued making vermicelli in the factory in Macao until the lease on the building expired and the owners insisted on raising the rent. There had been other difficulties as well. Transportation of the vermicelli had created problems and once, they lost twenty crates worth $4,000 when the junk conveying them to Hong Kong sank. Then when the first son was released by the Communists, he went to work selling vermicelli that the second son produced in Lung Shing. The latter finally accused him of not turning in all the money from the sale of the vermicelli and refused to have him around. Apparently, the first son had become more than reasonably addicted to gambling and other forms of rash expenditure. In the end, he was reduced to working for a few dollars at the gold-silver paper trade, an unhappy man who died not long afterward while still in his thirties.

Despite losses and tragedies, the Enterprising Woman was undaunted, and looked for new ways of making money. A large two-story building primarily for storing rice was constructed near the pass high on the hill where it had been customary to dry vermicelli. When it was completed, the Enterprising Woman moved into the second floor with her unmarried children. Pig raising was promising large profits, especially as there were always some spoiled vermicelli to use as feed, and she wanted to share in them. Concrete sties had consequently been erected on two sides of the new building.

Looking over the pass at the inviting unoccupied land bordering the blue bay of Sai Mi Wan, she decided to invest in another twenty-five pens in that area, and she obtained a Crown Permit for about 240 feet of frontage along the inner end of the bay. When she was unsuccessful in her application for an extension of the public water supply to her house near the pass, she had a well dug on her Sai Mi Wan property that provided an unfailing supply, which she had pumped to her new home. Unfortunately—although it seemed logical at the time—she chose to construct the new pigsties with the small granite gravestones that covered the adjacent hill slope, many of which had been used for paving during or after the Japanese occupation. The reviving British authorities decided to stop such desecration, however, and the Enterprising Woman was fined several thousand dollars, which clipped the wings of her ambition.

Discouraged in her attempts at large-scale pig raising, she observed that the Lung Shing inkmaker Fei had no competition in a business so profitable that he had opened a branch in Tung Pak Wan. One of his experienced workers who knew the processes involved was attracted to Sai Mi Wan, and a sizable one-story concrete house was erected twenty-four feet back from a breakwater with the necessary boiling stove and concrete ink vats built on the intervening flat. The Enterprising Woman also managed to have a line of three pens constructed nearby in which she thereafter raised pigs.

The ink business itself, she turned over to her third son who had come back from Macao. He operated it with changing partners for several years, finally giving up his share of the undertaking for $150 a month and spending the money to no great advantage. As usual the overall direction fell back on the shoulders of the Enterprising Woman who owned all the physical assets. With her help, the third son set up his own rice vermicelli business in Yuen Long in the New Territories (Fig. 1.1).

Soon after her investment in Sai Mi Wan, the Enterprising Woman rented forty-five feet of her frontage for the establishment of a paper factory. Then about 1955, she began to raise pigeons behind the ink plant. She says that she lost $2,000 just feeding the birds over a two-year period and finally gave most of them away. A year after the demise of the pigeons, she built a wheat noodle cake factory on the site, which she operated for one year. Also in 1958, she rented rooms in the ink factory house to a family of Seagoing Tailors and then the intervening 100 feet of beach property between it and the Papermakers to two groups of Duck Raisers. About 1959, she conveyed the northernmost twenty feet of her beach frontage to the Fish Dryers for $500 as they wanted to add it to the adjacent strip they had obtained. Actually, the drying of fish had started a few years earlier when some friends of the Inkmaker had been allowed to use the end of her beach land for that business, which they later sold out. Thus the Enterprising Woman created a whole industrial area which has given to Sai Mi Wan its immediately recognizable aspect.

When we met our intelligent informant, she was keeping a daily watch on her properties and planning new activities. A tall, rather heavily built woman with sharp eyes, she welcomed us, answering our questions easily and asking her own. She wore Japanese style composition slippers below commonplace black trousers (fu) with a blue and white checked sam, her long black hair drawn into a bun at the back of her head. In her ears were gold earrings set with bits of jade, and on the third finger of her left hand she wore a gold ring bearing a deep blue stone. These were her working clothes, commonplace enough. On important occasions, such as going to see one of her married daughters in Kowloon, she puts on a cheong sam, which no one thinks strange.

She still lives in two rooms on the second floor of the building near the pass where her second son uses the first (ground) floor as a bead factory. In Sai Mi Wan, she has two sows and about fifty chickens, which supply eggs to sell, but she does not bother with any other animals. Neither does she have any fruit trees. The well mentioned previously provides plenty of good water. It is pumped up by a small electric motor run on the same house current that supplies her with light. She does not have a meter for power.

The life of the Enterprising Woman has become somewhat simplified by the fact that her second son, who lives at the bottom of the stairway path leading to Sai Mi Wan, has one of his seven children bring her food at each mealtime. She is not one to eat in a son's house when the son has in her opinion unwarrantedly taken over the position of head of the family.

The Enterprising Woman enjoys food and drink, but with reasonable restraint. The habit of smoking she acquired during the Japanese occupation. Cigarettes at that time could be obtained only with a ration ticket, but she had a friend who bought cigarettes from people who did not smoke and sold the packages on the black market. This woman gave her a package once in a while and that started her habit.

If our Enterprising Woman has any form of self-indulgence, it is apparently expressed in her enjoyment of the movies. She laughed when she told us that she scolded her children when they were young for wasting time and money at the cinema. They went without her knowledge, however, and if the picture was very good, they would buy her a ticket, telling her she must see it. She would give in, as she says, so as not to waste the money they had spent. Thus she came to regard the pictures as colorful and entertaining, although she admits that she really does not understand them. She attends whenever there is a new film at the Jade Theater in Lung Shing, or about twice a week, buying a fifty-cent seat. If a picture is well-recommended, however, she will even cross the strait to see it, but she insists that she cannot afford to do so very often. As for mah-jongg, she does not know how to play, and she has never been swimming. Her greatest pleasure is looking after her various business ventures and talking to people who may suggest other ways of making money. She walks to the central district of the town almost every day, but seldom goes farther. She has been to Tung Pak Wan but, like most people, did not know of the existence of Chung Nam Wan.

By and large, the health of the Enterprising Woman has always been good. If something bothers her, she drinks a little medicated wine or goes to either a Chinese doctor or an unlicensed physician with Western training who she says helps her if she has stomach trouble after eating. She did have trouble with her teeth from the time she was thirty. They finally became black and painful. When about fifty-six (or ca. 1953), she had an itinerant dentist give her an anesthetic and pull them all out. The dentures he made cost her over a hundred dollars and have never been comfortable, so she wears them only when she eats or goes out. She says that she cannot really chew anything with them.

Political matters seem to have little interest to a woman devoted to business unless a government upsets the traditional procedures, and that the British do not. She says that she pays about $300 a year in taxes, obligations which informants do not tend to minimize. She thinks the rate is a little high but, on the other hand, she states that she always knows what she owes and does have a peaceful life under the British, whereas the Chinese not only extorted what they could in taxes but were very rude. The fact should certainly be recorded that she can neither read nor write. Also she has never joined the Kaifong Association.

In one way, the Enterprising Woman seems to have little regard for religion but in another, she does give attention to the matter. For example, she burns incense on the first and fifteenth of each month. She also celebrates the Earth God's birthday on the second and sixteenth of each Chinese month by burning more incense and candles. Then she has a special meal including pork, chickens, and wine, which are first offered to the God and afterward enjoyed. She makes similar acknowledgments to the God of Heaven on the 15th of the 7th month and celebrates the 19th of the 2nd, 6th, and 9th months as birthdays of Kun Yam (Kuan Yin). This means that she indulges in at least sixteen annual feasts besides that at New Year's.

She states that she sends all the gods to heaven—specifically the God of Heaven, the Door God, and the Kitchen God—on the 24th of the 12th month. The Earth God is not included, as he always remains where he is. To the Kitchen God, she offers rock candy before his departure, and she asserts that he always returns on the 4th of the 1st month, never earlier. Her theological knowledge is extremely limited, but she believes that the God of Heaven is associated with happiness and the Earth God with the forgiveness of sins. Honoring the gods, she says, was begun by intellectuals, and the common people like herself simply follow along. At one or two o'clock on New Year's morning—as determined by the almanac—she lights candles and incense, kowtows to the gods, and burns gold-silver paper money in a large, brown stoneware jar with yellow dragons on it that stands in her yard. The base of the jar is broken at one side to provide the necessary draft. Finally she sets off some firecrackers as an end to this ceremony of hoi nin (k'ai nien), or Opening the Year, as it is called.

It is also significant that the Enterprising Woman goes to one or the other of the Lung Shing temples two or three times a year, but she limits the number of such visits because such religious activities cost money. It is noticeable that the ridgepole of her house at the pass is painted red and has a red cloth draping down about two feet on each side. At the ends of the cloth are pockets containing things needed in the house, such as rice, charcoal, twelve kinds of seeds, and other materials she can no longer remember. The ridge pole was raised on a day determined by the almanac, a book on which she has always depended for important decisions, such as dates for marriages, starting new business ventures and, most important, knowing which direction one must first walk on New Year's Day. Of course, a specialist had to be consulted to read it for her.

On a table in the corner of her sitting room is an eight-inch high statue of a God sitting in a chair, which the Enterprising Woman picked up in the street following a typhoon. She refers to it as a Buddha, but that assignment seems gratuitous. Above on the wall are two framed pictures under glass. One is an impressionistic photograph of a figure said to be Kun Yam

(Kuan Yin); the other on the right is a photo of a God with two attendants in a Swatow temple. We were informed that he has the reputation of almost always granting requests, but that if one turned one's back to this God when leaving, one would be bitten by a tiger. We politely backed out of the room.

The Enterprising Woman experienced a blind marriage, but her children were married semi-blind, which she believes incorporates the good features of both other systems. Asked about preferential mating, our informant expressed the belief that neither the marriage to a father's sister's son nor to a mother's brother's son would be proper, but that a marriage to a mother's sister's son would be traditionally desirable. Family matters are somewhat of a sore subject for the Enterprising Woman as she frankly admits that her sons have been more or less of a disappointment. Of her four daughters, two are married and living in China, another is married and resides in Hong Kong, while the youngest, not yet married, works in a cotton factory at Tsuen Wan in the New Territories. All are getting along satisfactorily.

Her eldest son, she put through Middle School, but he would go no further. He died leaving three sons and a daughter. His widow, however, has proved her capacities by earning $10 a day in her husband's trade. Also the eldest grandson now earns $180 a month of which he gives his mother $40, while the second grandson makes $60 a month and still goes to school in the afternoon. The third grandson, aged ten, is also attending school. The granddaughter is sixteen.

The Enterprising Woman's second son runs the original rice vermicelli business in Lung Shing. His mother says he is unfair because he is gaining control of the family finances illegally. We must add for his part, that as the eldest son of a mother approaching seventy, his action in this respect is at least comprehensible. Later she admitted that about 1957 under some duress she had made a division of her property. The eldest son's widow received the vermicelli machinery from Macao; the second son, the Lung Shing vermicelli business; the third son, the establishment near the pass; and the fourth son is to get the Sai Mi Wan property, but she still holds it in her own name despite some pressure. The daughters received no share but the elder (in Hong Kong) was given jewelry by the Enterprising Woman during her most affluent period after the occupation, and the younger was able to save the money that she earned. Notwithstanding the time spent in all her other activities, the Enterprising Woman says that during the period when the gold-silver paper business was profitable, she and her daughter always had a long table set up on which they could do block printing in their spare time and each make about three dollars a day.

On the other hand, the Enterprising Woman blames the second son for afterward trading the third son some vermicelli machinery for the property at the pass because the latter could not pay the taxes. It was perhaps a shrewd deal. Furthermore, his mother complains that the second son has invested about $100,000 in the bead factory and extensive adjacent pig pens, whereas he has not given his mother a cent for the last eight years. More serious is her charge that her second son disregards the interests of her other children. He asked his unmarried youngest brother and sister to move from the upper floor of the building where they were living with their mother, and then rented the space to another family. At the time, this unmarried sister worked in the family rice vermicelli factory. At first, the second son had paid her $50 a month, then $30, and then nothing at all, says her mother. At least, the girl is now earning from $180 to $200.

This crisis in the family came about when the mother complained that her second son was not paying his sister. He reportedly scolded his mother and then used the resultant turmoil as an excuse to tell his siblings to move out. They became angry and left. There are always two sides of a story and this is but one. It also may be added that the Enterprising Woman has little admiration for her second son's wife.

The third son is admittedly the most esteemed by the mother who frankly states that her second son has protested that she has favored both this brother and their youngest sister. The third son still has his own vermicelli business in Yuen Long in the New Territories, but the Enterprising Woman says that he makes just enough money to take care of his family. In any event, it was noted that she makes no complaint about his not contributing to her welfare financially.

The fourth and youngest of her sons works in a soy sauce factory in Kowloon where he earns about $160 a month. He occasionally gives his mother twenty to thirty dollars and when he comes home, as he does frequently, he always brings her a bottle of wine or some other present.*

In 1961, with her noodle cake factory not functioning, the Enterprising Woman set to work manufacturing the more commonplace uncooked wheat flour noodles. She employed one man to help her but she says things go slowly because of her inexperience. The noodles, for example, which are cut thirty-six inches long are folded once to one-half that length, then in half again and twisted. She says it takes her two hours simply to fold twenty catties of noodles whereas an experienced worker could do it much faster. She was manufacturing forty catties of noodles a day and said that if she makes money, she will hire men and expand her production.

Before recording more of this remarkable woman's newly established activities, it will be well to enlarge on her past accomplishments and the developments in Sai Mi Wan as a whole, so we shall now turn to the affairs of her ink factory.

---

*For the anthropologist it should be stated that this biographical sketch was pieced together from notes taken periodically between 1961 and 1966.

16. The Purple Ink Factory

The Enterprising Woman has had the ink factory in operation for about ten years. During that time, one partner has replaced another and there have been a series of employees. Sometimes a partner works, thus earning a salary as well as a share of the profits, and sometimes he does not. Sometimes the factory operates at full capacity, and sometimes competition has curtailed the demand and production slows down of necessity because the ink will not keep. Such was the situation at the time of our study. Only one inkmaker was working and this long surviving man among the partners had come into the group between one and two years after it had begun. It was he who finally explained that the business had actually been started by the one man in Lung Shing who learned the trade before leaving China. All the other inkmakers on the island have acquired their knowledge from him or his pupils.

The most significant historical fact about this original Amoy inkmaker (who has now gone to sea on a large ship) is that he is the brother of the Mrs. Fei whose husband had the first ink factory in Lung Shing and later in Tung Pak Wan. The man who actually made the ink quarreled with his sister and her husband and left them to start a new factory in Sai Mi Wan on the property of the Enterprising Woman and under her guidance as has already been explained.

The present producer, or the Inkmaker as we shall call him, lives in one room or cubicle of the factory house (Fig. 14.2). He is forty-five years old. He left his home in the Chang P'u district of Fukien, about four hours by boat southwest of Amoy, in 1950 soon after the Communists took control and came to Hong Kong. As he was rich enough to own a grocery store and a sixty-foot junk, he thought it a wise move. For over a year he lived with friends in Tiu Keng Leng, which is on the west shore of Junk Bay across from Shau Kei Wan (Fig. 3.2). There he was unsuccessful in the rice business. Through friends he met the Enterprising Woman who persuaded him to come to Lung Chau. He had left two sons and a younger daughter of fifteen in Fukien with his wife. The latter did not come to Hong Kong until about 1957 and since that time she has been working as a servant for a family in Hong Kong. Consequently, we never saw her in 1961. She is a native of his district and has not learned Cantonese well enough to be intelligible. After ten years, he himself speaks Cantonese with a strong accent. He seems like a lonely man, and no doubt he misses his children.

The Inkmaker is tall and rather gaunt with individual silver hairs in his crew cut hair and his smile reveals gold caps on both second upper incisors. When working, his simple costume of shirt and pants shows the purple stains of the ink that he manufactures, and his hands and rubber boots become bright red, a brilliant color that fortunately washes off with no great trouble. Dressed in his best clothes, a sam fu type of dark suit with a fountain pen in the breast pocket, he is momentarily unrecognizable as he looks at his wristwatch.

The Inkmaker had only one or two years of schooling and his wife with whom he was joined in a blind marriage had none. He admits to a fondness for movies and he sees the Cantonese productions shown at the Jade Theater in Lung Shing at least two or three times a month. Once with the Enterprising Woman we saw him watching a game of mah-jongg and when we asked if he played, she interpolated with laughter that he only watched when he had no money. He laughed in apparent admission that there was some truth in the fact. Although working at the edge of the bay, he said he did not go swimming as many other Sai Mi Wan men do. The Enterprising Woman, made her frequent appeal to humor by saying he was too old to drink salt water. The quickness of her response drew laughter from the group.

It was not surprising that the Inkmaker who had visited the ink factory in Tung Pak Wan long ago had never heard of Chung Nam Wan as no one was living there at the time. When told where it was, he said he had never climbed over the gap. On Lung Chau, busy men seldom go where they do not have to, and the Inkmaker usually puts in long hours as we shall see. Furthermore he has over a hundred pairs of pigeons in a house-sized cage at the east edge of the factory which require his attention. Curiously, neither the Inkmaker nor his wife drink even on feast days, but he smokes cigarettes. Obviously, not a very religious man, he does say that they honor the gods.

Since a presentation of the operation of an ink factory is necessarily somewhat technical, we have organized the material into sections and attempted to write our descriptions of equipment and procedures in as simple language as possible. To avoid unnecessary complications, the economic analysis is based on full production, as partial operation introduces endless variables which our informants could not calculate themselves. The figures for a theoretical half or quarter scale production, of course, can be easily computed.

The factory. The establishment for making purple ink, as has been said, was the first of any kind at Sai Mi Wan, and it required the building of a stone breakwater along the beach at the end of the bay. With this wall at the southerly side, a flat area was filled in and covered with concrete, behind which was erected a sizable house. The house now has little to do with the factory except that one cubicle is kept for the use of the men making ink, although only one of them now sleeps in Sai Mi Wan as has been said. The remainder of the house is rented to two brothers, the Seagoing Tailors, and their families. The brothers do not get home very often.

The flat area, which extends about sixty feet along the shore and is twenty-four feet in width, contains a stove for boiling the wood from which the coloring comes, and six groups of concrete tanks for the ink (Fig. 16.1). Besides these constructions one sees baskets for holding the finished ink, bright purple cloths into which the ink is poured in those baskets, conical ladles, sections of hose of various sizes through which the ink is siphoned, and a few minor utensils. A partitioned-off section of a building behind the house previously mentioned may be included as part of the factory since it is used for storing the ground wood from which the ink is made, and a section of a row of pig pens bordering the westerly edge of the flat should be included on similar grounds since it is used for storing completed ink. All in all, the factory is colorful, if not actually imposing.

Boiling the wood. The ink vat stove is essentially similar to a common pig food stove with the areas above the pans built up to form vats, one for hot water at the rear and a slightly larger one at the front for ink. There is also a small cement tank built up for straining the boiling ink to the east of the ink boiling vat. The straining tank is 23″ wide, 26″ long, 18″ high (above the surface of the stove), and has walls about 3″ thick. When one faces the stove one has the sea behind one to the southwest. There is a pile of coal to the right between the stove and the first group of cooling tanks.

The part of the ink boiling vat that is above the surface of the stove is made of vertical staves of wood in the form of an inverted tub, the top being of slightly smaller diameter than the bottom. The staves are held in place by means of three bindings of wire as well as by cement around the bottom. The staves rise 15″ above the cement and the opening is 28″ in diameter. There is a wood slat cover with a wood handle in the center. The cover stays in place by virtue of being 2″ in diameter larger than the ink boiling vat itself (Fig. 16.2).

Just behind the ink boiling vat is another vat identical in construction for heating water. The height of the stoves is the same, but the opening is only 26″ in diameter.

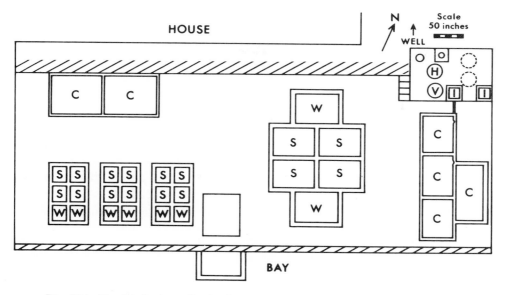

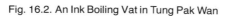

Fig. 16.1. The Ink Factory. C—Cooling tank; H—Hot water vat; I—Straining tank; S—Sedimentation tank; V—Ink vat; W—Water + shik fui tank.

Fig. 16.2. An Ink Boiling Vat in Tung Pak Wan

Behind the hot water vat and to its right is the chimney which rises 82″ as a concrete construction two feet square, 26″ more as a cement cone, and is then continued upward by three and a half lengths of tile drain pipe held in a vertical position by four iron straps wired equidistantly around them, to which are fastened three steel guy wires.

Next to the chimney at the west side is a small opening on which one can place a kettle two feet in diameter to make the last use of the stove's heat for cooking pig's food or what one will. The whole area of the top of the stove is 138″ x 90″, but this includes the unused east half which has a second straining tank and two holes for the pans of unconstructed hot water and ink boiling vats. The top of the stove is 30″ above the flat which contains the tanks and is flush with the floor level of the house.

The Inkmaker in charge of boiling proceeds to his work by climbing the five steps at the left of his stove. Water is fed into both the ink boiling vat and the hot water vat at the beginning of the day by means of a hose leading from a small cement cistern adjoining a well eighteen feet behind the stove. The capacity of the ink boiling vat is given as nine five-gallon cans (U.S.), or 45 gallons, whereas that of the hot water vat is slightly less. The well from which the water comes lies at the base of converging hills, and is certainly the most abundant producer in Sai Mi Wan. Water can be introduced into the cistern either by hand or by help of a small electric pump.

With the vats filled with water, the inkmaker dumps twenty-five catties of ground ink wood into the ink boiling vat, using a shallow basket 24″ in diameter and 5½″ deep to do so. The ink wood,* originating in Thailand, is purchased in Hong Kong, and then ground in Kowloon. About 3,000 catties are purchased for the factory at one time. The ground ink wood is boiled for twenty minutes—or heated in hot water and brought to a boil in that time—as was determined empirically. Informants gave the time on different occasions as twenty-five minutes, and later thirty-five to forty minutes. Obviously some variation occurs as a result of the heat of the fire. For each boiling, seven to eight catties of coal are burned. Most significant in estimating the length of the boiling cycle is the fact of whether the time for straining (five minutes) is included, and also the interim between undertakings. When the Inkmaker looks into his vat and decides the boiling is active enough, he stops the action by adding a can or two full of hot water from the hot water vat. Sometimes, if he is not watchful enough, the ink boils over, and then he rushes to add more hot

---

*The so muk (su mu), or ink wood, is sapan wood, a product of *Caesalpinia sapan* L. Hobson, 1851–58, in his section on medicines (pp. 21–22) in his fascicle on internal medicine, states that so muk is used by the Chinese for dye, and medicinally as a specific against diarrhea, one ounce of so muk being boiled in one and one-half catties of water until one catty of the liquid remains. The dosage is one ounce three times a day.

water which is the method of keeping the ink from becoming too hot. In any event, once real boiling occurs, he begins to transfer the ink into a straining basket which rests on top of the straining tank, using a conical metal ladle 13¼″ in diameter and 11″ deep with a short wood handle to do so. Most of the ground ink wood remains in the ink boiling vat, but toward the end of the operation, a good deal is caught in the straining basket. The ink flows from a hole in the bottom of the straining vat through a metal pipe a short distance to an open trough formed on the edge of the nearest cooling tank and then splashes into it. The ground ink wood caught in the straining basket is then dumped back into the ink boiling vat which is again filled with hot water from the hot water vat by means of a five-gallon can with a horizontal wood handle set into the middle of its top. The use of hot water obviously functions to hasten the next boiling of the ink wood.

Five boilings are carried out with no addition of ground ink wood. The odor of boiling ink is not noticeable to anyone a few feet away from the vat and has no particular distinction in any case. Before the ink is removed from the fifth in a series of boilings, the equivalent of a large rice bowl of shik fui (shih hui), or lime* is poured by means of a cup into the ink boiling vat to get as much ink out of the wood as possible before it is discarded. When the fifth vatful of ink is strained, the residuum is thrown on a pile at the right of the stove, to be later dried and used as fuel in the noodle cake factory. Full production for a day amounts to four series of five boilings, or twenty altogether, using 100 catties of ground ink wood in total. This means ten hours of actual work for the ink boiler at a minimum (assuming thirty minutes for each boiling), but the work day is said to be fourteen hours beginning at five or six in the morning at times of full production.

Treating the ink. There are six cooling tanks in the factory, one group of three (plus an unused one) in front of the stove and a second group of two more in the northwesterly corner of the work area. The first group has cement walls about 6″ thick which are 34″ high. All three tanks in use are 49″ wide (inside measurement), but they vary in length, the one nearest the stove being 60″, the next, 68″, and the third 64″. The capacity of each of these tanks was estimated as forty-five to fifty five-gallon cans or from 225 to 250 gallons. (The unused tank on the east side of the row is 45″ wide, 94″ long, and has the same height and width of walls as the others, except for one unsupported east wall which is almost 9″ thick.) The

---

*Shik fui is said to be a substitute for pak fui (pai hui). The former may cost about 15 per cent less but leaves a muddy texture in the ink according to another inkmaker. Shik fui, it is claimed, is made from rock, pak fui from shell. The latter, a local product, is sometimes suspect since the dealers may dilute it with fine sand.

second group of two cooling tanks, some distance away seems to have walls only about 4″ thick and 29″ high. The inside measurements of both are 64″ by 84″.

When the first tank is filled from the straining tank, the second is filled from the same trough by closing the outlet to the first with the rags which had been used for the second. When two tanks are full, the others are filled from the full tanks by siphoning with (plastic?) hoses (1¼″ inside measurement). The siphoning is commenced by sucking and spitting out a mouthful. Even the ink in the cooling tanks can be tolerated as it is no longer hot enough to burn one. The siphon hoses, once in use, can serve to keep the ink in adjacent tanks at the same level. The ink remains in a cooling tank for two days before being removed for further treatment. The contents of the cooling tanks are not stirred before removing, the first sediments being cleaned out of the tanks once every month or two and discarded. When dry, this refuse may be burned.

Once cooled, the ink is siphoned into sedimentation tanks, 1¼″ (inside diameter) hose being used (Fig. 16.3). The sedimentation tanks are in four groups, each with adjoining tanks for water plus shik fui. The centrally located group consists of four tanks. The inside measurement of each tank is approximately 46″ x 68″. The walls are about 7″ thick and stand 48″ high. Against the middle of each of the long sides of the rectangle that the tanks thus form is a tank for water plus shik fui. Each of these two tanks has an inside measurement of 51″ x 70″. The walls are about 6″ thick and 54″ high. The capacity of each of these latter tanks was estimated as ninety to a hundred five-gallon cans, or 450 to 500 gallons.

The second, third, and fourth groups of sedimentation tanks are parallel to each other in the southwesterly corner of the work area, each comprising four sedimentation tanks with two matching water-plus-shik fui tanks, making a total of eighteen tanks. Each has inside measurements approximating 24″ x 27″ and walls about 6″ thick. The twelve sedimentation tanks are 30″ high, but the six water-plus-shik fui tanks are 34″ high.

When the ink has been siphoned into the sedimentation tanks, the water plus shik fui is added by siphoning with a 1″ or 1¼″ (inside diameter) hose in the proportion of two parts of shik fui plus water to one of ink, which also happens to be the reverse proportion of shik fui to water, thirty five-gallon cans of shik fui being previously mixed with sixty five-gallon cans of water in the adjacent water-plus-shik fui tanks. In the central group, the water-plus-shik fui tanks are emptied and cleaned once in twenty days.

To the mixture of ink and water plus shik fui, pak fan (pai fan), or alum, is immediately added. This material, which has the appearance of lumps of ice is placed in a basket 16″ in diameter and 9″ deep with two vertical loop handles and is dipped up and down repeatedly in the ink.

Fig. 16.3. Cooling and Sedimentation Tanks for Ink in Tung Pak Wan

The ink remains a day in the sedimentation tanks and then the upper two-thirds of the liquid, cleared by the pak fan, are either drained off or ladled out of the tanks and returned to the water-plus-shik fui tanks. The central group of sedimentation tanks has plugged holes one-third of the way up from the bottom. A wood and rag plug is knocked out, and a section of 1¼″ diameter (inside) hose is inserted. No packing is used; if some of the liquid leaks out onto the concrete floor, no one cares. A 29″ x 35″ concrete drain tank is set into the ink floor at the edge of the sea wall between the first and second groups of sedimentation tanks, and there is a larger one, 39″ x 63″, beyond it extending out from the sea wall. Actually this latter tank was originally planned to hold water. From the second, third, and fourth groups of sedimentation tanks, the excess liquid is removed by ladling, as no drain holes are available.

Removing the ink. When the excess liquid has been taken out, the residual ink is removed from the bottom of the sedimentation tanks by means of a conical ladle like that described in the boiling of ground ink wood except that the handle is larger. The process can be accomplished even more quickly when the Inkmaker climbs into the tank with his rubber boots on and ladles out the ink with a five-gallon can into a 22″ square metal tank 11″ deep which has two straight metal spouts (5½″ L) on the front. To these are fastened a pair of hoses leading to the draining baskets, which are thus filled two at a time. This distribution tank is placed on top of four empty five-gallon cans resting on two boards across the top of a tub in order to bring its top flush with the outer edge of the sedimentation tank. The ink pours into baskets 25″ in diameter and 19″ deep into which large cloths have been placed (Fig. 16.4). In these cloths, it is allowed to drain for two days and is then ready for the market. It may drain longer if no purchaser is immediately available.

Economics. The product of the factory is a purple ink which is good only for paper. It washes from the hands readily by rinsing them in a pak fan solution and can be washed out of clothing. The purchasers of the ink are the factories which make gold-silver paper money for the dead, and it is rarely sold as far away as the town across the strait. Furthermore it will keep for only twenty days. The basic materials which are consumed in making the ink are ground ink wood, coal, shik fui, and pak fan. The ink wood costs $25 per 100 catties, $10 more to grind, $1 to deliver to the town across the strait, and $.30 to bring to Sai Mi Wan, making a total of $36.30 per hundred catties. Coal costs $7 per 100 catties delivered in Sai Mi Wan. Shik fui costs $12 to $13 per 100 catties in the town across the strait, and

Fig. 16.4. Ink Draining in Baskets

pak fan $30 to $33. Thus we compute a day of full production to cost approximately as follows:

100 catties of ink wood	$36.30
150 catties of coal	10.50
120 catties of shik fui (lime)	15.60
50 catties of pak fan (alum)	15.75
Total	$78.15

To this figure must be added another item which is significant. Three men's labor is required for a day of full production. These have been stated to be paid by boilings as follows:

Boiler's wages at $.35 per boiling	$ 7.00
Experienced tank man at $.60 per boiling	12.00
Tank man at $.40 per boiling	8.00
Total	$27.00

An additional item in the cost of production is the $80 per month paid for rent. For convenience we can compute production at twenty full days a month and add $4 a day to the costs.

Finally minor items should be considered such as cloth to line the baskets. Two yards are needed for each basket (which holds sixty to a hundred catties of ink). Cloths cost $1.20 to $1.40 and last about a month and a half. The three sizes of hose cost $1, $.80, and $.40 cents a foot respectively, but last a long time (hoses in use are two years old and are in good condition). Baskets for ink and straining baskets cost $4 each, a flat basket tray $4, and so on. At least another dollar can be added each day of full production to meet these charges. This gives a total daily cost of $110.15.

The ink sells for $.38 a catty which, computing on the basis of 400-catties production a day, indicates an income of $152. The difference between cost and income indicates a daily profit of $41.85 which, divided among four partners is $10.46 each. There is also the possibility that there is some excess in the product, and if the yield of the same material were 450 catties, the additional income would be $19 which would add $4.75 more for each partner or a total of $15.21. One of the partners said an income profit of $2 to $3 per 100 catties was the best that could be expected.

Finally it may be stated that the entire plant, including sea wall, ink factory equipment, and house, cost approximately $5,000, in 1951 (the electric well pump with hose required $400 alone). Ten per cent per annum return would be $500 per year. The ink factory may return $960 and the house $600 more. When business is good, the Enterprising Woman has obviously done very well, and when it has fallen off, she still has not done badly. We can now turn to the efforts of another investor who dreamed of making a fortune by raising pigs.

17. The Hotel Man's Establishment

When things have occurred a long time ago, it is often very difficult to ascertain the details and this was particularly the case with respect to the Hotel Man who had not lived in Sai Mi Wan for many years before our first visit. According to the Enterprising Woman, a Fukienese who operates a hotel in Hong Kong received a Crown Permit soon after she did for some land bordering her own and extending easterly along the Sai Mi Wan beach. On the other hand, the Fortunate Wife of the Farmer, whom we shall introduce shortly, claimed that she was in Sai Mi Wan a few months before the Hotel Man, but the burden of evidence has piled up against her. It was many months before we finally met the Hotel Man himself, but when in the course of his own account, he gave a date three years earlier than that stated by the Fortunate Wife of the Farmer and, unaware of any contradictory opinion, claimed that he was second to take up land in Sai Mi Wan, we accepted the latter statement and adjusted the former to conform with the pressure of additional information. In any event, we shall put down the date of his arrival as 1952.

The Hotel Man came to Hong Kong as a young man of about twenty in 1934. For many years before acquiring land on Lung Chau, he was engaged in the travel business, chiefly arranging for the transportation of his countrymen between Fukien and Hong Kong. He became aware of Lung Chau because it was a place in which numerous people from the Fuchou and Amoy areas lived, and he discovered the bay of his future residence by climbing over the hill for a holiday picnic.

When the Communists finally took control of the mainland, his travel business was ruined and, in casting around for something else to do, he decided to raise pigs at Sai Mi Wan. Having acquired the land, he built a sizable stone and concrete gable-roofed house perpendicular to the beach with a double row of pig pens beyond it (Figs. 14.2 and 17.1).

The Hotel Man, who has cultivated a manner of unusual formal politeness—no doubt a complement of his professional activities—lived in Sai Mi Wan with his wife and several children for about two years before he discovered that making a profit from pig raising was more complex than he had anticipated. His lack of aptitude as a farmer led him to leave the island and he settled himself as the proprietor of a small hotel, which he leased, in Hong Kong.

Fig. 17.1. The Hotel Man's Establishment (Fish Dryer's in left foreground)

When we viewed the Hotel Man's Establishment in 1961, it was occupied by representatives of five different families, which were as difficult to disentangle as the historical account just presented. When it is realized that four of the families comprising a total of twenty-one individuals, including eleven adults, were crowded into the space erected for his own nuclear family, our problem becomes understandable. Actually, shelter was only achieved by extending shed roofs from each side of the original house, thereby providing cooking areas (Fig. 17.2).

After the four families had all become residents of Sai Mi Wan, the Hotel Man rented the open area between the house and the property of the Enterprising Woman to another man who was more confident of his ability to raise pigs. The latter constructed a large block of concrete pens and has pursued his business ever since with the help of three workers, two of whom live on the premises. As a preliminary to clarifying the succession of occupants of the Hotel Man's Establishment, we shall refer to the families in the house as A, B, C, and D, and to the pig raiser as Mister E.

Actually, the coming of the four families is not hard to explain when once the key facts have been exposed. Mr. A is the younger brother of the

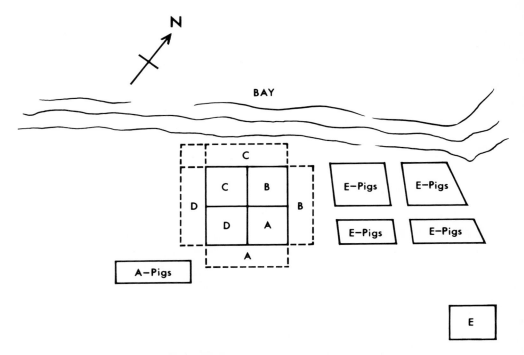

Fig. 17.2. Hotel Man's Establishment. Letters refer to inhabitant families.

Hotel Man's wife and at the time the latter returned to Hong Kong, the A family was invited to move in and look after the place. Soon they in turn invited some friends to join them—three related families also from Fuchou who were living together in Shau Kei Wan where Family A also lived briefly—and thus provide some income for the owner. Family B occupied two of the small cubicles into which the house was partitioned, paying $15 for one and $10 for the other. Family C and D each had their own segment for which they also paid $15, thus providing the Hotel Man with $55 per month, plus $35 for the rental of land to Mr. E. Later, the space occupied by Families A, B, C, and D was equalized.

Family A. Although Family A is very poor, the members are still better off than those of Family B, according to their neighbor, the Fortunate Wife of the Farmer. What seems certain is that at some time formerly they have been on a higher economic level than most of the people in Sai Mi Wan. Now, with eight members in the household and business misfortunes, things do not look well. The family consists of Mr. A and his wife, sons of six, five, and less than a year, and a daughter of three, plus Mr. A's father and mother.

Mr. A came to Hong Kong from a small village close to Fuchou in 1948, his wife and parents joining him in 1951. He had been in the export-import business dealing in various kinds of groceries among which canned goods, noodles, and salted fish were mentioned specifically. He had known some of the Fukienese people in Lung Shing who make gold-silver paper for the dead and hoped that by settling in Sai Mi Wan he could find work in that specialty, but his ambitions were apparently unrewarded. It is clear that he has lost money in several ventures since coming to Hong Kong, and most recently when he attempted to make wheat noodle cakes in Sai Mi Wan having purchased a machine for the purpose early in 1961. Following this failure, he rented the equipment to a group of partners, but the machine broke down, so the Enterprising Woman loaned them her factory to use up their flour which otherwise might have become moldy.

Mr. A does not give the appearance of a man who lives regularly in Sai Mi Wan. He looks like a well-to-do business man who has relaxed for a holiday at the seashore. Our memory of him is always that of a round-faced, half-smiling man in a suit of striped white pajamas. His parents, on the contrary, are not given to smiling. His father has a melancholy face and his mother one that is stern and forbidding. It somehow suggests that she would be happier if her son would just try a little harder to make a living. It would seem that she has little to complain about in her daughter-in-law who works constantly.

Mrs. A presents a sad picture of family affairs and certainly in some ways she is painting it slightly worse than it is. She states that they have only congee for their three meals, but in a later visit admitted that they kept a few chickens to eat. Also they have two or three pigs, but we concede that Mrs. A is correct in her assertion that they are unsuccessful in raising these animals. They get sick and die too easily, she says. The family has no ducks, pigeons, dogs, or cats, and there is no place for a garden or fruit trees. A well, first reported as a poor one, was later said to produce good water. The fact that no one in the family either smokes or drinks can hardly be viewed as an economic matter. Neither is the fact that none of the children are in school, since the oldest is just six. The women in the family cannot read or write, but Mrs. A did have two years of primary education. Mrs. A spends her spare time pasting silver foil squares on paper for one of the gold-silver paper factories in Lung Shing. Her mother-in-law, who can devote herself almost uninterruptedly to the task, can make five or six dollars a day. Two dollars is paid for the pasting of a bundle of sheets 26″ high. Unquestionably the women work hard. The neighbors say that Mrs. A is particularly industrious; besides tending pigs and helping to make noodle cakes, she sometimes dries a kind of small fish and makes a sauce which is a specialty of Fuchou. This we shall mention again in writing of Mrs. B who spends more time in sauce production.

During the hot summer, we always found Mrs. A in her under sam and under trousers, the latter cut well above the knee, a most convenient costume for working and feeding the baby. The material had an attractive orange, brown, and black pattern, and somehow it did not seem strange to discover that Mrs. A owns a few cheong sam although she does not wear them. Also, she had wood shoes with one red and one blue plastic band. Her hair is bobbed and has been waved, and she wears a wristwatch with a stretch band, the metal matching the gold ring on the third finger of her right hand. Speaking of gold, one becomes particulary conscious of the cap on her upper right second incisor. Her mother-in-law dresses in a conservative style black sam fu and has gold earrings.

As has been stated, Family A shares a house for which families B, C, and D pay the rent, as they individually attest. Family A has one room plus a shedlike extension in which the cooking is done on a kerosene stove. On the other hand, there is not only electricity but an electric fan, apparently like the dish cabinet, an inheritance from more affluent days. There are also two chairs with backs, plus several more ordinary stools. There is a spittoon on the cement floor, which the children use for urination.

Mrs. A, who was married blind, does not want any more children. Her three older ones were born at the Alice Ho Miu Ling Nethersole Hospital in Victoria and the last in the new clinic in the town across the strait in 1961. She claims that she was not told that she could obtain advice and assistance with respect to contraception. Everyone in the family except the baby received the single injection given for cholera in 1961, and there is no question but that doctors with a Western type training are generally preferred. There are other leanings toward the West. The family was first claimed to be Christian by Mrs. A who said that they do not go to church or, she added rather wistfully, get any material help. Later it was clear that Mrs. A was only trying to identify with the ethnographer, an American who was presumed to be Christian. Finally we discovered that a friend in Taiwan had entrusted some money to a Protestant minister who was coming to Hong Kong. After it was delivered to Mr. A, the contact was developed by additional meetings. Mr. A said eventually they had planned four or five years ago to become Christians, but then they did not have the time as the minister's church was in Kowloon. They do not belong to the Kaifong Association.

Mr. A unhesitatingly states that the British Government performs excellently in Hong Kong, and that the Chinese could not do as well. Mr. A, we might add, completed a primary school education and went through junior high school in Fuchou. He is the one person in Sai Mi Wan we saw reading books. He likes to go to the movies and he not infrequently takes his wife and all their children to the cinema in Lung Shing and less often to one across the strait. It may not have been a compliment to his guests when he said that he prefers films from America. He knows how to play mah-jongg but claims that he has no time to do so. There is no radio in the house. Mr. A says he can swim, and the older children certainly play in the water. Mr. A has been to Tung Pak Wan but he had never heard of the settlement at Chung Nam Wan. It is notable that he has visited Taiwan where he has a brother.

Family B. Like the others in the Hotel Man's Establishment, Family B shares things in common with Family A. They are Fukienese from near Fuchou, "pro-Christians" who have never been to church, and friendly people. They also have sons aged nine, seven, and three. The father was born about 1922 and his wife at thirty is ten years younger. Mr. B, like his friends, Mr. C and Mr. D, is a tailor who works in Wan Chai (Fig. 3.2). More specifically he is a pants cutter who comes home to spend the night sometimes as often as once a week. His widowed mother lives with them and the day of our first visit she brought us a glass of bean curd liquid to which her daughter-in-law added some sugar, a memorable courtesy to one unaccustomed to the drink.

Mrs. B, who has deep walnut-colored eyes and bobbed hair with a twist in front was wearing a patterned blue sam fu that day, but the sam and fu did not match. She also had red strap slippers as did her mother-in-law who was dressed in black fu and a faded blue sam. The older lady had some gold capped teeth and her hair was gray. Mrs. B said that she had one cheong sam which had been made for her wedding, but that she had never owned a wristwatch.

The women in the family have had no education and the husband only a few years of schooling. The two oldest sons attend School B. They were born in Tsan Yuk Maternity Hospital in Sai Ying Pun, while the third son was born in the Tung Wah.

The members of the family seldom go to the movies, they have no radio, and they play no games. Mrs. B has been to Tung Pak Wan, but she had never heard of Chung Nam Wan. She says the family has no religion, but the two oldest sons attend the Catholic Church without having been baptized.

The most interesting thing about this quiet, almost pretty, little woman is that she runs a small-scale fish sauce business. In the yard beyond her shed-roofed porch are forty-seven pottery jars about twenty inches in height and the same in diameter with heavy cement covers on them. In these jars Mrs. B makes the sauce which is a specialty of the Fuchou area and, if business is good, she sells about 2,000 catties a year.

To make this much appreciated condiment, she buys what are called ch'ik ü (ch'ih yü), a kind of sea catfish the length of her first finger, for eight to ten dollars a 100 catties in the 5th or 6th month.* To eighty catties

---

*All months numbered in Arabic refer to the Chinese lunar months. See Appendix C.

of small catfish, she adds twenty to thirty catties of salt (at $7 per 100 catties) and a very little water. This mixture is put into the pots and allowed to stand for a year. Periodically, she removes the heavy covers of the pots and allows the sun to warm the contents but there is always the danger of the chickens adding a few droppings. There is no rule as to when the covers are removed, just as there is no measure of the amount of water in the original mixture. All we could discover is that if there is too much water, the sauce will not be of good quality. In any event, when the sauce has stood its time, there are only fifty to sixty catties left from the original 100, or 110, plus water. This residuum is finally boiled for a few minutes, brown sugar, raw ginger, aniseed, and cayenne pepper being added beforehand. The work thus completed, the sauce is put into old beer bottles holding one catty four ounces (which cost empty only $3 per 100) and peddled to fellow Fukienese in Hong Kong for $.60 each, Mrs. B making a trip every few days to the Central Market area in Victoria or to families in Wan Chai that she knows. Thus she can make a net profit of about $40 a month. The sauce is said to improve if kept in the jars as long as two or three years, but she generally sells it before it reaches that age.

Family C. The smallest cubicle in the Hotel Man's Establishment is occupied by the wife and six-year-old daughter of Mr. C who sews pants in Wan Chai and comes home perhaps once a week. Since he makes only about $200 a month, as do the other two tailors, it is not surprising to find the rest of his family busily working on gold-silver paper for the dead. Their work space is very cluttered and Mrs. C is the first to express the fact that there is really not enough room for them all even when there are no visitors.

Mrs. C, who is thirty-six, and eight years younger than her husband, was wearing a green patterned sam with pale silver fu and blue strap slippers when we first called on her. She had gold button earrings and her two upper left incisor and canine teeth were all capped with gold.

Like Mrs. B, Mrs. C had no education and her husband only a few years of schooling. She does go to the movies occasionally, but they have never owned a radio. High on the wall of the house under the shed roof where Mrs. B and Mrs. C do their cooking is an elaborate red box with a picture of a God inside with a ten watt bulb to illuminate it, electricity having been provided for all the families soon after they came. The bottom of the box has a small railing behind it in which is a vase with artificial flowers. Around the altar is a border of flags of Nationalist China. Also above their common door to the house is a commonplace pat kwa (pa kua) plaque (Fig. 17.3). Below it is a wood tablet containing two lines of six characters each, which are not easy to translate intelligibly, but refer to the Earth God, the Dragon God, and the Money God. Mrs. C was no help, commenting that she was not very regular in worshipping the gods.

Fig. 17.3. A Pat Kwa (Pa Kua) Plaque

Family D. The fourth Fukienese family in the Hotel Man's Establishment comprises a very sensitive man of thirty-two, his wife who is a year younger, and two sons of five and three. They all occupy a room on the opposite side of the house from Family B and C and share their porch with Family A. In this complex of people sleeping under one roof, we finally discovered that Families B, C, and D are related, although for some reason our original informant had denied it. Later she confirmed the fact that Mister D is the son of Mr. B's father's sister. Also Mr. B and Mr. C are sons of two brothers.

Mr. D, like his cousins, dresses in Western style clothes, as might be expected of a professional tailor. Mr. D, however, makes a special impression because of the perfection of his even, white teeth. He had moved from Fuchou to Amoy where he was practicing his trade when he left for Hong Kong in 1950. Arduous and continuous labor has always characterized his life. In Wan Chai, where he works with Mister C, in theory he gets up at eight, starts sewing at nine, and continues with brief interruptions until midnight or even sometimes until one in the morning. He is induced to follow this heavy schedule because he is paid by piece work and can thus considerably augment his income by such long hours. In the summer season, however, business slacks off and he admits that his schedule is less rigid. Also he has a vacation of a few days at New Year's.

It should be noted that the families living in the Hotel Man's house follow the typical Fukienese pattern of eating three meals a day with congee in the morning and evening and boiled rice with dishes at noon. Mr. D himself neither drinks nor smokes. None of the three tailoring families keep any animals or attempt to raise vegetables, we must add.

The D family, like the B and C, does not own a radio. Mr. D had three years of education, but his wife had none. He enjoys movies made in the West but he seldom has time to see one. He never goes to swim in the bay as he has never had time to learn how. None of the families belong to the Kaifong Association.

The two sons in Family D were born in Tsan Yuk Hospital. In a discussion in which Mr. A joined, it was said that no child of any of the families in the Hotel Man's Establishment had been born at home and specifically in Sai Mi Wan, it being pointed out that it was more convenient, safer, and less expensive for a woman to bear a child in a hospital. Mr. D, like the others in the group, was married blind. Mr. D, we may conclude, claims to have no religion, but his wife occasionally burns incense to the gods, as did his mother.

Mister E. The fifth family should be remembered as Cantonese and wholly unconnected with the others on the Hotel Man's estate. Also, Mister E did not enter the group until 1956. The owner of the property wanted income from it and he rented the unused area for $35 a month to Mister E, who has a vegetable stall with his father at the Central Market in Victoria. The license for the stall costs $150 per month which is cheaper than those near the entrances. Actually in 1961, the license fees were standardized and everyone pays according to category rather than on the basis of cost at the time of first application. Meat stalls we might add cost three to four hundred dollars, and fish stalls, five to six.

Mister E comes to Sai Mi Wan every afternoon to check on the activities of his three employees, one of whom is the head of Household Three in Tung Pak Wan, and on the health of his pigs of which he has over fifty. There are also the vegetable fields to be looked at with an eye as to salable produce (Fig. 14.2, area 2E). What grows is sold at the family vegetable stall, but for the most part they must depend for stall vegetables on purchases at the Kennedy Wholesale Market west of Victoria, or at the Yau Ma Tei Market in Kowloon (Fig. 3.2). They also have over a hundred chickens and ten pairs of pigeons, but no ducks. Obtaining water in Sai Mi Wan is a problem, for Mister E has sunk as many as four wells to the depth of thirty feet to get enough of that precious commodity. It is pumped out by means of an electric motor.

The first day we talked to Mister E, we were interrupted by two potential women customers, apparently boat people, who were interested in buying some pigs. He offered them some young animals for $50 each. One woman asked, "Are you sure they won't die after a few days?"

"In two weeks they will be worth $70," he answered immediately. Then he went on to explain that he sold pigs of eighty catties for $220.

The woman countered by telling of a bad experience she had with a pig dealer and how she was once cheated by fifteen catties on the weight of an animal. The woman looked at some more pigs but no business was done.

Shortly afterward, Mister E complained to one of his workers that he was losing money all the time, implying that his difficulties were caused by the fact that a few families were producing so many pigs and chickens in Tung Pak Wan.

The E family, originally from Nan Hai, commonly known as Fat Shan, near Canton, has lived in the Colony since about 1938 and did not leave during the Japanese occupation. For the first ten years the members resided in the town across the strait and then they moved to Victoria. Consequently they have long known of Lung Chau. Before Mister E, or perhaps technically his father, rented the establishment in Sai Mi Wan, he worked as a delivery man. He is now about thirty years old and has recently married. According to his statement, he has to get up at four in the morning to be at the market, which opens at five and does not close until eight in the evening. He works at the stall during the morning, and his wife is there much of the day also. Business, he admits, is passable, which may be interpreted as signifying that it is really very good.

Mister E went through four years of primary school before the Japanese occupied Hong Kong. Later he attended night school for a year or two. He says he still likes association football which he played in school. When we saw him he was dressed in black cloth shorts, black socks, and dirty blue tennis shoes. Over a once white T-shirt, he wore a black coat.

Whatever else may be said, the E family has no time left on its hands. Fortunately, the basic Chinese foods are always in demand, whereas if the family were engaged in a business, such as papermaking, there would always be the danger that the product would become unsalable.

18. The Papermakers

As we have mentioned, the Enterprising Woman became involved in the papermaking business, at least to the extent of renting the westernmost forty-five feet of her beach frontage in 1953 to five Swatow men who wanted to build a factory to replace one that they had been forced to abandon in Lung Shing because of new construction. At the time we began our study the men had been in partnership about ten years suffering various vicissitudes which had brought their joint undertaking close to an end. Already some of the partners were devoting much less than half time to papermaking, and one we never saw. Fortunately, the most dynamic man still remaining among them was sympathetic toward our inscribing a record of what appeared to be a fast dying industry on Lung Chau, and most of what we learned was the result of his tutelage. Before going on to a description of papermaking itself, we will introduce our friend.

This Papermaker is a tall man, so thin that his clothes always seem suspended from the high points of his body rather than embracing it. His face is of pale ivory color, and glossy in its smoothness, a quality which extends to the top of his head on which one can count the hairs, each separated from the other in a strange, uniform dispersal. At work, he usually wears only very short blue shorts and blue Japanese style slippers, plus a wristwatch. When going into Lung Shing, he may add a white sweatshirt or black cotton jacket, although there is nothing strange about appearing bare to the waist in his favorite restaurant during the hottest months. This distinctive looking man was born about 1927 in Ch'ao Yang, an unlocated community (consequently not on our maps) that is said to be about an hour's journey by boat to the southwest of Swatow, in the northeast corner of the province of Kwangtung. He was one of seven or eight children of a reasonably well-to-do father who was engaged in the prescription and sale of Chinese medicine. Asked why he did not go into the profession himself when he asserted that he had been given considerable training by his parent, he replied with a feeling that lent authority to his excuse that he was afraid that he would poison someone. We immediately liked him even better.

Business in Ch'ao Yang suffered under the Japanese occupation and his father suggested that his future might be more secure if he emigrated to Hong Kong. This he did when he was eighteen. There was the usual linguistic problem as the people of his area speak the Ch'ao An dialect of Chinese which is not understood by the Cantonese. It took him a year to learn the new language and while he did so he lived with some relatives in Mong Kok in northwest Kowloon (Fig. 3.2) who were engaged in the import-export trade. Then he went to Cha Kwo Ling and opened an accessory store. When he was twenty-two his parents sent for him to come home, and he was married to a girl he had never seen until the ceremony took place.

After his return to Hong Kong with his wife, a friend persuaded him to move to Lung Chau where he learned the papermaking trade. He and his wife had a shack behind a barbershop on Main Street, but when the property was taken over for new construction, he was given $800. Of this amount he spent $700 on a new shack higher up the hill and just below a gold-silver papermaker's establishment, a fellow Ch'ao An speaker to whom he sold much of his paper.

A strange looking man is our friend, and he has a stranger looking house. It is approached as though through a tunnel and then one climbs a stepladder twelve inches wide and crawls into a room which is a cube of approximately six feet in each direction. Stranger than strange, the floor is of glossy linoleum and the occupants take off their shoes before stepping on it. Part of the extreme limitation of space results from their having rented out the room beneath for $15 a month. Cooking is done in the entryway. Within the cubicle itself, various shelves of considerable size project from the walls and on these sleep his three sons aged nine, five, and three. Fortunately, at the time of our visit it was possible to squirm down out of the cubicle in the opposite direction as our host promptly did since there was not room for all of us in his home at one time. Our host quickly explained that the extra exit was most valuable as a fire escape, a fact we could well believe looking down over the shacks below us as we eased ourselves along the ledge which led into the gold-silver paper man's backyard.

Fortunately, as our friend reports gleefully, his wife will have no more children. A local midwife was taking care of the delivery of their first child when the birth became difficult and the mother was rushed to the Queen Mary Hospital. At the time his second son was born, he was short of money and obtained a nurse from the Tsan Yuk Maternity Hospital. She could not manage the delivery, however, and his suffering wife was taken to that hospital. When the third pregnancy occurred, he again took his wife to Tsan Yuk. At first they did not want to keep her, but he persuaded them to do so because of her record of difficult birth. After the third child arrived, she was made secure from further impregnation, a fact which delights them.

His wife, as is the case of most women of her class and age group, was given no formal education. The Papermaker, however, finished primary school and had started high school before he had to give up. He has high hopes for his sons, however, the eldest of whom attends School D in Lung Shing. Interestingly enough, the three children are bilingual, but they know Cantonese better. They usually reply in Cantonese when spoken to in the speech of Ch'ao An, and when the eldest reads aloud he can only voice the characters in Cantonese, whereas his father can only do so in the Ch'ao An dialect.

The family does not belong to the Kaifong Association. Politically, the Papermaker holds that the British do better at administering the government of Hong Kong than the Chinese could. As for the governments in Peking and Taipei, he has as little regard for the one as for the other, and that is indeed small.

Personally, our friend says he cares nothing for religion, although he has always enjoyed eating the offerings made to the gods by his parents and his wife. In his father's house there were ancestral tablets and he had to kowtow before them under threat of his mother's spankings. At the paper factory, incense is burned to the Earth God and food and drink offerings made. This is done by the men's wives who take turns at this duty. It was pointed out that anything that one likes can be placed before the Earth God, including cigarettes and wine. The Papermaker, incidentally, smokes American Lucky Strike cigarettes when he can afford the $1.10; English Capstans for $0.90 when he has coughing spells because he thinks the Virginia tobacco is "softer," and when he is short of money, he rolls his own. On those occasions when there is not even enough money to eat, he stops smoking altogether.

The Papermaker's real weakness, however, is strong wine. He started drinking when he first came to Lung Chau almost ten years ago. Usually he would prefer "Double Distilled" at $3 a bottle, but the quality of the liquor he drinks depends on the condition of his purse. Cheaper brands, he says "are all mixed up" and not dependable. As for French cognac, he can "drink it like beer, it's so smooth." But it costs over $20 for the standard size bottle. Our friend even says he does not like to make too much money, as he will then drink to excess. On the other hand, when he is without funds, he does not find the desire for drink imperious, and gets along without liquor. He admits that his fondness for alcohol is not a good thing by and large, but he says that he loves strong drink, and that it is his one real consolation. This hardly makes his wife, who does not even smoke, any happier. She would prefer to use the money to go to the movies, but he is bored by them.

It is perhaps a peculiarity of this factory that the papermakers are all fond of liquor, and some of them are more dissipated than our friend as we ultimately learned. The process of making paper by hand and foot is not

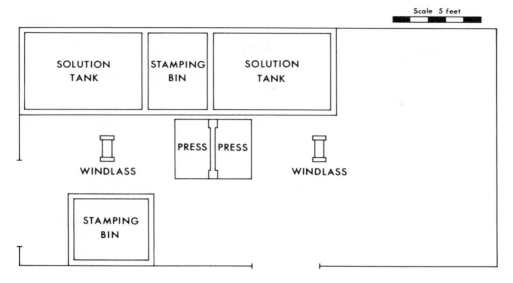

Fig. 18.1. The Paper Factory

difficult except for the screening and stacking of new sheets which requires kinesthetic imagery beyond the power of a pen to convey. It is time now to present primitive papermaking as well as our ability allows.

The factory. The building comprises a single room twenty-seven by fourteen feet parallel to the beach (Fig. 14.2). Basically it is a clapboard structure on low concrete walls with a gable roof which has been extended two-fifths of its total size by a wood frame covered with metal sheathing which in part opens up as windows. The older section has two windows also. Perhaps it would be more correct to say restored rather than extended, since the papermakers spent about $600 to rebuild the first structure they had made after it was blown down by Typhoon Mary in 1960, the men doing the work themselves. The floor of the factory is concrete, but it is very rough and dirty. Six and a half feet in front of the establishment is a new well about thirty feet deep which produces very good water despite the fact that its center is only 128″ away from the edge of the retaining wall which prevents the sea from flooding the area at the highest tide.

The factory equipment consists essentially of two low concrete stamping bins, two concrete paper solution tanks, and a primitive wood, double-faced, pressing mill (Fig. 18.1). This basic equipment originally cost about $2,000. One stamping bin is isolated to the left of the door; the other is roughly opposite the first between the two paper solution tanks at the rear of the building. The pressing mill stands against these latter constructions, its center about even with the common wall of the stamping bin and a solution tank. Besides these large pieces of equipment there are the large bamboo screens which press down the pulp in the solution tanks, the poles used to stir up the solution, the framed nylon screens on which the paper is lifted from solution, some metal buckets and pans to transfer the liquids and pulp, and a few tables and stools. There is a single electric light bulb on a line extended from that at the ink factory building.

Perhaps one's attention should also be drawn to the small round tray on the window sill with its diminutive and distinctive Yi Hsing ware teapot and five tiny handleless cups from which the papermakers imbibe their thickly brewed Kun Yam (Kuan Yin) tea, as is customary among natives of Swatow and the Fukien coast to the east. Also one may note the bottles of strong, colorless spirits near the tea things which, according to their own statements, symbolize the main pleasure of the papermakers. The wine is drunk only at the principal meals which are eaten at one or two in the afternoon and seven or eight in the evening. Unless they are short of money, each man drinks a catty a day, most of it at night. Asked if they do not feel the effects, one quickly answered, "No. The more you drink, the more energy you have." The men also have a breakfast at six or seven in the morning and some congee at ten. There is a pot stove and also one which burns kerosene on which the men cook their midday meals, the earlier and later ones being eaten in Lung Shing. One papermaker commented as we made notes, "You think we look dirty, but we wash our rice bowls in boiling water." We smiled at each other. Close to the front door is a can painted red to hold incense sticks burned for the Earth God. None of the men sleeps at the factory, the doors of which are always unlocked. Most of them, like our principal informant, are married and live in Lung Shing.

Stamping the pulp. The process of making the paper begins by a man searching the bottom of a stamping bin for any extraneous material left there, such as twigs, bits of metal, or string. The bin, which stands by itself, is 44″ wide and 50″ long with a flat cement floor and cement walls around it about 4″ wide and 15″ high. The man, once satisfied, tosses a few armfuls of small scraps of paper taken from a large bagful purchased as remnants from the makers of paper money for the dead. Then a few panfuls of solution transferred from one of the tanks are poured onto the paper (fresh water would serve, but the solution is near at hand). When ten minutes have been consumed thus, the Papermaker adds more paper, spreading it and picking out more unwanted material, the procedure requiring a second period the length of the first. The scrap paper as it soaks up the liquid solution takes on a distinctive smell which can be oppressive to the unaccustomed nose if the day is without a breeze. Content that the material which he has been treading underfoot is sufficiently free of unwanted debris, a third armful is added and the process of stamping begins

Fig. 18.2.
Stamping Paper

(Fig. 18.2). A bare foot is thrust out in one direction after another, no particular force being concentrated on any part of the foot. One simply stamps naturally and not too hard. After a few minutes, the Papermaker may use his other foot; it is a matter of personal inclination, naturally guided by the need for rest plus the facility in stamping in opposite directions without turning around. More paper and more water are added as the process continues. About fifty catties of scrap paper are stamped in one batch, and about 280 catties of water mixed in with it. The whole process requires about two hours of one man's time. The papermakers take turns carrying out the different parts of their task, although sometimes, if pulp is needed, a second man will step into the stamping bin with the first. When sufficiently stamped upon, the pulp appears dry, but some water oozes between the toes of the Papermaker when he finally treads on the pulp.

Molding the paper. The second stage in the papermaking begins with the transference of the stamped pulp in a metal pail to a solution tank. The concrete tank is 44″ wide, 80″ long, 39″ high, and has walls about 4″ thick.

The solution—water with the remnants of pulp—reaches within 6″ to 8″ of the top. It is never completely replaced, but more water is added as needed each morning. When the pulp has been dumped into the tank, a screen of split bamboos the size of the inside of the tank, is floated on the solution. The bamboos themselves are 1½″ wide and tied together loosely. The papermakers estimated that there were twenty-four or twenty-five bamboos in each one, but only fifteen by actual count were used in the screen of the east tank and nineteen in that of the west. Then a couple of boards are placed crosswise of the bamboos (and crosswise of the tank) and a large stone is added which sinks the screen to the bottom of the tank carrying most of the pulp with it. The latter, however, gradually seeps up into the solution, which remains at more or less the same consistency, although this factor is controlled by a periodic pounding of the bamboo screen with a pole having a flat, oval piece of wood about 9″ long and an inch thick fastened to its end, and then by a vigorous whipping around of the solution with a plain pole.

The solution must stand for half an hour and then one of the paper-makers can begin to screen off sheets of new paper using a framed screen, or mold, to do so. The screen is made of nylon and by itself measures 19″ wide and 28″ long, the same as the resultant pieces of paper. The screen is supported by ten small steel bars stretching the width of a wood frame about an inch high. These molds are relatively inexpensive, costing about $20. One will last six or seven years. The nylon screens can be repaired with fine fishline. In the Swatow area, from which the whole process has diffused, bamboo screens were used, but they lasted only six months and had to be continually repaired. The wood frame of the nylon screen is 23″ wide and 32″ long.

Lifting the paper out of solution is actually the most demanding part of the operation as the thickness of the product is thus entirely controlled. The Papermaker reaches out over the tank and lowers the mold vertically in an arc until it is horizontal, then pulls it up to the surface, allowing the water to run off as he does so (Fig. 18.3). He will normally lift the right side of the mold a little toward the near corner and run the solution off toward the diagonal one at the far left. A thin layer of paper pulp is thus spread over the top of the nylon screen. If necessary, the solution can be cleaned by simply turning it over and allowing it to float in the water a few seconds. The process looks simple enough, but skill is required. All the workers have it, and they take turns in molding as in other stages of the work. When the Papermaker lifts his mold out of the solution, he makes a quarter turn to the left (or to the right, depending on which tank he is using) and deposits his mold upside down on a stack of previous sheets stacked on one side of the paper press. A slight pressure causes the new sheet to adhere to the previous one (to begin, a few sheets from a previous run are left on the paper press). The start is always the most difficult part

Fig. 18.3. Molding Paper

of laying the paper as it does not readily stick to the wet sheets below it, extra pressure having to be applied to the screen. The mold fits into three vertical wood guides so that the paper sheets are stacked evenly. There is one of these at the outer side and two at the back. They are made of wood 1½" square and are 35" high (Fig. 18.4). Water runs down continuously from the stack of paper as each piece is pressed on the preceding one, and a trough around the edge of the stack carries the liquid into a metal bucket which either overflows or is picked up by the Papermaker and its contents poured back into the solution tank. Periodically, he stirs the solution to break up any lumps of pulp. After stirring, the mold needs only to be slipped under the surface of the liquid to collect sufficient pulp. Also, the Papermaker can tell when there is insufficient pulp in the solution by feeling the bottom of the tank with his stirring stick. When the pile of paper in the stand is about 26" high, it is ready to be pressed. Such a pile is said to require about four hours of work to produce. In theory, paper can be molded at a rate of about five sheets a minute.[1] During our observations, production was desultory, the workers being discouraged by the poor state of the market and consequently readily distracted by us. The remanent solution can be left untouched for ten days if need be.

Pressing the paper. The new sheets of paper do not have to be immediately pressed but they usually are. The press is of simple construction and consists of a 42" x 52" cement base into which two 5" x 6" rectangular posts reaching seven feet above the floor have been inserted (Fig. 18.5). A

1. Cf. Fei and Chang, 1945: 189–90.

Fig. 18.4. Paper on the Press

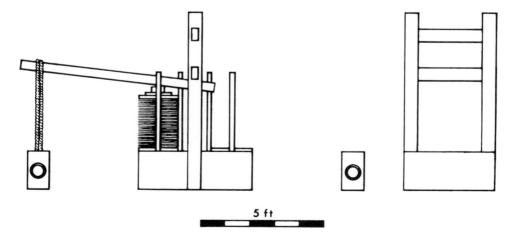

5 ft

Fig. 18.5. The Paper Press

foot from the top of the posts, a heavy horizontal piece is mortised into the verticals and about a foot below the first, a similar second one. A pressing lever 90″ long made of a 5″ x 6″ timber fits under the lower of the two cross pieces when pressing is to be done. About six feet from the vertical members of the press (in opposite directions) are rough wood rollers 7″ in diameter set into vertical wood blocks. The rollers, which can be turned by a steel bar, form windlasses. As may be construed from the above description, the pair of windlasses makes it possible to press the paper stacked between the wood guides on either side of the vertical members of the press. Two men may pile their sheets of paper at the same time, but the pressing must be done on one side at a time.

The stack of paper actually rests on a smooth wood plate one inch thick, 19″ wide, and 28″ long, which in turn rests on a heavy wood tray 1½″ thick, 28½″ wide and 36″ long with walls 2½″ high (one inch inside). The greater size of the tray leaves a trough all around the edges of the wood plate (and paper stacked on it). There are drain holes at various places in the trough but these may be plugged. At the outside corner of each tray, the vertical wall has been cut down to the top of the tray so that water can run out into a pail below.

When ready to press the stack of new paper, the Papermaker adds a few sheets of dry paper to the top of the pile, then a wood board 1½″ thick the size of the paper and with blocks fastened both ways on it. After clearing the trough of pulp which surrounds the base of the pile, he brings the heavy pressing lever into position, carrying it on his shoulder. With one end slipped under the lower cross member of the main vertical pieces of the press, he allows the other end to fall slowly. As the lever encounters the wood board on the pile of paper, the water begins to rush out of the stacked paper from the pressure. The Papermaker still supports the lever, letting it fall little by little until at last the paper supports its weight. Two or three minutes have perhaps passed in the process, and the Papermaker empties the bucket of exuded water into the solution tank. (The bucket is 11″ high and 14″ in diameter at the top.) Then he presses a little on the end of the lever. More water comes out. Then he raises the lever on his shoulder, placing a block under it on top of the board on the paper. The lever reaches upward at an angle of about fifteen degrees from the horizontal. This done, he fastens a 1½″ rope around the windlass roller, overlapping its own part to hold it, then loops it over the top of the lever and back around the windlass roller, again overlapping its own part. Then he empties a second bucket of expressed liquid into the solution tank and, inserting a steel bar into the windlass, gradually draws down the lever to a horizontal position. Ten minutes have gone by since he started, and he empties a third bucket of liquid and then a fourth. Lifting the lever, he adds a second block above the board, raising the horizontal beam as before. The water runs out again, and the Papermaker rubs the sides of the pile of paper to clean away the fibers. Then he empties the bucket for the fifth time. From this juncture, the windlass becomes harder to turn and he presses on the steel bar first with one foot, then with both. A second man comes to help, both naked except for blue shorts with underpants beneath. When the bar is horizontal, a sixth bucketful of water is emptied into the tank. For the last time the lever is raised for the insertion of a third, but smaller, block which raises the lever only ten degrees above the horizontal. Little water is still running into the bucket. The pile of paper has been reduced in height from 26″ to 9½″. Twenty minutes have elapsed since the start of the operation. The two men turn the windlass, but the rope slips. One man inserts a piece of paper behind the rope and in another five minutes the bar is horizontal. The bucket is emptied for the seventh time. The stack of paper, only 9″ high, scarcely feels wet. The Papermaker estimates it weighs a little less than fifty catties.* The pressing has taken twenty-five minutes.

Drying the paper. As a final stage, the pressed sheets have to be sun dried and, in order to do so, they must be separated (Fig. 18.6). The pile of paper is removed to a low table and a man picks up the top sheet by a corner and doubles it back, then the next, but leaving the end extending a half inch out beyond that of the first. Eight sheets are done in this fashion, to form a group. Usually the pile is beaten in the center—first with the fist, then with a wooden mallet or an empty wine bottle—which forces up the edges. Tears made in the process of folding are repaired with the fingers.

The sheets separated in this manner are carried to the front of the factory, to the beach, to a neighbor's flat, or to the nearby hillside and spread out to dry (Fig. 18.7). Any available space is used. If the sun is strong, eight sheets can be left together; if less strong, half that number, and so on. A heavy rain will destroy the damp paper, and the makers must also guard their product from heavy wind. In ideal weather the paper dries in four or five hours and is soon brought in and separated into individual sheets. The lots of eight sheets, once loosened, are shuffled like playing cards in the short direction, then made even lengthwise by using the fingers. The stacks of dried paper are thus finally readied for sale.

---

*There is some inconsistency in such judgments. Another partner on another day estimated a pressed stack 11″ high would produce only about forty catties of dried paper. Part of the difficulty comes from the fact that one batch of paper may be pressed a little more than another. Ideally, a 35″ stack should be pressed in half and produce eighty catties of dry paper.

Fig. 18.6. Separating Paper

Fig. 18.7. Drying Paper

Economics. The primitive process of papermaking, or really remaking, is limited to three products: paper for the manufacture of money to be burned for the dead, toilet paper, and cardboard. The first type is the one commonly produced.

The raw material is the waste from the manufacturers of gold-silver paper money for the dead, as well as other sources of discarded paper such as stationers, and it is brought to the factory in large bags weighing twenty to thirty catties each, which cost $2 to $6 depending on the kind and amount (we shall presume that the average cost of 100 catties is $16). Rent for the factory is $200 a year. Other costs, such as electricity for light are minimal.

At full operation 200 to 300 catties of paper can be produced in a day. This requires an equivalent amount of scrap which costs $40 if we assume the amount to be 250 catties. Each man figures on a salary of $15 for his day's work, or a total of $75. There are no taxes or other expenses to consider except rent which we can compute as amounting to $.75 a day, giving a total of $115.75.

If 250 catties of paper for paper money were produced, they would bring $130 at $52 per hundred. Toilet paper on the other hand sells for $65 per hundred, but less can be made. Computing twenty per cent of the latter gives an average daily income of $136.50. The profit, here figured at $20.75 above the basic $15 a day salary, when divided among the five partners would give each an additional $4.15 and a total of $19.15.

Unfortunately the paper making business does not function that ideally. First of all, a sudden heavy rainstorm on the accumulated paper laid out to dry may cause a very high loss (the raindrops riddle the wet paper with holes and render it worthless). Or the demand for paper may fall off, and the prices may drop. When paper is exported from mainland China, the price drops in half and the factory closes. In 1961, there was no competition from that source. Cardboard is very seldom made in the factory because of the uncertain demand and variable price ranging from $40 to $70 per 100 catties. Up to 500 catties of cardboard can be produced in a day, however. Curiously enough, it is not always possible to obtain enough scrap because of its demand by the building industry (it is pulped and used to fill in gaps in concrete). Finally, competitive factories should be mentioned. One man produces paper in Lung Shing and two more do so in Little Tung Pak Wan with a total capacity of almost 150 catties a day. Each uses exactly the same kind of equipment (one stamping bin, one solution tank, a screening tray, and a wood press), but with much less working room than the Sai Mi Wan factory. Indeed, the Lung Shing papermaker works in a cellar so dismal it seems like a pit.

As a result of this situation, as has been said, not all the partners work regularly at Sai Mi Wan. During the summer of 1961, one of the men took employment at a plastics factory in Sai Wan (Kennedy Town) west of Victoria (Fig. 3.2), where he can make at least $15 a day in only about seven hours. Those who still make paper buy their own scrap and operate individually except for selling, but each knows the amount of his own paper. One assiduous worker tries to make $15 in a long, strenuous day and he is quite miserable when an unexpected rain cheats him of a three-day profit. Of the paper produced, most is sold to the makers of gold-silver paper in Lung Shing, but in the past some has been sold in Hong Kong. Ultimately, the papermakers report with pride, a small part of their produce reaches America where paper to be burned for the dead is sold in the Chinatowns of the large cities.

19. The Fortunate Wife of the Farmer

In 1954, three years after the Enterprising Woman began to foster the commercial enterprises which have in part been described, a new and independent development occurred in Sai Mi Wan. It was new because it represented the immigration of a family who came to settle on the land in order to develop a farm, and independent since the people were native Cantonese rather than coming from the Province of Fukien as did the Enterprising Woman and most of her associates. Even the papermakers, we will remember, were Ch'ao An speakers, a language more closely related to Fukienese than to Cantonese although indigenous to the Swatow area of northern Kwangtung. In a relatively short time the new-comers had acquired first 10,000 square feet of hill slope above the foot of the bay and then 15,000 square feet more. Even the Enterprising Woman whose land they have cut into behind and above states that these Cantonese farmers have been very clever about the business—and she says it as though they have been almost too clever. One thing is certain, if there is a woman in Sai Mi Wan of comparable astuteness to the one who first developed the area, it is she whom we shall call the Fortunate Wife of the Farmer, and we shall now present her story.

This woman was married to her present husband more than a quarter of a century ago. They both came from the neighborhood of Shih Lung which is not far from Tung Kuan and almost due east of Canton (Fig. 3.1). Soon after 1920 when he was a boy of fourteen, the husband was brought by his parents to the town across the strait. He was born about 1907, and his wife six years later. She remembers as a young girl of eighteen being taken in a sedan chair from her house to that of his parents in the ancestral village. It was not the custom for a bridegroom to fetch the bride from her house, but he came out of his own on her arrival. Then she was carried into his home on the back of a woman. Later that evening, men gathered to tease her and her husband, but in his village this was done only by the young male members of his tsuk (tsu), or lineage. Almost immediately she came to Hong Kong as a bride. There the young couple lived with the parents of the husband who worked in a grocery store.

Some time before the Japanese invaded Canton in 1938, her mother left China and joined them. The latter began to deal in bamboo, and in consequence she became familiar with the Lung Shing sauce factories to which she delivered bamboo for use in binding kegs. The mother of the Fortunate Wife decided that the small island would be a good place for her daughter to live, and in about 1937 the family moved there.

In Lung Shing, the family engaged in selling eggs and stoneware to the fishermen. The eggs were mostly those of ducks, the whites being used to coat fish lines. The business suffered, however, because so many of their customers promised to "pay later," but could not or did not. By 1951, after a new plastic covering for fish lines was beginning to be used, the end of their trade was in sight and they were forced to look for other means of livelihood. About this time, they acquired shares in a rope business. There were ten partners and three main kinds of line were manufactured. One was machine-made hawser up to two inches in diameter essential for ships; another was a thumb-thick line that was made by hand; and the third, bamboo line that was used for constructing furniture.

There was still not enough income to take care of the many children in the family and, recognizing the extremely high price paid for pigs, they decided to raise some. This could not be done in town because of a recent regulation, so the government authorities were asked whether any nearby land was available. Thus they were directed to Sai Mi Wan. At first, they did not intend to live there but a house was built to provide a home for their workers. As things turned out, the husband and children became permanent residents of their new home in 1954 while the Fortunate Wife remained in the old one to attend to the rope business which was expanding. Needing more factory space, she offered the main floor of the Lung Shing house on Ferry Street which the rest of the family had abandoned. They had lived in it for almost twenty years and paid only $40 a month rent. When it was used for rope making, however, the owner demanded more money, which the Fortunate Wife flatly refused. The case went to the courts on the grounds that she had sublet the house illegally. In the end, after great expense for which she had to borrow the money, she states that the court decided in her favor, but that she was nonetheless obliged to pay more rent. Later, a beam in the building having come loose, government inspectors suddenly appeared and she was ordered to move out on the grounds of safety. She had no choice but to comply and thus joined the rest of her family in Sai Mi Wan. Her old home, she added, was quickly rented for $200 a month as a barber shop which still occupies it. The rope business from which she then withdrew, also continues, but there are now only two partners.

Nothing that has so far been reported explains why the mistress of the family should be termed "Fortunate," and this must be done without further delay. In the course of her married life, the Wife has borne ten children of whom only five survive. By 1948, after many years of marriage, her living offspring were all girls. The lack of a son had become only too obvious, and following age-old Chinese tradition, the good Wife accepted her husband's decision to add a concubine to their menage. He occasionally made trips to his ancestral village to visit the graves of his family and on one of these he brought back a girl. The following year, less than two months apart, each woman gave birth to a female child. Joy was not unrestrained in the house. Then, wonder of wonders, in 1951, the aging Wife bore a son who still lives. Thus she achieved the status which all Chinese wives have traditionally aspired to at a time when to do so had been looked upon as hopeless. Furthermore, since the birth of that son, four more children have been added to the family including one by the Wife, but all of them again are daughters. What in her own mind could be better proof of her guiltlessness in not having produced more sons, and in a polygynous family, what could more rightfully give her the title of Fortunate Wife than being the mother of the only male child?

The family chose an excellent location for its story-and-half concrete house on a flattened area about half way down the hill (Fig. 14.2). It is reached by a level path which turns off to the left as one descends from the pass setting off Sai Mi Wan from the town of Lung Shing (Fig. 19.1). The southerly view out over the deep narrow bay is delightful from the flat in front of the house. The flat is partly covered by a porch, the building of which required a special permit. Stretching out generously from this artificial embankment is a plane tree and to the right a vine-covered trellis sets off a small garden area containing more than a dozen potted plants with such a profusion of colorful flowers that we wondered if perhaps they were for sale, but the mistress of the household smilingly retorted that they were not good enough which was a modest way to refer to the lack of business given florists.

Less than thirty feet farther along the hill is a second smaller house, and beyond it, a series of pig pens and chicken houses in front of which is a large bamboo. The area is also dotted with papaya and guava trees.

A second examination of the main house showed one large room on the ground floor with an open stair ladder to the second. It was built with a permit allowing construction fourteen feet high. The house has a flat concrete roof. The upper floor seems somewhat crudely made, but the Fortunate Wife says that she can stand up in it. One large window in front swings outward from the top. There are three front windows on the main floor, one to the west of the central door, with ten horizontal iron bars and double side hung sashes, and two to the east without bars. When the question of inconsistency was raised, the Fortunate Wife said that the

Fig. 19.1. House of the Farmer

barred window was a secondhand purchase and that the bars were really unnecessary as there were no thieves in Sai Mi Wan anyway.

The interior of the house seems fantastically cluttered. At the front of the main room one is struck by an old footpowered Singer sewing machine and nearby on a windowsill rests a bottle of oil for its worn bearings. Crowded onto the sewing machine stand are a small electric cooking plate, a pair of large scissors, and a coil of wire. A few feet away rests a table with drawers and on it a school bag, a newspaper, an abacus, various articles of wearing apparel in small plastic bags and above the table on the wall, hangs a roll of toilet paper suspended by string. Above the toilet paper appears a large framed piece of glass under which are interlaid numerous snapshots of the members of the family. Against the rear wall an enclosed stand rises higher than a table and on it cups, a flashlight, bottles, cigarettes, and a hairbrush. Next to it is a tall wardrobe with a glass mirror set into the front; on the other side a table with a teakettle, three bottles, and some bowls. In one corner of the room is a European bed frame of attractive quality with an ordinary Chinese bed of wood horses and boards mounted in and over it. From an adjacent corner a ladder leads to the half floor above. Since a few feet of space remain, twelve separate items of clothing or rags hang from nails on the crossbeams. The kitchen, which lies directly behind the main room, or north of

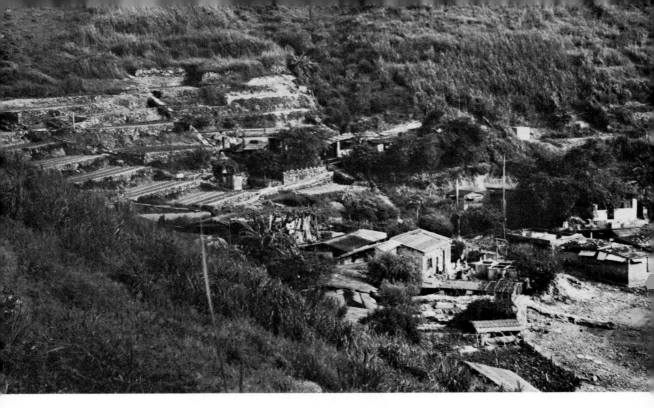

Fig. 19.2. Terraces of the Farmer

it, contains two large stoves and a cement tank for water as major fixtures, besides the usual accumulation of cooking appurtenances. As the concubine states with a recognition of the facts, it is dirty.

On the west end of the house is a roughly made narrow extension with pieces of tin forming a covering on the outside. It has a separate entrance in front. To the east is another shed used as a bean curd factory. Since about 1955, electricity has been available for lights of which there are some even in the pig house, and there is also a power meter for the operation of a pump. A covered well is conspicuous at the easterly end of the flat in front of the house. About two years ago, a second well was dug about thirty feet west of the house at a cost of approximately 1,000 dollars. It is only 19″ in diameter but approximately thirty-eight feet deep as is the other. Unfortunately, it provides less water and even with this augmentation of the supply there is periodically a shortage, which has caused difficulties with the owners of the bean curd factory.

In the house, live four adults and eight children. These comprise the Fortunate Wife, her husband, the concubine, three daughters of the Wife, aged thirteen, twelve, and five, plus her son who is ten, and four daughters of the concubine aged twelve, eight, seven, and a baby of six months. Three of the children were born in Sai Ying Pun Hospital, Hong Kong, two in a hospital now torn down, and the rest in their various homes including the youngest in Sai Mi Wan with a nurse from the clinic across the strait in attendance. Actually, the wife has lost five children including a son, and the concubine one daughter, most of them from pneumonia, it is said. Finally, there is a middle-aged male farm laborer. Also, as a member of the family but not living at home is the eldest daughter of the Wife who works and lives in a suburb of Kowloon. The hired man and the son share a double-decked bed in the tin-covered extension. The rest of the family is divided unevenly between the two floors of the house, the Fortunate Wife being the only permanent occupant of the ground floor. She says that the upper floor is too hot in summer and it is easy for her to move out on the porch when the temperature becomes unbearable. The household gives many indications of being an exceptionally happy one, and the Fortunate Wife seems as devoted to the concubine's children as to her own.

The head of the house is a mild-mannered and unusually quiet man who seems to be totally without aggression (although even with two wives and nine children one never can be sure). Although he had no previous experience as a farmer, or even the intention of becoming one before taking up property in Sai Mi Wan, his farm is a model of neat agricultural terraces (Fig. 19.2) on which he has learned from his workers how to grow at least sixteen kinds of vegetables according to the schedule given in Table 19.1.

TABLE 19.1
Vegetable Growing Schedule

Vegetable*	Growing Periods (by Chinese months)
Beans, green string (ts'eng tau kok)	1st to 7th
Cabbage, Chinese white (paak ts'oi)	all year
Cabbage, flowering Chinese (paak ts'oi sum)	all year
Carrot (kam sun)†	anytime
Chives (kau ts'oi)†	all year
Chrysanthemum, garland (t'ong ho)	10th to 12th
Garlic (suen t'au)	end of 8th to beginning of 1st
Kale, Chinese (kai laan ts'oi)	7th to after 1st
Lettuce (sang ts'oi)	8th or 9th to 2nd
Onion, Chinese green (shui ts'ung)	3rd month to 9th
Onion, Chinese green (siu yuk ts'ung)	7th through 2nd
Parsley (uen sai)	all year (but 6th or 7th difficult)
Spinach, Chinese (in ts'oi)	2nd (or 1st) through 8th
Spinach, water (ung ts'oi)	1st to end of 6th
Sweet potato (faan shue)	all year but winter best
Tomato (faan ke'e)	all year (but 6th or 7th difficult)

*Transliteration of Chinese words follows Herklots, 1947.
†Rarely grown.

The retail prices per catty for some of these vegetables in 1961 were given as:

Cabbage, Chinese white	$0.70
Cabbage, Flowering Chinese	1.00
Kale, Chinese	0.80
Lettuce	0.40
Spinach, Chinese	0.40
Spinach, Water	0.30

We might note that he does not grow foreign (European) onions or any kind of melons and that the sweet potatoes raised are eaten by the family while their greens provide food for the pigs. Unquestionably the men work very hard in the fields and sometimes a man who was formerly a regular employee comes in temporarily to assist. Certainly unusual on the island, if not unique, is the use of an electric light on a long extension cord to make it possible to harvest a crop in the pre-dawn darkness. At this chore, the concubine helps.

Twice a day the head of the house and his concubine, using baskets and carrying poles, convey the produce, which the latter has washed, to the market area in Lung Shing where the family owns the number one license among vegetable dealers which costs $100 a year. The farmer is usually there from 7:00 to 11:00 A.M. and from 1:00 to 3:00 P.M. The concubine does the family shopping and returns home to take up her household duties while her husband sits on his stool and purveys the enticing fresh vegetables spread out in front of him.

The family also raises a few pigs and even provides a pen for a sow belonging to a woman in Lung Shing. Unfortunately the visiting sow aborted its last litter. Perhaps this might not have happened if it had belonged to the Fortunate Wife as she once claimed that she was the only one in the family who knows how to take care of pigs. It is a responsibility that keeps her almost constantly at home. There is no longer the profit in raising the animals that first attracted her to Sai Mi Wan, however. She recalls that in 1953 and 1954, people were paying $300 per 100 catties for full grown animals (although the best price she ever received was $260), while young pigs cost as much as $700 per 100 catties since they were in such great demand for raising.

Much of her energy is also taxed by the chickens she owns, there being approximately four hundred at the time of our first visits. They are kept in small cages for most of the four months it takes to raise them, but they have an area in which to run during a period of two weeks just before they are sold and after they have received an injection. Most of the eggs that are laid serve to provide replacements, but chicks are also purchased every month. Feed comes from China and consists of more than ten ingredients including fish powder, meat powder, refuse of bean curd, and

Fig. 19.3. Some Members of the Farmer's Family

peanut residue (from oil making). Some of the fowl, the farmer sells in the Lung Shing market, while the rest are taken to Sai Mi Wan where there is a large wholesale chicken market (Fig. 3.2). The family has never had any pigeons.

The four or five papaya trees and approximately thirty guavas supply little more than the children's appetites. Before the typhoon of 1960, there were also a few banana plants which the wind had not yet uprooted.

For much of the year, the members of the family eat their meals at a large table on the covered flat outside the house, and it was there that we saw them together (Fig. 19.3). We were always made to feel welcome despite the search for more stools and the necessity for quieting down the five dogs and two cats that veered around one's legs. The nameless cats were quickly justified as rat catchers, and the dogs—well, the Fortunate Wife says they simply do not seem to get rid of the puppies, and by the time they grow up they like them too much, behavior which we can regard as another instance indicating the amiability of the family. One of the dogs, called "King Boy," belongs to the male worker. Another dog named "Black Boy" and two bitches named "Dolly" and "White Girl" are offspring of a third called "Yellow Girl." The mother and her female progeny were notable in having double dew claws on their hind feet. The father was probably "Black Boy" as he has six claws also.

Normally the children are given breakfast at seven in the morning as they have to go to school at eight. They have either congee or bread of various kinds. If the parents are too busy, the children may be given some money to buy themselves food in town. Theoretically, the adults do not eat until the regular meal about eleven. Then the basic food is rice, with some small fish, and a little meat with salted vegetables. About four in the afternoon there is a break for sweet soup or a few noodles. Then between seven and eight comes supper with rice and various other dishes as in the late morning, there being little difference in the content of the two meals. The Fortunate Wife says they often have soup made from mussels which she digs at the edge of the bay. The concubine does most of the cooking, although the children help. When we visit, we are given tea.

Coming upon them at the midday meal, we noted a large aluminum container of congee on the table with a tub of dry rice at one side. Also on the table was a dish of chopped pigs' legs, one of Chinese white cabbage, one of small fish, and one of ham ü (hsien yü), or salted fish. The concubine ate in the house and then moved out when her husband left the table. She could have brought a stool but she did not bother. It was she who cleaned up afterward. The husband seldom opened his mouth during the meal except to put food into it, while the Fortunate Wife cheerfully commented that the Cantonese will always spend a little money to have a few dishes whereas about food, the Fukienese are miserly. The Fortunate Wife is very conscious of Fukienese and the adjacent people of the Swatow area as they practically surround her. She also speculated that the Yünnanese especially enjoy hot dishes because they eat so much congee.

After that she picked up the concubine's six-month-old daughter who had just awakened and held the child by its upper legs between her own, at the same time making a repetitive sound as though she were trying to whistle. Soon the baby urinated, causing a tiny stream to run under the table until it was blocked by the sleeping dog of the worker.

The Fortunate Wife has a fondness for smoking cigarettes, which she herself rolls into a long conical form using a strong Chinese tobacco called shang ts'it (sheng chieh). Her husband, who seldom indulges, was seen once in a while with an expensive American brand named Lucky Strike, while the worker buys cheaper ones. As for the concubine, she never smokes.

The family of the Fortunate Wife is most unusual in that it makes clothing at home. For this purpose they own a sewing machine and an electric iron, and all the females who are not babies use them. Only the older ones do the cutting, however. The regular dress of the women and older girls is the sam fu. As noted one day, the twelve-year-old daughter of the concubine was wearing a blue patterned material while her mother had on black fu (trousers) above Japanese style slippers and a green sam bearing a black diaper design. The latter woman has a pleasant, guileless face and when she smiles, as she does frequently, she shows nice white teeth. She dresses her hair in a straight bob and wears no earrings.

The Fortunate Wife is less predictable in her clothing. That day she had on a faded yellow sam fu with the trousers cut off above the knees. We presumed it to be an old sam fu used as a sleeping costume and specially shortened for the practical problems of one who must splatter water in washing pigs. Her wood-soled shoes with red plastic straps were also functional. The Fortunate Wife is not one to be constrained by formal patterns in any event, and one's gaze is immediately drawn to her sensitve and striking face emphasized by sharp eyes under spectacles with black tortoise shell framing on top only, and the long handmade cigarette clamped beneath two upper right gold-capped incisors. Her hair is straight and ends in a pony tail which is distinctive because it is tiny. She wears a pair of long, curved combs, but no earrings. She does have a green jade bracelet on her left arm, however (Fig. 19.3).

Another day we saw the Fortunate Wife in a new gray sam fu with white vertical stripes. She looked so distinguished, we immediately asked if she would like a cheong sam. She promptly replied that she had never owned one and did not hope to. This was not exactly the truth for about three weeks later she remembered that she did have a cheong sam but had worn it very rarely because people laughed at her when she did so. The fact had come to mind because her eldest daughter had visited her the previous day and brought home several cheong sam which she had tried on.

Another occasion demonstrated still further how readily the Fortunate Wife could forget her clothes. One day we saw her in town taking one of her neighbor's workers to the doctor. She was dressed only in her fu and under sam, extremely unusual street wear for a woman.

The summer costume of the men of the household consists of white T-shirts and shorts, dark blue for the head of the house and khaki for his helper. At home they go barefoot. In fact the husband of the Fortunate Wife seldom uses slippers even in town, which is very unusual. He does wear a jade bracelet on his left wrist, however, as she does. For inclement weather, the head of the house has a black rubber raincoat and a large straw hat.

It is notable that this quiet man can read and write, although more so that his Fortunate Wife can do so as well. Even their worker can decipher some characters. Only the concubine is wholly illiterate. Therefore it is not inconsistent to find that the eldest daughter of twenty-five went to a Catholic high school after finishing two years of Chinese middle school. Few children from the island are better educated, and she now holds two positions, one as an assistant in a Chinese travel agency in Kowloon and the other as a salesgirl during periods when the agency is closed. She rarely returns to Lung Chau and then only for an hour, but her mother goes to see her once a month at which time she is given a share of the daughter's salaries. Four of the younger children, including the boy, attend School D in Lung Shing. The family has belonged to the Kaifong Association for many years. Also, three of the five children belong to a school medical insurance group which costs five dollars a semester. The others do not as there is a limit on the number in a school that can be insured. The Fortunate Wife favors doctors with Western type training but primarily on the basis of cost. There are refugee doctors without licenses for practice in the Colony of Hong Kong to whom one can go for fees of only two or three dollars.

The Fortunate Wife says she has no time to attend movies, but admits that the children go once in a while. The family also has a radio. On a hot day we have seen the worker taking four or five of the children swimming about four in the afternoon. Half an hour later the Fortunate Wife followed with a pail to collect mussels. Occasionally, the adults play mahjongg in the evening, which is the only game that they know.

The lady of the family has definite views on the government of the Colony as on most everything else. She thinks well of the British and makes it clear that most of the practices of which she disapproves emanate from lower grade Chinese officials who have direct contact with the people. She frankly admits that their Crown Permits for the land cost about a thousand dollars in gifts and that even to put up a porch roof on two columns extending out from the front of the house had to be arranged by unofficial payments. Also, health inspectors have to be paid off. She concludes that even the British officials are being corrupted and especially those with Chinese wives. "Go see my wife," has become a recognized suggestion.

There is said to be no graft with respect to the annual payments on property made to the Crown, however. The house tax was recently raised from $90 to $165, but that was because her permit did not originally cover her family. Included is $10 for a well. A single pig pen also costs $10. The tax on the additional 15,000 square feet of farm land is $190, recently raised from $150. Police seldom ever appear in Sai Mi Wan, but they did so briefly at the end of 1960, looking over the hills for a prisoner who had escaped.

The family is nominally traditionalist in religion, but several of the daughters have been converted to the Catholic religion; the Fortunate Wife does not think they are very serious about their beliefs, however. In the house is an altar with a picture of a god attended by two other deities. There are also papers representing the family ancestral tablets. The Fortunate Wife takes such matters more or less for granted. She explicitly states that no feng-shui was involved in either locating or orienting the house. If she feels strongly about anything connected with religion, it is the Chinese who work for the Christian missions, her *bête noire* being a woman employed by the Pentecostal Holiness Church of Lung Shing. This woman is said to have charged fifty cents to people who wanted to share in the distribution of free gifts made through the Church. Furthermore, this woman is said to have paid people to get in line for the free food and then give it back to her. Some other women blackmailed her and received twice as much food as they should have. Also there was reputedly direct stealing from the stock of supplies early in the morning. Through these various forms of dishonesty, this Church employee is said to have obtained enough money to purchase a flat in the town across the strait.

As has been said, the Fortunate Wife had a considerable expense when she was forced into court over the use of her house for rope making. Most of the $1,600 that the legal fees cost her, she borrowed from some friends in the bean curd business. In lieu of interest on the money, she agreed to let them use part of her property in Sai Mi Wan for a period. But of this development, we shall delay discussion so as to deal with it in its chronological order in the growth of the community.

20. The Caretaker

The most distant house to be seen in Sai Mi Wan is occupied by the family of a Ch'ao An man who came to this outlying area as a caretaker for the property of the Man Who Retired of whom we shall tell later. Like so many others in Hong Kong, he is a refugee from the Communists. In 1949, he and his father escaped from a village "two roads away" from Lu Feng close to the coast of Kwangtung where the family owned considerable land (Fig. 3.1). The son left behind a wife, who has since remarried, and a thirteen-year-old son. At first he and his father settled in Pok Fu Lam village in the northwest part of Hong Kong Island (Fig. 3.2) where they worked for the Dairy Farm, a long established firm in the Colony. In 1954, his father died, and the next year the Caretaker went to work on a new government water reservoir project. There he met the Man Who Retired and the latter persuaded him to look after property in Sai Mi Wan that he had just begun to develop. After eight months, the Caretaker felt that he should earn more money and through a cousin found more remunerative employment in a cotton cloth factory in Hung Hom, southeast Kowloon. That was in 1957.

The year was a memorable one because in the factory he met a young Hakka woman of twenty-four from Tung Kuan east of Canton to whom he was attracted and they communicated with each other in their somewhat limited Cantonese. After knowing each other four months, they decided that they would like to face life and its difficulties together. She had already experienced a great many, having been brought to Hong Kong by relatives in 1955 for medical treatment after an illness that had persisted four years. The name of the disease she does not know, but she states that she was yellow and swollen all over. With proper drugs, she had made a full recovery in two years.

In seeking the necessary papers for their wedding, they were sent from one government office to another. His first wife had obtained a People's Republic of China divorce, and then married another man, which complicated the matter. Finally the young couple gave up and did not register the new union. As the Caretaker also pointed out, to do so would have cost about $20. His wife soon became pregnant and before long was unable to continue working in the factory. Since his own earnings were insufficient for their needs, and the Man Who Retired sought to recover his services, they decided that Sai Mi Wan would at least be a secure place to raise children.

Heaven blessed the household that same year with a son, in 1960 with another, and in 1961 the Caretaker was hoping the next child would be a girl. She arrived promptly on schedule. Then the Caretaker said that the family was large enough, but his wife claimed that they could not help having a child every year. The first two boys were born in a maternity home in the town across the strait. The nurse told the mother that she could arrange to have no more children and that the fee would be only $6. A neighbor and friend of the wife has strongly recommended an operation, but her husband fears that it would be dangerous since she might lose her strength. When the wife was nine months pregnant with her third child, the doctors at the new clinic across the strait told her that she should remain in the hospital, but she would not as there was no one to care for the other two children. She finally returned to the hospital with no time to spare.

In commenting on preferential marriage, the mother said that in her opinion, a union with either a father's sister's son or a mother's brother's son would be improper. She added that things have changed recently in China and that her younger sister had married their father's brother's son. The Caretaker, hearing again of this sacrilege, added with some feeling that he had even heard recently of a brother marrying his sister in China. As it did not seem probable that we could verify the latter statement, we let it pass.

The most obvious case of sibling rivalry we noted during our study was demonstrated by the second son of the Caretaker toward the newly arrived daughter. He was fifteen months old and he bit and slapped his five-week-old sister. When his mother prevented this direct display of aggression, he then bit his one year older brother. Observed in the days before he was caught between two siblings, he had seemed quite angelic sucking on a pacifier. He contentedly threw an imitation jade bracelet on the floor while there was still a plastic lion within reach as well as some similar toys.

One thing that made the Caretaker's family particularly significant was that, apart from producing children so continuously, they were engaged in the process of building a home with their own hands. This came about through the combining of natural desire with necessity. As has been stated, the father of the family had found a place to live as the Caretaker for the Man Who Retired, but in 1961 his services were no longer needed and he was forced to look for another home for his enlarging family. Having to move was certainly something of a strain but there was no bitterness toward his patron. He simply described him as a government official who had received his pension in a lump sum and proceeded to spend it in developing a sizable property not always successfully. His patron had tried to make soy sauce but had lost a large sum of money. Then he rented part of his shore land to people who raised ducks profitably, but when he tried to do so himself, again he lost money. As the Caretaker suggested, the Man Who Retired was more ambitious than successful in business, but we shall give consideration to that question in its turn.

Soon to be dispossessed of the house he had occupied for several years, the ex-Caretaker's immediate problem was to find a new place to live. Above and beyond the property of the Man Who Retired is a gap in the high westerly ridge along Sai Mi Wan. Down the other side at the edge of the strait is a small factory in which salted fresh water fish from China are washed and re-dried. It is operated by a few men who come there by boat, coasting the shore from Lung Shing. There are also three widows who have settled in the immediate vicinity. Two of them keep pigs, and one makes leung fan (lian fen), a kind of Cantonese jelly contrived from agar-agar. It is a muddy, unprepossessing place which has no fresh water, the latter having to be purchased from boats that purvey it at a cost of ten cents for filling two five-gallon cans. One of the widows has a sweet potato patch in the pass in order to feed the vines to her pigs. To do this, she told us she has to buy ten buckets of water every other day when it does not rain. We mention this tiny settlement in passing as being part of the environment, although it has no other connection with Sai Mi Wan than the widow's accusation that someone in the latter place had been stealing her sweet potato vines that were growing in the pass, the most likely candidate being one of the Duck Raisers.

Beyond the pass is the steep, mountainous, uninhabited end of the island. The British built a concrete pill box there in anticipation of the 1941 invasion, a gesture which may have provided the Japanese with a lookout post but has remained otherwise unappreciated. On the far slope, about thirty feet higher than the pass itself, there was a small hut of stones used before the occupation by a government watchman over the then existing pine forest. Then the hut was demolished by the typhoon of 1960. It is there that the Caretaker decided to build himself a new home, and we were privileged to watch part of the process and to see the family move in. Technically the house might be said not to be in Sai Mi Wan, but we have rationalized its inclusion not only on historical grounds but also because it would otherwise be in nowhere. Also it is tied to that bay settlement by being dependent on it for water and because the Caretaker's chicken coop is in the Sai Mi Wan drainage (Fig. 14.2).

Fortunately, the Caretaker is a mason by inclination if not actually by trade. With the remnants of the hut cleared away, he constructed a concrete, gable-roofed, one-story house in a small leveled space snugly against the hill (Fig. 20.1). The outside measurements are 102″ x 140″, the narrower dimension being that of the front with its door facing the inner end of the bay called Sai Mi. The roof, sloping down over the door, is 90″ from the ridge to the cement floor, which has a concavity about a foot in diameter to the south of the door so that any rain water that comes in may be dipped out. The less exposed walls, southerly and easterly, are made of small stones and earth, while for the other two walls, more rectangular and larger stones were used. All four walls are faced with smooth white cement on the inside and the more exposed northerly and westerly ones on the outside as well. The roof is made of clean boards four to six inches wide and one inch thick supported by a ridgepole and a pair of new two-by-two purlins evenly spaced on each side between it and the side walls. The roof boards are covered with tar paper, the northerly and southerly edges of which are reinforced with a neat row of speckled white granite grave-stones from the nearby hill.

There are two tiny windows 10″ high by 5″ wide in the rear wall and two in the front without either frames or glazing. Each has a section of tile projecting out above it. In the northerly wall, 42″ from its east end is a

Fig. 20.1. The Caretaker's House

fifth window opening 40″ above the floor. It is 27″ high by 18″ wide and contains three vertical iron bars. The front entrance is 72″ high by 32″ wide and is closed by double doors which swing inward and are covered with galvanized tin on the outside. Notable is the fact that the ground outside the house has not been cleared to the level of that inside. For instance it is only 29″ below the large window. Also the low point of the eaves at the rear of the house is 62″ above the ground, but 76″ at the front.

When we look inside the house, we see that a double-decked bed extends from wall to wall at the rear. The lower part can be enclosed by a white mosquito net, and there are quite a few mosquitoes about which are presumed to thrive in the grass on the hills. On the upper deck of the bed are stored two woven bamboo suitcases and a cloth bag. On the lower is a red plastic mat with a pleasant design. Under the large window is an ordinary table containing a screened food area beneath its top. On it is a small tea cup and a cylindrical porcelain teapot with a double wire handle. Above, on the windowsill, is a commonplace small kerosene lamp, a ball of string, and a box of matches. On the wall to the east of the window is a pad calendar with a sheet for each day. There are both a low stool and a high one in the house. In the northeasterly corner leans a split bamboo carrying pole and a stone hammer with a bamboo handle. Between the table and the bed, a plain reed mat is rolled up. Under the bed glistens an aluminum spittoon presumably used as a chamber pot. As might be expected, there is no electricity.

Outside the house, a crowbar, a woven sifter for sand, a basket to carry dirt, two cut-open gasoline can buckets in which to convey water, and a straw sun hat are visible. There are also a small stove, a few dishes, and some baskets. We mention these things because they represent practically a complete inventory of family possessions, except for the clothes that are worn.

Two months later, the Caretaker had built a neat stone and cement stove against the hill three and a half feet in front of the door. It is of typical form, although a little smaller than usual being roughly 42″ wide at the front, a little more at the back, 38″ deep, and 28″ high. The fire hole for inserting grass and twigs is 8″ high and 7″ wide and has a flat stone at the bottom. For cooking there is a 20½″ movable lens-shaped pan with two handles. Over the stove extends a light shed roof made of slats of tin, tarpaper, and corrugated asbestos. The stove having been built, the energetic Caretaker was utilizing spare time to level off a sixty-inch wide area for storage between the house and the steep rising ground. Already a chicken coop had been built on the Sai Mi Wan slope of the hill. When first seen from the opposite side of the bay we thought it was the residence of a family we had failed to visit. A month later the Caretaker's family had acquired about twenty chickens. We immediately made certain that they had obtained no pigs, pigeons, or ducks, nor any pets. The fact that four five-gallon cans (U.S.) of water already have to be carried up a considerable distance from the well of the Man Who Retired practically precludes the possibility of raising vegetables, but the owner of the new home has planted gourd seeds in an old soy sauce jar in front of the door, and the vines are running over the hill.

The Caretaker smokes homemade cigarettes of finely-cut Chinese tobacco, which he twists in a cone of special paper, bending over the large end and biting off the small. If he works hard, he says he also has to drink a little, but his wife unfortunately breaks out with a rash if she consumes any alcohol and consequently will not do so even at the most traditionally desirable times, such as following a birth. Both enjoy tea, however. They have a breakfast of congee between seven-thirty and eight before the Caretaker goes out to work; then their main meals at noon and again between six and seven in the evening. The family does not have much money to spend, but it does not starve.

At home, the Caretaker's wife wears black cotton fu with a blue sam and red Japanese style slippers. She has never owned a cheong sam. On our early visits, her hair was tied in a long pony tail, but after her third child was born, she had it bobbed and waved. Jewelry she has none unless we count the numerous gold caps on her upper left front teeth. She says that her teeth are so bad that she has a hard time chewing and consequently digesting her food. Her physiological defect she attributes to the fact that her father was a sugar maker who did not prevent her from eating sugar all the time. One result is that she gives very little of this sweet food to her own children. She would like to have dentures but states that at a cost of $7 a tooth, she cannot get enough money at one time. She dresses her older boy in a sam fu also, while the younger is content in only a shirt. Her husband, when at home, may be seen in a white T-shirt, blue short drawers, and yellow tennis shoes, but on going to town he will add dark blue trousers and his wristwatch.

They go to the settlement across the strait occasionally, but although the husband has sometimes worked in Tung Pak Wan, they had never even heard of Chung Nam Wan. They were surprised when the hamlet was described to them.

It is convincing when this family says they are too busy for many amusements. They attend a movie perhaps two or three times in the year. A radio cannot be afforded and neither of them knows how to play mahjongg. As might be expected from the Caretaker's having been a refugee from the Communists, he prefers the security of a British government in Hong Kong. Both favor doctors trained in the Western tradition as being more quickly effective and cheaper.

The family is nominally traditionalist in religion but the members do not visit any temples. The Caretaker is not above having superstitions, however. His second son shows four birthmarks at the top of his head. One is smaller than the other three. The Caretaker says that he pounded three large nails and one smaller one into the wall of his house in exactly the same pattern on the night before the child was born. The Caretaker states specifically, however, that he does not believe in feng-shui, and for some time there were no symbols of religious faith in the home. A month or so after they took up residence, however, we noted the four characters on kü lok ip (an chü lo yeh) painted on red paper and pasted outside above the door, which we can translate as meaning "Live peacefully and work happily." Also on the ground to the right of the door was a can for incense sticks and a paper pasted above it with the four-character legend po ngo p'ing on (pao wo p'ing an) which we shall translate as "Keep us safe." Inside the house the Caretaker had put up a small red shelf with a paper ancestor's tablet for his father and above it a photograph of the deceased. On the shelf itself were an incense burner and some flowers.

Shortly before our arrival, the Caretaker had collected his father's bones from the government cemetery and was trying to find someone to take them back to his native village. It was difficult because, not being a writer, he had lost contact with his mother and brother. Friends coming from the neighborhood simply said they had disappeared. Thus he was faced with a problem as something had to be done. The government had designated the place of original burial and borne the cost of interment, but he had to collect the bones by the seventh year if he wanted them. To do so earlier, he said, was prohibited as unsanitary, and later the bones would not be complete or any longer cared for. It appeared that he would inevitably deposit them on the nearby hill.

21. The Carpenter

There was an interval of at least three years after the farming family had settled in Sai Mi Wan before anyone else came to take up land along the easterly shore. Perhaps it was because the most accessible areas near the town had been preempted by the Enterprising Woman, the Hotel Man, and the family of the Fortunate Wife. Afterward a newcomer had to make his way farther along the shore of that bay into places where the bank was precipitous and the sources of fresh water were uncertain.

Finally, in 1957, a carpenter pushed on past the buildings of the Hotel Man on the easterly side of the bay and cut a flat place out of the steep, rocky slope thirty to forty feet above the sea. There he constructed his house (Fig. 21.1). He did not build without giving great thought to the matter, for like all traditional Chinese carpenters, he had a real concern for feng-shui. Otherwise, as he says, how could one build the windows and doors in the right direction? The Carpenter realized that he was faced with a problem since his site was blocked by the high range of hills on the opposite side of the bay. To counteract this influence, he oriented his door along the slope toward the south as much as was possible without actually turning in toward the rising ground behind the house. The classic appreciation of an opening toward the south had not escaped him, and to the south was the open sea. To the north, he planted bamboos, and a lighter variety of the same plant to the west. On being questioned, he explained that the view north across the bay is never good, and that one should not see the ultimate limits of the water (Fig. 14.2).

The house, of modest dimensions, has a concrete floor and the first four feet of its side walls of the same material (Fig. 21.2). On top of the concrete, rests studding which carries the board walls to a two-story height and a gable roof, the ridgepole of which extends about two feet beyond the wall to the southwest. The construction of the wood area is of a special kind, however, which the Carpenter learned from observing the way the Japanese built houses in occupied Swatow while he was young. Its virtue, he claims, lies in its resistance to wind, and the Carpenter proudly

[353]

Fig. 21.1. The Carpenter's Estate (with Mr. E's garden in left foreground)

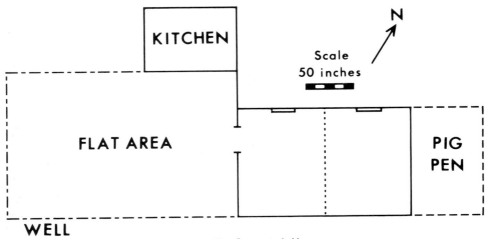

Fig. 21.2. The Carpenter's House

reports that his home was the only one in Sai Mi Wan to survive the typhoon of 1960 completely unscathed. The exposed walls are made of 8″ wide vertical boards that are a half-inch thick with the lengthwise joints covered with strips 1¾″ wide and three-eighths of an inch thick. The upper floor covers the length and width of the house except for an opening for a ladder with steps in the middle of the easterly side. The ceiling is only 54″ high. The three older children sleep on a bed at one end, and the linoleum floor is covered with a litter of papers they do not bother to clean up. The lower floor is divided into two rooms by means of a one-eighth inch masonite partition, a material imported from the West. There are double sash windows without bars on the bay side of the house. Since the whole house is only fifteen feet by nine feet eight inches on the outside, a large bed takes up most of the space in the inner room. It is there that the father and mother with their two younger children sleep.

In front of his door the Carpenter has created a sizable flat area about twenty feet long, part of which he cut from solid rock with a hammer and chisel. This area is also floored with cement. At the back of the flat he has a pool-like well that is fed by a spring, which provides sufficient good water except during the 11th, 12th, and 1st months of the year when he has to go to the inexhaustible well of the Enterprising Woman at the head of the bay. She gives him water free for the carrying. He had tried to sink another well below his house near the beach, but salt water came in. A smaller one a little farther back does produce water for washing, however, and he has constructed a small cement surfaced flat nearby for drying clothes.

On the seaward side of the flat area southwest of the house is the kitchen, open toward the hill, and with a shed roof sloping toward the bay. As in the house, the floor is concrete with four-foot side walls of concrete. The rest of the walls and roof are covered with boards of varying sizes and lengths, but they are smooth and have been placed tightly together. It has an additional important function in shielding the flat working area from the sun on hot summer afternoons. At the opposite end of the house are a few pig pens. These represent a temporary arrangement as the Carpenter wants to build new sties away from the house so that the area of the latter will be clean. This project will have to wait until he has more money since he has already spent the $3,000 he had saved for his new home.

The Carpenter, who is a Ch'ao An speaker, came from a small place which is three or four hours by sea from Swatow on the east coast of Kwangtung. This was in 1946 after the Japanese had been evacuated. He had learned his trade in his native city where his father and grandfather had also been carpenters, but thought he would make more money in the Colony of Hong Kong. For the first three years he lived in Shau Kei Wan

(Fig. 3.2) and then moved to Sai Wan where he built himself a shack without a Crown Permit. When the Government finally requisitioned the land on which he had squatted, they offered him as a substitute a place to live in Ho Man Tin, which is almost in the center of Kowloon. He chose Lung Chau instead since he had heard from friends that the island was a good place with many small industries in which people invested their money. He lived in the town of Lung Shing for four years and then obtained a permit for the land in Sai Mi Wan. The primary motivation for the last move was the commonplace desire to raise pigs in order to increase his income, and pig raising is an activity that is permitted only in the outlying areas. The obvious esthetic attractions of his new locale, he sets aside with a smile as having had no influence whatsoever on his decision.

The Carpenter married not long after coming to Hong Kong and chose his wife himself, or perhaps it would be more accurate to say that they decided on marriage together. She had come to Hong Kong with some girl friends just before the Communists came to her town. The girls had heard there would be no more jobs in which they could make money. They settled in Shau Kei Wan where she worked as a servant for a family. Her eyes twinkle when she says that she soon met the man whom she married. He says if one is a good man with no bad habits, friends naturally will introduce one to prospective wives. It is clear that his wife, who was born in the same town as himself, has no regrets, nor does he. He was about twenty-two and she eighteen when the choice was made. Now they have five children who contribute to their happiness. The oldest is a girl of thirteen, the next two are boys of ten and six respectively; then there is another girl of five, and another boy of two. Now at thirty-six years of age the Carpenter, who obviously likes children, says that he is not going to have any more, his wife having undergone the necessary operation when their last child was born at the Tsan Yuk Maternity Hospital in Sai Ying Pun. The mother was dubious that the problem of having so many children could be so easily solved, but she is becoming pleasurably confident that such is the case.

The Carpenter's wife is an intelligent woman with an animated face that has not lost its attractiveness because her two upper second incisors have gold caps. Her musical laughter constantly intersperses our talks, making her face into a melody of tiny wrinkles and tightening the skin on her narrow, button-ended nose. His face is a marvel like some wonderful theatrical mask. Its contours are round and he has a mushroom-like nose set between a triangle of bulging cheeks and mouth. On his upper lip short hairs twist in various directions but those on his head are a real distinction, thrusting four inches straight out like a visor of a cap. He adores his wife who he says works unceasingly, and it is obvious that if she were not shy, she would make the equivalent statements about him. She, like her husband, speaks Cantonese with a Ch'ao An accent, but the children have none. The whole family is bilingual. The Carpenter says he can understand the speech of Amoy people, but not those from Fuchou.

We met them on hot summer days in the kitchen area somewhat shaded by a wood trellis with ch'au p'i kwa (chou p'i kua) and shui kwa (shui kua) vines growing over it. In the center was a round four-legged table and some boxes to sit on. Most conspicuous were great stoneware jars with a deep, overall, brown glaze and paintings of dark yellow dragons on them. These, as the Carpenter knew, were made in the area of Peking or Tientsin and were sent to Hong Kong as containers for pickled eggs which, being sold, the jars could be purchased for a few dollars each. They are now used to store water and pig food. Along the edge of the cliff between the house and the sea stands a row of lovely bamboos. Adjoining the latter is a bush which is said to cause a rash if touched.

Beyond the wood trellis is a typical large pig food stove which is constructed to burn sawdust, which they can obtain without cost in the town. The family has three sows and one was expected to farrow so the Carpenter had stayed home from work. About four in the afternoon seven more pigs came into the world, which was about three less than that mother usually produced. Besides the newcomers and the three sows, there were also eleven half grown pigs. Periodically buyers appear in a boat to inquire if the Carpenter wishes to sell. Indicative of the value placed on the animals, it was noted that in hot weather the pigs were washed three times during the day.

Besides pigs, there is also a chicken coop with over twenty hens. The family specializes in selling eggs rather than chickens. In the winter of 1963–64, people ordered them at a price of one dollar for four, about four dozen being available each week. The young chickens are bothered by rats of which there are many, some weighing over a catty. We saw a small one crawling along the branch of a bamboo. There are no cats in the household. Forty or fifty pigeons occupy another cage, but the Carpenter says that raising them is not very profitable. He rarely sells pigeon eggs, although they constitute a very expensive dish to be found in most large restaurants where they become an expected part of any feast with a dozen or more dishes. The Carpenter does not eat any of the eggs himself, or any of the pigeons either.

As is usual, there were various gasoline-can-buckets, aluminum kettles, and enamelware dishes in the kitchen area, the expected adjuncts of meals. The Carpenter's family has congee about eight in the morning, then its two principal meals about one in the afternoon and seven in the evening. The Carpenter smokes moderately, buying Union cigarettes at twenty for fifty cents, while his wife abstains entirely. The Carpenter says he never drinks and never eats dogs. We asked because they have a dog and two bitches. One of the latter called Dolly had just given birth to four puppies while the other bitch had five that were older. The Carpenter who obviously likes dogs as he does children, says he will give the young dogs away. There is reason to believe, however, that the puppies will be sold to a fisherman who buys puppies to eat. The dogs are said to always bark at him. When I looked surprised, my informant said that the dog buyer may be an opium addict and that the animals distinguish him in consequence. The dogs, however, bark at most strangers. Only the bitch Dolly has been honored with a name. Unfortunately the shortage of fresh water has prevented the family from growing any vegetables, but they have planted a number of banana trees.

Sometimes we found the Carpenter's wife pasting silver tinfoil on paper for a factory in Lung Shing. She says that if she and the older children work fairly regularly all day they can make about $3.50 (1963). A man is sent from town to collect the paper every night. Her husband told her it would be better to stop this activity and give the children twenty or thirty cents less for candy.

During our first visit, the Carpenter was wearing blue shorts and a white T-shirt. His feet were bare. After the midday meal his wife set off to town dressed in a blue patterned sam fu and red Japanese style slippers. She carried a black rain umbrella as a protection against the afternoon sun and a shopping basket on her arm in which to bring home her purchases from the market. Although the family sells chicken eggs, she was going to buy some smaller ones imported from China as they are cheaper. Rather than lose a dollar for four of her own eggs, she would prefer to buy meat.

About four-thirty the Carpenter's wife returned. She was hot and promptly removed her sam fu. Her under coat, distinguished by short sleeves, a low collar, and two pockets above the lower front edges, was of a light patterned material, while her under trousers differed from her fu in being cut off near the knees. These underclothes, somewhat soiled, were more adapted for abbreviated home wear than they would have been if they had been made of a plain, light material. With her sam fu removed, the Carpenter's wife descended to the sea and proceeded to swim. When she returned, the single thickness of thin and soaking wet cotton clinging to her skin revealed with certainty that the under coat and under trousers had been her only remaining garments. In a moment she retired and then shortly returned in a set of dry underclothes. This modern young woman with curled, bobbed hair told us that in China before she was married she had owned a cheong sam. She has not owned one since. Her ears were pierced when she was an adolescent and for some years she wore gold circlets in them. Then a few years ago her ears became inflamed and the holes enlarged which she said was very ugly and she does not want to wear earrings anymore. She would like some other jewelry, however. The Carpenter told us that he had owned a wristwatch before he was married. Later, when seen working in town, he was wearing blue slacks, his usual white T-shirt, and Japanese style slippers with blue straps.

When the ten-year-old son came home from the afternoon session of School D, which he attends with his older sister, he was wearing blue shorts, a white shirt, and Japanese style slippers with red straps. After depositing his school satchel and plastic water bottle—if he did not carry water he would have to buy soft drinks as no boiled water is available at the school—he, too, went swimming. It is one of the main pleasures of the family. Because they live in such an excellent location for this activity, the Carpenter and his three older children, one of whom is only six, have learned well enough to cross the bay (perhaps eight hundred feet) and come back. They use the breast stroke while the children's mother swims free style, but not nearly as well. The younger girl and her two-year-old brother play in the water at the edge of the shore while their father watches.

Other pleasures are less often indulged in. None of the family goes to the movies very often or to football games. They are just too busy, it is said. There is no radio in the house, and no one knows how to play mah-jongg. The six-year-old son who impressed us as being very bright had made a tiny box out of a piece of newspaper with a paper tube a half inch in diameter and six inches long to slide through it. The box even had a paper handle. He called this construction his telescope. Also he makes curious crayon drawings which his parents occasionally paste on the door. One looked like a flying mouse.

Education has been limited in the family. The wife has had no formal teaching, and the Carpenter only two years of primary school. Their children were late in gaining admission to School D in Lung Shing, and the ten-year-old boy is only in first grade while his thirteen-year-old sister is in second. When there is illness in the family, the Carpenter says that he goes to a doctor with Western training by whom one can get cured quickly for a dollar, which certainly is a bargain. He added gratuitously that he does not trust doctors with traditional Chinese training.

A box of old carpenter tools, mostly of Japanese origin, rests under the kitchen shed. The owner has not been using them recently as he has found a convenient and more lucrative position working in the newly-opened bead factory owned by the Enterprising Woman's second son. Since it is just over the pass on the road to Lung Shing, the Carpenter does not get around the island as much as he did formerly. He has been to Tung Pak Wan, however, and he knows that Chung Nam Wan can be reached by continuing around the south shore from his house, but he has never been there. Once a year he goes into Victoria to pay the annual Crown Rent on his property which he says amounts to about $300 a year. The Carpenter evinces no other interest in the government, or in who governs. He says that what is important is to have money and to have food to eat. In 1963, he was charging about $10 a day for his services, but there were numerous short periods when he did not find work.

The family's religion is traditional in the Chinese sense, but the members do not go to any of the temples. The only deity that they worship is the Earth God, but they do periodically make offerings to the ancestors. The Carpenter bluntly states that an interest in the old-time religion is no longer fashionable. Despite his professional involvement in feng-shui, he claims that he not only never consults the almanac, but does not honor the gods in any specific direction on New Year's morning. In conclusion, he stated that his mother who lives in Lung Shing became a Catholic because she attends a Catholic clinic for treatment.

22. The Seagoing Tailors

Almost everyone in Sai Mi Wan agrees that it is important to have money, and few families enjoy more cash income than the Seagoing Tailors. We met only the elder of the two brothers as they have an opportunity to come home but once or twice in a year. His visit was particularly enjoyable to us as he is the one resident of Sai Mi Wan who speaks English, but no doubt the visit was even more appreciated by his wife. She is twenty-five, ten years younger than he, and they have four children, a son aged six, a daughter of five, another son aged three, and a daughter of two. They do not want any more children but to avoid having them raises a problem. The younger brother likewise has a wife but only two children, a daughter of three and a son less than a year. The brothers' mother also lives with them.

It was in 1957 that the elder Seagoing Tailor learned through Fukienese friends, Family A in the Hotel Man's Establishment, that the Enterprising Woman, a native of Fukien herself, had some space to rent in a house at Sai Mi Wan (Fig. 14.2). Thus the families of the two tailors came to occupy three of the four small rooms in the building adjoining the ink factory. Actually there is what constitutes a fifth room which is the passage that separates the others, two on a side, and this area they at least dominate. The younger Mrs. Tailor has the room on the right as one enters, the elder Mrs. Tailor lives behind her, the mother across the passage from the latter, and the Inkmaker in the remaining room in front. They all do their cooking in a little shed at the westerly end of the house which overlaps the front of the Duckraisers' residence. There seems to be no particular distinction in the rooms of the Seagoing Tailors unless it is the fluorescent light which serves both of the young wives' rooms by being hung above and parallel to the dividing masonite partition. It is perhaps significant that the elder of the two did not know the surname of the Inkmaker who lived in the same house for many years. Of course, the Seagoing Tailor was seldom at home. When he was, he spoke of his neighbor by his nickname which is Ts'au (Ch'iu), or "Autumn."

Without question, the elder Seagoing Tailor is something of a character, as we would say in the West. He talks incessantly, whether in English or Cantonese, neither of which languages he speaks well. Everyone in the family speaks some Cantonese, it should be noted. He has a sharp, acidic personality for which he periodically apologizes with smiles. He is prejudiced against the British, and not wholly without reason. When he was encouraged to tell us about his life, he did so with singular frankness.

He was born on the outskirts of Fuchou about 1927. His father was a very clever man, our informant reported with a sparkle in his eye while he told of watching his parent pour hot metal into a small mold that had been made with great care. What he was making were silver dollars of the Yüan Shih-k'ai regime (1913–1916). From this artistic activity he became only "a little rich" because he never had a chance to develop mass production. Twice he was apprehended by government authorities and twice he was released for lack of incriminating evidence. The machinery of his trade he always buried in time, and we are assured that it can still be found somewhere under his house. Harassed in his creative undertaking, the father retired as a farmer and died before the Japanese invasion of Fukien. The son who watched these parental labors with such interest at the age of seven or eight became apprenticed to a tailor in Fuchou for three years when he was nineteen and thus learned his trade which he feels, if less artistic than his father's, can be even more frustrating at times.

In 1947, the young tailor left Amoy when he was warned that he could not carry on his trade after the Communists took control. Arriving in Hong Kong, he was faced with the problem of learning Cantonese since he was not content in remaining among the Fukienese speaking tailors of Wan Chai. His ambition carried him forward with reasonable success, and about 1954 he returned home to Amoy to marry the girl chosen by his mother who had found her through relatives. After returning with his bride, our friend arranged for his younger brother also to emigrate to Hong Kong. This brother, about five years his junior, had practiced the trade of a noodle maker in Fuchou, but under the Communists he had been forced into a union and was paid only enough money to live on but not sufficient to marry. Arriving in Hong Kong around New Year's time 1955, the younger brother planned to continue his trade, but he was not very successful so his elder sibling arranged for him to learn tailoring under the tutelage of a friend. Within four months he had learned enough to go to work for another tailor at a salary of more than a hundred dollars a month.

In the meantime, the elder brother accepted a position as tailor on a British naval vessel. After his first son was born in 1956, he was fired with ambition. With four partners including his brother, the Orient Custom Tailoring Company was formed and a shop acquired on a fashionable Kowloon road. One of the leading cinema actresses of Taiwan cut the ribbon across the door on the opening day, or at least that is the way the lady in the picture which was shown to us was described, and her appearance did not belie the account. A few months later, however, one of the partners absconded to New Zealand with all the cash in the Company and it promptly went bankrupt. That was in the first half of 1958. The elder Seagoing Tailor who had invested $20,000 in the business was left with the task of paying the larger part of it back to the bank from which it had been borrowed at 10 per cent interest. His younger brother was slightly better off, having put only $10,000 into the venture.

After this fiasco, the elder brother was fortunate enough to find a place with a friend on another ship of the British navy. There he has remained despite the fact that he always becomes seasick in rough weather. On this survey frigate they have three rooms for which they pay nothing, but in return they have to accept all the tailoring commissions of the crew and, it would seem, take charge of the laundry. In addition, they run a little store and sell various luxury items such as cameras, dark glasses, and similar articles. They do have to supply their own food, but the cook on the vessel is generous when paying for his own tailoring.

Working on ships indeed would be a profitable arrangement were it not for one thing. A certain percentage of the crew apparently will not pay for the clothing they order, and since the losses so incurred devour much of the profits, it puts the Seagoing Tailor in a rage when he tells of it. Undoubtedly some of the English crew also treat him with contempt, as he unconsciously demonstrates to us in many ways. What he actually says is that only one Englishman in ten has been friendly. On the other hand he has repeated the story of the officer on one cruise who indirectly forced recalcitrant members of the crew to pay their tailoring debts before leaving the ship. The problems thus described are so commonplace in the world that they would hardly merit recounting were not the informant one's courteous host in a peaceful and happy little home on the bay of Sai Mi.

Just before New Year's 1959, the Seagoing Tailor's mother found the younger son a bride, this time choosing the pretty daughter of her mother's father's brother's daughter, or less precisely, a maternal second cousin once removed. Although the girl belonged to the next generation older than the bridegroom, she was eight years younger than the groom. On this occasion, the mother came along with the bride and the wedding was performed in Hong Kong. A few months earlier, the elder brother had found them all a home in Sai Mi Wan. Soon after the wedding the younger brother who had been unemployed for eighteen months went to sea on an aircraft carrier in a similar position to that held by his brother.

The Seagoing Tailors are relatively sophisticated individuals. The elder brother, for example, has visited Japan and various parts of the South Seas. He never heard of Chung Nam Wan, however, and has not been to Tung Pak Wan but, as he points out, he is seldom at home. On the other hand, exploration of the home area is not part of the family pattern.

His mother, for example, says that she once walked as far as the house of the Man Who Retired but came back because she did not like the barking of the dogs. She has not been as far as Tung Pak Wan either, and she finally admitted that the only homes she has visited in Sai Mi Wan are those of the four Fukienese families who live in the adjacent Hotel Man's Establishment.

It is not strange, considering his shipboard shop, to discover that the elder brother has a camera and a tape recorder, as well as a radio in his house. He is fond of the movies and is particularly attracted by Communist films that he sees at the Cathay Theater in Wan Chai. His indulgence in movies must be slight, however, compared to the women of his household, one or more of whom seem to make an almost daily pilgrimage to the Jade Theater in Lung Shing when he is not home. His mother also states she prefers pictures from the mainland, but she cannot seem to explain why. No one in the family swims unless we credit the elder brother with doing so when he laughingly says that he can dog-paddle.

Our friend, the Seagoing Tailor dreams of sending his six-year-old son to college in Peking after he has finished a preliminary education in Hong Kong. University training, he states, is too expensive in the Colony. As for himself, he studied over a period of nine years but, since the decade was one of war, some years he was in school only two or three months. He never received a primary school certificate whereas his wife did, being ten years his junior. He is very proud of his elder son who started in the School C kindergarten at the age of five and was transferred to first grade before the end of the year. The boy was reputedly the brightest student in his class and demonstrated to us his ability to spell and pronounce every word in his English primer, an achievement he undertakes by rote. As is to be expected in Hong Kong, his pronunciation is impenetrable, but that is merely a reflection on the inadequate phonetic abilities of the teachers of this exotic language.

The Seagoing Tailors quite understandably wear standard European type clothes, but the women in the family remain attached to sam fu and in the very hot weather find underclothes cut above the knee quite sufficient at home. It is significant that both the young wives do own cheong sam, whereas their mother-in-law does not. The latter is a handsome woman in her black sam fu. She has unusually fine teeth that show off well with her slightly silvered black hair drawn tightly back and twisted into a bun at the rear of her head. She wears small gold button earrings and has a jade ring in a gold setting on the middle finger of her left hand and a plain gold one on the same finger of her right one. When we admired them, she said that in Fuchou she had a lot more rings and bracelets which she was not allowed to bring with her. We noted that her youngest grandson sports a silver anklet on his left foot which the grandmother says is worn just for fun.

Our friend, the Seagoing Tailor, told us that the members of the household are all Confucians, but with the warning that Confucianists are not concerned with the existence of God. His mother later said that the family has no religion, having given up all the customary practices since coming to Hong Kong. Even in her husband's house, incense was burned only at New Year's and at the time of major festivals. Her own parents, however, also burned a little incense on the second and sixteenth of each month. Interestingly enough, however, the Seagoing Tailor's mother never eats beef and abstains from all meat as well as fish at the morning meal, taking only congee and vegetables in the belief, as her elder son confided, that by this sacrifice she will pass on strength to her sons. He himself recognized Buddhist doctrine behind her behavior. He concluded with the statement that as a child he did believe in the prognostications of the fortunetellers in the temple who use bundles of sticks to divine the past and the future.

Another unusual thing about the grandmother is that she is the only one of the whole household who smokes. Every three days she consumes one package of Robin Hood cigarettes which cost $.60. She formerly smoked a typical Fukienese silver water pipe (which she says all Fuchou ladies used), but she has been unable to acquire one in Hong Kong. She also drinks on occasion as do her two sons. The women raise a few chickens, but keep no other birds or animals. The grandmother still runs the household quietly but firmly. Each of her two sons contributes a specified sum to her each month for the expenses of the family. This includes $50 a month rent to the Enterprising Woman, we were told by the eldest son, who added that he also gave his wife twenty dollars as pocket money. Congee with "dishes," as the Chinese say, is provided about eight in the morning, then there is rice with "dishes," at noon. Sometime between six and seven in the evening there are more "dishes," but with congee again.

The old lady points out that one of the differences between the Cantonese and the Fukienese is that the latter have three meals a day while the former have two (a meal without rice is simply not classed as a meal). Also she thinks that the Fukienese are more fond of soup. Further, she explained that whereas a Fukienese woman who has just given birth is provided with six meals a day, three with boiled chicken and wine and three with fine wheat vermicelli, a Cantonese woman in the same situation is served a mixture of ginger, eggs, vinegar, and other such foods. Indeed, she cannot understand how the Cantonese can eat so much ginger anyway. Although comprehending very well, we did not attempt to explain.

One day we found the Seagoing Tailor's mother breaking up pieces of dried glutenous rice flour for further drying in basket trays. On showing our interest, she promised to cook some t'ong t'ün (t'ang t'uan), a kind of special dumplings, if we would come back the next day, and inevitably we did. The process begins with washing some glutenous rice mixed with some ordinary rice in a container by swirling it around in covering water. The rice is then soaked for a day and ground in a small stone mill that is like a large wedding cake on a stone plate. The wet rice is poured into a hole in the upper stone which is perhaps sixteen inches in diameter and six inches thick. A heavy white liquid is discharged from under its serrated bottom surface and collected in a bag at the lip of the plate. When the contents of the bag have been dried, the flour is broken up into pieces for re-drying. This done, it can be cooked in various ways. Our hostess made little balls about an inch in diameter, dropped them in boiling water whereupon they immediately sank. After a while they rose off the bottom and she took them out and rolled them in sesame seeds, bean powder, ground peanuts, and sugar. Such balls may be eaten warm or cold; they taste sweet and doughy. Children love them. They are usually eaten with very thin congee. Most people on Lung Chau, it may be added, cannot afford these glutenous rice dumplings except at feasts and most particularly New Year's. With this sense of luxury in mind, we can pass on to consider the Villa of the Shipbuilder's Son.

23. The Shipbuilder's Son's Villa

One of the richer men connected with Sai Mi Wan is the son of a shipbuilder in Lung Shing. He obtained a Crown Permit for the steep land on the westerly side of the bay before one reaches the property of the Man Who Retired (Fig. 14.2). This was done about 1957 according to the latter who had not applied for this area nearer the town because the adjoining land farther out was much more open and adaptable to building.

Despite the topographic limitations of the property—or perhaps partly on account of them—the Shipbuilder's Son has developed what is probably the most esthetically appealing estate in Sai Mi Wan (Fig. 23.1). The structures occupy two terraces on the hillside, the lower and broader of which, lying about twenty feet above the water, is distinguished by a row of papaya trees large enough to bear fruit and over fifty pots of various kinds of flowering plants. Behind them are two concrete gable-roofed houses side by side. The roofs are of a corrugated composition material. The larger and more southerly house is reserved for the owner, while the smaller yet still quite sizable one is occupied by the caretaker and her husband. Straight out from between the houses is a double row of hedge enclosing a path that ends in concrete steps descending to the beach. These have been partly broken away by the sea. In front of the main house the flat is covered by an arbor thickly entwined with leafy vines. In one corner under it is a well and a large tank with a sign on it which says the water is unfit for drinking. The caretaker says the water itself is palatable but that rusty pipes and the pumping machinery contaminate it. In any event there is a second well. Regrettably, there are also mosquitoes.

Somewhat to the north and on a terrace above is a long building with the lower part made of concrete. This structure serves as a chicken house, but there are only about twenty hens in it. As one approaches this building one becomes aware of what the caretaker calls a wood-oil tree, a large ornamental about twenty-five feet high. Beyond the tree and chicken house is an unusually elaborate toilet made of concrete. At the east end of the property stretches a row of pigpens only periodically used. There is no electricity at the Villa. As the gossip goes, the Shipbuilder's Son has spent about twenty thousand dollars on the place, or at least that is the figure

Fig. 23.1. The Villa

estimated by the Fortunate Wife of the Farmer. The caretaker said the Villa had recently been offered for sale, but that an offer of fifteeen thousand had been refused.

The caretaker and her husband have been at the Villa for only a few months, having learned of the opening from a neighbor who held the position and decided to leave. The pay consists of $110 a month plus the use of the small house. The husband works at the golf club at Deep Water Bay, Hong Kong. This couple came from the Pao An district of Kwangtung a few years before the Communists took control of the province. They have children living in China.

The caretaker is alone much of the time but she says that she keeps busy and does not mind. She has no radio and seldom goes to a movie. When her husband comes home, he sometimes takes a swim, but she never does. Occasionally in the evening she visits other families. There are no pigs or pigeons to take care of, but she plants a few vegetables for the family. When we visited her, she was making some clothes for her husband's brother. Of religious beliefs, she claims to have none.

Unfortunately, we did not meet the owner of this unusual place, but we did talk to his family in Lung Shing. They are Hsin Hui people (Fig. 3.1) who own one of the principal slipways on the island. It is the second son who was born about 1928 who acquired the property in Sai Mi Wan because, as his mother says, he wanted a place to sleep and plant trees, motives which struck us as most rare and reasonable for a resident of Lung Shing, one of the noisiest and close-quartered of towns. She remembered his buying the wood-oil tree when it was only five feet high. "He just loves that place," she concluded.

The mother, a charming and perhaps dominant woman, left little doubt that she had not and did not approve of the Sai Mi Wan venture financially. Neither had she approved altogether of his marrying a girl of his own choice with whom he had associated for four months beforehand. On the other hand, she was fair enough to say that he was a good man who had always worked hard and had put his own savings into the Villa. "He just could not help it," she insisted.

Clearly, here was an exceptional person, one who had been forced to leave school at the end of his primary education because of the Japanese occupation. After the war he did study English at night school. It was by no means out of character to discover when we tried to seek him out that he had gone to New York, or that his wife preferred to await his return in the home of her mother.

24. The Man Who Retired

The Man Who Retired did not do so until a year after had been expected because there was a delay about replacing him in his responsible position as a foreman on the staff of the Waterworks where he had forty men working under him. He had reached the retirement age of fifty-five in 1957, after being first employed by the Government as a young man. Born in Kowloon about 1903, he was taken back to Shan Wei in eastern Kwangtung (Fig. 3.1) at age eight for his primary education comprising four or five years in a private school with over a hundred students. Then on his return, he attended a now defunct Chinese high school in Kowloon. His family were Ch'ao An speakers, but he learned Cantonese early as a native of Hong Kong. He also claims to know Hakka. Thinking back on his career, he told how he had gone into the import-export business with an uncle. This enterprise having failed, he then worked for the water department as a common coolie, and once having found an opening in the department, he recounted how within five years he had worked his way up to be a foreman, a position which he had held ever since. With a salary of $400 a month and housing for nominal rentals of from $7 to $25 a month, it was a respectable life which allowed him some leisure and aspirations about what he would do when he had more. During his leave of one month each year, he went looking for the ideal place in which to retire and by 1954 he had wandered over most of the New Territories and the islands around Hong Kong proper. Having friends in Lung Shing, it was natural that he examined that island. It was there that he discovered Sai Mi Wan and he made his decision at once. He admired the way the two ridges of hills enclosed the finger of sea. Also the site was a place reputed to be both cool in summer and warm in the winter, while the water provided the opportunity to swim. As he described it, the deep bay was like an armchair, a nice place to sit. We should add that the Carpenter says that it has excellent feng-shui, it facing south and being where the strength of the ridge lies (Figs. 14.2 and 24.1).

At that time, no claim had been made on the northwesterly limits of the bay, and the Man Who Retired applied in 1954 and ultimately received a Crown Permit for about 20,000 square feet, much of it shore frontage. As a government servant of long standing, this grant was perhaps less

Fig. 24.1. The Establishment of the Man Who Retired and of His Friend

difficult to secure than it might have been for some other person. By the date he had expected to retire, a large flat area had been cleared and a nicely-built one-story gable-roofed, concrete house had been erected facing the bay well above the beach (Fig. 24.2). As there was the previously mentioned delay in leaving the waterworks, a Caretaker was allowed to occupy the dwelling for a year, but in the meantime more construction continued as it has ever since.

First there was a smaller house built a hundred feet north for the Caretaker, and then even more ambitious developments. The Man Who Retired truly gloried in the florescence of his seaside estate. By 1958, when he and his family had moved into their new house, he had persuaded a close Friend who owned a sesame seed oil business to take an additional 20,000 square feet of land on the shore nearby to the east. Then when the Friend recognized that the land of the Man Who Retired was better for building, the latter traded him part of his property for the westerly half of the Friend's. Soon the Retired Man set up a sizable establishment for raising ducks along the beach. He was not very successful, so he rented

Fig. 24.2. The House of the Man Who Retired

the buildings to a doctor, and when the doctor developed a profitable business, he later constructed another duck house to the north of it for himself. When he first gave up duck raising, the Man Who Retired went into partnership with his Friend in the soy sauce business. This was disastrous. The undertaking was a financial failure and the factory itself was ruined by a landslide in 1959.

Not mentioned was the chicken house and extensive yard westerly of his home (Fig. 24.3), or another small building for a seventy-four-year-old man, the father of his elder brother's wife. This old man has two sons who are well off—each owns a grocery store—but he does not get along with them. When the Caretaker first came, the old man would appear once in a while and he has been a permanent resident since March, 1960 when the little house was built. Outside the door, it has a tiny garden in which he grows water spinach protected by a reed fence and nearby is a small chicken house with gourd vines covering it.

Three wells have been dug on the property of the Man Who Retired, two near the shore which are sixteen to eighteen feet deep to supply water for the ducks, and a third near the house only fifteen feet deep which the owner says always has water in the morning although by afternoon that well is often dry. The water supply has been tested at the Waterworks and the quality reported as good. The water is boiled for home use nonetheless.

In his enthusiasm, the Retired Man admits to having spent about 20,000 dollars on his estate, enthusiasm which does not seem greatly diminished by heavy losses in connection with the sauce factory or a recent deficit of 2,000 dollars in the last four months of his own duck raising enterprise. For a Retired Man of property, such things must be accepted —or so it would seem. In any event, there cannot be much left of his pension of $32,000 which he took in a lump sum on leaving the employ of the government.

The household of the family comprises the Retired Man, his wife who at fifty-eight (Ch) is a year younger than he, their thirteen-year-old daughter and eight-year-old son, a worker who takes care of the ducks, and the previously referred to old man. Also the Man Who Retired and his wife have a third child, a daughter now twenty-three. She was sent back to Shan Wei in 1942 with her father's aunt. Later she wanted to return but was not permitted to do so by the Communists. The parents have not seen her since she was a child but they have a picture they showed us. She now has a son, having married by free choice. Her father thinks this is now the best way, pointing out that in his day all marriages were arranged. Soon after the World War I when he was seventeen or eighteen, his parents went back to Shan Wei and arranged for his marriage.

Fig. 24.3. The Chicken Yard of the Man Who Retired

When we first met him, the head of the family was wearing blue shorts, slippers with a plastic strap, and a white T-shirt. What made the costume unusual was not the wristwatch on his left wrist or the carved jade bracelet beside it but the fountain pen clasped in the neck of his shirt and the old piece of carved jade at his belt. The pen, of course, was the symbol of his considerable education, and we learned that the Man Who Retired has a pit ho (pieh hao), or pen name, which is an estimable acquisition. As for the jade piece, which was said to be over a thousand years old, it was somewhat more surprising to learn that it conveyed the specific advantage of preventing the wearer from falling down and breaking his bones.

It somehow seemed consistent that when the Man Who Retired was asked whether he preferred to patronize doctors with Western or with Chinese type training, he modestly admitted to practicing Chinese medicine himself, at least to the extent that he or his family had need of treatment. He corroborated our suggestion that his efforts in curing were successful, but with further details of his therapeutic methods, we were not rewarded. He did say, however, that he had studied with a teacher in the evening during the period he was in high school. He did not continue as he considered medicine a "shaky" profession, or one with too much dangerous responsibility. There is an advantage, he thinks, in treating the body as a whole as the Chinese physician does, rather than attempting to cure the localized appearance of the disease in Western fashion. Acupuncture, such as we observed in Lung Shing, he regards as valuable therapy, but says it is a specialty that he knows nothing about (see pp. 812–13).

Turning back to the subject of dress we noted that his daughter also wore blue shorts which went very well with her blue and white shirtwaist, while a handkerchief over her head added another mark of a young lady influenced by Western culture. Both she and her mother wore Japanese type slippers. In other respects, however, the mistress of the house in her black fu and white patterned sam was the most conservatively dressed member of the family. Her curled bobbed hair also would have been so considered compared to her daughter's black pony tail. Neither one has ever owned a cheong sam. Both displayed gold earrings—the mother's being circlets while the girl's were simple buttons. The older woman also wore a green jade bracelet on her left wrist and a reddish brown one on the right, while the younger had a silver chain showing at the neck. This, as we immediately suspected, bore a Catholic medal, for we learned on questioning that the daughter had been converted when she began school in Pok Fu Lam village on Hong Kong Island (Fig. 3.2). This fact seemed to create no schism in a family that was otherwise not only conservative in religious beliefs, but more than usually concerned with them. Following the great tradition of tolerance, her father immediately pointed out that all religions depend on one's conscience, adding that his daughter did not try to convert her parents.

Discussing religion, the Man Who Retired surprised us by suddenly assuming the cross-legged position of a meditating priest which we presume most adult Chinese are not capable of doing. He said that on visiting some of the larger temples he had seen individuals sitting that way and had consequently practiced until he had learned how to do so himself. No specific knowledge of Buddhism or other manifestations of its practice evidenced themselves in our discussion. Over the door of the house was a pat kwa (pa kua) symbol, the ancient and widely used design of eight groups of three long or bisected lines. The Man Who Retired said that it helped to keep evil away from the house.

Broaching the subject of feng-shui, we were pleased to discover that the head of the family had positive ideas. Taking our lead, he expressed the opinion that carpenters are not necessarily effective in their knowledge of the art, and he then commented on the Carpenter's house directly across the bay as being in a poor location—that it was "pressed in" and facing wrong. We remembered the builder's own explanation of his problem, but were immediately distracted by the statement that the Man Who Retired had used a little feng-shui himself in planning his buildings. Unfortunately simple questions did not lead to simple answers and all that could be certain of the process was that an instrument something like a compass had been utilized, an instrument that belonged to someone else and was not available for us to see.* We were led to believe by the Man Who Retired that it might have been better to employ the specialist who lived in Lung Shing, but he had moved to another island.

Since one of the days on which we visited the Man Who Retired was the 7th of the 7th month, we asked if he would celebrate the feast. As an educated man, he of course knew the legend of the lovers meeting on the Milky Way and that rain was to be expected from the tears of their parting. He said that it would be proper to burn incense at midnight, as well as paper combs, lipstick, and powder for the girl, and then have a feast, but that his family, like most on the island, would not do so. The wife of his Friend's nephew, who had just dropped in, added that the powder to be burned on such occasions is real and can be kept to cure small children of swellings and various other ailments. She also remarked that the 7th of the 7th month is a night especially celebrated by amahs who have sworn to remain virgins.

The daughter and her mother made no comment, although the former may have felt superior in such matters as she attends fourth grade at the morning session of School D, whereas her brother is in first grade at the

---

*For a detailed description of the geomancer's compass, see Eitel, 1873: 33–44.

afternoon session and consequently was not present. The mother, we might add, is illiterate as might be expected of her generation. The Man Who Retired, incidentally, expects to put his children through middle school if he can afford to.

Whatever may be said of the state of knowledge and belief in the family, their home is very pleasant. The house is larger and better constructed than most, and is distinguished by the fact that the gable roof is of tile and overhangs the door by two or three feet. At each side of the entrance is a window with five vertical iron bars. The windows have the common double sashes which swing open outwardly and are glazed in two sections, top and bottom. There is a cement slab porch several feet off the ground with a board and bamboo trellis high above it covered with a mass of vines bearing ng chau t'ong (wu chao t'ang), a trumpet-shaped lavender flower, which makes it very pleasant to sit at the table beneath it and look over the bay.

Inside the house, the furniture is perhaps slightly more ornate than in the average house, and this is especially true of the tables. There is a commonplace plank bed, however, and a double-decked one, both with mosquito nets which it is said serve primarily to keep dirt from dropping from the roof rather than to protect from the reputedly few insects. On the wall opposite the door hangs a pendulum clock in a large dark wood case and beneath it on a shelf is a blue-and-white baluster-shaped vase of near contemporary period. There is no electric current in the house, but the lines were expected the following year.

In the area easterly of the house is the usual shed roof kitchen and a small storage building. To the west spreads a sizable grape arbor with large clusters of fruit, which the daughter seemed to enjoy although the taste was very sour. Our host said they were an American variety and that they did become sweeter in the fall although the poor character of the soil apparently spoils them. A considerable number of papaya trees have been planted on the property, but only three or four have reached productive maturity. There are also a few guava trees, but no bananas.

The household food seemed similar to that of other well-to-do families in Sai Mi Wan but with perhaps more meat. Breakfast consists of congee with secondary dishes, whereas the two main meals comprise plain boiled rice with various dishes. The Man Who Retired says they prefer pork to either chicken or beef. Sometimes the members of the family eat noodles in a restaurant as a change from rice. Also mussel soup is a common dish at home, these shellfish being readily obtained from the beach in front of the house. Shrimps, crabs, and fish are also eaten. The Man Who Retired has a small purse seine, but he says it takes too much time to fish, so they usually buy them. Actually, he is fond of the sea and owns a sampan which both provides pleasure on the bay and serves to bring supplies from the town on the other side of the island, although if enough are ordered, they will be delivered free. Curiously, he has never been to Chung Nam Wan which is only a short distance along the south shore, although he knows of the settlement.

The Man Who Retired and both his children swim every day, sometimes morning and evening. They cross the bay and return using the breast stroke most of the time. He reports that he has never seen any sharks in the bay at Sai Mi Wan. The other principal diversion of the family is attending movies and they not infrequently go to the superior of the two cinemas in the town across the strait which has a large screen, better seats, and is air-conditioned. It is also more expensive. There is no radio in the home, and they do not play mah-jongg. The master of the house admits to doing a little drawing and painting occasionally, but he says the latter is too much work. No one in the family drinks or smokes.

Farming is limited to one area of activity on the estate of the Man Who Retired. No pigs are raised and no vegetables grown, although flowers are planted before New Year's when the annual demand makes their sale profitable. It is planned to have some pigeons but there are none now. It is chickens and ducks that receive the principal attention as a source of income. Between two and three hundred chickens provide bits of color moving over the large fenced yard south of the house. A considerable part of this area is covered with either shed roof or vine covered trellis. Most of the fowl are sold at an age beginning at four months for a price of about five dollars a catty, one more than is usual because no injections are given. Both the restaurants in Lung Shing and people in the public market buy them. Hens begin to lay at an age of six months. Most of the eggs are saved for hatching; others are sold at a price which may be forty to fifty cents each. When a hen sits on a nest and does not lay, they take her off and tie her legs so that she cannot escape one of the handsome pair of roosters that preside over the yard. Sometimes hawks attack the chickens, but few are caught. The little ones run and the roosters will fight to protect them as well as themselves. There are not many rats, says the Man Who Retired, and there are two nameless cats to chase them away and three dogs, including a bitch, for further assistance. The dogs are named Dolly (Tao Li) and Hak Tsai (Hei Tzu), or Blackie, and the bitch is called A Ts'oi (A Ts'ai), or Rich.

The Man Who Retired is still raising ducks, but that activity we shall discuss later after we present the story of his Friend's establishment which grew up because of the short lived soy sauce business.

25. The Friend of the Man Who Retired

The Chinese are a gregarious people and the Man Who Retired to the far end of Sai Mi Wan is no exception. He thought it would be nice to have his Friend, a well-to-do man in the sesame oil business in Shau Kei Wan, apply for an adjacent piece of land, and the Friend, whose family also originated in Shan Wei, was persuaded to do so with the inducement of making money by establishing a sauce factory. Soon after acquiring his land, the Friend had a large terrace constructed high on the hill above and northeast of the house of the Man Who Retired. This terrace has a stone block retaining wall about six feet high and forty feet long behind which a concrete apron stretches thirty feet wide broadening to fifty-four feet at the back. The apron lies in front of a small, ornate, white concrete building with a tile roof and a concrete projection in imitation of a beam end near the upper corners, each bearing a character impressed on the face. The left character is luk (lu), the right one is fuk (fu), which, when read right to left as is proper, mean "Happiness and a prosperous career." There is a window at each side of the door with double sashes that swing outward as well as a window at each end. All are protected by vertical iron bars.

The peculiar things about the building are that it is only about twelve feet square—which is really too small for a sauce factory—and that it has practically no back wall remaining. Not long after its construction, when sauce production had been well started, heavy rains caused a landslide of the earth and rock cliff cut away in making the terrace, and in this deluge, the back wall was overwhelmed. The clay was never cleared from the interior.

Inside near the door rest six huge jars and outside on the terrace thirty-seven more are turned bottomside up. All are plain except two which have the yellow dragons characteristic of egg-shipment jars. They are mute indication that the terrace continued to be used after the preliminary disaster.

After his misfortune, the Friend decided to erect a large building nearer the beach in which to make sauce. Less precipitous land was leveled and a second unusual building, certainly the largest residence in the whole settlement of Sai Mi Wan, was erected (Figs. 14.2 and 24.1, lower right). Originally put up as a factory, it has been used as a house since the failure of the business. It is a gable-roofed structure with clapboard sides on a concrete base with walls which are 21″ high. The roof is made up of boards covered with tarpaper, the ridgepole being twelve feet above the top of the concrete walls. In shape, the house is interesting as it is said to be a copy of those in the Hai Feng area of Kwangtung, except that the latter have walls of stone cemented over and roofs of red tile. The building, which is only fifteen feet wide, is almost thirty-five feet long with a setback of 16″ in the middle twelve feet of the front wall (Fig. 25.1). The pair of doors, which close the only entrance of the house in the center of the setback, swing inward and are a full seven feet high above two concrete steps which themselves make a 14″ rise. The large windows, in the middle of each section adjoining the door, have twin double-sash frames that swing outward. These are set 27″ above the cement wall whereas the smaller pair of windows in the rear wall are sixty inches above the concrete wall. There is also a window at each end of the building and these (which are slightly to the rear in order to avoid cutting the posts supporting the ridge pole) are 48″ above the concrete. The windows at the rear and ends are protected by vertical iron bars and those in front by horizontal wood slats. This unusual exterior appearance of the building is emphasized by the frayed paper picture of a traditional Gate God posted on each panel of the door.

Entering the house one faces a table set as an altar with a picture of another God above it. Somehow, the house, which has been divided into three rooms by masonite partitions, is more imposing than any other in Sai Mi Wan. The cement floor is relatively clean and on it in the bedroom

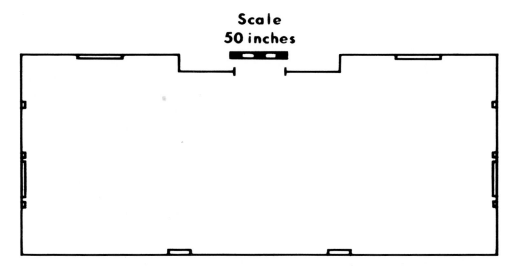

Fig. 25.1. The Friend's House

section, set off by a blue patterned curtain at the entrance, is a colored straw mat. Also in the bedroom is a black cabinet with doors which lock, and even more unusual, a Western type bed with a mosquito net over it. In the center room besides the altar there are two folding chairs and four square wood stools. In the corner is a dining table with each of its four legs in a can filled with water to prevent ants from reaching the food. Two stoneware bowls and several thermos bottles stand on the table. Against the back wall not far from the altar is a wood toilet stand with a large enamelware bowl, a covered cup of the same material, and a pink towel. A pair of portrait photographs of an elderly woman hang above one of the two barred windows at the rear of this room. The third and westerly division of the house, which is used for storage, is characterized by the numerous large stoneware jars it contains, relics of the soy sauce venture. In some of them, rice, vinegar, and other foods are preserved. Electricity is not available.

Outside at the easterly end of a cement flat is a shed kitchen walled with rusty tin. In it is a stove so carefully made that it might well be considered a model for the local type. The kitchen, like the house, is exceptionally clean except for ants in the process of being poisoned. On the shore side of this shed there are two small rooms. Between the kitchen and the front door there is a large cement tank for water which comes from one of the wells dug for the Man Who Retired.

The regular occupant of this menage is a young woman of about thirty who is the wife of a nephew of the Friend of the Man Who Retired. Her husband, who is about ten years older than she, works for the uncle in his factory in Shau Kei Wan making rubber shoes, and it is too expensive for him to come home more than once or twice in a week as he earns only $120 a month besides such extras as free rent in Sai Mi Wan and his meals. He lives somewhat under a cloud because he persuaded his uncle to invest in the soy sauce factory in partnership with the Man Who Retired. Actually, the latter had introduced the man who knew how to make the sauce to his neighbor, the nephew of the Friend. Besides soy sauce, a fish sauce and vinegar were also made. The quick decline of the business made the wife, our informant, even discredit the sauce maker's honesty, and when her husband was so ashamed that he could not inform his uncle about the way things were going, she told the uncle that it was better to close down the business before he lost any more money. Naturally, the uncle blames his nephew for being the cause of his having lost more than $10,000 on this venture which was begun in 1958. The Retired Man's statement is simply that they were in the sauce business temporarily, but that sauce is hard to sell.

The nephew's family are Ch'ao An speakers from Hai Feng near Shan Wei. The nephew's mother, widowed before her only child was born, still lives there at the age of seventy-two. She would not leave the country when others in her family did, saying that she preferred to die on her own land. Now they have to send her sixty-five dollars worth of food and other materials every month and then she has to pay money to obtain the gift. For example, a bottle of cod liver oil pills cost $3 in Hong Kong and another $.40 for postage. On receiving it the mother has to pay $4 in People's Republic currency (ca. HK$10). In a 1961 letter, it was reported that the people of her district had only one catty of yams for each person a day and that a doctor's prescription was needed for sugar. They were forced to eat young grass and individuals were swelling in the stomach and feet. The photograph portraits, previously mentioned, are of the nephew's mother. The first was taken when she was particularly worried because her son had been accused of having a conservative viewpoint and consequently could obtain no work. The other was taken after he reached Hong Kong in 1956 and had sent her some money.

The nephew of the Friend of the Man Who Retired has an unusual personality. He is very reserved and extremely hesitant to meet strangers. He finished middle school and reads a great deal. He had a wife who was brought into the home by his mother when he was a child. She is now dead but a son of twenty survives. The nephew's second wife whom he married as a widow about 1956 bore two daughters who died before she gave birth to a son in 1953. This boy, the Communists would not allow to leave the country and he still lives with his grandmother. The husband suffers because he has not been able to make much money since he came to the Colony. He has even offered to work as a laborer, but his wife persuaded him not to. As she sees it, a man with a middle school education and no real experience can be at the greatest disadvantage in Hong Kong. In his wife's eyes, however, he is a very good and conservative man who does not drink or become involved with other women.

Our informant, the wife of the nephew of the Friend of the Man Who Retired, is an exceptionally gracious woman. When we first met she was wearing a very worn black fu with a white undercoat with blue flowers. Her feet were bare, but on the floor was a miscellany of footwear—wood shoes with blue straps, Japanese style slippers in red, tennis shoes, and rubber overshoes. On the wall hung a broad-brimmed straw hat. She is specially memorable, however, as she sat on a neighbor's bench in a classic pose with her bare left foot pressing against the thigh of her opposite leg. She was wearing the same black fu but with an undercoat of a slightly golden brown with small clusters of white daisies. The material was silk and surprisingly attractive as it faintly outlined her diminutive breasts. Her black bobbed hair was brought back loosely along the sides of her head and done up in back in a European style. She wore as jewelry only small studs of gold in her ears and a plain wedding band on the third finger of her left hand. She told us that day, incidentally, that she does not own a cheong sam.

This young woman first came to Hong Kong in 1945 because her parents lived in the Colony, and then went back to her husband in China periodically. Now she misses her son very much, and for some reason she cannot understand, she is unable to conceive again. In any event, she says that she does not want any more children. Much of the time she is not very busy, for except to care for a sizable flock of chickens in a large wired area above the house, she has only her few rooms to take care of. They have neither ducks nor pigeons, and they grow no vegetables. When the Friend of the Man Who Retired obtained his permit for the land, however, he also acquired one to raise pigs, and they hope to obtain some soon or otherwise it will expire. There are two or three guava trees on the property, and what is much more unusual, three small peach trees. There is one dog named A Fi (A Fei), or Fatty, who stays in the chicken coop, and also six or seven cats. The wife eats two meals a day, one about ten in the morning and the other at five or six in the evening. One of her few pleasures is smoking a large old bamboo waterpipe, the tobacco for which costs $.60 an ounce and an ounce lasts ten days. In this indulgence, her husband also shares. Actually, as she admitted, she would prefer to smoke Lucky Strikes but they cost $1.10 a package.

Once a day, or once in two or three days, she walks into Lung Shing to shop, and perhaps once a month she goes to a movie. She has not been as far as Tung Pak Wan and has never even heard of Chung Nam Wan. Occasionally, she goes to Shau Kei Wan with her husband. She has no radio, never plays mah-jongg, cannot swim, and unfortunately is unable to read since she never went to school. Were she ill, she would go to a doctor with Western training because she believes he would cure her quicker and less expensively. They do not belong to the Kaifong Association and do not go to the temples although there is a definite religious atmosphere in the house. As we left one day, we observed a small red cloth draped tightly under the ridgepole, and were told it is a ceremonial talisman that was placed there when the beam was raised. As usual, we stopped next door to look at the ducks.

26. The Duck Raisers

About 1958, three unrelated men came to Sai Mi Wan to raise ducks. We shall call them Mr. One, Mr. Two, and Mr. Three. They were all Ch'ao An speakers from a single village in the Swatow area of the east coast of Kwangtung, and they had all previously worked together raising ducks at Wong Chuk Hang, a settlement on the south coast of Hong Kong Island (Fig. 1.1), for the uncle of Mr. Two. When they decided to go into business for themselves, through a friend they met the Enterprising Woman who offered them an excellent location on the beach and a house of three rooms at the foot of Sai Mi Wan (Figs. 14.2 and 26.1). They agreed to pay fifty dollars a month rent.

Family One. Since Mr. One had a wife and four children with him, it was logical that his family would occupy one of the rooms and the other two men without their families would take another, leaving a common room between. It was also reasonable that Mr. One would pay half of the rent. Mr. One developed his duck pens on the hill behind and above the house and beyond that of his friends. The other two men, who worked in an equal partnership, built theirs to the west along the beach. The two men cooked for themselves.

Mr. One, aged forty-one, has two sons, thirteen and six, and two daughters, one aged four, the other only three months. The three older children were born in one of the Tung Hua hospitals, the youngest at home. Their mother, who was married blind at twenty-two is two years younger than her husband. She is very conscious of a shortage of money and says she would like to give some of her children to a rich family that can educate them. None of them goes to school. During the threat of a cholera epidemic in 1961, she insisted that she could not afford to let them have cholera injections, although she believes in Western medicine as more effective than Chinese. It was a matter of time, not money, as almost everyone queued up and received the shots free. The family does not belong to the Kaifong Association. Mr. One can play mah-jongg, but his wife does not know how. She has heard of Tung Pak Wan but not of Chung Nam Wan, and she seldom goes any place, even into town. She says she would like to go to the movies but claims that she cannot because of the children.

Fig. 26.1. The Duck Raisers at the Outer End of the Bay

Mrs. One has waved bobbed hair and no visible jewelry, but she wears attractive sam fu, which is a matter of taste. Once we noted a matched set of pale blue with a blue flower design, another time a modern print of blue and white rectangles and lines. She has never worn a cheong sam. Her feet were bare. In the very hot weather, Mr. One wears only shorts and Japanese style slippers while working. He took a job as a coolie when he first came from China about 1952.

The bedroom of Mr. and Mrs. One is large, but of ramshackle construction. They put the room together themselves for an expenditure of only $200, although it probably was somewhat abused by the same Typhoon Mary that killed all but about a hundred of their ducks. In the room is a larger than usual bed made by placing six boards on wood horses. They have no other furniture of any value or distinction, however.

The middle room of the house, which was built as a kitchen, is open in front toward the sea except for a wire screen and three large pieces of bag burlap that slide on a wire to provide a curtain. The family eats on a piece of furniture made by putting the square top of an old-fashioned table on a low tub. There are four typical wood stools and various small ones. Basket trays hang from the ceiling and there are two stoneware jars, one of which holds water. Actually, the Duck Raisers have a well not used by others that has a constant supply. There is a radio which is said to belong to everyone in the group, and electricity is available in the bedroom. A mirror, obviously by the inscription originally a gift to some restaurant, hangs from a post.

The family of Mr. One has congee for breakfast between eight and eight-thirty; rice and dishes for the main meals about two-thirty and again very late between seven-thirty and eight. There may be an addition of sweet soup, however, about four in the afternoon, and sometimes they have congee at night if the children prefer it. A duck is eaten only on feast days. Mr. One enjoys a drink and also smokes tobacco pinch by pinch in a pipe a foot long that looks like a section of a man's cane, but his wife indulges in neither pleasure. The adults drink very concentrated tea, as is the Swatow custom. Food is cooked on either a movable pot stove or one which burns kerosene. There is a large pile of kindling stacked in the corner, but the wood is primarily for one of the two pig food stoves at the rear of the room that in this case is used to prepare food for the ducks. It is of unusual construction in that the upper foot has a circular depression above the pan, thus making it possible to cook more than the pan itself will hold. The other stove burns sawdust.

The family has no cats but has two very good dogs that do not bother the ducks—a male called Hing Tsai (Hsing Tzu), or Prosperous Boy, and a bitch named Li Tsai (Li Tzu), or Beneficial Girl. The children were recently given a black puppy by someone. The dogs catch rats and are said to protect the ducks from other people's cats (the Fish Dryers have two). The dogs are said to eat fish from those piled up for the ducks.

Mr. One has no pigs, chickens, or pigeons, and he grows no vegetables. He does have one guava and three papaya trees, and a banana tree that has spread. Mrs. One says they have no religion, which in her mind is no contradiction to the fact that they burn incense before Mr. One's ancestral tablet.

Mr. One's day is almost completely occupied in caring for his ducks. There are hundreds and hundreds and they must be kept very clean. They are divided into three groups by age, not counting those just born: those less than twenty days old, those between twenty and forty, and those over forty. At the age of seventy days the ducks are sold. The ducks rest in a shed on one-inch wire screens a few inches off the ground which allows their excretions to drop through and be cleaned up. Each group also has a sizable shaded yard containing a pool with water that is changed two or three times a day. The beach sand on the surface of shed and yard is shoveled up and replaced once every day. The yard, used when the ducks are not resting, is screened only vertically at the perimeter. The sand is cool and wet and the ducks can choose their own place to sleep.

The ducks are fed four times a day: early in the morning, at noon, about four in the afternoon and late in the evening. Each meal is the same and consists of cheap fish purchased at the wholesale fish market across the strait that are mixed with green vegetable remnants, the refuse of bean curd, wheat, wheat chaff, broken rice kernels, beans and corn. This food is cooked in the pig food stoves four to five hours and then dumped in several piles onto mats in the pens when cool. The ducks go to the piles, some eating more, some eating less. The hungriest will show the greatest greediness but then will be less aggressive the next mealtime.

The supply of ducks is replenished by purchasing either incubated duck eggs almost ready to hatch brought from the New Territories, or newly-hatched ducklings. The price for the latter was $1.20 each. We observed a man delivering a load in two baskets said to have 160 or 170 in each. Altogether, 359 were counted. They were of the local breed of ducks that likes water, not the Taiwan type that likes mud. They were not fed before delivery as that would cost money. A six-by-ten-foot pen was made for them from a long piece of checkerwork matting which when set up on end stood 15″ high. Dry straw from old fruit containers was pulled apart and spread on the floor of the pen to keep the ducklings warm. The ducklings were pulled from the baskets by their heads, it being said that even very rough handling does not hurt them immediately following their birth, although they become sensitive thereafter. Mr. One took a duckling in each hand and dipped its bill momentarily in a pan of water to teach it to drink. Then he threw them in pairs into the pen where they immediately began to peck at the straw. They are capable of eating in a few hours, but they are generally not fed until the next morning. For the first few days they receive steamed rice; after that, regular food.

When the time approaches to sell the seventy-day-old ducks, which by then average a little over three catties each, the Duck Raiser calls his dealer at the poultry market in Sai Wan (Kennedy Town) and makes an appointment for one of the coming mornings. On the appointed day, he rises at two in the morning, eats a bowl or two of congee, and begins to tie each duck's legs together, putting fifteen or twenty of the birds into a large, flattened hemispherical basket made specially for the purpose. By five o'clock when the sampan he has arranged for arrives, over a hundred caged birds are ready to be ferried around the island and across the strait. When the ducks are landed and the sampan owner is paid his $6, the baskets are transferred to a truck and the driver sets off with them to Sai Wan where they all arrive about seven o'clock when the market opens. This part of the journey costs another $7. The price paid by his dealer, who is one of seven or eight, may vary somewhat according to the needs and supply of the day, but the Duck Raiser will know the approximate amount beforehand. By eight, he is on his way home by bus, and thus within three days he can dispose of five hundred grown ducks. Profits are said currently to be small because so many people have gone into the business.

Mister Two and Mister Three. Part of the competition, of course, comes from the efforts of Mr. Two and Mr. Three who say they have over two thousand ducks. Mr. Two's family was originally in the bean and sugar business in Swatow and it was his uncle who started raising ducks in Wong Chuk Han. Mr. Two learned the business from him. Mr. Two's wife with their three sons and a daughter are still in China, he having applied unsuccessfully over many years for permission to bring her out. Mr. Three came from China about 1950. Both partners wear merely shorts and slippers, Mr. Two preferring those of Japanese style and Mr. Three, wood ones with black plastic straps. When it is very hot, they go into the sea and bathe. Humorously, they say they have to swim in their business.

Their room, where Mr. Two sleeps—really a kind of shed with a concrete floor—is piled up with bags of duck food. It is very clean and the front is made from new clapboards, a restoration after the damage caused by Typhoon Mary in 1960, which not only knocked down the building but killed all their ducks. They consider it lucky that they survived themselves. Application was made for disaster assistance, but although the local examiner wrote out a certified report on their loss, they received no compensation. They, too, spend almost all their time caring for their ducks. Mr. Two, however, likes the movies and goes quite frequently to the cinema in Lung Shing, but Mr. Three seldom attends. Both have visited Tung Pak Wan, but neither knew of Chung Nam Wan.

Mr. Three is "over fifty" as he stated on various occasions, avoiding precision. Actually, he is fifty-three and fifteen years older than his partner. His black hair is shot with white, but he is still strong enough to hoist heavy bags of sawdust onto the sea wall from the sampan which brings them. Like most of the Duck Raisers, his legs are usually bare. He sleeps on a board bed at the northerly end of the duck pens in what was originally a pig sty. There is an immediately adjacent window that looks out on the sea. It can be closed by a sliding panel of thin boards. No ducks are allowed in his small sleeping section, and he is accustomed to having them a few feet farther away. Like his partner, Mr. Three has a wife and a number of children in a village near Swatow.

The men take turns in preparing their meals. Usually on the second and sixteenth of each month they sacrifice a duck in honor of the Earth God. They chop the duck up into small pieces and boil them in very little water. When the meat has become more or less tender (Chinese ducks are tough compared to American), a little soy sauce and sugar are added and the duck cooked a little more. Sometimes they eat a duck without the sauce, one bird lasting four or five meals. Duck should be sixty days old to taste right, we are told, as the meat of a young duck is not properly developed. Besides these bimonthly occasions, Mr. Two and Mr. Three also celebrate New Year's, the 5th of the 5th month, the 15th of the 7th, the 15th of the 8th, and Tung Chih. Mr. Three enjoys San Miguel beer and both like a strong, clear, rice wine called Mau T'oi (Mao T'ai) which comes from Kweichow and costs $4.30 for a half-catty bottle which will last one of them for six to eight occasions. Also, Mr. Three smokes Robin Hood cigarettes which cost only $.60, saying that the Lucky Strikes preferred by his partner are too expensive.

The partners added to our knowledge of duck raising. The little ducks under fifteen days are fed only rice mixed with milk powder. Afterward all meals are the same. They are made up mostly of fish heads and fish bones purchased from restaurants plus the residue of bean curd since these are the cheapest foods. Until they are forty days old, the ducks are fed four times a day, then three times a day until they are sixty days old, and after that only twice a day. The ducks are force fed before selling. Lights are kept on all night in the duck pens so that they will eat and drink more, consequently growing fat faster. Also, in the crowded pens without light they pile up and hurt each other. Ducks do not fight with one another. When they are twenty to thirty days old, however, the ends of their upper bills are snipped off so that they will not pluck each other's feathers. The snipping hurts a little and they will not eat for one or two meals thereafter. A Duck Raiser has to figure on a 10 per cent loss in ducks no matter how careful one is. Some ducks become ill and will not eat. They are also sensitive to wind and sudden changes in temperature.

As does Mr. One, so do Mr. Two and Mr. Three usually dispose of their ducks in the Sai Wan market, but from the 8th to 11th month inclusive, they prefer to sell to a company in the New Territories that preserves duck for export largely to the U.S.A. This company paid $3.50 a catty during the short season, whereas sales in the Sai Wan market have been bringing only $2 to $2.10. Mr. Two, who works very hard, says that they can make money if the price is $3 a catty or over. It costs over $5 to raise one duck of about three catties. Obviously, at the time, the Duck Raisers were on the verge of losing money which may explain Mrs. One's anxiety.

Mr. Two's Grandfather. A clansman from the same village referred to as Grandfather but only distantly related to Mr. Two, came to stay with the latter in Sai Mi Wan a few months after the two partners started raising ducks there. He is an elderly man of fifty-eight and still comes in to see them on occasions. His costume appears distinctive because of his black Chinese slippers. He had not been around Sai Mi Wan very long before he was employed to raise ducks for a nonresident Ch'ao An speaking medical doctor with Western type training who is a friend of the Man Who Retired. The latter rented his duck pens on the beach in front of his house to the doctor, who now owns about four hundred birds under the supervision of Mr. Two's Grandfather. The latter employs two younger men, also Ch'ao An speakers from Swatow, and it is they who do most of the work (Fig. 26.1).

Mr. Two's Grandfather entertained us with strong Fukien tea, as did Mr. Two himself. The Grandfather emptied a whole ten-cent packet of leaves of the type called Kun Yam into a tiny Yi Hsing ware pot, but the diminutive cups he brought out were indeed very special—white Ching-te-chen porcelain of almost eggshell thinness. Both pot and cups rested in a high-lipped metal tray which caught the excess boiling water with which he flooded both teapot and cups. In a few minutes he threw out the water from the cups and filled them with the bitter tea.

Inevitably, we asked from whence came the cups. He smiled and explained in rather heavy Cantonese how he had escaped from the Communists in Swatow about 1950 and had come to Hong Kong leaving his wife, three sons and a daughter behind. In the Colony, there were the usual problems of adjustment for an older man with his education. He had finished high school in China and after forty years can write and speak a few words of English as he demonstrated. He had no special training, however, having sold fertilizer and rice in his home village. Fortunately he did possess some talent in calligraphy and art. Pressed to make a living, he found employment painting porcelain in a factory in Sai Ying Pun, west of the Central District of Hong Kong. There he added standard designs in five-color enamels to the white porcelain of China afterward re-fired in a muffle kiln. He showed us also a few special pieces that had been preserved with his calligraphy on them. It was pleasant to look at. With the passing of time, however, his eyes had given out and rheumatism had made his hand unsteady. "I am old," he announced with a plaintive smile, climbing up on his bed to bring down pictures and business cards of the more successful members of his tsuk (tsu), or lineage, some of whom he said had become rich in Bangkok. It was such men who paid him respect by calling on him when they journeyed to Hong Kong.

Mr. Two's Grandfather says that he prefers Chinese doctors for help with his rheumatism or any trouble of the bones. Also, he pointed out that if he went to a doctor trained in the Western tradition he would have to take the day off and perhaps stay in the hospital which would leave no one to supervise the duck farm.

As might be expected of one who suffers from rheumatism, he does not go swimming. Also he attends the cinema only a few times a year and without preference for one kind of picture or another. He does not belong to a Kaifong Association and says that he has no religion. We noted the familiar red can to hold incense sticks before the paper tablet to the Earth God. He said that it was there when he came. Consequently he burns a little incense so as not to give offense, adding that he is always willing to conform to customary religious practices.

The younger of the two workers came from northern Kwangtung to

Hong Kong in 1955 at the age of sixteen. For some time he was employed in a plastics factory in Kowloon and he wishes he still lived there. It was not until four months before we met him that he came to Sai Mi Wan, having heard of the position through friends. At the time, the country seemed attractive but now he would like to be back in the city. He looks after his thirteen-year-old brother who stays with him. The rest of his family is in Swatow. Despite his short stay on the island, he has been to Tung Pak Wan, but he has never heard of Chung Nam Wan. Every night that he has time, he walks into the town of Lung Shing. Although he much prefers Victoria, he can get to the capital city only once or twice a month at best.

At the farm he wore only short drawers, but one Sunday when we met him on the ferry, he was wearing a Philippine style shirt, long dark trousers, blue-gray socks, and black Oxfords. He looked fresh and clean and was carrying a six-dollar umbrella. His younger brother matched his style in a white shirt, blue shorts, socks striped horizontally in red, chartreuse green, black, plus several other colors, and black loafers. Their costumes would not have suggested their residence.

The Duck Raisers all live rather crudely in a shedlike house behind the duck pens, but not unpleasantly. There is a kind of porch in front with one bed on it, a table, and various tools. A radio, which is greatly enjoyed, hangs from the eaves, and there is a pot and small cups for the strong tea of the Ch'ao-Fu-Hui people.* They eat three meals a day with congee for breakfast. The younger worker smokes Indians, which cost $.60 and he likes to drink on occasions, as does the Grandfather of Mr. Two.

They have a few chickens at the duck farm but no pigs or pigeons, no cats and no dogs, and they do not grow vegetables. Most of the time there is much to be done, but the younger worker does have some fun. He likes to swim and can cross the bay and come back. He likes the cinema in Lung Shing and he likes to play mah-jongg once in a while. He also likes girls but says it is not easy to get one for the most important thing is money. He states flatly that he will not think about marriage until he is thirty. At present he has no feelings about the government. His parents held traditional Chinese beliefs, but he, like Mr. Two's Grandfather, says he has no religion. He also has never been to school.

The ducks are kept almost exactly as in the establishment of Messrs. One, Two and Three, only the view at the outer limits of the bay is more charming, a fact which may not be generally appreciated. The view across the shaded duck pens and their pools leads straight out to sea (Fig. 26.2).

---

*For the definition of Ch'ao-Fu-Hui, see Appendix F and pp. 462–63.

Fig. 26.2. View from the Duck Raisers'

The several hundred birds are divided into the same three classes by age. At night, since there is no electricity, kerosene lamps are lighted and placed in the pens. One day while we were there, the younger worker sold two to a woman who had come to the farm to buy them. Before delivery, he force-fed and watered them through an ordinary tin funnel so that they would need no food until the next day (Fig. 26.3). At this period, almost two months after our first observations on duck raising, the price had gone up to $2.80 a catty because the importation of food from China had been stopped as a result of the cholera in Kwangtung. Mr. Two's Grandfather says they can break even with a price of $2.30 a catty, for ducks averaging from three to three and a half catties, the latter having each cost approximately $5.00 to feed and selling at about $7.50, indicating $2.50 in other expenses.

The Man Who Retired. These successes in duck raising once again led the Man Who Retired into the business, as already has been indicated. His descriptions of the workings of his establishment are almost identical with those of the others, and our observations added little. He did include wheat germ and locally grown grass in the usual list of duck feed, and he

Fig. 26.3. Force-feeding a Duck

did have more confidence than his competitors in the future of the preserved duck business. He is a consistently optimistic man. Even the price,
which fell to about $2 a catty for ducks, did not seem to disturb him,
although he admitted a considerable loss at the time. He pointed out that a
sixty-day-old duck weighs about two and a half to three catties. Ducks, he
confirmed, do not fight with each other, whereas chickens will fight ducks
and win. Also, he claimed to have two thousand ducks with the expectation of having half as many more by winter. For some reason, Mr. Two
had a definite impression that the Man Who Retired had only a few
hundred. We did not count them.

27. The Bean Curd Maker

It may be remembered that the Fortunate Wife of the Farmer had agreed to let some friends use part of her property for the manufacture of tau fu (tou fu), or bean curd, in lieu of interest on a debt contracted because of legal difficulties involving her rope factory. We shall now consider these people who came from Swatow about 1946 and, after living in the town across the strait from Lung Chau thirteen years, moved to Sai Mi Wan in 1959 (Fig. 14.2). The impetus for the change in residence came from the fact that their home was taken by the government in order to make room for a new hospital. The authorities offered them accommodations behind a cinema, but they decided that they wanted a place in which they could raise pigs and thereby make the best use of the residue from their bean curd production. Through a mutual friend in the fish paste business, they met the Fortunate Wife of the Farmer who offered them an unusual proposition. But more of that later.

The Bean Curd Maker and his family are Ch'ao An speakers who have been in the same business since before they left China. The choice of their destination in Hong Kong came about because of friends from Swatow. The Bean Curd Maker's father joined them in 1957. Technically, his home is still in the town across the strait with a younger son who works as a laborer but, in the summer of 1961, he was sleeping on a crude bed in the room which serves as the bean curd factory. He is so old that he can walk only with difficulty. The Fortunate Wife of the Farmer says his children do not treat him as well as they should, or more specifically that they do not share with him the best of their food and also leave him the task of doing his own laundry.

In the Bean Curd Maker's family there are also his wife, who at forty-five is nine years younger than he is, their five children—four daughters aged twenty-three, seventeen, ten, and six, and a son of four. The eldest daughter is married and her thirty-year-old Ch'ao An husband works in a plastics factory in Sai Wan. They have one son who is less than a year old. He spends a good deal of time in a cloth carrier tied on his mother's back.

When the weather is hot, the Bean Curd Maker wears an abbreviated costume consisting of blue or black shorts and black loafers on his feet. His wife who has an animated face and waved bobbed hair seemed to be in a different outfit on each of our visits but with our interest focussed on the manufacture of bean curd, it was probably overlooked that some of the garments were underclothes, easily confused with sam fu unless one is interested in distinguishing them. In any event, we noted a green spotted fu worn with a brown and yellow diamond pattern on a white sam, and another day, a smart green and black diamond-patterned sam fu. While working in the factory, her feet were bare and she had removed her sam leaving a blue-patterned undercoat. She had a green jade bracelet on her left wrist, however, gold loop earrings, and a gold chain around her neck. Her two elder daughters, both of whom also have waved bobbed hair once appeared in identical, flowered mulberry fu but different unmatched sam. They also wear no shoes when working on the wet floor of the factory, but the eldest daughter put on green strap Japanese style slippers later. She, like her mother, wears gold loop earrings, a gold chain around her neck, and a gold band on the third finger of her left hand. Another time we saw her working in a light-colored white and blue fu and a yellow spotted undercoat. Her next younger sister put on a matching sam when she finished work. She, too, owns gold earrings and also a wristwatch as does the elder sister. They bought the wristwatches with money that they earned while working in a factory across the strait. "All the girls had wristwatches," one of them explained. Interestingly enough, the two older girls own cheong sam, but the elder says they seldom wear them.

Besides the bean curd factory to take care of, the family has a sow and four young pigs as well as over a hundred chickens. They even have one pigeon as a pet. They grow no vegetables, lacking both space and time. There is one cat but no dog in the family. The Bean Curd Maker and his wife enjoy drinking all kinds of liquor very much, and both he and his father smoke.

Amusements do not take an outstanding place in the family. No one admits to any great interest in movies but all go occasionally. No one knows how to play mah-jongg. They do not own a radio, but that is perhaps irrelevant since that of the Fortunate Wife of the Farmer is often playing loudly only a few feet away. The married daughter says she does not know how to swim, but her father claims that he can. Sometimes his wife goes into the water.

No one except the son-in-law goes to Hong Kong very often. The parents walk to Lung Shing daily to sell their bean curd, and the married daughter goes there often after dinner, just for a walk or to attend a movie. She knows of Tung Pak Wan but has never been there, and she had not heard of Chung Nam Wan. This daughter had six or seven years of formal education in China. The oldest unmarried daughter goes to a government night school on Monday, Tuesday, and Friday evenings in the town across the strait. The school has only two years of middle school and she is in the first. Her father has also had a primary school education, but her mother has had none. The latter has not only never been to Tung Pak Wan but said about Chung Nam Wan that there was no such place on the island.

One of the most interesting things about the Bean Curd Maker's family and that of the Fortunate Wife of the Farmer is the lack of social interaction. They live and work a few feet apart as though the other family did not exist. We never observed these juxtaposed neighbors exchange a remark, yet they seem to be superficially friendly. Even more notable, there are a dozen children in the two families, but we never saw any of the two family groups playing together. In the course of time, however, we discovered that there was a problem that caused discord. The Bean Curd Makers say they had been promised that there would be sufficient water for their business in the family well. But the Farmer needed considerable water also, and it has consequently been necessary for the Bean Curd Makers to go down to the seemingly inexhaustible supply of the Enterprising Woman and then climb back half way up the hill with water, a wearisome and time-consuming task.

The Bean Curd Makers, as has been suggested, acquired their residence under peculiar conditions. It was when the Fortunate Wife of the Farmer needed money to pay the debts contracted on account of litigation. At her proposal, an agreement was made between the two families whereby the Bean Curd Makers loaned her $1,500 for the right to residence and working space on the other's Sai Mi Wan property for seven years, at the end of which time the money is to be repaid and the Bean Curd Makers are to move out. After a few years in Sai Mi Wan, not only the water situation disturbs the Bean Curd Makers, but they find the distance to the market unnecessarily great.

They do not mention the inconveniences of a house that is patently too small for their sizable family. The single story building is built up of clapboards on a low concrete wall with a shed roof of wood and tarpaper sloping toward the house of their juxtaposed neighbors. A four-foot roof has been added over the porch. A window on the front and one on the hill side can be closed by clapboard shutters that swing from the top. The inside of the house is divided in two by a masonite partition. It is not a place into which one goes to visit as there is literally no space to turn around, and even outside, the porch is cluttered to its roof with baskets and five-gallon cans. The explanation of this concentration of impediments lies in the fact that the house was originally a pig pen enclosing an area ten by fifteen feet square minus the thick walls.

The grandson in the Bean Curd Maker's family was born free of charge in the new clinic across the strait where mothers must supply their own food, however. He became the eighth person who sleeps in the house. In general, doctors with Western training are preferred in the family because they are said to cure more quickly. The eldest daughter admits that she would like to have two or three more children which will almost certainly force her to find a home of her own. She seems to be happy in her marriage which was one of free choice. Her parents were married semi-blind, having been allowed to see each other once. Her mother is of the opinion that it would be improper to marry either a father's sister's or a mother's brother's son, but that to marry mother's sister's son is all right.

The family appreciates the British Government in Hong Kong because, as they say, life was not so good in China. The married daughter states that she has no religion but this point of view does not conflict with the traditional religious behavior of the household. For instance, the whole family enjoyed a feast on the 16th of the 6th month to honor the Earth God who keeps devils out of the house. Actually, such ceremonial recognition is appropriate on the 2nd or the 16th of any month, but the 16th of the 6th is the most popular date. At the feast, there was a sizable fish and roast pork. The married daughter said the family, rather than eating chicken, preferred buying a bigger than usual fish. On the 15th of the 7th month, they will also have a feast. Other feasts are enjoyed on Ch'ing Ming, on the 5th of the 5th month, the 15th of the 8th, at the Winter Festival, and, of course, at New Year's. We noted a commonplace pat kwa (pa kua) plaque with its octagonal design of whole and broken lines above the door of the house. It is there "to keep the house safe," we were told. Also over the door is pasted a horizontal orange-red paper with the characters chiu ts'oi wong seung (chao ts'ai wang hsiang) which can be loosely translated as "welcome money—prosperous mien."* Beside the door on the right hand side (as one faces it) is another red paper with t'in ti fu mo (t'ien ti fu mu), or "heaven-earth-father-mother" in black, and below it, four feet above the floor, is fastened a can painted red to hold incense sticks for the Earth God. Also, it was said, sometimes the family visits the Hung Shing temple near the ferry.

The bean curd factory. Factory is perhaps too imposing a name for the place in which bean curd is produced at Sai Mi Wan since the establishment is nothing more than an area about twenty feet square covered by a shed roof. In fact, if the stone mortar were removed, it would appear to be the kitchen of the Fortunate Wife of the Farmer's house to which it is juxtaposed. The area has a concrete floor and concrete walls at the rear and to the south along the hill. The north wall is that of the house and on the west, there is no wall at all, a curtain of bag cloth being pulled down when the rain drives in. The well with inadequate water is just outside the area. At the rear of the factory is a typical pig food stove of the sawdust

---

*By rare coincidence, the Mandarin and English words "mien" are practically synonymous.

burning type, an important piece of equipment in the manufacture of bean curd. It has a tile chimney extending through the roof, the pipes being held rigid by three bamboos wired equidistantly around them. The shed roof, which has a wood frame, has a small section at the higher north end which can be pushed up to give ventilation. Near the stove is a red can and in it are some burned incense sticks. The additional and distinguishing feature of the factory is the gasoline motor-driven stone mortar which is located at the front of the kitchen and away from the house (Fig. 27.1). There is no electricity despite the fact that the near neighbors have it.

Cluttering up the relatively small amount of open area are buckets for the liquid curd, trays in which to form the cakes, bags and cloths used in the process, brass ladles, gasoline cans converted into water containers, four assorted stools, and several baskets of sawdust, besides various odds

Fig. 27.1. The Bean Curd Machine

and ends which chance seemed to have deposited so long ago that they are no longer noticed as useless appurtenances of the place. As has been mentioned, since the Bean Curd Maker's eighty-two-year-old father came to stay with him, a double-decked wood bed has been put up next to the pig stove for the old man to sleep on, which addition supplies a most homely, domestic touch to the factory despite the rusty tin cans, empty bottles, and cobwebs encrusting the bed's upper surface. Fortunately, the aged one resides in the driest corner of the area for, when it rains very hard, it is wet in the factory.

Grinding the beans. The initial stage in producing bean curd is the grinding of the yellow soy beans, which are imported from the United States. Ten to twenty catties are soaked in water four or five hours (three hours in summer, since they get soft if soaked more at that season). From a large enamel bowl, they are slowly poured by means of an enamel cup into the top of the mortar, which has a metal rim forming a hemispherical repository 5″ high. Slowly the beans go down through a hole in the turning stone and the white curd immediately begins to stream from underneath the turning stone into a trough around it and out of a rusty metal spout in front into a wood bucket. The stone mortar is 18″ in diameter and 5″ high. It moves counterclockwise against a lower matching stone and is revolved normally at a speed of thirty revolutions per minute by a vertical steel shaft 36″ in length with a pinion gear on top 7½″ in diameter. The latter is turned by a small interlocking gear on a horizontal shaft 18″ long with a wheel on the end 18″ in diameter. This wheel is moved by a belt connected to a small wheel 22″ below it on a one-cylinder gasoline motor that makes an infernal racket when running.

Some of the first bean curd is poured back into the mortar with additional water. Then more beans are added and more water. The bucket below the mortar gradually fills, and a second replaces the first. Often the curd wells back into the bowl-like top of the turning mortar and sometimes the strain of grinding is too much for the old equipment and the vertical shaft breaks loose from the heavy disk, which looks like granite. The Bean Curd Maker calls it "mountain stone." Then the vertical steel shaft is lifted out and the small steel socket which fits into the stone is slipped off. The latter is fitted to the hole in the stone by pouring lead around it. This metal, when the fitting breaks loose (it is hoped not more than once a month), is melted in an old sardine can on a kerosene stove and poured back around the socket, the can being held by a pair of pliers. After a minute it is hardened by splashing some liquid bean curd around it, and the grinding continues. Such a break requires fifteen to twenty minutes to repair. A stop in the grinding operation also occurs when the motor runs out of fuel. The little tank hung on the wall is taken down and rested in the trough around the grindstone while several cupfuls of gasoline are poured into it and then a small amount of oil. Only a minimum gets into the bean curd trough. After it is hung up again, and its short plastic pipe is pushed out of the way, the motor is started with a pull of a rope. Such a delay consumes only five or six minutes. Unfortunately, the equipment is getting old and the vertical shaft periodically rises up out of its socket slipping the crosspin out of the vertical sockets in the pinion above, which makes one loose half-turn and catches the pin again, the shaft falling down with a sharp bang. If one subtracts these various delays, forty-five minutes may be considered an average time for grinding.

When all the beans have been fed into the mill and ground, water is run through to clear it. Then the mortar is stopped and the grindstone is lifted by hand, fingers being put into one of the two opposing small notches in its side. Then a second person pours water in the top, which comes streaming through. The cleansing is reasonably thorough as it is necessary to prevent souring the next batch of curd.

Straining the curd. The two buckets of curd collected from the mortar are poured one at a time into a bag made of a special cotton cloth which is folded into a double square 31″ on a side and sewn along one edge, leaving two open. The bag rests in a shallow wood tub 15″ in diameter with two solid opposing semicircular wood handles projecting horizontally near the top and a second set of four near the bottom which support the tub in the top of a larger one. The latter is 17″ in diameter at the top and 10″ high. The smaller tub, in which the bag of ground meal rests is also 10″ high and has four holes spaced evenly around the edges of the bottom which result from the fact that two of the wood pieces from which the bottom is made do not quite reach the vertical sides.

With the tubs in position, the ground soy meal in the bag in the upper tub is squeezed by picking up the long, pennant-like ends of the bag, twisting them first together and then around the neck of the bag with one hand, both hands being used thereafter to knead the bag, thus expressing the liquid curd which drains from the upper tub into the lower one. In the final straining, the neck of the bag itself is twisted tightly. The straining process requires only three or four minutes. The liquid that falls into the lower tub is the desired product, the residual meal being dumped into a gasoline can and ultimately fed to the pigs.

Cooking the curd. In preparation for boiling the curd, a couple of quarts of water are thrown into the pig food stove pan and whisked around to wash it, then scooped out. The first bucket of strained bean curd may then be dumped into the pan perhaps fifteen minutes before the fire in the stove is lighted. This latter act is accomplished by using paper and kerosene, sawdust then being gradually added, pushed down onto the grate with a wire periodically, and coaxed to burn evenly with a frayed bamboo fan. The second bucket of curd is added to the first and the undiluted liquid is gradually brought to a boil, which requires about forty minutes. Infrequently, the bean curd is stirred with a wood paddle, but one must be careful that the liquid does not burn or boil over. Once boiled, the curd is removed with a metal ladle into buckets 15½″ in diameter and 16″ deep. A large enamel bowl being held under the ladle to catch any drippings. The last remnants of the boiled curd are scooped out with a shovel-shaped spoon, after which any burned material adhering to the pan is scraped off and consigned to the fire. Pig food is then cooked in the hot pan from which the curd has been removed.

Solidifying the curd. The next stage is to put two heaping spoonfuls (Chinese porcelain spoon) of shik fui (shih hui), or lime,* and one of tseung sham fan (chiang shan fen), or starch, into a little of the bean curd liquid which had been left unboiled in the tub into which it was first strained. This mixture is stirred with the hand. The boiled bean curd is then poured on top of it. The latter sets in about ten minutes. The one inch of foam which appears on top of the solidifying curd is scraped off and added to the pig food cooking on the stove.

In the first grinding of the day, about five catties of bean curd are destined for deep-frying, squares about an inch on a side and a half inch thick, as well as some two inch squares, being dipped into boiling peanut oil. On the top of curd used for this purpose, a small brass ladle of salted water is sprinkled after the foam has been removed. The whole process of readying the boiled curd requires ten minutes and the deep-frying only ten minutes more.

Making the curd cakes. Without waiting for the curd to set further, the makers begin ladling it out into small cloths placed in wood forms on trays. These implements must be described. The forms are made from crossed pieces of wood ¼″ wide and 1¼″ high so arranged as to make enclosed squares. The forms are of two sizes: one with twenty-five squares of 2¾″ on a side, the other with sixteen 4″ squares. The forms rest loosely on square trays made of several boards with a pair of cross pieces on the bottom ends to hold them. The area of the boards is 19″ by 17″, being slightly greater than the maximum covered by the forms. To ready a form of either size for the bean curd, it is placed on a board, and 8″ square napkins of the same material as the previously described bag are laid over alternating squares of the form, the sides of the napkins being oriented

---

*This is a much more expensive form of lime than that used in making purple ink. Two years later we were told by the Bean Curd Makers that they were using only shik ko fan (shih kao fen), or gypsum.

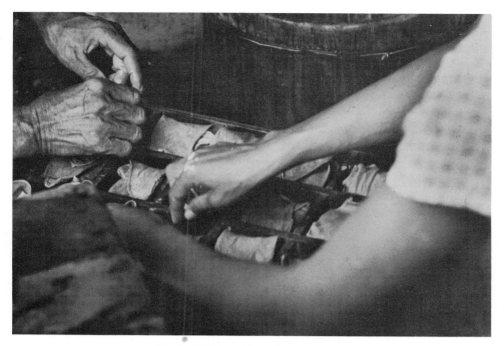
Fig. 27.2. Wrapped Bean Curd Squares

diagonally to the sides of the form. Then the corners of the napkins are folded in. This done, the remaining squares are covered with napkins, but the corners remain folded out.

It is these latter squares that are filled first, the custard-like curd being transferred from the bucket with bright, shiny, handleless ladles of brass 5¼" long and 4" wide. The corners of the napkins in the squares that have been filled are then flipped back over the curd, and the corners of the napkins in the alternating squares opened out. The remaining squares on the tray are then filled with curd and the tray is passed on to another worker with half of the curd squares exposed.

In the next stage of the work, the exposed squares of curd are tightly wrapped by pulling the corners of the napkins over them with enough force so that the cloth seems smooth. Then the first half of the napkins, already folded, are rewrapped to make them as tight as the alternate group (Fig. 27.2). This done, the tray is put on a stand (actually a box) and the form lifted off leaving the cloth-wrapped packages of curd which are then pushed together in the center of the tray. As each set of forms is completed the tray of packages is placed on top of the previous one, thus by its weight suppressing some liquid from the packages below. Ladling out all the curd into eleven trays with smaller squares (275 cakes) and partially filling a larger one (eleven cakes) required thirty-five minutes of two adults' time. It should be mentioned that in making the larger cakes, a small rectangle of bamboo (1¼" x ¾" x ⅛") is placed momentarily on top of the curd to impress its own design, no reason being attributed for doing so except custom.

The final stage in the production of bean curd is unwrapping the packages and placing their contents in a gasoline can half full of water in which they are transported to the market. This can be done as soon as the last form has been removed from a tray of squares. On one occasion it was noted that when only four trays of curd were made, an empty fifth tray was put on top and then a gasoline can two-thirds full of water added for twenty minutes to aid in suppressing the remaining liquid. Finally, it may be recorded that removing the 286 cakes of curd from their wrappings and placing them in water (including the removal of the bamboo pieces from eleven) requires less than half an hour of two adults' time, one of whom stopped shortly before the task was completed. The cakes of curd are then of such a consistency that they do not suffer from the necessary minimum of handling. Also, if not broken, they do not absorb the protective water in which they are carried and which keeps them fresh. It may be mentioned that to keep the napkins from souring after they have been unwrapped, they are put into a large enamel bowl and kept wet until their next use just before which they are rinsed out in fresh water. Straining bags are washed after each use, however.

Economics. The usual product of the factory is small squares of pressed bean curd. Some squares of a larger size are made however, as also much larger pieces, which are cut according to a customer's purse. Also, fried bean curd squares are produced. The raw material is yellow soy beans, which cost $.50 per catty. Several hundred catties are usually purchased at one time. Sawdust for fuel costs $.50 for a large basket and somewhat more than a basket is used each day. Shik fui (lime) costs $.50 a catty as it is bought in lots of 5 to 10 catties at a time. Starch costs $.40 a catty. Gasoline costs about $3 for a five-gallon (Imperial four-gallon) can, but only $1 to $1.50 worth is used each day. About six Chinese ounces of peanut oil are used to fry five catties of curd, and the oil, sold by weight, costs $1.20 per catty (16 Chinese ounces), making a daily expense of about $.40. There are also other expenses which are minor. The stone mortar (which originally cost $600) has to be resurfaced twice a year by a professional stone cutter who charges $10 each time. The 8″ square napkins cost $9 per hundred and the bags of the same material, a little over a dollar. These articles, curiously enough, because of the character of the cloth, can only be purchased in Sham Shui Po, in the southwest corner of the New Territories adjacent to Kowloon and a long way from Sai Mi Wan. They last about a year and a half, however. The napkins, which are always kept wet, in time turn coffee-colored and reddish brown in the center.

Normal daily production of the factory consists of two grinds of beans totaling twenty-five to thirty catties (the lesser amount in summer, the larger in winter). Taking the small figure we can estimate the cost as $12.50. For sawdust, $.60 may be added, for gasoline and oil, $1.50, for peanut oil, $.40, and perhaps $.50 would cover all other expenses.

The income can be computed on the basis of 560 small squares, four of which sell for $.10 producing $14, and sixteen large squares which sell two for $.10 yielding $.80, plus two large soy cakes which add $1.20, plus five catties of fried squares selling for $1.20 a catty or $6, making a total of $22. There are also about sixty catties of residual meal each day. This sells for pig food at $.05 per catty adding $3 to the daily income.

Expenses and income can be summarized as follows:

Expenses

25 catties of soy beans		$12.50
Sawdust (for fuel)		.60
Gasoline and oil		1.50
Peanut oil		.40
Misc. (lime, starch, etc.)		.50
	Total	$15.50

Income

560 small squares at 4 for $.10		$14.00
16 large squares at 2 for $.10		.80
2 large soy cakes		1.20
5 catties of fried squares at $1.20		6.00
60 catties of residual meal at $.05		3.00
	Total	$25.00

The profit by this rough computation is $9.50 per day or $285 per thirty-day month. The Bean Curd Maker himself keeps no records and claims to be unsure of his monthly profits.

The question of rent should be mentioned. Actually the Bean Curd Makers pay none as their factory and house are supplied to them in lieu of interest on money loaned to the owners, as has been explained. Perhaps $20 should be subtracted from the income, however, to cover the assumed rent of the factory area.

Fortunately, full production can be maintained almost every day, and the personnel consists of only one family. The husband and wife do most of the work although they receive significant assistance from their married daughter who lives at home, and less certain help from a grown unmarried daughter who sometimes works in a factory. Also the seven-year-old daughter is effective at placing the napkins in the trays, and the five-year-old son tries to do likewise, but his father discourages him for obvious reasons. Nevertheless, the child pats a curd square affectionately

Fig. 27.3. Bean Curd for Sale

whenever he has a chance. It is perhaps not surprising that none of the family eats much of the product. The parents occasionally consume a few pieces of fried squares but the children will eat no bean curd at all. They say that they see enough of it without facing it at meals.

The bean curd is manufactured twice a day, grinding being carried out first about 4:00 A.M. and then between 10:30 and 11:00. The product is carried into Lung Shing at 7:30 to 8:00 in the morning and again about 2:00 in the afternoon and sold on the street near the market (Fig. 27.3). To do this no permit is needed. If a little of the bean curd is not purchased in the morning, it can be held over to the afternoon, and the fresh afternoon cakes may last until the next day but, on the other hand, the squares spoil easily. Happily, there is not much competition in the business, there being only one other manufacturer on the island. Many people make tau fu fa (tou fu hua), or bean curd flowers, however, which is the name given to the commonly eaten yogurt-like curd before it is made into cakes and pressed into the consistency of a jelly. It is only the latter procedure which requires the fine grinding by a machine and time-consuming hand labor.

Business is at its best at Chinese New Year's when as much as fifty catties of fried curd squares may be sold in a day. For the rest of the year, however, production is not stopped unless there is a typhoon. Sales are direct to the consumers and they buy just as much when it rains. As the Bean Curd Makers say, "After all, one must eat."

There are also minor sources of income. One day the Bean Curd Maker's wife was observed selling seven gunnysacks (in which soy beans were delivered) to a man who came specially to buy them. They were of various quality and, after some pretty bargaining, the lot went for $4.20.

28. The Fish Dryers

The fish drying plant. At the foot of the bay between the Papermaker's and the Shipbuilder's Son's Villa is a fish drying plant (Fig. 14.2). It consists of two sizable buildings: the larger extending along the beach northerly to the end of the property, the smaller perpendicular to the beach. Between the two structures is a generous passageway that ends at the back in steps which go up ten feet to a twenty-five foot wide terrace leveled off on the hill. In front of each building is a wood platform extending out some twenty feet over the beach from the retaining wall which rises three and a half feet above the pebble beach. The platform, of which the northerly part is removable, is supported at the outer edge on beams stretching between a row of concrete pillars about twenty feet apart. Twenty-five feet seaward of these pillars is another parallel row of solitary pillars now unused. Under the platform in front of the larger building are two concrete salting tanks five feet deep, six feet wide, and more or less eight feet long. Between the two platforms, concrete stairs go down to the beach and extend in a yard-wide walk forty-five feet to provide for the loading and unloading of boats (Fig. 28.1).

The larger building of the fish drying plant is essentially a shed with a flat wood and tarpaper roof at the same level as the adjoining rear terrace via which fish that have been spread out to dry are brought on racks. This shed, used primarily to store fish, is approximately fifty feet long and half as wide. The stone abutment of the terrace serves as a rear wall and five concrete pillars in median and front lines provide the other supports of the roof. There is a concrete floor in the shed and waist high concrete walls between all but two of the outer pillars. Otherwise the shed is open, although curtained in rainy and cold weather with burlap sacking as much for the protection of the workers as for that of the fish. It should be added that in 1960, Typhoon Mary collapsed the whole roof with a consequent loss of about 10,000 dollars.

The smaller of the two buildings has a gable roof of tarpaper and wood and is placed perpendicularly to the sea wall. It is twenty-five feet long and about twenty feet wide along the bay. It has a concrete floor and eighteen-inch high walls with one concrete corner at the southerly end of the property. Only the southeasterly half of the building is enclosed, one wall reaching up to the ridgepole. The material is very rough clapboards and, near the top at one side, sheet metal. Besides serving as very primi-

Fig. 28.1. The Fish Dryers

tive sleeping quarters for the two male fish dryers, this building is piled full of baskets, tubs, boxes, and crates of various descriptions and sizes. Under the roof of the open half, the men scrape the fish near a platform scale. At the end of the building is a large area partly cut into the hill and covered with a shed roof which, since it contains a pig stove and meals are cooked there, may be called a kitchen, although it too is dominated by baskets and tubs. There is no electricity in the establishment.

This drying plant is owned by two brothers who have inherited their fish business in Sai Ying Pun west of the Central District of Hong Kong, where they live. The elder, who comes to Sai Mi Wan not infrequently, is a grandfather at forty-six, while the younger, about thirty, is remarkable in having nine sons and no daughters. They have an agreement to supply 15,000 to 17,000 catties of salted fish each month, which are sold to the government for prisoners' and refugees' meals. To produce this food the owners buy cheap fish (which are mostly small) in the wholesale fish market across the strait. If the fish are fresh, they have some of them taken to Sai Ying Pun where they are salted, but there they have space to spread out only about twenty drying racks, a disadvantage that led them to find more room and set up the establishment at Sai Mi Wan. The remainder of the fish is brought by their sampan directly to Sai Mi Wan. The sampan comes irregularly since obtaining fish for prisoners' food depends on whether any of the poor grades are available, and also on the price. They also dry better grades of fish for both export and local sale, however. These likewise are transported on the sampan to the island plant.

Drying the fish. The fish arrive in Sai Mi Wan in baskets containing about sixty catties each. They are picked over by the workers and certain odd types of fish over five inches in length are cut open and cleaned. Thus readied, the fish are taken to the salting tank which, after being washed out and the drain replugged, is covered on the bottom with a few shovelfuls of salt. Then more salt is spread over the surface of the fish in a basket and worked in among them. This done, the basket is dumped into the salting tank with a motion that spreads the fish. This process may be continued until the tank is full, but that is not usually the case as a tank holds approximately 12,000 catties equivalent to two hundred baskets of fish, which are much more than ordinarily purchased. (Actually, when only small amounts of fish are obtained, they are salted in tubs.) One man, who does the salting and pouring, can load one of the large tanks in three or four hours. Fish are left in the tank for two nights. One the second day the fish exude a good deal of water which is released through the drain before the fish are removed.

Once salted, the fish are shoveled into baskets again and removed from the tank, a ladder being used when needed. Then the scales are scraped off almost all fish with a knife made by splitting an eight-inch section of bamboo that has grown to an inch and a half in diameter. Fish that arrive in such poor condition that they are in danger of being broken apart by such scraping are not scaled, however. Following removal of the scales, the fish are soaked in sea water for half an hour to eliminate the excess salt. Curiously, although the hands of the workers are in water much of the time, they say their skin never cracks, a fact they attribute to the oil from the fish.

Finally, the salted fish are laid out on bamboo slats half an inch wide and 46″ long which have been tied with six evenly spaced rows of twine into lengths of 112″. Each bamboo mat has first been stretched over two heavy, parallel wood poles extending perhaps ten inches beyond the mats. On these, the fish are transported by two workers to the drying areas on the roof of the shed, on the adjoining terrace, on the front platforms, and sometimes also on any nearby area that is flat enough to support them.

In good weather, two or three days are required for drying—only two toward the end of the year which is usually ideal for the purpose, but often much longer in the rainy spring or summer typhoon season. At the threat of rain, the fish racks are stacked. The first rack is extended between two boxes; then a piece of wood two inches square in cross section is put across the parallel bars at each end. Next, a second rack is added and the process repeated until there are half a dozen, the group then being covered with a large canvas which is tied in place. This is also done every night as no one can be sure that it will not rain.

When dry, the salted fish are reloaded onto the owners' sampan, then taken around the island and across the strait to be trucked to Sai Ying Pun. Fish to be sold locally are sent out in baskets which cost $5 each when new, but are actually acquired for no extra payment when the fish are first bought. Tubs likewise are included with purchases of the fish that come from China. Dried fish for export, if small, are shipped in burlap bags or, if large (over five inches long), in wood boxes.

Actually, the types of fish that are dried are innumerable. One of the better grades is called wong fa (huang hua), or yellow flowers (yellow croaker).* These actually come from China so salted that they are considered inedible by the cats, which will steal one or two of the others. This amount of preservative, however, enables the Chinese authorities to hold the fish off the market indefinitely if they choose. Once in hand, the scales have to be scraped off with a bamboo knife. Then the fish are soaked in sea water an hour. With much of the salt thus eliminated, they are once again dried and thus become ready for shipment. Such fish are sold to feed Chinese miners in Borneo.

It should be noted that these Chinese salted fish lose only about 25

---

*For more precise identifications of the fish mentioned in the text, see Appendix D.

per cent of their weight in preparation, while ordinary fresh fish dried for prisoners' meals will lose 30 per cent. It is theoretically possible to process about 1700 catties of Chinese salted fish in a day at the plant in Sai Mi Wan, thereby producing between 1200 and 1300 catties for sale.

Another type of fish is acquired after they have been salted locally. These small filefish known as sha mang (sha meng), five inches or less in length, are merely redried after peeling off the skins, a laborious process which necessitates wearing gloves. Afterward, the fish are put out in the sun. Because of the effort involved and the loss in weight of fifty-five per cent, sha mang sell at a relatively high price.

More desirable are the hung sin (hung hsien), or red goatfish, ranging from five to nine inches long, which are brought fresh from the wholesale market across the strait. Despite the name, they have a distinct chartreuse yellow line running along both sides when observed in the baskets at the Fish Dryer's. This is simply because the red disappears when the fish are taken out of the sun. They are processed in the same manner as are the fish salted for prisoners' food. None is eviscerated. When dry, they are packed into boxes and shipped off to Singapore where they are much appreciated by the overseas Chinese.

One of the rarer and more expensive products of the fish drying plant are dried fish for export to the United States where they are ground up for poultry feed. Tiny fish called kung ü (kung yü), or anchovies, are obtained from the wholesale market. These little fish have to be steamed, after which they are dried on twilled mats. No salt is used, and the other distinguishing feature is that their dried weight is only 15 per cent of what it was before steaming. This factor, of course, is largely responsible for their high selling price.

Even more expensive, however, are the ts'o pak (chiu pai), or white herring, a slender dark fish which measured from fifteen to eighteen inches long. These are salted in tubs. Before putting them out to dry, the head and gills are covered with a wrapping of thin paper to make sure that no worms can get through these openings. A piece of sha chi (sha chih), a kind of tough paper, about nine inches square is placed under the head of the ts'o pak after the fish has been washed off in a tub. Then more water is added to the paper to make it stick. This done, a second sheet is added, and then a third after which the tops of the forward edges of the papers of one side are wrapped over the nose of the fish, then a next fold pulled up toward the head, and so on, with more applications of water by wetting the hand. The paper which is thin and strong adheres tightly. Sha chi costs $8 for forty large sheets, each of which is cut into nine small ones, thus adding a little over two cents to the cost of drying each fish.

Ts'o pak require four or five good days of drying before they are packed in peanut oil in cans for shipment to America where they must pass inspection by government officials. It is interesting to note in the case of these fish that not only are they never eviscerated but also they do not even have the scales removed as there would be a meaningful economic loss in so doing.

Sometimes the wong fa previously mentioned come refrigerated from China and measure from fourteen to twenty-one inches in length. As might be expected, they have a distinct yellow color which is characteristic of the ventral areas. These fish are distinguished by being salted in brine for only one night. They, like the ts'o pak, then have their heads and gills covered with paper. After drying the usual period, some are sold on the local market, some shipped to Singapore.

A still larger fish is the tai ü (ta yü), a kind of pond-cultivated carp which falls into the class of that delicacy known as mui heung (mei hsiang), or rotten fragrance. These fish, which have a split tail, are already dried in a peculiar manner before being acquired for the Sai Mi Wan plant. Although measuring from twenty-three to twenty-six inches in length, they are neither cleaned nor soaked in salt brine. They are merely laid on the racks where salt is worked into the gills. The final drying requires expert care and space that is not available to the people who first preserve them. This type of fish, which costs more than pork, is greatly appreciated by the affluent Cantonese.

Scores of species of fish have been processed in the salting plant during the years of its operation and on almost every visit we saw new ones. The methods of treating the fish, however, seem to conform essentially to those that have been described above, although without doubt many minor mysteries remain in the unconscious practices of the manager.

The fish drying business in Sai Mi Wan began about 1959 when, following the death of their father, the owners decided to expand the family concern and obtained a Crown Permit for the land. Tax on the property is about $400 a year which is said to be twice what a farmer would have to pay for the same area. Two Fish Dryers are employed who live at the plant, and usually two women come in to work by the day, although the number will vary according to need.

Economics. The daily cost of operation, which includes only the salaries of four persons and their food, other things being supplied, comes to $30. Of this amount about $3 is expended for food. The women are paid $4 a day, but the manager's assistant, an old man, makes only $75 a month. The manager himself labors consistently and with the even disposition of a man who feels himself well paid; it would seem that he makes about $500 a month. Working hours are from nine in the morning until about six in the evening.

Since the amount of preparation, and the type, quantity, and prices of fish vary, it is difficult to reduce the economics of fish drying to one tabular statement, and even our intelligent informant, the plant manager, is unable to do so. We can produce some figures, however.

Ideally, the cheap fish salted for prisoners cost $7 to $8 a hundred catties, but sometimes they are not available, and other fish may have to be bought that cost up to $15 if the contract is to be fulfilled. As $30 a hundred catties is paid for finished salted fish, they may then have to be supplied at a loss since the processing costs about $15. Fortunately for the owners, they can present their problem to the wholesaler, and then government agents who are thoroughly aware of the prices for fish on the market will recommend an adjustment in payments which at least allows for a minimum profit. It may be added that there is an incidental increment from the fish scales that are scraped off and sold to farmers who pay $20 per 100 catties for this fertilizer delivered in the New Territories.

Such security cannot be expected from other sources, and losses or near losses can consequently follow. For example, in the case of wong fa of the type that comes salted from China, we can indicate prices adjusted to a theoretical four-day schedule as follows:

Expenses

6,800 catties at $24 per 100	$1,632
Labor for four days at $35 per day	140
	$1,772

Income

5,100 catties at $36 per 100	$1,836

Here a profit of $64 is an inadequate return for four days.

In another case, that of the salted sha mang, the figures are even more instructive.

400 catties at $6.50 per 100	$ 26
Labor for four days at $35 per day	140
	$166
180 catties at $45 per 100	$ 81

Here there is an actual loss of $85.

When the manager was asked while we watched the staff of four people working what sense there was in laboring to lose money, he pointed out, courteous as always, that there had not been one good day in five for drying and, that since they had nothing else to do, by working there would not be a full loss for his time. Sha mang would not be profitable even if another woman were hired, thus cutting the labor costs to $13.50 a day. As the manager pointed out, only once or twice before had the owners bought them, apparently realizing the cost of the processing but having no choice of fish to fill their contract.

In other cases, on paper the profits may seem high. For example, fresh hung sin may cost $13 per 100 catties and sell from $32 to $35 per 100. The process of drying will cause a loss of 30 per cent in the weight of the fish, however. Salt costs $8 per 100 catties and 2,500 catties will be used for a theoretical full tank load of fish (12,000 catties). Thus we can compute:

Expenses

12,000 catties of fish at $13 per 100	$1,560
2,500 catties of salt at $8 per 100	200
Labor for four days at $35	140
	$1,900

Income

Sale of 8,400 catties of fish at $33 per 100	$2,772

The seeming profit of $872 in four days is misleading. The owners can seldom buy or sell so much hung sin at one time. The owners' salaries and other business expenses are not included. Furthermore, there is only space to dry 2,000 catties of these fish at one time. Finally, and what is most significant, the weather may preclude drying for days on end. In the winter months the fish will not spoil, but in the summer, even dried fish have to be refrigerated to be kept very long as they will otherwise become too infested by worms.

In theory, one of the most profitable kinds of fish to process are those that are shipped to the United States for poultry food. They sell for $120 to $130 for 100 catties, whereas the cost of production is from $80 to $90 per 100, leaving a profit of about $40. Since these fish lose 85 per cent in weight, only a few hundred catties could be produced in a day were it possible to obtain so many fish, so much help, and the necessary demand for the product.

The same conditions apply to the ts'o pak which are bought for $360 to $370 per 100 catties and sell for a hundred dollars more, with a loss of only 20 per cent of weight. Frozen wong fa from China cost only $130 per 100 catties and sell for $170, with a loss of 30 per cent, while tai ü cost $240 and sell for $370 with a loss of 35 per cent in weight.

The market for the various types of dried and salted fish is furthermore affected by various unexpected factors. Some years, for example, charitable organizations from abroad have given money to have fish dried for the poor. In 1961, however, such money seems to have been used for the purchase of rice. Considerable losses can be brought about by weather conditions, as previously mentioned, and rats do some damage, although two cats are employed to worry and kill them. In consequence the rats tend to stay away. Hawks or other birds, incidentally, are no problem.

Our personal attachment to the fish drying plant was reinforced by a small and curious gray bitch who would not give up barking at a stranger no matter how much discussion we had. No doubt she was influenced in part by certain feelings of insecurity recently instilled by giving birth to three puppies. She also inspired a certain affection because of her unusual name which we added to our vocabulary of Cantonese slang. She was called La Cha Kwai (Hsia Cha Kuei*), or Dirty Ghost, which seemed singularly apt.

The Fish Dryers. The master of Dirty Ghost was a forty-eight-year-old man who came to Hong Kong in 1950 when the Communists took over his rice store in the Hsin Hui district of Kwangtung (Fig. 3.1). He is a laconic looking individual with a wonderful tuft of long brown hairs growing from a mole one inch below the left corner of his mouth. This Fish Dryer served in the Chinese 19th Route Army from the time he was sixteen years of age, finally holding the rank of p'ai ch'eung (p'ai ch'ang).† In the course of such a life, he has traveled over much of China or at least as far as the Russian border. He has also been in Taiwan. Soon after he left China his wife, who had been chosen by his mother, died, and in 1952, his son, then five years of age, was brought to him in Hong Kong by his concubine, whom he chose himself. She was lonesome in Hong Kong, however, and returned to China where she, too, has since died. In 1961, the son was working as a messenger in the Education Department of the Hong Kong Government, having refused to remain in the high school to which he had been admitted following graduation from primary school. The manager of the fish drying plant, who had six years of education in China himself, also has a second-hand metal shop in Stanley, which a friend looks after. This Fish Dryer who, as well as his associate, has worked at Sai Mi Wan for a year, wears a white T-shirt and shiny black fu plus wood-soled slippers with a band of red plastic.

The assistant, who is sixty-four, and also a Cantonese, dresses in a black sam and blue homemade shorts (actually fu cut off above the knees) with green strap Japanese slippers. He never went to school. He came to Hong Kong in 1951 from Macao, where his family has lived for generations. He has a wife whom he visits every week or two. She lives with his eighty-six-year-old mother in a flat-bottomed boat that is tied up across the strait from Lung Chau. One son of thirty-three works as a fisherman as he formerly did himself, and another, aged fourteen, is a uniformed

---

*The Mandarin hsia cha does not have the meaning of the Cantonese la cha.

†Our informant said that the 19th Route Army was divided into a hierarchy of units involving 12, 36, 108, 960, and 2,800 men. A p'ai ch'eung was in command of 36 men.

employee who opens the plate glass door for guests at a Kowloon hotel. This Fish Dryer also has a married daughter of forty-two in Macao who has seven children. He and his wife try to visit them every year.

The Fish Dryers sleep at the end of the shed in a double-decked bed draped with a pair of white mosquito nets. Over the door of their residence is a sign written on red paper which says chiu tsoi (chao ts'ai), or welcome money. The men cook their own meals when there are no women workers around to do it for them. Usually the manager goes into Lung Shing for yam ch'a in the morning, but his assistant does not.* About eleven they eat their first regular meal which may consist of rice, a vegetable soup with bean curd, and a dish of fried fish. This is not fish that they process but one that costs over a dollar a catty. Actually, they do not eat very much fish, especially in summer when the smell of wormy, cheap varieties is always present around them. The manager says that he does not drink, but we observed him sucking on a bamboo water pipe periodically. His assistant, on the other hand, does not smoke but will drink on occasions. The establishment has its own well, but no garden or chickens.

Both men are fond of swimming, an art at which they are unusually proficient. Sometimes the older man swims all the way to the mouth of the bay and back, a total distance that we calculate is about 2,200 feet. The younger of the two says swimming is the thing he does best, and that it would be difficult to put a limit on the measure of his abilities. He adds, however, that he does not have much time to swim. The manager goes to the movies occasionally, preferring the European and American pictures at the cinema across the strait, whereas the old man from Macao insists—and there is no reason to doubt him—that he has never seen a movie in his life. He also never went to school, which is not so unusual among fishermen.

There are the typical indications of the worship of gods at the fish drying plant. For these, the old fisherman is responsible as he spends a significant part of his salary for incense. Also it was noted that the owners make gifts of money for extra food on four feast days: New Year's, the 5th of the 5th month, the 15th of the 8th month, and the Winter Arriving Festival. Although enjoying this extra increment, the manager states flatly that he himself has no religion. His son, however, went to a Protestant school, and was apparently baptized by immersion, behavior that the father considers laughable. He described the minister as mumbling some words, then pushing the boy's head under water so quickly he gulped a few mouthfuls of water. His final comment was that if one is to become a Christian, it is advisable to be a Roman Catholic as that church gives away better food.

---

*For an explanation of yam ch'a, see p. 551.

29. The Noodle Cake Makers

In 1959, the Enterprising Woman decided that she would go into the wheat noodle cake business and so she purchased the necessary machinery. Then, before any noodles were made, she agreed to sublet the factory to three men who had been making noodles using the machinery of Mr. A whose elder sister is the wife of the Hotel Man. When Mr. A's machinery broke down the three men were very much in need of a factory where they could use up their stock of flour before it spoiled. It took them six weeks to do so.

The three men whom we shall refer to as the Noodle Cake Makers are all Fukienese and live in Lung Shing. They all came from the same place as the husband of the Enterprising Woman, but none are related to her. They call their company, which was organized in 1961, "Good Friendship," which we hope continues to represent their feelings for each other. One had previously been a sailor, and they were only in business for a few months altogether. When they gave up, they had about 1,800 catties of noodle cakes they could not sell. Even when the future of the company was most discouraging, they courteously helped us to understand the special processes which were amplified in detail by the owner of the machinery. We shall now do our best to organize and convey this information simply.

The noodle cake factory. The production of min ping (mien ping), or wheat noodle cakes, is carried on primarily in one large room (Fig. 14.2). The cooking and the drying, however, is done outside. Were it not for the stove, the factory might not be noticed at all, for the room is the farther, if larger, section of a building almost hidden behind the house of the Seagoing Tailors which faces the beach and the purple ink factory. The structure has its rear (east) wall of concrete, as well as its end walls, but there is a wood partition which separates the smaller western end which is the storage room for the ground ink wood belonging to the ink factory. The west wall is also of wood, creating a narrow alley between the noodle cake factory and the house. A high gable roof (with an axis north and south) does not prevent the factory from being on hot days one of the hottest in Sai Mi Wan. Two high openings left for windows at the top of the rear wall do not help much. The floor is of concrete with a gutter next to the concrete walls. A single fluorescent tube suspended from the center of the ceiling supplies light at night.

In the northeast corner of the floor, which is approximately seventeen feet long and fourteen feet wide, are the essential machines of the factory, an electrically operated dough mixer and powered with it, a special machine for rolling and cutting noodles. Almost as noteworthy is a European type platform scale on the table at the rear. Apart from these things, the contents of the factory appear ordinary enough and include one high table (at rear) and one low table (in front) consisting of boards on sawhorses, an old desk with drawers, one or two chairs and stools, a square wood platform in the center of the floor with bags of flour and a wood tub on it, several enamel bowls of various sizes, a brass wire sieve, and a bottle of dye. Nothing else is apparent except an old, discarded, hand-operated roller-cutter in one corner. The doors to the factory face each other at the west ends of the north and south walls.

Making the noodle dough. The commonplace Cantonese noodle cakes must be distinguished from ordinary Fukienese vermicelli in that the former are steamed and will last at least a year, and from rice vermicelli in that they are made of wheat flour like the more usual kind of vermicelli. The Noodle Makers begin their manufacture by scooping seventeen catties of flour from a bag into an enamel bowl, carefully weighing it on the scale, and then sifting it into a wood tub resting on a wood platform about six feet square placed in the center of the floor to keep the flour dry. The tub is 23½″ in diameter and 10″ high whereas the sieve is 10″ in diameter and 3″ high. The screen of the sieve is made of fine brass wire set in a wood frame. It is a well-made instrument. To this first batch of flour, a second consisting of three catties of flour of an inferior grade is added by sifting. All the flour is then transferred to the motor driven mixer, after which seven catties of water are weighed in an enamel ware bowl. To this, an unmeasured teaspoon of soda is added (the Enterprising Woman said salt, not soda) and about five tablespoonfuls, or one-third of a cup, of yellow coloring fluid. This combination is gradually poured into the mixer after the latter has been started, the contents being mixed for three minutes and then ejected onto a wood tray 24″ by 30″ in size.

The mixer, made in Japan and bearing the name Otake, is a globular metal bowl 16″ high and 12″ in diameter with a turning arm in the bottom. It stands on the same metal frame as the roller-cutter next to it, a machine, also made in Japan, which consists essentially of a pair of adjustable smooth metal rollers 5″ in diameter and 8¾″ long with a second pair of removable cutting rollers below them. The cutting rollers are 1½″ in diameter and the same length as the smooth rollers. They have 100 cutting grooves (rollers with 200 grooves are used for noodles to be dried but not steamed). Above the rollers is a wood tray 27″ long and the width of the rollers. At the sides of the tray is a pair of metal uprights (which may be folded down) with slots in the tops for the insertion of a single wood roller 1½″ in diameter. The metal uprights extend 8″ above the bottom of the tray. The first pair is 9″ from the outer end of the tray, the second pair 13″ from the first. A third pair extends out in front of the metal rollers.

Below these metal rollers and extending in the opposite direction is a second wood tray of the same width but five feet long, its end resting on a stand made for the purpose. Seven inches from its outer end is a pair of wood uprights extending 9″ above the bottom of the tray, and there is a second pair 13″ from the first rising 8″. Each pair of these uprights has slots in the top to hold one of the same wood rollers used in the upper tray. The lower tray has wood sides 2¾″ high along the half nearest (and under) the machine; 3½″ high along the sides and end of the other half. No machine of this type for making noodles is said to be manufactured in Hong Kong. Primitive machinery did the same work in China.

Rolling the dough. About one third of the mixed dough is put into the upper tray of the roller-cutter and made into a flat cake the width of the tray. This flat cake is then fed between the smooth metal rollers which have been adjusted to leave a quarter of an inch between them. The rolled dough falls down into the second wood tray below in a jagged-edged band which is turned back on itself through the rollers to make a continuous band. To this loop more dough is added. Keeping one's fingers from getting between the rollers when forcing in the thick dough is an important element in the operation, as well as its major hazard. As the band extends, it is cut, and a continuing strip is folded back on itself on the lower tray. Then, after this five minutes of rolling, it is all removed to the upper tray. Quickly the lower tray is swept clean of flour and tiny scraps of dough, and these are added to the band which has been removed to the upper tray. Next, the smooth metal rollers are tightened to within one-eighth inch of each other by turning two turnscrews at the ends of the rollers.

The second rolling of the dough then begins. As the thin band of dough appears on the lower tray, it is slapped with a small bag of flour in the left hand of the Noodle Maker to keep the folds from sticking together. Rapidly, he inserts a 1½″ wood roller into the nearer set of uprights of the tray and winds the end of the band of dough around it from underneath. Somehow, without stopping the machine, he manages to keep the thicker part of the band of dough feeding between the metal rollers, to dust the thinner extruding band with flour, and then to roll it up on the wood roller. Finally, the Noodle Maker tears off the last two feet of the thicker band and lays it aside to facilitate the starting of the next rolling. The second rolling requires only two minutes, making a total of seven for both.

Cutting the noodles. With the dough rolled into a thin band, it is transferred on the wood roller to the pair of similar uprights on the upper tray and the lower tray disconnected from the machine and set aside. Then cutting rollers are inserted below the flat rollers and the teeth (facing grooves) cleaned with a toothbrush by pressing the bristles into the grooves after the machine is turned on. This done, a wood tray conforming to the 11½″ width of the machine and 27″ long is slipped under the cutters to receive the noodles. This tray has little edges ¾″ wide and ½″ high leaving a flat area 10″ wide.

The thin layer of dough is slapped with the before-mentioned bag of flour as it passes from the top of the unwinding roll—the bag has been conveniently suspended from the ceiling on the end of a string so that it hangs near the roll as the Noodle Maker drops it out of his right hand for a moment—and is fed into cutting rollers. With his left hand, the Noodle Maker pulls out the tray below the cutters a little when a pile of noodles has been formed the size of a small loaf of bread. Five of these piles are made in succession before the roll of dough is completely cut, an operation which requires only two minutes and allows the folders to start working.

Continuation of rolling and cutting. The cut noodles are passed on to those who will fold them, and the longer lower tray is replaced. Then a second third of the dough is put into the upper tray and the whole process started again. This time, however, the beginning of rolling is facilitated by the use of the two-foot piece of the band first rolled. Otherwise, the rolling proceeds as before. When a thin roll has been wound, however, the spool is temporarily transferred to the farther of the two sets of uprights on the lower tray (as the folders are still busy), and the last third of the mixed dough is rolled, beginning with a two-foot section saved from the second rolling. Then the lower tray is removed, the cutters are inserted, and each roll is cut in turn. This procedure saves removing the tray and putting in the cutters once. The time involved is listed below:

Mixing the dough in machine	3 minutes
First rolling of dough (⅓ batch)	6 minutes
Second rolling of dough (⅓ batch)	2 minutes
Cutting of noodles (⅓ batch)	2 minutes
Total	13 minutes

By adjustment, this makes a total of thirty-three minutes for twenty catties of material. Loss of interim time between operations brings the elapsed time between taking the flour in hand and delivery of cut noodles to approximately forty-five minutes.

Folding the noodles into cakes. The cut noodles (or rolled dough) can be kept for about four hours, but the Noodle Makers normally work on it at once (mixed dough must be rolled immediately, however; otherwise it would change color). The piles of noodles are spread out on the large table at the front of the room which has a smooth cover of patterned floor linoleum. Usually two workers pick up the noodles in wisps about two and a half feet long (five feet of noodles), and break off the ends. The wisps are deftly folded in two, then once again, and finally placed in a special circular steaming tray with one more fold added at the end. The steaming trays are 20″ in diameter with bottoms made of cross slats of fine wood woven into place and supported by six-layered wood rims 2″ high. Each layer of the rim, which is one inch thick, is a little lower than the one inside it so that the surface is stepped down and outward. This peculiarity of construction locks the tray into position when stacked. Each tray holds fifteen or sixteen noodle cakes. To fold twenty catties of cakes requires thirty-five to forty minutes of two people's time, although they can speed up the process ten minutes.

Steaming the cakes. The trays of noodle cakes are removed to the steamer which is merely a sawdust burning pig food stove with two wood cross-pieces fitted into the lens-shaped pan 29″ in diameter so that ten trays can be stacked on top of them. Over the trays is lowered a large cylindrical metal cover 26½″ in diameter with conical top (Fig. 29.1). The cylindrical part is 34″ high and the cone 10″ more. The cover can be raised

Fig. 29.1. The Noodle Cake Steamer

up and down by a rope which passes through a small pulley above the stove and is fastened to a metal loop at the top of the cone. The stove is fired with residue from the neighboring ink plant, and old ink cloths, bright purple in color, are wrapped around the edge of the cover just inside the pan to keep the steam in. The noodle cakes are steamed approximately forty minutes.

Drying the noodles. When the cooking has been completed, the trays of noodle cakes, which have turned bright yellow, are dumped onto drying frames and then spread out in orderly fashion. The drying frames are 35″ wide by 57″ long. They have edges made of wood (1½″ by 1″) with a single cross piece in the middle. To these wood supporting pieces, hexagonal wire screen (roughly ½″ by ¾″ mesh) is nailed. These frames, loaded with noodle cakes, are laid out in the sun for two days, or longer if the sunshine is not constant. When nearly dry, the noodle cakes, about four inches long and almost as wide, are examined with the fingers. Dried cakes are removed and others rearranged on trays for further exposure to the sun. Well-dried noodle cakes will keep for at least a year and are ready for eating when put in boiling water for ten to fifteen minutes. There is little spoilage in drying the noodles as they are simply not made unless the weather is good.

Economics. The single product of the factory is steamed noodle cakes which require flour, water, soda (salt), and food coloring for their manufacture. The production in a full day is two to three hundred catties of noodles, the same amount of flour being needed in their making. The work day is said to be twelve hours, but the three men who operate the business (with part-time assistance of boys) were starting at five in the morning and finishing at six or seven in the evening.

Taking production to be 250 catties of noodle cakes, the major investment is for flour. The better grade cost $.35 to $.40 a catty in 1961, the inferior (which is purchased from people who receive it from free distribution) only $.33. Computing 15 per cent at $.33 and the other 85 per cent at $.37½, we come to a figure of $12.38 plus $79.69 and a total of $92.07. The additional cost for soda (at $1.20 to $1.60 a catty) and for coloring matter may be estimated at $.13 bringing the final cost to $92.20.

The wholesale price of noodle cakes is $.50 a catty (about nine cakes to a catty). This means an income of $125 with a profit of $30.93 to pay for salaries, rent, and return on the investment. This is not enough for the business to survive.

It may be noted that the basic Japanese machine used in the noodle factory was purchased by the Enterprising Woman for only $800 as this roller-cutter had been on exhibit some years (the regular price was reported as $2,500), but the installation cost nearly $1,000 more and the motor $300. Also the platform scale would cost about $80 if new, and the steaming trays $3 each. The twenty to thirty drying frames ($7.50 each), the stove and steamer ($180), as well as the building itself (ca $1,300) were initial expenses which further complicate the economic analysis. Before we completed our analysis, the noodle cake factory went out of existence, a portent of what would happen in the future to the whole of Sai Mi Wan.

30. Summary and Analysis

The People

The census. We can clarify the overall view of the culture of Sai Mi Wan by presenting the data on population in Table 30.1. We have listed 113 individuals of whom eighty-eight regularly sleep in Sai Mi Wan, thirteen come in to work by the day, and twelve can be treated as visitors insofar as their actual presence in the settlement is concerned, although about half of them are the permittees for property and the others are spouses or children who return to Sai Mi Wan only once a week or even much less often, such as the Seagoing Tailors, for example.

Age. When we consider the age of these people, we must once again mention the special problems involved in recording birth dates among the Chinese.* We have dismissed the fact that a Chinese is one year old at birth and two years old on the first day of the following year, by simply subtracting one year from the person's age if he is at least two or older, thus deriving the year of his birth. The error this manipulation entails seems insignificant compared to the difficulties of obtaining an absolutely accurate statement from a person as to how old he is. Chinese like most people almost everywhere make misstatements as well as actually forget their age. In any event, in most cases, we used various checks and concluded that for a general picture of the community our efforts were sufficient. Regrettably we were not able to obtain the necessary data from a few people who left the community before we had completed our survey.

As one can quickly compute from Table 30.2, there are forty-four individuals, or 46.31 per cent, under twenty-one years of age. Of these, twenty-three are boys, or as close to half as can be. In the total population, there are 55.78 per cent males, which is not unreasonable.

---

*For an interesting statement of these, see *Hong Kong 1961 Report*, 1962: 12–14.

TABLE 30.1
Population of Sai Mi Wan by Households

Individuals	Status*	Sex	Year of Birth	Language†
The Enterprising Woman				
Widow	W	F	ca. 1898	Fu
The Purple Ink Factory				
Inkmaker	R	M	ca. 1916	Fu
Inkmaker's Wife	V	F	ca. 1918	Fu
The Hotel Man's Establishment				
The Hotel Man	V	M	ca. 1913	Fu
Family A				
Mr. A	R	M	ca. 1924	Fu
Mrs. A	R	F	ca. 1933	Fu
First Child	R	M	ca. 1956	Fu
Second Child	R	M	ca. 1957	Fu
Third Child	R	F	ca. 1959	Fu
Fourth Child	R	M	ca. 1961	Fu
Mr. A's Father	R	M	ca. 1896	Fu
Mr. A's Mother	R	F	ca. 1897	Fu
Family B				
Mr. B	V	M	ca. 1922	Fu
Mrs. B	R	F	ca. 1932	Fu
First Child	R	M	ca. 1953	Fu
Second Child	R	M	ca. 1955	Fu
Third Child	R	M	ca. 1959	Fu
Mr. B's Mother	R	F	ca. 1901	Fu
Family C				
Mr. C	V	M	ca. 1918	Fu
Mrs. C	R	F	ca. 1926	Fu
First Child	R	F	ca. 1956	Fu
Family D				
Mr. D	V	M	ca. 1932	Fu
Mrs. D	R	F	ca. 1933	Fu
First Child	R	M	ca. 1957	Fu
Second Child	R	M	ca. 1959	Fu
Family E				
Mr. E	W	M	ca. 1932	C
First Worker	W	M	ca. 1917	H
Second Worker	R	M	—	—
Third Worker	R	M	—	—

(cont.)

*R—resident
V—owner or family member
   who appears only as visitor
W—incoming day worker

†Fu—Fukienese from near Fuchou or Amoy
  C—Cantonese
  H—Hakka
  S—Ch'ao An from Shan T'ou or Shan Wei areas

TABLE 30.1. Population of Sai Mi Wan by Households (cont.)

Individuals	Status*	Sex	Year of Birth	Language†
The Papermakers				
First Worker	W	M	ca. 1927	S
Second Worker	W	M	—	S
Third Worker	W	M	—	S
Fourth Worker	W	M	—	S
Fifth Worker	W	M	—	S
The Fortunate Wife of the Farmer				
Husband	R	M	ca. 1907	C
Wife	R	F	ca. 1913	C
First Child	V	F	1936	C
Second Child	R	F	1948	C
Third Child	R	F	1949	C
Fourth Child	R	M	1951	C
Fifth Child	R	F	1956	C
Concubine	R	F	ca. 1928	C
First Child	R	F	1949	C
Second Child	R	F	1953	C
Third Child	R	F	1954	C
Fourth Child	R	F	1960	C
Worker	R	M		C
The Caretaker				
Husband	R	M	ca. 1930	S
Wife	R	F	ca. 1934	H
First Child	R	M	ca. 1959	S
Second Child	R	M	ca. 1960	S
Third Child	R	F	1961	S
The Carpenter				
Husband	R	M	ca. 1926	S
Wife	R	F	ca. 1930	S
First Child	R	F	ca. 1949	S
Second Child	R	M	ca. 1952	S
Third Child	R	M	ca. 1956	S
Fourth Child	R	F	ca. 1957	S
Fifth Child	R	M	ca. 1960	S

*R—resident
V—owner or family member
   who appears only as visitor
W—incoming day worker

†Fu—Fukienese from near Fuchou or Amoy
C—Cantonese
H—Hakka
S—Ch'ao An from Shan T'ou or Shan Wei areas

[424]

Individuals	Status*	Sex	Year of Birth	Language†
The Seagoing Tailors				
Husband	V	M	ca. 1927	Fu
Wife	R	F	ca. 1937	Fu
First Child	R	M	ca. 1956	Fu
Second Child	R	F	ca. 1957	Fu
Third Child	R	M	ca. 1959	Fu
Fourth Child	R	F	ca. 1960	Fu
Husband's Mother	R	F	ca. 1907	Fu
Husband's Brother	V	M	ca. 1932 or 1931	Fu
Husband's Br. Wife	R	F	ca. 1940	Fu
First Child	R	F	ca. 1959	Fu
Second Child	R	M	1960	Fu
The Shipbuilder's Son's Villa				
Owner	V	M	ca. 1928	C
Husband	R	M		C
Wife	R	F		C
The Man Who Retired				
Husband	R	M	ca. 1903	S
Wife	R	F	ca. 1904	S
First Child	R	F	ca. 1949	S
Second Child	R	M	ca. 1954	S
First Worker	R	M	ca. 1888	S
Second Worker	R	M	—	—
Third Worker	R	M	—	—
And His Friend				
Nephew	V	M	—	S
Wife	R	F	—	S
The Duck Raisers				
Mr. One	R	M	ca. 1921	S
Mrs. One	R	F	ca. 1925	S
First Child	R	M	ca. 1949	S
Second Child	R	M	ca. 1956	S
Third Child	R	F	ca. 1958	S
Fourth Child	R	F	ca. 1961	S
Mr. Two	R	M	ca. 1923	S
Mr. Three	R	M	ca. 1908	S
Mr. Two's Grandfather	R	M	ca. 1904 or 1906	S
First Worker	R	M		S
Younger Worker	R	M	ca. 1940	S
Younger Worker's Brother	R	M	ca. 1949	S

(cont.)

TABLE 30.1. Population of Sai Mi Wan by Households (cont.)

Individuals	Status*	Sex	Year of Birth	Language†
The Bean Curd Maker				
Husband	R	M	ca. 1908	S
Wife	R	F	ca. 1917	S
First Child	R	F	ca. 1939	S
Second Child	R	F	ca. 1945	S
Third Child	R	F	ca. 1952	S
Fourth Child	R	F	ca. 1956	S
Fifth Child	R	M	ca. 1958	S
First Child's Hu	R	M	ca. 1932	S
First Child's Son	R	M	1961	S
Husband's Father	R	M	ca. 1880	S
The Fish Dryers				
Owner	V	M	ca. 1918	C
Second Owner	V	M	ca. 1934	C
Manager	R	M	ca. 1914	C
Assistant	R	M	ca. 1898	C
Worker	W	F	ca. 1927	C
Worker	W	F	—	C
The Noodle Cake Makers				
Worker	W	M		Fu
Worker	W	M		Fu
Worker	W	M		Fu

*R—resident
V—owner or family member
  who appears only as visitor
W—incoming day worker

†Fu—Fukienese from near Fuchou or Amoy
C—Cantonese
H—Hakka
S—Ch'ao An from Shan T'ou or Shan Wei areas

Family composition. Since Sai Mi Wan is so largely industrial, simple though the products may be, we find only fourteen families that are actually resident in the community. We note that they have forty-four children under twenty-one. Of the fourteen families, ten are nuclear including only a husband and wife and children. In one of these there is also a concubine. Two of the remainder, which include one or both parents of the husband, we consider as enlarged nuclear families, rather than extended families, since the parents arrived by force of circumstances after the married children had set up nuclear families. In the third case, besides a husband's father, there are also a married daughter and son-in-law with their child making four generations in one small house. We are inclined to consider it a stem family by adoption. In the fourth family, there are two brothers,

TABLE 30.2

Age Classes

Age	Male	Female	Totals	Age	Male	Female	Totals
0-5	16	12	28	46-50	2	1	3
6-10	5	3	8	51-55	4	1	5
11-15	2	5	7	56-60	1	2	3
16-20	0	1	1	61-65	2	2	4
21-25	1	4	5	66-70	0	0	0
26-30	4	3	7	71-75	1	0	1
31-35	6	5	11	76-80	0	0	0
36-40	4	1	5	81-86	1	0	1
41-45	4	2	6				
Grand Total					53	42	95

their wives, their children, and the brothers' mother. This joint family is also an economic family, or one with a common purse, as are all the other thirteen. We may add that to the best of our knowledge there is no adult in our census who has not been married.

Lineage. In each of these families the normal identification with the ancestral tsuk (tsu), or lineage, has greatly weakened if not been altogether broken. On the other hand, there is a strong sense of dependence on extended familial relationships in some cases, as, for example, when a widowed mother manages a household containing two daughters-in-law.

Provenience and language. From the island viewpoint, the chief distinction of Sai Mi Wan is that it has so many people from Fukien and the east coast of Kwangtung who speak a language collectively referred to as Ch'ao-Fu-Hui that is unintelligible to the Cantonese who make up 79 per cent of the population of the Colony.* From our census list we tabulate forty-five Ch'ao An speakers from the areas of Shan T'ao (Swatow) and Shan Wei (Shabue), and thirty-nine from Fukien, which make a total of eighty-four or 77.77 per cent of the 108 known cases. Even of the remaining twenty-four cases, two are Hakka, leaving only 20.37 per cent of Cantonese. It is expected, of course, that most of the children in these Ch'ao-Fu-Hui families will sooner or later displace their parental speech with Cantonese.

Approaching the matter from household and work groups, we can present Table 30.3 based on language.

Again we have evidence of the preponderance of the non-Cantonese.

Hong Kong 1961 Report, 1962: 10.

TABLE 30.3
Languages Used

Group	Language			Total
	Ch'ao An	Fukien	Cantonese	
Family	6	6	2	14
Work	3	2	2	7
Total	9	8	4	21

The Historical Development of Sai Mi Wan

Chronology. As has been made sufficiently clear, the founding of the settlement and much of the impetus for its early development stemmed from the efforts of the Enterprising Woman, a Fukienese widow. Indeed, many people on Lung Chau call Sai Mi Wan by the name of Fukien Ch'ang, or Fukien Place. Actually the interspersal of people of the different groups was fairly even as the development continued, as Table 30.4 shows.

Interrelationship of groups. Of these fifteen groups, 1, 2, 4, 8, 12, and 15 are related to the extent that the Enterprising Woman controls the land. Groups 5 and 13 were tied together in a similar way when the Fortunate Wife of the Farmer took in the Bean Curd Maker. Also, establishments 6, 10, 11, and 12 are linked around the Man Who Retired. To these three principals, we have to add the Hotel Man, who has been responsible for five subgroups coming, as well as the Carpenter, the Shipbuilder's Son, and the Fish Dryers.

Individual motivations for settlement. Apart from the matter of association in language and business interests, there is also the question of individual motivations. The four earliest of the seven principals just mentioned were attracted to Sai Mi Wan as a place to raise pigs, and this was also an important factor for the Bean Curd Maker. Hog raising was profitable in the nineteen-fifties. The coming of the fish drying plant is also readily understandable from an economic point of view. What is truly exceptional is that in the case of two of the principal permit holders, it was the physical and esthetic attractions of Sai Mi Wan that first drew them to this isolated settlement. Both wanted escape from the clamor and crowding of urban life. This same feeling does not seem lacking in the case of some other individuals, such as the Hotel Man, but most of the people flatly deny any esthetic considerations whatever.

TABLE 30.4
Date of Settlement

Establishments	Date of Settlement	Language of Settlers*
1. The Enterprising Woman	ca. 1949	Fu
2. The Purple Ink Factory	ca. 1949	Fu
3. The Hotel Man's Establishment	1952	Fu
4. The Papermakers	1953	S
5. The Fortunate Wife of the Farmer	1954	C
6. The Caretaker	1956	S
7. The Carpenter	1957	S
8. The Seagoing Tailors	1957	Fu
9. The Shipbuilder's Son's Villa	1957	C
10. The Man Who Retired	1958	S
11. And His Friend	1958	S
12. The Duck Raisers	1958	S
13. The Bean Curd Maker	1959	S
14. The Fish Dryers	1959	Fu
15. The Noodle Cake Makers	1961	Fu

*Fu—Fukienese, S—Ch'ao An, C—Cantonese.

Food, Drink, and Tobacco

Pigs. As hitherto made clear, the desire for economic profit by raising pigs was an important motivation for most of the early settlers to move to Sai Mi Wan. The groups who continue to raise pigs are:

    The Enterprising Woman
    The Establishment of the Hotel Man: Mr. A and Mr. E
    The Fortunate Wife of the Farmer
    The Carpenter
    The Bean Curd Maker

It seems apparent that in Sai Mi Wan the people who do not raise pigs fall into several categories. First, there are a few families that do not have adequate space and in which the men of the family do not come home every night. It is not that women cannot raise pigs by themselves, but at times a man is most useful. In a second category are the late arriving well-to-do people. Raising hogs demands physical labor, and for such people to engage in it means that they must employ workers and consider the undertaking as a business. Only Mr. E goes in for pigs in this fashion and he started relatively early. Since then, the profit in hogs has declined and people are preferring other investments. Third, and the most clear category of all, is that of establishments devoted to some other special form of production. Pigs are not a natural complement to making ink, drying fish, raising ducks, or producing paper. The workers simply have no time. Finally, we might say that there is no really large producer of pigs in Sai Mi Wan, although Mister E is moving in that direction with over fifty animals.

Chickens. As for chickens, almost everyone has a few, the factory people again being the exception. Three people—the Man Who Retired, Mister E, and the Fortunate Wife of the Farmer—have over a hundred and the latter more than four times that many. Somehow it seems consistent with her character that she is an expert at injecting chickens, while the Man Who Retired seems most logical in being proud that his chickens grow naturally.

Pigeons. Pigeon raising seems to be an adjunct activity. Many people try to raise them, and it is not clear why some people fail. Residents who have enough space but do not raise pigeons are as likely as not to say that they expect to. On the other hand, the Fortunate Wife of the Farmer makes herself clear when she states bluntly that having pigeons around is a nuisance.

Vegetable growing. In Sai Mi Wan there is only one real farming family in the sense of cultivating vegetables for sale, although Mister E has made gestures in that direction. The reasons are clear. It is significant to note that both the Farmer and Mister E have their own market stalls.

Ducks. Duck raising is an industry in Sai Mi Wan and four groups are involved, each claiming to have 1500 to 2000 birds of various ages. In two of the groups, the workers are the owners, while in the other two, which were started because of the success of the former, workers are employed. No one has only a few ducks, and those who have many are most conscious of an unfavorable trend in the market.

Dogs and cats. There is the usual multiplicity of dogs and cats in Sai Mi Wan, with dogs in the majority. Dogs are rationalized as protectors of the house, and there is no evidence of their being eaten by the residents. Cats are the discouragers of rats. Two of the families that have no dogs—the Seagoing Tailors and the Bean Curd Makers—seem adequately secure in being juxtaposed to neighbors that have many.

Meals. A knowledge of the people in Sai Mi Wan made clear that they eat relatively well according to Lung Chau standards. The pattern in Fukien and Ch'ao An speaking families is to have three meals a day, the first and last fortified with thick congee, the noon meal with plain rice.

These Ch'ao-Fu-Hui speakers also serve concentrated tea to adults as is the custom in their homeland. The Cantonese eat two meals a day, having a light collation without rice for breakfast. The children usually have three meals, however. Cantonese men like to go to town and have yam ch'a, or tea with appetizers, for breakfast. The Cantonese, typically, also have extra food about two to three o'clock in the afternoon, as their first regular meal between ten and eleven is early. This special dish to break the long interval before dinner consists usually of a soup, sweet or otherwise.

Actually, as might be expected, hours of eating vary in different groups for one reason or another and there are individual variations as well, but the ideal procedures are clearly recognized.

Drink and tobacco. A few facts become clear, but none of them particularly surprising. More men drink and smoke than do women. There are one or more heavy users of strong Chinese wine (spirits), clearly an individual matter. More extraordinary is the number of abstemious families, some of which do not serve wine even on feast days. On such days, however, most adults do have a few drinks. The use of metal water pipes by older Fukien women is exemplified. Smoking seems to begin at a later age than might be expected, especially among females. Poorer individuals usually buy cheaper grades of cigarettes or roll their own.

Dress and Adornment

Clothing. The dress of most of the people in Sai Mi Wan is superior to the average of Lung Chau, it would seem. Many resident families are better off, and most visiting owners belong to a different economic world. Even the poorest give the impression of being actively upward mobile.

Two things are specially indicative of the higher standard of dress. In at least a half dozen of our groups, one or more women own cheong sam. Clearly, younger women are more likely to have them than older, and certainly none of the women wear them very often. The other notable thing is that in two homes, those of the Fortunate Wife of the Farmer and the Seagoing Tailors, there are sewing machines which are used for making almost all of the family clothing.

Personal adornment. Almost every woman in Sai Mi Wan has bobbed hair with a more or less permanent wave. Only the oldest women are exceptions. Men have western style haircuts, the Carpenter's being somewhat exceptional. Almost every adult in Sai Mi Wan owns a wristwatch and most women have rings, bracelets, and earrings. Some of the well-to-do families have quite a lot of jewelry, and more did have before they left China. This does not indicate articles of adornment of any great value, however. Plain gold bands on the fingers, jade bracelets of poor quality stone, and gold button earrings are the standard pieces, but there are others, and particularly jade or less expensive stones set into rings. The cost range of such pieces of jewelry is probably between ten and a hundred dollars. On the other hand, at festivals, especially New Year's and that of Hung Shing, we noticed the women of the Hotel Man's Establishment, as poor as they seemed to be, and those of the Seagoing Tailors, as well as those of the Bean Curd Maker, all wearing gold chains tightly on the outside of their collars, the loose sections being tucked inside at the front of the neck. Such chains cost up to several hundred dollars. It is perhaps significant that these chains were noticed specifically on Ch'ao-Fu-Hui women.

As conspicuous absences, we should note a complete lack of the use of cosmetics. At least we never saw a woman wearing lipstick in Sai Mi Wan, and only the FortunateWife of the Farmer was seen carrying a conventional handbag.

Housing and Services

Type of construction. In the thirteen establishments that we have considered in Sai Mi Wan, there are ten buildings (or sets of buildings) constructed as residences and five as factories. A second building has been put up as a factory by both the Man Who Retired and His Friend. Of the fifteen structures, nine are made of stone and cement. Certainly in some cases more cement was used, as for example in the home of the Fortunate Wife of the Farmer, while in that of the Caretaker, only a minimum of this expensive commodity was provided.

Of these nine stone and cement buildings, all roofs except the flat one on the house of the Fortunate Wife of the Farmer are gabled. Of the gable roofs, all are wood covered with tarpaper except those on the house and factory of the Man Who Retired and the house of His Friend, which are tiled, and on the twin houses (counted as one) of the Shipbuilder's Son's Villa, which are made of a prefabricated composition material in corrugated form.

Of the wood structures, the Carpenter has built his home with vertical boards whereas all others are essentially clapboard. All of these also have wood and tarpaper gabled roofs except the Bean Curd Maker's house and one section of the Fish Drying plant which have shed roofs.

Toilets. The home of the Fortunate Wife of the Farmer is distinguished by an outhouse set below a point halfway on the path leading to their home. It is a fragile wood structure in which a six foot man cannot stand up. Standing almost in the middle of the vegetable fields, it provides a kind of public privacy. On its concrete floor is a ten-inch groove which runs out under the back and continues as a concrete duct down into a large fertilizer basin. In this outhouse a pair of two-gallon cans of water are normally used for flushing. Users bring their own paper when needed. A better-made but similar facility of stone and cement has been erected at the edge of the sea wall on land cultivated by Mr. E of the Hotel Man's Establishment. It empties onto the beach below. The Shipbuilder's Son's Villa is reported to have a toilet room removed from the houses and a concrete bathtub long enough to lie down in. Most people in Sai Mi Wan, we must presume, use buckets in obscure corners of their property.

Electricity. Electric lines provide light in the various establishments on the property of the Enterprising Woman and on those of the Hotel Man. The Fortunate Wife of the Farmer has not only electric light but also a meter for power as does Mister E. All others in Sai Mi Wan do without electricity.

Wells. Every house and factory has its own well, or one adjacent to it, except the residence of the Caretaker. He has to carry water. Only one of the wells belonging to the Enterprising Woman has a seemingly unlimited supply of good water although most establishments get along comfortably most of the time. The Carpenter runs short as does the Bean Curd Maker. The wells on the northwest shore have more or less salinity but their waters are drunk nonetheless.

Finally, it may be noted that there is no telephone in Sai Mi Wan, and in no home is there a female house servant.

Domestic Life

Childbirth. There are seventeen mothers with children residing in Sai Mi Wan. Thirteen of these women have borne children since they came to the settlement but, of these, only two were delivered at home, the rest having first seen the light in various hospitals or maternity homes in Hong Kong. Although numerous mothers are strongly opposed to having more children, and some want to give away a child already in the house, only one woman has had an operation to prevent the unwanted increase in her family.

Marriage. Of all the married women in Sai Mi Wan, only six apparently were not married blind. There is one case of semi-blind marriage that took place in the nineteen-thirties, and there are five cases of free marriage including that of the one concubine living in the settlement. Two of these were in the late nineteen-forties and the other three in the fifties. An occasional old woman still favors the idea of blind marriage, or at least a semi-blind marriage, for her children, but none of the younger women entertain such conservative notions.

Among the older women with whom we discussed the question of preferential or taboo choices in a spouse, the responses were consistent. A boy's marriage to either his father's sister's daughter or his mother's brother's daughter was considered undesirable if not actually bad. A good choice for a boy, however, was his mother's sister's daughter. To marry a father's brother's child, of course, has long been taboo since the individual would belong to the same lineage and surname group. Before leaving the subject of marriage we may note that there was no adult woman in Sai Mi Wan who had never been married.

Home activities. In Sai Mi Wan it is expected that everyone over seven years old should spend most of his waking time working or going to school and, from our observations, behavior follows the rule. A considerable number of adults seem to be uncomfortable if they are not working, and most of the children are made to work also. If there are vegetables, pigs, chickens, or pigeons to care for, these require considerable effort on the part of both women and children. In Sai Mi Wan, few men who are heads of households devote much time to such labor, as most are professional men. Even the Fortunate Wife's husband is more of a vegetable seller than a farmer, spending many hours of the day sitting at his stall in the Lung Shing market.

Child rearing. Raising children is probably the mother's most time-consuming task. Babies demand almost incessant care, and when there are older siblings first to share and then to take over the task, there are usually more babies. Considering the necessary interruptions, children are carefully watched and therefore kept within close range. Within that eye's distance, however, there is a generous license for the young child to do what he wants. There is rarely any limitation on noise, for example. When a slightly older child is put in charge of a younger, authority can be as forceful as necessary as long as no weapons are used. There are conflicts and crying and a regular progression of small accidents, but all things considered, the life of the small child in Sai Mi Wan seems not too unpleasant. Certainly young children are much loved in most families, and the early years can be considered among the happiest of one's life.

Gold-silver paper. Children who are home from school, besides sharing in the various domestic duties of their parents, participate in special activities such as pasting tinfoil on gold-silver paper for the dead or overprinting it with a wood block coated with purple ink. Indeed this type of activity is commonplace among at least seven families in Sai Mi Wan, and the Enterprising Woman is an old hand at it herself. There are some families, however, that are too busy with their own undertakings, such as those of the Fortunate Wife of the Farmer and the Bean Curd Maker. Also, this may be the reason we did not see gold-silver paper at the house of the Man Who Retired or that of His Friend.

Education and Amusements

Education. In Sai Mi Wan, at least four men claim to have had more than a primary school education. Also, three finished primary school and two more almost did. Another five, at least, had some formal schooling. On the other hand, we find only one woman who has had more than primary school training, another who completed primary school, and three more who had some formal education. The remainder, it would seem, had none.

All the children who might be expected to be in school are in school with the exception of one boy, a son of a Duck Raiser. The lack of individuals in the sixteen- to twenty-year-old range should be noted.

Amusements. Sai Mi Wan is enclosed by precipitous slopes and the buildings line its shores. Lung Chau is hot a large part of the year, and the Chinese in such climates like to bathe. Therefore it perhaps should not be surprising that many residents go into the water in summer, but it is a little extraordinary that so many really swim. The manager of the fish drying plant is an expert, and his assistant unusual. Two families have members that lustily cross the outer end of the bay and return. Of these one is a mother.

As for attendance at the cinema, the population seems to divide into two aggregates, plus one man. There are those who like the movies very much and go once a month or much oftener and those who go seldom, perhaps a few times a year, plus the assistant to the manager of the fish drying plant who has never seen a motion picture in his life. Most of the adults and almost all of the children like Chinese films, but a few sophisticates prefer pictures made in the West. Indeed, the manager of the fish drying plant will not go to any others. He says he has not seen more than two or three Cantonese pictures in his memory. They bore him, he insists. The week that we questioned him on the subject he had seen three non-Chinese pictures in the leading cinema in the town across the strait. That many foreign films in a week was unusual for the theater, and consequently unusual for him even though he seldom misses a Western picture when one is shown.

There were few radios in Sai Mi Wan in 1961; only three according to our count. Each of these served a considerable number of people, however. The Duck Raisers at the end of the bay owned one in common for eight individuals to enjoy. The Seagoing Tailors next door had another which served thirteen people some of the time and ten regularly. The third radio belonged to the family of the Fortunate Wife of the Farmer with twelve resident members, and its sound could hardly be escaped by the Bean Curd Maker's resident nine.

Two families, the Farmer's and the Man Who Retired's, said they played mah-jongg occasionally for pleasure. The Inkmaker has a reputation for doing so. Otherwise mah-jongg was a game of which few people even admitted knowing the rules.

Political and Economic Considerations

Political considerations. The political views of most residents in Sai Mi Wan are colored by the fact that they are refugees from the economic system of the People's Republic of China. None of these men and women suffered any physical abuse under that government. They left their ancestral homes either because they anticipated that their small businesses could not endure under Communism, or because they simply wanted to make more money in Hong Kong. The shortages of essential goods on the mainland which reached a peak about 1960 has, of course, not made life in the provinces from which they came any more appealing.

A second group only slightly smaller in size is made up of those who can be called old-time residents of Hong Kong, meaning individuals who have been in the Colony since before the Japanese occupation and consequently before the Communist control of southeastern China. The raising of political questions seems to evoke a minimum of feeling among these people, although there was little enough among the refugees in the group previously mentioned.

A question, such as, "What can you see that is good about Communism?" was quickly deflected by informants into what was bad about Hong Kong. Only one man seemed to be really favorable toward the People's Republic, and even his attitude was touched by the spurious quality of being based on resentments derived from personal contacts with the British. On the other hand he did make a positive point in asserting the value of free education in contemporary China.

Attitude toward the British. Only one person voiced dislike of the British, and that was a special case. Indeed, only a few of the residents of Sai Mi Wan have had more than the most casual relationships with the non-Chinese subjects of the Queen. Toward the government of the Colony, opinion was overwhelmingly positive and favorable. Fearing the influence of talking to a Westerner, we countered statement with questions. "Would not a democratic government by Hong Kong Chinese themselves be better?" The response was so generally consistent that it seemed amusing. "The Chinese could not do as well." And why? Because the corruption of petty Chinese officials in Hong Kong is ubiquitous, the symbolic evil hand that pulls money from the pockets of almost every citizen. This one really bad thing would become intolerable without the British.

Trying to reverse the flow of judgment and create the still mirror of objectivity, one or two people admitted there were some worse aspects to the irregularities under the Kuomingtang regime on the mainland. In Hong Kong, at least, one was not personally insulted or physically frightened; there was only the uncontrollable, illegitimate drain on one's finances.

Economic considerations. Money is important to the people of Sai Mi Wan, but so is pride, which is closely related to the concept of "face," frequently spoken of in connection with the Chinese. No one is starving in the settlement, and there is no resident who does not claim to be poor, which is a reasonable attitude in terms of the larger Hong Kong society. The visiting investors in the settlement certainly can be classed as a group with superior economic status. Apart from these well-to-do nonresidents, two other groups may be distinguished. One of these comprises poor families who themselves make clear that at least things have been worse. In short, they are economically upward mobile. The Carpenter and the Caretaker are specific examples. Contrariwise, there is the group of families that has clearly come upon hard times. Mister A of the Hotel Man's Establishment is a case of a man whose position has declined and who shows little sign of being able to reverse the trend. About him and the Man Who Retired, one develops the feeling that they are not accustomed to manual work, whereas all other residents and most visiting members of the population do labor with their hands, although a few have done much more of it recently since coming to Hong Kong.

Of the various business ventures in Sai Mi Wan, none seems to be making a fortune for those who have invested their time and their money. The outlook appears good for the Bean Curd Maker, and apparently the Fish Dryers know how to maintain a consistent profit. Complaints, however, rise from the Inkmaker, the Papermakers, and even the Duck Raisers, that the forecast for business in their fields is bad. In most instances, they seem to accept the situation with equanimity. The Man Who Retired is a special case as he has a record of failures since coming to Sai Mi Wan which is obviously no pleasure for him to relate.

For the professional people, such as the various tailors and the Carpenter, things are, ma ma ti, or "passable," a colloquial Cantonese expression which conveys an admission that things are going well. The Seagoing Tailors considered collectively as a family almost certainly have the highest cash income of any group living in Sai Mi Wan. The other tailors and the Carpenter have less, but they are "getting by."

The produce people, by which expression we refer to the Farmer and Mister E of the Hotel Man's Establishment, also seem secure. Both are protected in having their own retail outlets, and whereas the Farmer has a built-in work force, Mister E seems to have built-in energy and ambition.

Religion and Health

Religion. Almost everyone "worships gods," in Sai Mi Wan—at least nominally, that is. In each house and factory except one there is a red can to hold incense sticks. Offerings are usually made to the gods at the beginning and the middle of the month and on at least five of the numerous feast days of the Chinese calendar. These are always New Year's and usually Ch'ing Ming, the 5th of the 5th month, the 15th of the 7th month, 15th of the 8th month, and the Winter Arriving Festival.

It would have been a more satisfying record if informants could have been more explicit about the gods they worship. The Earth God and God of Heaven were most frequently mentioned, but the whole approach to religion is not particularistic in Sai Mi Wan. Very often a person will say he has no religion. To "worship gods" is a traditional activity that most people carry out as proper. Clearly some individuals, especially older ones with no education, are afraid not to do so since they regard the simple ceremonies as protective. Only one or two of the residents admitted to visiting either of the two temples on the island. Others among the religious group denied going, giving such reasons as the lack of time or money.

One or two residents are more seriously religious in the traditional sense but without really distinguishing themselves or their beliefs by so being. All daughters in one family and one in another have been converted to the Roman Catholic faith, but there is no family in Sai Mi Wan in which all members are Christians. Naturally, the girls hope that there will be.

Even more outstanding are the several positive agnostics in the community. Two men are convincing skeptics in their disavowal of religion, and two others present an attitude that is more forceful than the usual denial of a belief in any God. Finally, the whole family of the Seagoing Tailors has given up any formal signs of religion.

Two individuals positively assert the value of feng-shui. One is the Carpenter whose profession gives him a certain vested interest in appreciating the value of orienting buildings according to the proper geomantic influences. The other is the Man Who Retired who has a predilection for the more exotic manifestations of religion. Most other people disavow any interest in feng-shui, but that does not mean that they do not believe in it.

Many individuals who "worship gods" make use of the almanac before engaging in significant undertakings such as arranging for a marriage or starting a new business.

If the "traditional" religion is weak in Sai Mi Wan, Confucianism, which might be expected to manifest itself in ancestor worship, is weaker still. Only in the Caretaker's and Bean Curd Maker's houses did we find the evidence of a paper tablet. In several cases, however, we received the logical explanation that the tablets were in the ancestral village.

Health. Few residents in Sai Mi Wan see a physician except during childbirth. Then it is almost certain to be a doctor with the Western type of training at one of the modern Hong Kong hospitals or maternity wards. Most informants said they preferred doctors with such training in any case because they cured faster at less cost. Apart from childbirth and critical illnesses when hospitals are again resorted to, local doctors are called upon for assistance, usually men who are refugees from China and do not have licenses to practice in the Colony but are not necessarily otherwise unqualified. From the patients' point of view, these doctors have the advantage of being cheaper than licensed practitioners.

A few individuals uphold the virtues of traditional Chinese medicine. The Man Who Retired claims knowledge himself as does one of the Papermakers although the latter has disavowed personal practice in favor of the new type of physicians. Some of the older people admit that they see advantages in the traditional healers and consequently patronize them for the relief of various pains, and many other residents have probably been treated by them at various times.

The great number of gold-capped teeth in the collective mouths of Sai Mi Wan adults indicate contacts with dentists, but the concentration of so much gold on the upper incisors suggests that perhaps a good part of the motivation in having the work done should be classed under the heading of personal adornment.

Conclusions

Having summarized our data on Sai Mi Wan, we shall present our personal commentary, the validity of which stands on a different foundation.

Age. The most notable thing about the distribution of people by age is the fact that there is only one individual in the 16–20 age group. This can be explained by the facts that (1) most parents who reside in Sai Mi Wan have not been married long enough to produce children that old, (2) some who were married long enough lost young children during the period of the Japanese occupation, and (3) some children of this age group were not brought out of China when it was possible and later permission for them to leave could not be obtained.

Lineage. The tsuk (tsu), or lineage, bonds have largely disintegrated not only because the residents have left their traditional homes, but also because in those homes the old social patterns have been torn asunder by Communism. Also, such factors as economic independence, free marriage, lack of communication, and Western cultural values have played their part in weakening the tsuk. To some degree, common provenience and language have created compensatory groupings.

Linguistic groups. There is considerable oppositional feeling between the Ch'ao-Fu-Hui people on the one hand and the Cantonese on the other. The Cantonese consider themselves superior to their coastal neighbors to the east, insinuating that they are miserly money makers who are even parsimonious about the food that they give themselves. Members of the minority group on the island apparently do help each other, and perhaps they are shrewder in business although this hardly seems possible. It is more likely that there is a selective factor operating with regard to the people the Cantonese encounter since the Chinese who go to alien places are often those most determined to make money. Just how the Ch'ao-Fu-Hui group feels about the Cantonese is somewhat less clear, but if the former are labeled *shrewd,* then the reciprocal term may be *sharp.* The minority does not altogether trust the integrity of the majority.

Overtly, the expressions of distaste are restrained, being most apparent in avoidance. Most particularly, the people born in the two areas almost never intermarry. This is not merely a matter of language as demonstrated by the acceptance of Hakka and Ch'ao-Fu-Hui unions. What will happen in the next generation is another matter, as the children are mingling and sharing a common native language which is Cantonese.

Historical development. It is not difficult to recognize that a desire to raise pigs was the primary reason for Sai Mi Wan being settled. This type of undertaking had recently been forbidden within the town limits of Lung Shing, and hog raising was profitable in the nineteen-fifties since China had curtailed its exports. Then, which is unusual for such a poor area, the pristine beauty of Sai Mi Wan attracted two men, the classic Chinese appreciation of nature having touched them. The industrial character of Sai Mi Wan, one might guess, may have been largely due to the concentration of non-farming Ch'ao-Fu-Hui people determined to make money.

Food and tobacco. Sai Mi Wan offers little attraction to him who cultivates the soil. The one unprecipitous area with a reasonable supply of water for growing vegetables was pre-empted early by a Cantonese family. Steep hillsides do not encourage cultivation and water must be available. As for ducks, there are certain advantages in raising them at the seaside. Duck pens have to be kept clean and by using a mixture of beach sand and gravel, which can be returned for the cleansing of the tide, this is effectively done. Also, the protected bay provides cheap transportation facilities, not only for ducks but for the tons of fish that are dried along its shore.

We noted a limitation of smoking among younger adults, and especially females. This may well result from a lack of cash, since indulgence is relatively expensive, a package of the better cigarettes costing almost as much ($1.10) as a woman can make in a whole day through extra work in the home.

Dress. In an isolated settlement such as Sai Mi Wan, one might not expect to find the quality of clothing that exists, but the explanation seems clear. Many of the families originated in urban areas or, if they did not, at least they did not belong to the lowest social stratum of the villages. Generally speaking, they were not farmers. Consequently, whether downward or upward mobile, the men usually own Western style clothes and many of the women have a cheong sam. Also, the comment should perhaps be made about the heavy gold chains worn by the latter. Such objects not only satisfy feminine desires for personal adornment but are realistically the savings accounts of the women.

Housing and services. Stone and concrete have been the standard building materials for residences throughout Sai Mi Wan history. Wealth shows itself in the roofs. Tiles are traditional and expensive. Corrugated composition roofs are expensive and modern. Most people have to be content with tarpaper-covered wood whereas more reinforced concrete might be expected. Accessory buildings and factories are largely clapboard structures with shed roofs because nothing is cheaper. The Carpenter has an unusual house because he takes pride in his distinction as a professional builder.

The reason for the pattern of the distribution of electricity in Sai Mi Wan is self-evident. Those having it are in a solid cluster at the foot of the bay, which is the area closest to Lung Shing from which the lines run. Extending new lines out around the bay will be expensive.

The water situation is equally comprehensible. The one good supply is near the bottom of the constricted area also at the foot of the bay, a fact one can attribute to the land structure. Sooner or later, to have an adequate supply for all the people of Sai Mi Wan, water will probably have to be piped from Lung Shing.

Domestic life. Too many children is the greatest problem of Sai Mi Wan. Ignorance with prejudice prevents birth control at one end of the line, and the lack of a free and easy solution impedes it at the other. In theory, it is not complicated to resolve the problem permanently for a woman after she has had four or more children including one or two sons since hospitals will then perform the operation on request, but for most parents, that is too many and too late. Besides, in practice it does not prove so easy. All women do not receive the essential information and less receive the necessary help. That is the report from Sai Mi Wan.

The marriage methods in Sai Mi Wan follow the changing mores. The older people (and some not so old) were consistently married by their parents with little or no consultation. A middle group (with few representatives, so it happens, in Sai Mi Wan) were allowed to meet the prospective spouse, while the most recent unions have come about through free choice. The trend to the latter method which has been furthered by the great change in customs under the People's Republic of China seems unmistakable and irreversible. Also girls have the choice of not marrying at the usual early age which, although more unusual, is exemplified by one case in Sai Mi Wan.

In the old American rural community, women typically had what was referred to colloquially as "chicken money." It was the name given to money that they earned by raising chickens and which traditionally did not go into the family purse, but was spent at will. Money from raising chickens certainly is not so regarded on Lung Chau, but the income from working on gold-silver paper in some households may be. There are, of course, a certain number of families which, being in difficult circumstances, depend on such work as a business. There are some individuals, relatively well off, who take it up at periods when demand slightly raises the reward for this home labor. Others do it almost entirely for the sake of something to pass the time, or as extra work to keep the children occupied. Working on gold-silver paper fits in with the ideal that people must be doing something continuously. For the more casual workers, it means buying something extra. For example, one father annoyed at so little reward being returned for so much effort, commented that it would be better for the children to give it up and get along with a little less candy. This seems to be an appropriate place to interpolate the observation that Sai Mi Wan people, no matter how poor, regularly give their children ten-cent pieces to buy special things to eat.

Education and amusements. The more urban backgrounds and the higher average economic level probably account for the amount of education among Sai Mi Wan adults. With new facilities developing in Hong Kong, the children give every sign of achieving more schooling than their parents did, a fact which is especially true of the girls, one of whom has practically educated herself out of the community.

The bay is unquestionably inviting on a hot summer day and that fact is alone responsible for some of the swimming that has developed in Sai Mi Wan. Only coincidence can explain the presence of such swimmers as the Fish Dryers, however, for their abilities were developed before, not after their arrival. The almost universal appeal of the movies is best satisfied in lone men and in women with not too much to do and the necessary money. Some people who want radios cannot afford them. As for mah-jongg, it is clearly not a game for the poor, and even less one for the busy.

Political and economic considerations. The strong anti-Communist flavor in the attitudes of some of the residents of Sai Mi Wan once again reflects the fact that they were not of the poorest stratum of old China. Most left just before or just after the assumption of power by the Communists and have no reason to hate as some late-leavers do who were physically hurt. On the whole, the people in Sai Mi Wan are too busy in the attempt to make a living to care about political matters one way or another. Curiously, on Lung Chau, one has to be reasonably well off to be really interested in Communism.

Money is what interests the people and the commonplace grafting practiced by petty officials is what they hate most, but again one has to be reasonably well off before much cash can be regurgitated. Perhaps the most pitiful of the Sai Mi Wan residents from an economic point of view are those who came from a non-laboring group and cannot successfully compete for a living. Their experience is inadequate to enable them to conduct independent businesses successfully, while heavy physical labor, even in one's own interest, appears psychologically, if not physically, impossible.

Even for those who accept the challenge of hard work and new business ventures, life can be difficult. Small capital industry is readily susceptible to the effects of change in the economic scene beyond the producer's purview. Hong Kong is particularly vulnerable because of the influence of mainland China and the political disturbances in southeast Asia. The produce market is affected by what the Chinese authorities decide, and from the external view, their decisions may seem capricious. Disruptions in smaller countries readily curtail the manufacture of gold-silver paper which in turn may be ruinous for papermakers and inkmakers. Still, the men in Sai Mi Wan seem to accept the challenges of the Communist system and, when things are at their worse, they simply look for the means to start over.

Religion. A few simple and sometimes familiar conclusions can be drawn from the data on religion in Sai Mi Wan. More women are religious than men. Form is more important than meaning in the customary observances. The "worship of gods" must be graded as a weak aspect of the culture and the people are generally disinterested in it. This is especially true of the children who have not even the classic traditions to sustain them and have consequently become more susceptible to the teacher of other religions. Except for a few children, the Sai Mi Wan of 1961 was still largely untouched by the Christians who will through their influence in the schools almost certainly, however, captivate more of the young people as time goes on.

Confucianism, toward which the Christians have less antagonism than toward the adulterated Taoism of Hong Kong, seems doomed. Always depending on lineage strength and classical learning, the remnants of emigrant faith are being destroyed at their roots by the Communists, it would seem.

Comparisons with Chung Nam Wan and Tung Pak Wan

In our study of the three small communities which are set apart from the urban center of Lung Chau, we can now distinguish clearly certain similarities and differences. To begin with the latter, Sai Mi Wan's population (113) is slightly larger than that of Tung Pak Wan (98), while both numerically overwhelm the hamlet of Chung Nam Wan (20). On closer examination, however, we note that there are actually more families in Tung Pak Wan (18) than in Sai Mi Wan (15) and, more significantly, the families of the former settlement to a greater extent are related by marriage or blood. Provenience, we infer, was more important than lineage in the historical development of Sai Mi Wan.

No contrast in the three communities can take precedence over the cultural-linguistic differences, however. Chung Nam Wan was in origin a Hakka hamlet that grew out of Tung Pak Wan with its mixed groups from which the Cantonese were to emerge as the dominating group. The alien Ch'ao-Fu-Hui people, represented by only a few families in Tung Pak Wan, appear as the majority element in Sai Mi Wan where there are almost four times as many such speakers as there are of Cantonese, while the Hakka component is negligible.

Economically, all three outlying settlements came into being because of a need for land, and the growing of vegetables together with the raising of pigs played an important part from the beginning. Only in Chung Nam Wan, however, did vegetable growing retain its priority. Pig raising, which ultimately was even more significant, developed in Tung Pak Wan beyond a point that anyone probably could have anticipated, while the specialized raising of chickens became only second in importance. Sai Mi Wan, to the contrary, with its lovely enclosure of blue water, became a natural center for the breeding of ducks.

Generally speaking, one receives the impression that the population of Sai Mi Wan is on a slightly higher economic level than the average of Tung Pak Wan. There is more diversity of business undertakings and the families came from backgrounds with somewhat more education and wealth. This advantage may be reflected in the frequency with which the Sai Mi Wan people attend motion pictures and especially the superior ones shown in the town across the strait. It does not account for their unusual amount of swimming, however. The physiographic character of Sai Mi Wan can be credited with that. We would like to correlate the small number of radios (3) in Sai Mi Wan with a certain sophistication of the people, but we fear that to do so is not valid, so we shall merely note that the number is peculiarly small compared to Tung Pak Wan where 50 per cent of the households have them. With the case of the cheong sam, the assertion of economic advantage and sophistication is given support, for this garment is as common in Sai Mi Wan as it is rare in the other two communities.

The smell of political opinion also varies. A pro-Communist odor is quite obvious in Tung Pak Wan and an anti-Communist one is equally pungent in Sai Mi Wan. In Chung Nam Wan the dominant scent is pro-Western. The latter character can be quickly accounted for in the small hamlet since two-thirds of the families are Christian. Tung Pak Wan, on the other hand, contains households with a wide gamut of beliefs which contribute to the social disunity of the settlement. Sai Mi Wan, on the contrary, is a community in which Christ has still gained no special standing among the various gods.

Similarities—as well as differences—characterize the settlements, but they are not quite as conspicuous. We find extremely few adults who have never been married. Nuclear families predominate in all the settlements. Most of the buildings have been constructed of concrete with distinction appearing only in the relatively recent houses of wood. Physicians with Western training are preferred by the majority of individuals, as is a free choice in seeking one's spouse, but there are still concubines living in all three communities. Schools and hospitals not only are everywhere appreciated but also are taken advantage of by most of those eligible. The British Government is respected but in large part for the degree with which it permits people the freedom to make a living and at the same time curtails the corruption that vitiates their satisfaction in doing so.

Finally, we must emphasize the fact that all three communities share a common dependence on Lung Shing, the growing metropolis of the island with its eight to nine thousand people. It is unlikely that any of these suburban settlements could exist without the town, although Sai Mi Wan, because of its multiplicity of activities is the most directly subsidiary to Lung Shing. Indeed, as we have already affirmed, one cannot really understand such a suburb of small industries without a fuller knowledge of the population center on which it depends. To comprehend Lung Shing, however, is not so simple. But let us try.